# Subject to Change

GENDER AND CULTURE

Carolyn G. Heilbrun and Nancy K. Miller, *editors*

GENDER AND CULTURE
A SERIES OF COLUMBIA UNIVERSITY PRESS
Edited by Carolyn G. Heilbrun and Nancy K. Miller

In Dora's Case: Freud, Hysteria, Feminism
Edited by Charles Bernheimer and Claire Kahane

Breaking the Chain: Women, Theory, and French Realist Fiction
Naomi Schor

Between Men: English Literature and Male Homosocial Desire
Eve Kosofsky Sedgwick

Romantic Imprisonment: Women and Other Glorified Outcasts
Nina Auerbach

The Poetics of Gender
Edited by Nancy K. Miller

Reading Woman: Essays in Feminist Criticism
Mary Jacobus

Honey-Mad Women: Emancipatory Strategies in Women's Writing
Patricia Yaeger

Thinking Through the Body
Jane Gallop

Gender and the Politics of History
Joan Wallach Scott

Inspiriting Influences: Tradition, Revision, and Afro-American Women's Novels
Michael Awkward

Plotting Women: Gender and Representation in Mexico
Jean Franco

*Nancy K. Miller*

# SUBJECT TO CHANGE

## READING FEMINIST WRITING

COLUMBIA UNIVERSITY PRESS

*New York    1988*

Columbia University Press
New York    Guildford, Surrey
Copyright © 1988 Columbia University Press
All rights reserved
Printed in the United States of America

LIBRARY OF CONGRESS
LIBRARY OF CONGRESS CATALOGING-IN-PUBLICATION DATA

Miller, Nancy K.
Subject to change.

(Gender and culture)
Bibliography: p.
Includes index.
1. French literature—Women authors—History and criticism.
2. Feminism and literature—France.
3. Women and literature—France.   4. Feminist criticism—France.
I. Title.   II. Series.
PQ149.M54   1988      843'.009'352042      88-4341 CIP
ISBN 0-231-06660-0
ISBN 0-231-06661-9 (pbk.)
Book design by Jennifer Dossin
Hardback editions of Columbia University Press books are Smyth-sewn
and are printed on permanent and durable acid-free paper.

*For Carolyn*

# Contents

# Acknowledgments

THIS BOOK has been a long time in the making, and it would never have been finished without two crucial moments of very special support: a Non-Tenured Faculty Fellowship at the Mary Ingraham Bunting Institute in Cambridge in the fall of 1980 and the spring of 1984, and a Rockefeller Foundation Humanities Fellowship in 1985–86. For these gifts of time I am much indebted.

Other debts, accumulated more diffusely and more personally over the years, are less easy to account for. When I first encountered feminist criticism I was struck by what seemed to me *lists* of acknowledgment, whole paragraphs of people feminist critics would thank for reading their work and talking about it with them. I thought this was either pretentious or implausible (or both): who *were* all these people so generous with their time and counsel? Perhaps this proliferation of readers was part of the poetics of sisterhood (about sharing—something, growing up as an older sister, I always hated). Now I have come to see this implication of others as part of the feminist project itself; or rather, though writing tends of course to remain a lonely affair, there is, I think, an equally real sense in which the practice of feminist criticism by virtue of its status as a *collective* project necessarily involves a map of acknowledgment and recognition. The writing of other feminist critics, the responsiveness of readers, the efforts of colleagues who through conferences, journals, and institutes produce scenes in which to work (*for* which to work) finally seems to relocate any criticism "of one's own" beyond the borders of personal investment.

Given the nature of this book (its interventionist fantasies), I am particularly grateful to the organizers of conferences and panels who got me to produce this writing in the first place, to try out new material in public, to rehearse and perform it in context. To Nelly Furman at Cornell University; Patricia Spacks at the English Institute; Nancy Huston at Urbino; Susan Lanser and Michael

Ragussis at Georgetown University; Michael Riffaterre at Columbia University; Elizabeth Weed and Joan Scott at the Pembroke Center, Brown University; Teresa de Lauretis at the University of Wisconsin-Milwaukee; Nancy Rabinowitz and Patricia Cholakian at Hamilton College; Frederick Keener and Susan Lorsch at Hofstra University; Virginia Swain at Dartmouth College. I also want to thank here Myra Dinnerstein and the remarkable group of feminist colleagues at the University of Arizona who brought me to Tuscon to present my work on women's writing under the auspices of an NEH Curriculum Integration Project.

I am equally grateful to the audiences at colleges and universities where I was invited to read this work while it was still in progress for their questions, suggestions, resistances, all of which (especially, perhaps, the last), in different ways, have helped me to reformulate my positions or reform my views. I am pleased to be able to thank here all the friends and colleagues who, over the years, have graciously brought me to lecture at their campuses. I list here in (more or less) chronological order the places to which I traveled: the University of Michigan (at Ann Arbor), Harvard University, New York University, Miami University (Oxford), the Ohio State University, Dartmouth College, Hamilton College, the University of Arizona at Tuscon, Tulsa University, Princeton University, Amherst College, the University of Toronto, MacMaster University, the University of North Carolina (Chapel Hill), Emory University, Drew University, Rutgers University, Stanford University, the University of California (at Berkeley and Irvine), Mount Holyoke College, Boston University, Pomona College.

There of course have been less formal but often more elaborate exchanges. Nina Auerbach, Barbara Babcock, Jane Bennett, Peggy Brawer, Rachel Brownstein, Terry Castle, Joan DeJean, Helene Foley, Christine Froula, Carolyn Heilbrun, Marianne Hirsch, Myra Jehlen, Alice Kaplan, Susan Lanser, Christie McDonald, Sandy Petrey, Naomi Schor, English Showalter, Brenda Silver, Catharine Stimpson, Margaret Waller, and Carolyn Williams have at different but always (it seemed) desperate stages of various chapters given me generous feedback and sharp criticism. Ellen Bassuk, Caroline Bynum, Linda Gordon, Marilyn Massey, and Eve Sedgwick in the spring of 1984 at Cambridge provided me with a context of critical thinking that helped me to move on to the final stages of the book.

My feminist students at Barnard and Columbia have honored me by the patience with which they allowed me in our seminars to elaborate this material before it became writing. For the chance to practice and to think aloud I am deeply in their debt. I want especially to tell Peggy Waller and Kate Jensen how much their inimitable way of being there mattered to me.

Donald Petrey and Jane Bennett relieved me of much of the burden of word-processing; Jane invented ways to be helpful; Peggy Brawer and Simone Kahn mercifully supplied local research assistance; the Barnard Faculty Grants Committee provided stipends that financed most of that work. I have appreciated the support.

There are, finally, three people whose belief in my work has sustained me in various modes throughout what had to seem to them the endless amount of time I have taken to let go of this book; who willy-nilly have had to live with this project in one way or another from its writing to the always penultimate revision of "finishing." To Carolyn Heilbrun, with whom I have taught and edited, gossiped and soul-searched, done Barnard/Columbia business over innumerable dinners in our neighborhood for almost a decade, and to whom, in the end, the magnitude of my debt is condensed in the dedication to this book; to Naomi Schor with whom I have perfected the art of the feminist literary phone date in our twice weekly incarnation as "les parleuses" between Providence and New York; to Sandy Petrey *with* whom I wrote most of these chapters, and who has complicated their writing by his presence in my life, I am, as they say, eternally grateful.

VERSIONS OF a number of chapters in this book have been previously published, in some cases with slightly different titles, in the following journals and essay collections. "Emphasis Added: Plots and Plausibilities in Women's Fiction," in *PMLA* (January 1981), vol. 96, no. 1, and in *The New Feminist Criticism* (New York: Pantheon, 1985); "For a Dialectics of Identification: Women's Autobiography in France," in *Women and Language in Literature and Society,* edited by Sally McConnell-Ginet, Ruth Borker, and Nelly Furman, copyright © 1980 by Praeger Publishers (New York: Praeger, 1980); "The Text's Heroine: A Feminist Critic and her Fictions," in *Diacritics* (Summer 1982), vol. 12, no. 2; "Writing (from) the Feminine: George Sand and the Novel of Female Pastoral" in *The Representation of Women in Fiction* (Baltimore: Johns Hopkins University Press, 1983); "Arachnologies: The Woman, the Text, and the Critic," in *The Poetics of Gender* (New York: Columbia University Press, 1986); and "Changing the Subject: Authorship, Writing, and the Reader," in *Feminist Studies/Critical Studies* (Bloomington: Indiana University Press, 1986).

I am grateful for permission to reprint these essays here.

NOTE: I have on the whole made use of published translations where convenient, available, or practical. In the case of the *Peruvian Letters*, I have slightly modernized the translation throughout. If no English translation is listed in the bibliography, the translation is mine. Where two sets of page references are included in the text, the first reference is to the English translation; the referencing for chapter 2 constitutes an exception to this practice.

*Subject to Change*

# INTRODUCTION

## *Writing Feminist Criticism*

And it is but a twin fact with this, that in France alone woman
has had a vital influence on the development of literature; in
France alone the mind of woman has passed like an electric
current through the language, making crisp and definite what
is elsewhere heavy and blurred; in France alone, if the writings
of women were swept away, a serious gap would be made in
the national history.

> George Eliot, "Woman in France: Madame de Sablé"

The custom among the ancients—
as Priscian testifies—
was to speak quite obscurely
in the books they wrote,
so that those who were to come after
and study them
might gloss the letter and supply its significance
from their own wisdom.

> Marie de France, Prologue to the *Lais*

THE WRITING of this book has from the beginning been bound
up with two separate but for me always interrelated scenes,
the seminar and the academic conference. In that very particular
sense of a work's location, this book began to take shape in the
fall of 1977 when I taught for the first time a course on women's
writing I then called (daringly, I thought) "French Women Writers: Toward a Definition of the Feminine Text." In 1977 Elaine
Showalter's study of British women novelists, *A Literature of Their
Own*, had just appeared; Ellen Moers's *Literary Women: The Great
Writers,* the previous year. Although Moers's book included discussions of Staël, Sand, and Colette, and indeed as early as 1973
Germaine Brée had brought out a collection of public lectures on
a tradition of French feminist literature, on the whole it would be
fair to say that those of us working "in French" felt ourselves to
be without a critical tradition.

No course on women writers had ever been offered in the French Department at Columbia, and at the time I knew of no others to draw upon. This did not, however, seem an altogether bad thing: we might not have known just what it was, but we had the sense of doing something. From my admittedly apocalyptic point of view on things, moreover, it seemed almost subversive (a good thing) for an assistant professor to offer a course on the "feminine text" in the seminar room in which I had been a graduate student (and in which the subject, needless to say, had never come up). Looking back now after ten years, I run the risk of mythologizing the moment, but I think the students in the seminar took as much pleasure as I did in the complicities of a slightly dangerous (at the very least, we thought, professionally radical) experience behind closed doors in the paranoid corridors of the fifth floor of Philosophy Hall.[1]

It was in the spirit of that adventure that I accepted an invitation to speak on a panel at the 1978 annual Barnard "Scholar and Feminist" conference, whose theme that year was called "Creating Feminist Works." The lone scholar's voice between those of a painter and a poet, I spoke in terms I hoped might be both personal (not too academic) and representative (not too personal) about what I thought was at stake in the study of women's writing (an academic's idea of being creative).[2] What bothered me then and still bothers me now was a double problem of theory and language: on what grounds was it possible to locate the question of female authorship? In what metaphors could one figure the discussion? At the time I played around with a vegetarian tropology: I compared artichokes to onions. Following out the implications of an opposition which distinguished as separate critical activities the critique of men's writing (sexual politics) and the analysis of women's writing,[3] I contrasted in this account of my own work the stripping away of leaves in order to get—past the choke—to the heart of the matter, the (male) text's ideological core (textual politics), with the peeling away of layers that ends somehow without closure, without ever arriving at a discernible (somehow feminist) center. I opposed the excitement that comes from an emphasis on product, meaning unveiled, to a more diffuse and ambiguous erotics of process.

In the opposition of two modes of textual pleasure, I was of course reinventing Roland Barthes's theoretical wheel; even his metaphors, though I was blithely unaware of it at the time.[4] In an essay called "Style and Its Image," Barthes compares an *already* superannuated view of the text as a "fruit with a kernel (an apricot, for example)" with a more current critical perspective on literary acts: "an onion, a construction of layers (or levels, or systems) whose body contains, finally, no heart, no kernel, no irreducible principle, nothing except the unit of its own surfaces" (10). As I review this history of my critical moves, I am struck by the fact that from the beginning I have cast the issues of a predominantly Anglo/American feminist discussion of female authorship in terms that rehearse French post-structuralist paradigms of textuality, by way of a Barthesian poetics (this is especially true of "Arachnologies" and "Changing the Subject"). At the same time, if, over the years, Barthes has seduced me with an attractive point of departure, I invariably part company with him at a crucial moment in the journey. My difference typically takes the form of a resistance to the end point of the argument. Thus, though in this occasional piece for the Barnard conference I entertain the possibility that women's writing might not have an identifiable core or center, I do not draw Barthes's conclusion that therefore *nothing* is to be found beyond "the unit of its own surfaces," that the body of women's (onion) writing contains nothing but signifiers to gloss. In my homelier (kitchen) expansion of the onion metaphor, I argue, for instance, that the layers of an onion are perceived only by a cut through its body. For me, a supplement of experience comes to check a critical politics dependent for its practice on the free-play of signifiers. The question of experience requires a theorization that refuses to scrap the material of its formation.

Despite the inadvertent but implicit support offered by Roland Barthes, onions and artichokes did not finally seem specific enough to support a poetics of women's writing. But by the fall of 1978, when I began to take the question of women's writing on the road, I had arrived at a language in which to begin to talk about a poetics of reading women's writing: plots and plausibilities.[5] In a way, each of the chapters in this book constitutes a similar effort to find working metaphors for the problems involved in creating a critical discourse in which to talk about women's writing both within the field of feminist studies, and within the critical debates that have dominated literary studies in the United States over the past twenty years. (These have not usually been the same discussion.) Emphasis added, tropes and sensible shoes, female pastoral, coming to writing, performance, arachnologies, overreading the underread, changing the subject: these formulations have all been part of my desire to theorize female authorship and put on the table the textual and political stakes of female signature in the production, reception, and circulation of women's writing.

More locally, I have tried to articulate through a variety of critical modes and strategies the possibility of elaborating a feminist literary theory and practice that emerges from working at the junctures where French literature, theory, and the realities of American institutions intersect.[6] Put another way, this book is about *coming* "from French" and *being* in Women's Studies. It has mattered to me, for instance, in symbolic and material ways not always easy to define, but that I know have played a shaping role in my critical positioning, that most of the essays in this book were written while I was running the Women's Studies Program at Barnard, and teaching, some of the time, in a French department—across the street at Columbia—of which I was not a voting member.

IN *Subject to Change* I explore ways of reading women as writing subjects, of tracking the erratic relations between female authorship and literary history in a particular cultural context. Of the writers whose work is most centrally the focus of this book— Lafayette, Graffigny, Staël, Sand, Colette—only Graffigny's name is likely to be unknown to many readers. But if these writers, and especially Sand and Colette, function to some extent as figures in a national literary landscape, this does not mean that their work (with the exception of *The Princess of Clèves*) belongs to the history of rereadings that have come to constitute that literature's canon of self-reference. One of the aims of this book, then, is implicitly to call the canon of exclusions into question by repopulating the landscape, and at a closer focus, to display the writing of these figures and the figures of their writing.

At stake, however, is not simply the reconstruction of another feminist literature. To the extent that all critical models exist and operate in a dialogical relation with the literature they account for, to change literatures is to change the subject of their criticism. If I want to add to the repertory of feminist criticism the performances of *other writing subjects,* it is also in order to articulate other models, other metaphorics. Building more narrowly on Adrienne Rich's notion of a "politics of location," I'm proposing a "poetics of location" that would acknowledge both the geographics of the writing it reads and the limits of its own project. (In this sense, I'm working toward a more historicized poetics, which, in an emphasis on local specificities—comparative bodies of writing?—works against the temptations of a feminist reuniversalization.)

Despite the national emphasis and the focus on feminist writing, this is not a book about "new French feminisms" (or "French feminist theory") except to the extent that these imports to the U.S. scene emerge from the critical upheaval produced by the political events of May 1968 in France, and whose discourses operate now in complicated ways within both feminist theory and literary studies. Although the argument I will make here is deeply (if ambivalently) indebted to the kind of thinking that this movement has engendered, this is not the French connection I'm after. I'm interested in another kind of "traffic in women," the circulation throughout literary history of French feminist writing.

THE FIRST five chapters deal with the issues I see as central to the question of women's writing and feminist critical theory, foregrounding as exemplary instances for constructing the subjects of criticism—*The Princess of Clèves, The Mill on the Floss, The Portuguese Letters, Indiana,* and *Villette,* in addition to the autobiographical writings (writing fictions) of Sand, Daniel Stern, Colette, and Beauvoir. In chapters 6–9, under the thematics of "coming to writing," I take four novels of feminist signature to expose and work through a certain number of problems in contemporary critical theory, notably the question of (female) authorship itself. In the discussions of individual novels, *The Peruvian Letters, Corinne, Valentine,* and *The Vagabond,* which like "Emphasis Added" grew out of teaching situations and are structured as readings, I am especially concerned with articulating both a general critical matrix—women's writing as a feminist literature of dissent—and specific strategies of figuration: the revision of female plot and the reappropriation of cultural space by a challenge to the male gaze I call "writing from the pavilion." Unlike "The Text's Heroine," "Arachnologies," and "Changing the Subject," which, as I indicate in the frames that precede them, were all originally written for conferences that carried their own agendas, polemics, and cast of characters, these chapters were written as a return to the work of the seminar, by which I mean primarily a scene of novel reading. Taken together in this uneven weave of textures and origins, the chapters, I hope, will point to the ways in which the intersecting claims of pedagogy, literary history, and theory coexist materially in feminist practice.

Although the novels I take up are "representative" in the conventional sense of reflecting a recognizable historical spectrum of a national literature—1678–1910—choices have of course been made. Why these and not others? For the beginning of an answer I will turn briefly here to Gail Godwin's account of the *Norton Anthology of Literature by Women* (entitled in the *New York Times Book Review*), "One Woman Leads to Another." In Godwin's view the anthology's greatest flaw is that it is "organized to bear out Virginia Woolf's opinion that women's 'books continue each other' " (13). Godwin goes on to object that "the editors might more appropriately have subtitled their anthology "The Feminist Tradition in English . . ." (14). Presumably the recourse to Woolf is meant to invalidate the whole project. But when one returns to the context of Woolf's remark in *A Room of One's Own,* it is not at all clear that her discussion either supports Godwin's opinion or explains the absence of aesthetic criteria in the anthology that Godwin deplores.

Reading the first novel of Mary Carmichael, the novelist Woolf has invented to speak of a future of women's writing, Woolf's feminist subject reflects upon the critical approach to a work that may be concerned with "writing as an art, not as a method of self-expression" (83). Confronted with this new novel, she wonders how best to read:

> It seems to be her first book, I said to myself, but one must read it as if it were the last volume in a fairly long series, continuing all those other books that I have been glancing at— Lady Winchilsea's poems and Aphra Behn's plays and the novels of the four great novelists. *For books continue each other, in spite of our habit of judging them separately.* And I must also consider her—this unknown woman—as the descendant of all those other women whose circumstances I have been glancing at and see what she inherits of their characteristics and restrictions. (84; emphasis added)

While it is clear that Woolf is indeed talking about a tradition of women writers, the part of the sentence Godwin quotes—"books continue each other"—does not itself bear the "mark of gender" (Wittig, 63). Rather, Woolf makes a statement about reading and about what today we might want to call intertextuality: books are not individually authored works of art but textual productions caught up in a web of quotation and rewriting.

Woolf here speaks the universal from the woman writer. More

than fifty years later, the possibility of women engendering the universal has yet to become an operative critical reality, for as we see, Godwin assumes that Woolf's generalization refers only to women writers (more typically, the gender of generalizations goes the other way).[7] Thus, for Godwin to say with recourse to Woolf that the anthology should have been called one of *feminist* literature does not really carry the point (her anxiety about Authorship notwithstanding). Woolf's poetics neither legislates a particular thematics for a literature written by women nor distinguishes feminist writing from (women's) art.

If I have taken the time to rehearse the terms of this polemic as it has come to attach itself to the question of the *Norton*, it is not to defend the anthology as an object (this others have done elsewhere), but to object quite self-interestedly on theoretical grounds to the terms in which its *project* is attacked. Woolf's notion that "books continue each other" (just as do feminist critics) is central to the question of women's writing and to the critique of canon-formation feminist literary history performs by its very existence ("masterpieces are not single and solitary births" [68]). In France that history turns, not surprisingly, around questions of identity and difference. In *Women Writers in France: Variations on a Theme*, Germaine Brée organizes her discussions around the "querelle des femmes," a debate about woman's nature and women's rights that began in the early modern period and that in many ways remains a subject of serious controversy today (between feminists and the forces of the new right; between women, but also, between feminists). In part because this has always been a feminist question, and in part because the network of associations that attach themselves to the terms "feminine" and "female" create other problems of connotation, Brée chooses to call the women's writing she discusses "feminist literature," which she defines "as referring merely to literature written by women" (5). I will follow Brée's lead here, though I will say a little more about what I mean by feminist, and argue that the novels I take up here indeed supply examples of (another) French feminism.[8]

Brée takes Christine de Pisan as the first in a small group of early modern French women writers she calls "initiators" (16). Although in certain historical perspectives Christine has been seen to occupy the place of "*first* author" (Poirion, in Brée, 21), for the development of the novel as I see it, I want to reframe the inaugural moments of feminist authorship. In a gesture meant to blur the moment of origins, I prefer to evoke Marie de France on one side of Christine's writing while placing Lafayette on the other, both before and after.

In "Lafayette's Ellipses: The Privileges of Anonymity," Joan DeJean, connecting Marie de France's (twelfth-century) poetics of gender to Lafayette's, and placing Lafayette in a tradition of seventeenth-century women writers who precede her, argues that "the complex relation that Lafayette engineered between author and text provoked a new type of reading for women's fiction and may thus have altered the course of criticism in France" (887). Although DeJean does not make a historical claim for Lafayette's originary status, she identifies a moment of text production that will come to give the French novel and French women writers' relation to it a very particular alignment and coloration. In a variety of ways all the novels I study in this book rewrite the effects of Lafayette's signature: "the trace of her authority that must simultaneously assert her power and protect her person" (887). While only Graffigny, after Lafayette, literally withholds her name from the title page of her fiction, all the writers whose work is in question here understand and stage the drama of female signature for their heroines and their authors. The *Peruvian Letters* (1747), *Corinne, or Italy* (1807), *Valentine* (1832), and *The Vagabond* (1910) all may be said to "continue" *The Princess of Clèves* as *feminist texts*.[9]

As a poetics derived from a specific cultural production, the description of feminist writing that follows is not meant to bear the weight of a universal authorship. If it sketches a horizon of writing that will enable other cartographies and other scenes, it will have served its purpose. At a first level, then, feminist writing articulates as and in a discourse a self-consciousness about woman's identity. I mean by this both an inherited cultural fiction and a process of social construction. Second, feminist writing makes a claim for the heroine's singularity by staging the difficulty of her relation as a woman in fiction to Woman. Third, it contests the available plots of female development or *Bildung* and embodies dissent from the dominant tradition in a certain number of recurrent narrative gestures, especially in the modalities of closure that Rachel DuPlessis has called "writing beyond the ending."[10] Finally, through an insistence on singularity, feminist writing figures the existence of other subjective economies, other styles of identity.

In its attack on the fathers *Corinne* thematizes most explicitly an indictment of patriarchy (Colette's Renée Néré refers to the regime of "patriarchal laundry"). But from *The Princess of Clèves* to *The Vagabond* in a variety of tones the protest can be heard.

In these novels, for instance, we can read as feminist writing the princess of Clèves's celebrated "refusal of love" repeated in Zilia's decision not to marry Déterville and Renée's not to marry Maxime, and even (perversely, perhaps) reenacted in Corinne's choice of Oswald as the man *least* likely to marry her. The "refusal of love," of course, more pointedly seen as the critique of marriage as a political institution, is also at work in the clearly overdetermined failure of Bénédict and Valentine's love to culminate in proper marriage.

In another set of intertextual relations, the princess's forest pavilion as a representation of female-controlled space that would exist outside the demands of plot is reappointed in Valentine's pavilion on the estate of her patrimony, in Zilia's library, Corinne's Italy, and Renée's borrowed "Elysian refuge." These *places* all mark, to different degrees, a form of resistance to the plausibilities of patriarchal plot. On still another level of continuity, Zilia's refusal of marriage, which coincides with the literal mastery of writing itself, throws into relief the sense in which the princess of Clèves's most singular gestures—the confession, the rejection of Nemours, the final retirement to female spaces—speak a desire to control story by refusing its plots that constitutes the trope of the woman writer in France par excellence.

If the Inca princess's "writing lessons" in the language of the dominant culture by their insistence on the costs of "coming to writing" supply a metaphorics for all of these novels as instances of feminist revision—*rewriting* conventional expectations for female protagonists—that metaphorics must at the same time be understood as the effect (or language) of the critique of the ideology of a woman's identity that I have called "changing the subject." Under this attention to the *possibilities of cultural resistance* I emphasize the deconstruction of the gaze and the reconstruction of the scene of writing itself. Thus, if at one end of the scale the princess of Clèves chooses to desire the duke of Nemours in a representation she controls, looking at his portrait within the walls of her pavilion, and removing herself (or trying to) from the empire of his gaze, the better to inhabit her desire; at the other, Corinne represents herself theatrically in public, offering herself to her lover's gaze the better to bring him into a mode of pleasure outside the specular regime of patriarchy. The captive Peruvian princess, the anthropologist's exotic object, becomes the writing subject of an ethnography on colonial culture that challenges the universal claims of the Enlightenment subject. Renée, the star of ambiguous vaudeville shows, returns to a writing of which she is the visionary. In Valentine's short-lived feminist utopia, the woman, forgetting convention, and wanting to see for herself, fantasizes herself briefly as a painter. *Corinne* and *The Vagabond* boldly display in their texts the relations between writing and the gaze, the gaze and performance, performance and the scene of writing. But in both novels the attempt to change the subject through performance proves to be vulnerable to the cultural power of the dominant male gaze observing; in both cases, only the production of writing—an authored text—offers an escape from the surveillance of masculine regard. Writing gives form to the vision of an imaginary elsewhere.

In a way, however, the difficulty of imagining a beyond-the-male-gaze may be inherent to the plots of heterosexual fiction. If all the novels dissent from an ideal of love, suffering, and conformity to female plot, each ending suggests nonetheless that the daughter's destiny is somehow fatally blocked: the daughters all thus come to mark the end of the line, of a certain line, a refusal to circulate. It is not only that they do not marry: they will not become mothers. They are final daughters. Is this bypassing of maternity the ultimate effect of the indictment of patriarchy? The fate of the daughters who appear at the end of Corinne and Valentine's novels raises (without solving) real problems of interpretation. Is little Juliette or little Valentine the signature of a difference *as yet* to come to writing? It may be that after the great period of novel writing for women in France, these new daughters come to embody a way of imagining another tradition. It may be also be that the difference of another coming to writing requires an outside to heterosexual economies. At best we can say that the value of the new daughters' signs, like the currency of a new country, remains subject to change.

IF *The Princess of Clèves* is the new novel of 1680, seen by the critics of its time as a rupture with the idea of the novel itself (Rousset, 17–19), what about *The Vagabond* and the novel in 1910? If the conventions of literary history that grant *The Princess of Clèves* inaugural status as the first psychological novel add justification for that position in this partial account of women's writing, what of Colette in last place? Why end here, in 1910?

Woolf, in her 1924 essay "Mr. Bennett and Mrs. Brown," asserts famously and flamboyantly that "in or about December, 1910, human character changed" (320). In this reflection about " 'charac-

ter' in fiction" and "the question of reality" (319), the change Woolf
is interested in identifying is a shift in human relations, a shift
accompanied by "a change in religion, conduct, politics, and literature" (321). Much in the style of *A Room of One's Own*, Woolf
concretizes her argument in a story she tells about observing a man
(Mr. Smith) and a woman (Mrs. Brown) in a railway carriage. The
interactions of Mr. Smith and Mrs. Brown take Woolf to the question of representation—how to make Mrs. Brown "seem real" (326),
and how Mr. (Arnold) Bennett would have one do it. (Woolf's
essay may also be read as a parable about sexism and feminism
and what that means for the production and reception of women's
writing [Daugherty, 269]).[11] The problem for the "men and women
who began writing novels in 1910 or thereabouts," Woolf writes,
was that "there was no English novelist from whom they could
learn their business" (326). Concluding that to render Mrs. Brown
will require "tools" and "conventions" different from the dated
ones of earlier periods, Woolf recommends patience: "But do not
expect just at present a complete and satisfactory presentment of
her. Tolerate the spasmodic, the obscure, the fragmentary, the failure" (337). If we recall the language she uses to imagine Mary
Carmichael's imaginary novel, we see the extent to which Woolf's
vision of a future of women's writing is bound up with new forms
and practices of literature; practices already visible in Colette's
writing, even before 1910.

The question of 1910 is not only a matter of the continuities and
discontinuities of feminist writing and women's texts. Animated
by a rather different agenda, Alain Robbe-Grillet, in the opening
essay of his 1963 revisionary poetics *Pour un nouveau roman*, also
identifies 1910 as a watershed year in the history of the novel in
France: "Flaubert was writing the new novel of 1860, Proust of
1910. The writer must accept to bear his date, knowing that there
are no masterpieces in eternity, only works in history; and that
they survive only to the extent that they have left the past behind
them and announced the future" (10). Although Robbe-Grillet, one
knows, has remained unregenerately indifferent to questions of
women's writing, the language in which he makes his choice
of Proust in 1910 returns us to the question we raised earlier of
Colette's date and place in the conventions of French literary history. For if I have been arguing that books continue each other as
feminist rewritings in the verticality of a female affiliation, it is no
less the case that in the lateral positionings of a national literature
women's books exist alongside men's: what happens, for instance,

to Colette's date seen together with Proust's? Proust's with Colette's? To the extent that the study of canon formation is a question of locatable instances of reading, it also becomes important to take the signatures together: reading at the intersections.[12]

Colette's new woman writer in 1910, before Mary Carmichael, casts her gaze on the "infinitely obscure lives" of the "majority of women" whose stories remain unrecorded, and adds to the human comedy, portraits "of the other sex," like those of Mr. Woodhouse and Mr. Casaubon, which reveal "that spot the size of a shilling at the back of the head" (94). But if Colette's novel thus anticipates Woolf's poetics, does this mean that her work comes after "1910"? Yes and no. In *The Vagabond* Colette both continues and breaks with the traditions of writing from which she emerges. She clearly belongs to a line of feminist writers and yet begins to unravel its pact with the conventions of representation; her novel marks a shift in location.[13]

It might, finally, be more useful to place Colette like her heroine-writer, as a liminal figure in the history of women's writing; on the edge of another kind of literary production. Thus, while Beauvoir produces after Colette feminist novels that formally and thematically follow the lines of a pre "1910" novel, Duras, Sarraute, Wittig, Cixous—the list is both incomplete and arbitrary—produce works that radically break with the old plot and the very notion of "character" in fiction. In that spirit I would now propose Wittig's *Les Guérillères* (1969) as an emblematic "after" to that tradition. Wittig's revisionary epic replaces closure with circularity, and female subjectivity at radically oblique angles to compulsory heterosexual structures. In *Les Guérillères* the signifiers of women's names march across the pages in a textual adventure that leaves the women beyond both men and the representation of women; freed from the sign of Woman, the particular female subject becomes plural and potentially universal: *elles.*

I WANT TO return now to my retrospective of writing feminist criticism. When I began working on women's writing I felt, as I said then, that I somehow had to justify this act, by which I meant *theorizing* it. This is how I put it in 1978 (parodying myself through Woolf):

> But why, you might ask, does reading women's writing immediately translate into a compulsion to make theory?
> If a person whose function in this world is not to be a lit-

erary critic decides to read a woman writer, that person only has to decide after the fact whether she or he likes the work in question. If, however, the reader, not having Virginia Woolf's recommended income of 500 pounds a year, earns her living by writing and talking about texts in an institution (of higher learning), that reader has a rather more arduous task to perform. That reader, as she inscribes the critical act within the academy, must not only justify the choice of the work in the first place (because most women's writing has no obvious, i.e., canonical claim to consideration), but, if she is to survive, she must also for political and intellectual reasons say something about the writing *qua* women's writing. ("Creating Feminist Works," 19)

But to whom was this justification of the need for justification addressed? Since that study was on the face of it highly, even unambiguously valued within the precincts of a dominant feminist scholarship, whose authorization was I worried about? To the extent that I was vividly untenured, I of course worried at all times about everyone. But it seems to me today that my concern was really both more and less disembodied.

Having worked for years on male authors within an intellectual climate that took itself for the scene of theory and imagined no outside to its language, it was inevitable that good daughter that I was, leaving men's writing for women's would make me anxious. Reading male-authored texts for the ways in which ideology constructed Woman was one thing; seeing the ideology of a dominant tradition through its exclusion of women writers as the construction of literary history itself was another. Was that a subject of theory, subject to theory? I now wanted questions of women's writing to "count" as theory; I wanted my (feminist) theory to be persuasive to "them"; I wanted the discussion of women's writing to reveal to them that their theories of text, subjectivity, poetics, the canon, etc. were in need of revision (not the other way around!). I wanted these things, but at the same time I continued to worry about the grounds of my own position in *their* terms. (This is part of what is going on in "The Text's Heroine," "Arachnologies," and "Changing the Subject.")

But if the problems between "us" and "them" loomed large in institutional terms—tenure, promotions, journals, fellowships, etc.— the question over female authorship—how to authorize it—for me was equally bound up with another problem of alignment: the borders and range of positions structuring (and fracturing) the field of feminist literary studies, the famous "Franco-American Dis-Connection" that characterized so much of the rhetoric of the late 1970s and which is still with us.[14] In other words, from the beginning my desire to justify the question of female authorship was knotted from within internal tensions of feminist debate.

Debate is probably not the right word to describe the profound differences in assumptions about language, identity, sexual differ-ence, and politics that underlie unevenly and freight asymmetri-cally the discussions of this period. On the whole this has been coded as a polarization between Anglo-American and French ap-proaches to literature. It more accurately has had to do with one's relation to "theory"—construed as deconstruction, psychoanaly-sis, and neo-Marxism—and to a profound ambivalence within a certain feminist analysis to those bodies of theory as "male." (We could also see this as a problem of signature: a tension between the cultural and political force of unitary theory grounded by proper names as an effect of the "already read" and the attempt to theo-rize from a multiplicity of underread perspectives. Put another way, what seemed to some as "untheorized" may also be understood as the not-yet-theorized.) Since I analyze these issues at length in both "Arachnologies" and "Changing the Subject," for now I sim-ply want to point to the crucial thematics of the debate over theory as it played itself out in the study of women writers. This is the reflection on textuality that may be summarized in the title of Barthes's famous 1968 essay "The Death of the Author."

As someone "in French" I had two specific problems in coming to women's writing, a field whose outlines had been defined by critics working in English and American studies, or in Women's Studies. On the one hand, as someone who had (as theory) read Lévi-Strauss and Barthes *before* Virginia Woolf and Adrienne Rich (as feminism), it was no easy matter to invent a way to reembody the author (who had never been alive for me in the first place). On the other, the *women* "in French" (this of course includes some women "from English") whose work I most admired *because* it was theoretical were not interested in women's writing as a chal-lenge to the Dead Author in the ways that I was—as a politics of signature located in institutional pedagogies of exclusion. They, like the theorists with whom they engaged—Freud, Lacan, Derrida—insisted on the complexity of a feminine not necessarily attached to women's bodies, but as bound up in stories of sexual difference. I thus found myself caught between two conflicting attractions. I also found myself in an oscillation of my own ambivalence inhabiting two positions: a "formalist" to certain feminists, a certain feminist to my friends "in theory."

In 1977, for example (though the essay was published in 1980), Peggy Kamuf was already arguing that to reduce a "literary work to its signature" will "produce only tautological statements of dubious value: women's writing is writing signed by women" ("Writing Like a Woman," 285–86). Mary Jacobus, after Kamuf, writing in "Is There a Woman in This Text?" (1982), also sketches out the implications of such a position, naming it and placing it within Anglo-American positions on the woman writer, in contrast to a "French insistence on *écriture féminine*—on woman as writing-effect instead of an origin" (109). Jacobus holds (as do Showalter and Gilbert and Gubar on this), that "the category of 'women's writing' remains as strategically important in classroom, curriculum or interpretive community as the specificity of women's oppression is to the women's movement," but like Kamuf she draws the line at the question of signature: "And yet to leave the question there, with an easy recourse to the female signature or to female being, is either to beg it or to biologize it" (108). Like Kamuf, Jacobus refuses "to posit the woman author as origin and her life as the primary locus of meaning" (108). While Kamuf was taking as her example of "a certain feminist criticism" remarks by Patricia Meyer Spacks in *The Female Imagination* (1975), for most mainstream feminist critics the question of signature itself simply was not perceived as a matter of philosophical debate. For them the question was not so much on what theoretical grounds to place the discussion, as what claims could one make for the body of writing one had assembled: the various "heroinisms" of Moers's "literary women" (1976); Showalter's "literature of their own" (1977); Gilbert and Gubar's figure of "the madwoman in the attic" (1979). In those volumes, female authorship poses itself as a set of problems within a politics of literature that is *already* a grounded context.

If the challenge to the signature from deconstructive and psychoanalytic positions has not on the whole been picked up directly by the feminist critics working on women's writing to whom it seemed addressed, it has, however, continued to surface in other quarters, coming from other places. On the one hand, as we have just seen, a wariness about signature is central to the attack from the traditionalists on the Gilbert and Gubar Norton Anthology (1985) for its principles of inclusion or exclusion—the worry being that "literary art and individual talent" are sacrificed to feminist values (Godwin, 12; Donoghue, 147). Or, as another disgruntled critic of the volume put it: "Why might a woman writer prefer not to be a Woman Writer? Perhaps for the same reason a frog dislikes to be used as a demonstration of the nervous system. It's afraid that might be all there is to life" (Rose, 89). On the other hand, at the other extreme of the critical spectrum, we find the philosophical questioning of identity that engenders Kamuf's analysis of the trope "a woman writing as a woman" enlisted in Jonathan Culler's discussion of feminist criticism in *On Decon-struction,* "Reading as a Woman."

Thus we observe this curious situation in which the study of women's writing is put into question both by the believers in art, origin, meaning, intention, and the individual talent and by those who believe in none of the above. Is this necessarily what the alternatives boil down to? Essentialism or theory? Artichokes (apricots) *or* onions?

It seems to me that the study of women's literature has made it possible to unhook signature from the interpretive securities of Authorship by rematerializing the relations of subjectivity, writing, and literary theory in very specific ways. In the critical turns I have made since writing *The Heroine's Text* (artichokes), I have tried to imagine authorship as a more complexly contextual activity than I had dreamed of in my original training and incarnation as a hardline structuralist: as a matter of writing that includes the problem of agency—the marks of a producing subject; and as a question of reading that includes the gendered effects of critical and institutional ideologies.

In "Writing Fictions: Women's Autobiography in France" I suggest that locating the signature of a woman's writing across the body of writing allows feminist critics to reproblematize the question of authorship and biography as interpretive ground. It is in part for this reason that I have included that essay in the argument I am making here. The stories of Sand, Stern, Colette, and Beauvoir are accounts of coming to writing in a historical real. In this sense they provide a social field of contrast to the metaphorical accounts of coming to writing that I read in the novels of feminist writers.[15] But that relation of course is too simple, since it is as clear that becoming a writer for a writer is also about making texts. Seen together in fiction and autographics, the scenes of authorization layer our understanding of the writing project as a negotiation between the subject and the social.

For me, the signature of the woman writer who is also a feminist writer is the mark of a resistance to dominant ideologies; for the feminist critic, the signature is the site of a possible political disruption. To insist on a meaning that attaches to signature is to value the challenge it can bring to the institutional arrangements based on its exclusion. This is not to say that I ignore the dangers of the claim or the appeal of a headier (sexier, as these things go) destabilization from deconstructive, psychoanalytic, and neo-Marxist perspectives. On the contrary. The chapters of this book all testify to my awareness of their seductions. But in the end, the critical theory I am looking for goes other ways.

At the Pembroke conference (1985) at which I first presented "Changing the Subject," Naomi Schor addressed the problem of viewing feminine specificity (what I talk about as female signature) from the bridge of French post-structuralist theory. Articulating her own resistance as a feminist to the "discourse of sexual indifference/pure difference," Schor wondered whether the insistence on indifferentiation in Barthes and Foucault wasn't perhaps the "latest ruse of phallocentrism," and observed that a significant number of feminist theorists have adopted other strategies for "subverting the unitary subject," strategies that take the form of a *doubling* more complex than the simple erasure of the tell-tale marks of sexual difference. Like Myra Jehlen, whose argument for "the claim of difference" (the understanding that "the other will have to live as other") as the crucial piece in a critique of the "male universal norm" Schor enlists in her own polemic, Schor concludes that only the dissymmetry of difference can undermine the grounds of repetition; providing "perhaps the only chance we have to construct a post-deconstructionist society which will not simply reduplicate our own" (110).

When I say, then, that I want to make claims for the female signature but not in the name of a biocritics of intention, I am saying in part that I want to have it two ways (tropes *and* sensible shoes)—French *and* (North) American. I am also saying that those terms themselves give us false dilemmas and equally false choices.[16] While I myself have continued to invoke those two positionings as if this outline constituted a reliable map of the territory, that is to a great extent because I have had a role to play in it (it is part of my history), and because I have been located in it by others. At the same time I have come to find this relentless redrawing of the boundaries a narrowing process rather than a gesture of complication. I long to see a more international geo-graphics in feminist writing. It seems to me that as feminist critics we do ourselves in by playing the old Franco-American game of binary oppositions (theory and empiricism, indifference and identity) as though it were the only game in town, as though we knew all the rules by which it could be played, as though layers were all there is to an onion, a pit to an apricot, or a heart to an artichoke; as though there weren't also Italians, for instance.[17]

I ORIGINALLY WANTED to call my book *Changing the Subject*. By this I meant to evoke both a voluntaristic desire for change— let's change the subject (this is boring), let's talk about something else (women writers, feminist criticism), let's make the subject different (refigure the universal, change the canon), etc. But when I learned to my chagrin that a book with that title had already been announced for publication, I decided to change my title to a phrase that had appealed to me earlier.[18] Now, "subject to change," of course, typically is followed by "without notice," and for a while, I resisted the new title precisely because of a certain programmatic arbitrariness (and a certain resulting annoyance from its effects— higher prices, cancelled trains) implicit in it. It was close to the original, but did it take me too far? It seems to me now that a dose of the arbitrary is not a bad thing; that the phrase nicely reappropriates clichés of femininity (*la donna e mobile*) while announcing a resistance to closure and readiness for revolution: this is all vulnerable; it all can go.

Finally, I have come to feel that "subject to change" suits the gamble of this book; that I could bring together pieces from my critical history and let them inhabit a space with newer ones that while not perhaps presenting radical contradictions, at the very least contain their own reworking of the earlier formulations (I argue the same cases with different emphases). I have revised the essays in varying degrees, changing titles, playing with epigraphs, adding and deleting notes, intervening to clarify points now lost even on me, but it is certain that publishing as one goes builds in very real problems. The most obvious one, of course, is the constraint involved in reprinting pieces already taken up in dialogue, or anthologized. As much as I might have wanted to in places, I wasn't able to rewrite the history of the past ten years. It has also seemed to me that at a moment when writing *on* feminist criticism is tending to draw up positions (battle lines?) as if they couldn't change, as if no one's thinking evolved, as if nothing overflowed the neat paradigms we have been tempted to construct in order to have a history "of our own," it was worth running the risk of leaving in the traces of the difficulty and embarrassment of doing the work (its scenes, in all senses of the word) in the hope that we not—playing Athena to Arachne—cut ourselves off from a possible future of subjects to change.

## NOTES

1. The students in that graduate seminar, whom I thank collectively here for helping me begin, were: Louise Adler, Elvire Borenstein, Theresa Bowers, Mary Jane Ciccarello, Marie-Claude Hays, Claude Holland, Alice Jardine, Judith A. Low, Carol V. Richards, Sylvia Richards, Paulette Rose, Françoise Thybulle, Margaret Waller.

2. My contribution was published as an edited record of the proceedings in pamphlet form by the Barnard Women's Center, 1978.

3. This was the distinction betwen feminist critique and feminist criticism that Elaine Showalter had elaborated informally at an earlier "Scholar and Feminist" conference at Barnard, and that became the unevenly valued opposition of critique and "gynocritics" of "Toward a Feminist Poetics."

4. After the conference, Margaret Waller, then one of the students from the seminar on French women writers, gracefully brought Barthes's onion metaphor to my attention.

5. As it turned out, it was largely from the work of that first seminar that "Emphasis Added: Plots and Plausibilities in Women's Fiction" emerged. I wrote "Emphasis Added" for a public lecture at the University of Michigan at Ann Arbor (Fall 1978) where I had been invited by the French department to spend a week visiting and teaching in Michel Pierssens's seminar on criticism and theory. This was my first public lecture, and I had been asked to speak to an audience who would not necessarily be "in French." At the time, that request seemed daunting, and I smoked through the entire lecture. Looking back, I am grateful that I was asked to address myself to a more "general" public. Otherwise, I might still be in French.

6. This intersection of concerns is close in spirit to the configuration of relations mapped in the title of the important 1981 special—collectively edited at Dartmouth—issue of *Yale French Studies*, "Feminist Readings: French Texts/American Contexts."

7. I'm thinking of Elaine Showalter's remarks in "Women Who Write Are Women": "The female witness, sensitive or not, is still not accepted as first-person universal" (33).

8. On the history of Feminisms in France see *New French Feminisms*, edited by Elaine Marks and Isabelle de Courtivron, and Maïté Albistur and Daniel Armogathe's *Histoire du féminisme français*.

9. In the tradition I describe I would include before Sand works by Villedieu, Tencin, Riccoboni, and Claire de Duras. The writing that takes place in what appears to be a gap between Sand and Colette remains to be explored as a history. Some individual names are known—Louise Colet, Daniel Stern, Gyp, Rachilde, Juliette Adam—but for now their literary relations have

not been traced. Cheryl Morgan, a doctoral candidate in the French department at Columbia, has begun to explore the reasons for the feminist critical blank.

10. Despite the very different corpus with which she works, Rachel DuPlessis and I have quite similar ideas about a poetics of feminist writing. Thus, DuPlessis says of the writers she discusses: "These authors are 'feminist' because they construct a variety of oppositional strategies to the depiction of gender institutions in narrative" (34). I develop our contiguities more explicitly throughout the individual readings, especially in my chapter on Graffigny's *Peruvian Letters*.

In part because of these kinds of intertextual connections, in part because of the theoretical complications it raises (about reading literature in history), despite my sense that a poetics (even of gender) needs to be grounded, I have not sought to tie a definition of feminist writing to the historical moments of feminist movements or currents. In *A Literature of Their Own*, for instance, Elaine Showalter identifies feminist writing (as opposed to what she calls feminine and female literature) with the period 1880 to 1920 and women's right to vote (although she also reserves the possibility of a more fluid use of the term). And most recently, in the introduction to her new book, "Mothers, Daughters, and Narrative," Marianne Hirsch chooses to restrict the use of the term "feminist" to the feminist movement of the 1970s and 1980s, "an aesthetic connected to a movement of active social resistance."

11. Beth Rigel Daugherty's "The Whole Contention Between Mr. Bennett and Mrs. Woolf, Revisited," offers enormously useful detail about the actual exchange. I thank Brenda Silver for bringing the essay to my attention. "Mr. Bennett and Mrs. Brown" is the central fable of Mary Ann Caws's moving "Centennial Presidential Address 1983: Realizing Fictions"; and the writing fiction of a thoughtful position paper by Shari Benstock, "Reading the Signs of Women's Writing."

12. By this I mean that we have to find new ways to get at the weave of writing at a given historical moment in order to see what has been retained, and why. In *French Novelists of Today* (a book first published in 1955 and reprinted in 1967), for example, Henri Peyre, following Woolf's chronology, also locates a "revolution in French fiction" in 1910. In his survey, which is meant to appraise, Peyre, in passing, places Colette (whom he sees as "antedeluvian"). While he acknowledges her "skilled workmanship" and compares her use of the adjective to Proust's, he judges her qualities as a novelist to be "grossly overrated and . . . responsible for the sad plight of feminine writing in France up to the fourth decade of the present century" (276–77). Although a look at these moments of canon formation has not been my project here, I think now that the study of women's writing in the future will need to focus on these intergendered occasions in literary history.

13. To point to an area I have left underdeveloped in this discussion: before the twentieth century, the imaginary of French women writers under the sign of Lafayette is generally aristocratic. Although the question of money and productive activity for women subtly punctuates most of these novels, only in *The Vagabond* does the issue become a central feature of woman's identity as it is bound up with a scene of work. The attention to money, class, and work comes much earlier in the novels of English women writers.

14. I'm alluding to the arguments articulated in Domna Stanton's essay in

*The Future of Difference,* and indeed the premises of the conference ("The Scholar and the Feminist VI"), conceived and orchestrated by Alice Jardine, that took place at Barnard in 1979, and that led to the volume. This is the moment when French theory as a powerful intervention begins to have its day in feminist and nonfeminist contexts. Mary Jacobus identifies a similar chronology, and its importance to her own evolution in the preface to *Reading Woman.* Margaret Homans, who has rehearsed these issues in several essays, seeks in *Bearing the Word* to elaborate a productive practice through the "critical contradictions" (xiii) posed by Anglo/American and French positionings.

15. It is also the case that the essay on autobiography was my first attempt to come to terms with women's writing, and that to the extent that I am reconstructing my own history as a feminist critic I wanted to include it. In the notion of "a dialectics of identification" that constituted the first part of the essay's original title, I was rehearsing the notion of "overreading" that I develop in "Arachnologies." In the shift now to "Writing Fictions," I am concerned with promoting the attrition of genre. That I began working on women's writing by writing on autobiography has something to do with good fortune—in 1977 Domna Stanton invited me to speak at a panel she was chairing on women's autobiography at the meetings of the Northeast Modern Language Association—and something to do with the status of this material in the French tradition: the autobiographical writings of Sand, Colette, and Beauvoir are well known (and in print—Sand's autobiography in a Pléiade edition) and they provided me with an accessible point of departure (given the status of women writers in France as figures, this is not surprising). I needed more of an education to discover the texts of women's fiction.

16. I'm thinking about the reification of this polarization operated by Toril Moi in *Sexual/Textual Politics.* Moi manages to collapse each side of the American/French divide with an astonishing lack of concern for the bodies (and positions) under erasure. On the one hand, she declares: "So far, lesbian and/or black feminist criticism have presented exactly the same *methodological* and *theoretical* problems as the rest of Anglo/American feminist criticism" (86). On the other, she makes Julia Kristeva (whose reluctance to be identified with feminism is well documented) the heroine of French feminism and ends her book *in* Derrida's words. It would be the subject of another book to restore the complexities to "French" and "American" eradicated here, but more crucially to redefine the *"textual theory"* that supplies Moi's categories. Naomi Schor acutely reviews Moi's moves in "Introducing Feminism."

17. This is of course playful and serious. I'm thinking specifically of Teresa de Lauretis and Rosi Braidotti's critical projects, and the voices of Italian feminism. But I'm also thinking more generally of the necessity to look elsewhere, beyond the inevitable metropolitan references, for different locations and material, beyond the exclusions of another, feminist "already read."

18. When I then learned from Carolyn Heilbrun that Lois Gould had just completed a novel called *Subject to Change,* I had to acknowledge the futility of trying not to bear one's date.

# I

## *Reading Women's Writing*

# [ 1 ]

# *Emphasis Added: Plots and Plausibilities in Women's Fiction*

> Nothing came down the street; nobody passed. A single leaf
> detached itself from the plane tree at the end of the street, and
> in that pause and suspension fell. Somehow it was like a signal
> falling, a signal pointing to a force in things which one had
> overlooked.
>
> Virginia Woolf, *A Room of One's Own*[1]

IF WE TAKE *The Princess of Clèves* as the first text of women's
fiction in France, then we may observe that French women's fiction has from its beginnings been *discredited*.[2] By this I mean literally and literarily denied credibility: "Mme de Clèves's confession to her husband," writes Bussy-Rabutin to his cousin Mme de
Sévigné, "is extravagant, and can only occur in a true story; but
when one makes up a story it is ridiculous to ascribe such extraordinary feelings to one's heroine. The author in so doing was more
concerned with not resembling other novels than with using common sense."[3] Without dwelling on the local fact that a similarly
"singular" confession had appeared in Villedieu's *Les Désordres
de l'amour* some three years before the publication of Lafayette's
novel, and bracketing the more general fact that the novel as a
genre has from its beginnings labored under charges of *invrai-
semblance*,[4] let us reread Bussy-Rabutin's complaint. In a true story,
as in "true confessions," the avowal would be believable because
in life, unlike art, anything can happen; hence the constraints of
likeliness do not apply. In a made-up story, however, the confession offends because it violates our readerly expectations about
fiction. In other words, art should not imitate life but *re*inscribe
received ideas about the presentation of life in art. To depart from
the limits of common sense (tautologically, to be extravagant) is
to risk exclusion from the canon.[5] Because—as Genette, glossing

this same document in "Vraisemblance et motivation," puts it—
*"extravagance is a privilege of the real"* (74), to produce a work
not like other novels, an original rather than a copy, means paradoxically that its literariness will be sniffed out: "The first adventure of the Coulommiers gardens is not plausible," Bussy-Rabutin
observes later in his letter, "and smells of the novel [*sent le roman*]."

Genette begins his essay with an analysis of contemporary reactions to *The Princess of Clèves*. Reviewing the writings of seventeenth-century poeticians, Genette shows that *vraisemblance* and
*bienséance*, "plausibility" and "propriety," are wedded to each
other; and the precondition of plausibility is the stamp of approval
affixed by *public opinion*:[6] "Read or assumed, this 'opinion' is
quite close to what today would be called an ideology, that is, a
body of maxims and prejudices which constitute both a vision of
the world and a system of values" (73). What this statement means
is that the critical reaction to any given text is hermeneutically
bound to another and preexistent text: the *doxa* of socialities.
Plausibility then is an effect of reading through a grid of
concordance:

> What defines plausibility is the formal principle of respect for
> the norm, that is, the existence of a relation of implication
> between the particular conduct attributed to a given charac-
> ter, and a given, general, received and implicit maxim. . . .
> To understand the behavior of a character (for example), is
> to be able to refer it back to an approved maxim, and this
> reference is perceived as a demonstration of cause and effect.
> (174–75)

If no maxim is available to account for a particular piece of
behavior, that behavior is read as unmotivated and unconvincing.
Mme de Clèves's confession makes no sense in the seventeenth-
century sociolect because it is, Genette argues, *"an action without
a maxim"* (75). A heroine without a maxim, like a rebel without
a cause, is destined to be misunderstood. And she is.

To build a narrative around a character whose behavior is deliberately idiopathic, however, is not merely to create a puzzling
fiction but to fly in the face of a certain ideology (of the text and
its context), to violate a grammar of motives that describes while
prescribing, in this instance, what wives, not to say women, should
or should not do. The question one might then ask is whether this
crucial barbarism is in any way connected to the gender of its author. If we were to uncover a feminine "tradition"—diachronic

recurrences—of such ungrammaticalities, would we have the basis for a poetics of women's fiction? And what do I mean by women's fiction?

Working backward, I should say first that I do not mean what in a certain French feminism is called *écriture féminine*, which can be described roughly as a process or a practice by which the female *body,* with its peculiar drives and rhythms, inscribes itself as text.[7] "Feminine writing" is an important theoretical formulation; but it privileges a textuality of the avant-garde, a literary production of the late twentieth century, and it is therefore fundamentally a hope, if not a blueprint for the future. In what is perhaps the best-known statement of contemporary French feminist thinking about women's writing, "The Laugh of the Medusa," Hélène Cixous states that, "with a few rare exceptions, there has not yet been any writing that inscribes femininity" (878). On the contrary, what she finds historically in the texts of the "immense majority" of female writers is "workmanship [which is] . . . in no way different from male writing, and which either obscures women or reproduces the classic representations of women (as sensitive—intuitive—dreamy, etc.)" (878). I think this assertion is both true and untrue. It is true if one is looking for a radical difference in women's writing and locates that difference in an insurgence of the body, in what Julia Kristeva has called the irruption of the semiotic.[8] And it is true again if difference is sought on the level of the sentence. If, however, we situate difference in the insistence of a certain thematic structuration, in the form of content, then it is not true that women's writing has been in no way different from male writing. I consider the "demaximization" wrought by Lafayette's novel to be one example of how difference can be read.

Before I proceed to other manifestations of difference, let me make a few general remarks about the status of women's literature—about its existence, in my view, as a viable corpus for critical inquiry. Whether one believes, as does Cixous, that there is "male writing," "*marked* writing . . . run by a libidinal and cultural—hence political, typically masculine economy" ("Laugh of the Medusa," 879), or that (great) literature has no sex because a "great mind must be androgynous," literary *history* remains a male preserve, a history of writing by men.[9] In England the history of the novel admits the names of Jane Austen, the Brontës, George Eliot, and Virginia Woolf. In France it includes Lafayette, although only for *The Princess of Clèves* and always with the nagging insinuation that La Rochefoucauld had a hand in that. Staël,

George Sand, and Colette figure in the national record, although
mainly as the scandalous heroines of their times. Nevertheless, there
have always been women writing. What is one to do with them?
One can leave them where they are, like so many sleeping dogs,
and mention them only in passing as epiphenomena in every period, despite the incontrovertible evidence that most were successful and even literarily influential in their day. One can continue, then, a politics of benign neglect that reads difference, not
to say popularity, as inferiority.[10] Or one can perform two simultaneous and compensatory gestures: the archaeological act of re-
covering "lost" women writers and the reconstructive act of establishing a parallel tradition, as Elaine Showalter has done in *A
Literature of Their Own* and Ellen Moers in *Literary Women: The
Great Writers.* The advantage of these moves is that they make
visible an otherwise invisible intertext: a reconstituted record of
predecession and prefiguration, debts acknowledged and unac-
knowledged, anxieties and enthusiasms.[11]

Elizabeth Janeway, by way of T. S. Eliot, has suggested another
way of thinking about women's literature. She cites the evolution
in Eliot's attitude toward that body of texts we know as American
literature. At first he held, as many critics have about women's
literature, that it does not exist: "There can only be one English
literature. . . . There cannot be British or American literature."
Later, however, he was to acknowledge "what has never, I think,
been found before, two literatures in the same language" (344).
That reformulation, as Janeway adapts it to delineate the conti-
nent of women's literature, is useful because it locates the problem
of identity and difference not on the level of the sentence—not as
a question of another language—but on the level of the text in all
its complexities: a culturally bound, and I would even say, culturally overdetermined production. This new mapping of a parallel
geography does not, of course, resolve the oxymoron of marginality: how is it that women, a statistical majority in our culture,
perform as a "literary subculture" (Showalter, *A Literature,* 14–
15)? But it does provide a body of writing from which to begin to
identify specificities that derive from that relation. Because women
are both of the culture and out of it (or under it), written by it
and remaining a largely silent though literate majority, to look for
*uniquely* "feminine" textual indexes that can be deciphered in
"blind" readings is pointless. (Documentation on the critical reception of *Jane Eyre* and *Adam Bede,* for example, has shown how

silly such pretensions can be.)[12] There are no infallible signs, no failsafe technique by which to determine the gender of an author. But that is not the point of the *post*-compensatory gesture that follows what I call the new literary history. At stake instead is a reading that *consciously* recreates the object it describes, attentive always to a difference—what T. S. Eliot calls "strong local flavor" (in Janeway, 344) not dependent on the discovery of an exclusive alterity.

The difficulty of the reading comes from the irreducibly complicated relationship women have historically had to the language of the dominant culture, a playful relationship that Luce Irigaray has described as "mimeticism":

> To play with mimesis is, thus, for a woman to try to recover the place of her exploitation by discourse, without allowing herself to be simply reduced to it. It means to resubmit herself . . . to "ideas," in particular to ideas about herself, that are elaborated in/by a masculine logic, but so as to make "visible," by an effect of playful repetition what was supposed to remain invisible: the cover-up of a possible operation of the feminine in language. It also means "to unveil" the fact that if women are such good mimics, it is because they are not simply reabsorbed in this function. *They also remain elsewhere. . . .* (76/74)

This "elsewhere"—which, needless to say, is not so easily pinpointed—is, she adds, an "insistence" of "matter" and "sexual pleasure" ("jouissance").[13] I prefer to think of the insistence Irigaray posits as a form of emphasis: an italicized version of what passes for the neutral or standard face. Spoken or written, italics are a modality of intensity and stress; a way of marking what has always already been said, of making a common text one's own.[14] Italics are also a form of intonation, "the tunes," McConnell-Ginet writes, "to which we set the text of our talk." "Intonation," she continues, "serves to underscore the gender identification of the participants in certain contexts of communication," and because of differences in intonation, "women's tunes will be interpreted and evaluated from an androcentric perspective" (542). When I speak of italics, then, I mean the emphasis added by registering a certain quality of voice. And this expanded metaphor brings me back to my point of departure.

Genette codes the perception of plausibility in terms of silence:

> The relationship between a plausible narrative and the system
> of plausibility to which it subjects itself is . . . essentially mute:
> the conventions of genre function like a system of natural forces
> and constraints which the narrative obeys as if without no-
> ticing them, and a fortiori without naming them. (76)

By fulfilling the "tacit contract between a work and its public"
(77) this silence both gives pleasure and signifies conformity with
the dominant ideology. The text emancipated from this collusion,
however, is also silent, in that it refuses to justify its infractions,
the "motives and maxims of the actions" (78). Here Genette cites
the silence surrounding Julien Sorel's attempted murder of Mme
de Rênal and the confession of Mme de Clèves. In the first instance, the ideologically complicitous text, the silence is a function
of what Genette calls "plausible narrative"; in the second it is a
function of "arbitrary narrative" (79). And the *sounds* of silence?
They are heard in a third type of narrative, one with a motivated
and *"artificial plausibility"*; this literature, exemplified by the
"endless chatting" of a Balzacian novel, we might call "other-di-
rected," for here authorial commentary justifies its story to society
by providing the missing maxims, or by inventing them. In the
arbitrary narrative Genette sees a rejection of the ideology of a
certain plausibility—an ideology, let us say, of accountability. This
"inner-directed" posture would proclaim instead "that rugged in-
dividuality which makes for the unpredictability of great actions—
and great works" (77).

Two remarks are in order here. Arbitrariness can be taken as
an ideology in itself, that is, as the irreducible freedom and originality of the author (Bussy-Rabutin's complaint, *en somme*). But
more specifically, the refusal of the demands of one economy may
mask the inscription of another. This inscription may seem silent,
or *unarticulated* in/as *authorial commentary (discours)*, without
being absent. (It may simply be inaudible to the dominant mode
of reception.) In *The Princess of Clèves*, for example, "extravagance" is in fact accounted for, I would argue, both by maxims
and by a decipherable effect of italicization. The maxims I refer
to are not direct commentary; and it is true, as Genette writes,
that "nothing is more foreign to the style [of the novel] than sen-
tentious epiphrasis: as if the actions were always either beyond or
beneath all commentary" (78). It is also true that within the narrative the characters do comment on the actions; and although
Genette does not "count" such comments as "chatting," I would

suggest that they constitute an internally motivating discourse: an artificial plausibility *en abyme*. This intratext is maternal discourse; and its *performance* through the "extraordinary feelings" of Mme de Clèves is an instance of italicization. The confession, to state the obvious, makes perfect sense in terms of the idiolect spoken by Mme de Chartres: "Be brave and strong, my daughter; withdraw from the court, force your husband to take you away; do not fear the most brutal and difficult measures; however awful they may seem at first, in the end they will be milder in their effects than the misery of a love affair" (69/68).[15] Moreover, the confession qua confession is set up by reference to a "real life" precedent and is presented by the prince himself as a model of desirable behavior: "Sincerity is so important to me that I think that if my mistress, and even my wife, confessed to me that she was attracted by another . . . I would cast off the role of lover or husband to advise and sympathize with her" (76/76). Seen from this perspective the behavior of the princess is both motivated within the narrative and supplied with a pre-text: the conditions of imitation.

But the confession, which I may already have overemphasized, is not an isolated extravagance in the novel. It is a link in the chain of events that lead to Mme de Clèves's decision not to marry Nemours, even though in this instance, the maxims of the sociolect might support, even expect, the marriage. As Bussy-Rabutin again observes, "And if, against all appearances and custom, this combat between love and virtue were to last in her heart until the death of her husband, then she would be delighted to be able to bring love and virtue together by marrying a man of quality, the finest and the most handsome gentleman of his time." Mme de Lafayette clearly rejects this delightful denouement. Now, Stendhal has speculated that if Mme de Clèves had lived a long life she would have regretted her decision and would have wanted to live like Mme de Lafayette (111). We shall never know, of course, but his comment raises an interesting question: why should Mme de Lafayette keep Mme de Clèves from living in fiction the life she herself had led? The answer to that question would be an essay in itself, but let us tackle the question here from another angle: what do Mme de Clèves's "renunciation" and, before that, her confession tell us about the relation of women writers to fiction, to the heroines of their fiction? Should the heroine's so-called "refusal of love" be read as a defeat and an end to passion—a "suicide," or "the delirium of a *précieuse*" (Doubrovsky, 48; Rousset, 25)? Or is it, rather, a *bypassing* of the dialectics of desire, and in that sense, a pecul-

iarly feminine "act of victory" (Varga, 524)?[16] To understand the
refusal as a victory and as, I believe, a rewriting of eroticism (an
emphasis placed "elsewhere"—as both Irigaray and Woolf say),
from which we might generalize about the economy of representation regulating the heroine and her authors, let us shift critical
gears for a while.

Claudine Herrmann describes the princess as a heroine "written
in a language of dream, dreamt by Mme de Lafayette" (77). What
is the language of that dream, and what is the dream of that language? In the essay called "The Relation of the Poet to Daydreaming" (1908), Freud wonders how that "strange being, the poet, comes
by his material" (44). He goes on to answer his question by con-
sidering the processes at work in children's play and then moves
to daydreams and fantasies in adults. When he begins to describe
the characteristics of the mode of creativity, he makes a blanket
generalization about its impulses that should immediately make
clear the usefulness of his essay for our purposes: "Unsatisfied wishes
are the driving power behind phantasies; every separate phantasy
contains the fulfillment of a wish, and improves upon unsatisfactory reality" (47). What then is the nature of these wishes and,
more to our point, does the sex of the dreamer affect the shaping
of the daydream's text? Freud writes:

> The impelling wishes vary according to the sex, character and
> circumstances of the creator; they may easily be divided, how-
> ever, into two principal groups. Either they are ambitious
> wishes, serving to exalt the person creating them, or they are
> erotic. In young women erotic wishes dominate the phantasies
> *almost exclusively,* for their ambition is *generally comprised*
> in their erotic longings; in young men egoistic and ambitious
> wishes assert themselves plainly enough alongside their erotic
> desires. (47–48; emphasis added)

Here we see that the either/or antinomy, ambitious/erotic, is immediately collapsed to make coexistence possible in masculine fantasies: "in the greater number of ambitious daydreams . . . we
can discover a woman in some corner, for whom the daydreamer
performs all his heroic deeds and at whose feet all his triumphs
are to be laid" (48).

But is this observation reversible? If, to make the logical ex-
trapolation, romance dominates the female daydream and constitutes its primary heroism, is there a *place* in which the ambitious
wish of a young woman asserts itself? Has she an egoistic desire

to be discovered "in some corner"? Freud elides the issue—while leaving the door open (for us) by his modifiers, "almost exclusively" and "generally comprised"—presumably because he is on his way to establishing the relationship between daydreaming and literary creation. The pertinence of differences there is moot, of course, because he conjures up only a male creator: not the great poet, however, but "the less pretentious writers of romances, novels and stories, who are read all the same by the widest circles of men and women" (50). Freud then proceeds to identify the key "marked characteristic" of these fictions: "They all have a hero who is the centre of interest, for whom the author tries to win our sympathy by every possible means, and whom he places under the protection of a special providence" (50). The hero in this literature is continually exposed to danger, but we follow his perilous adventures with a sense of security, because we know that at each turn he will triumph. According to Freud, the basis for this armchair security, for our tranquil contemplation, is the hero's own conviction of invincibility, best rendered by the expression "Nothing can happen to me!" And Freud comments, "It seems to me . . . that this significant mark of invulnerability very clearly betrays—His Majesty the Ego, the hero of *all daydreams* and *all novels*" (51; emphasis added).

Now, if the plots of male fiction chart the daydreams of an ego that would be invulnerable, what do the plots of female fiction reveal? Among French women writers, it would seem at first blush to be the obverse of "nothing can happen to me." The phrase that characterizes the heroine's posture might well be a variant of Murphy's law: if anything can go wrong, it will. And the reader's sense of security, itself dependent on the heroine's, comes from feeling not that the heroine will triumph in some conventionally positive way but that she will transcend the perils of plot with a self-exalting dignity. Here national constraints on the imagination, or what in this essay Freud calls "racial psychology," do seem to matter: the second-chance rerouting of disaster typical of Jane Austen's fiction, for example, is exceedingly rare in France. To the extent that we can speak of a triumph of Her Majesty the Ego in France, it lies in being beyond vulnerability, indeed beyond it all. On the whole, French women writers prefer what Peter Brooks has described as "the melodramatic imagination," a dreamlike and metaphorical drama of the "moral occult" (20). There are recurrent melodramatic plots about women unhappy in love because men are men and women are women. As I said earlier, however, the suffering seems to have its own rewards in the economy of the female unconscious. The heroine proves to be better than her victimizers; and perhaps this ultimate superiority, which is to be read in the choice to go beyond love, beyond "erotic longings," is the figure that the "ambitious wishes" of women writers (dreamers) takes.

In the economy of Freud's plot, as we all know, fantasy scenarios are generated by consciously repressed content; and so he naturally assumes a motive for the "concealment" of "ambitious wishes": "the overweening self-regard" that a young man "acquires in the indulgent atmosphere surrounding his childhood" must be suppressed "so that he may find his proper place in a society that is full of other persons making similar claims" (48)—hence the daydreams in which the hero conquers all to occupy victoriously center stage. The content that a young woman represses comes out in erotic daydreams because "a well-brought-up woman is, indeed, credited with only a minimum of erotic desire" (48). Now, there is a class of novels by women that "maximizes" that minimum, a type of fiction that George Eliot attacks as "Silly Novels by Lady Novelists": "The heroine is usually an heiress . . . with perhaps a vicious baronet, an amiable duke, and an irresistible younger son of a marquis as lovers in the foreground, a clergyman and a poet sighing for her in the middle distance, and a crowd of undefined adorers dimly indicated beyond" (*Essays,* 301–2). After sketching out the variations of plot that punctuate the heroine's " 'starring' expedition through life," Eliot comments on the security with which we await the inevitably happy end:

> Before matters arrive at this desirable issue our feelings are tried by seeing the noble, lovely and gifted heroine pass through many *mauvais moments,* but we have the satisfaction of knowing that her sorrows are wept into embroidered pocket-handkerchiefs . . . and that whatever vicissitudes she may undergo . . . she comes out of them all with a complexion more blooming and locks more redundant than ever. (303)

The plots of these "silly novels" bring grist to Freud's mill—or rather, the grist I bring to his mill—in an almost uncanny way; and they would seem to undermine the argument I am on the verge of elaborating. But as Eliot says:

> Happily, we are not dependent on argument to prove that Fiction is a department of literature in which women can, after

their kind, fully equal men. A cluster of great names, both living and dead, rush to our memories in evidence that women can produce novels not only fine, but among the very finest;— novels too, that have a precious speciality, lying quite apart from masculine aptitudes and experience. (324)

(Let me work through her essay to my own.) What Eliot is attacking here is not only the relationship of certain women writers to literature but the critical reception given women's fiction. We might also say that she is attacking, the better to separate herself from, those women writers whose language is structured exactly like the unconscious that Freud has assigned to them, those writers (and their heroines) whose ambitious wishes are contained *entirely* in their erotic longings. And she is attacking these novelists the better to defend not those women who write *like* men (for she posits a "precious speciality" to women's productions), but those women who write in their own way, "after their kind," and implicitly about something else. Silly novels are that popular artifact which has always been and still is known as "women's literature"—a term, I should add, applied to such fiction by those who do not read it.[17]

Women writers then, in contrast to lady novelists, are writers whose texts would be "among the finest" (to stay with Eliot's terminology) and for whom the "ambitious wish" (to stay with Freud's) manifests itself as fantasy within another economy. In this economy, egoistic desires would assert themselves paratactically alongside erotic ones. The repressed content, I think, would be not erotic impulses but an impulse to power: a fantasy of power that would revise the social grammar in which women are never defined as subjects; a fantasy of power that disdains a sexual exchange in which women can participate only as objects of circulation. The daydreams or fictions of women writers would then, like those of men, say, "Nothing can happen to me!" But the modalities of that invulnerability would be marked in an essentially different way. I am talking, of course, about the power of the weak.[18] The inscription of this power is not always easy to decipher, because "the most essential form of accommodation for the weak is to conceal what power they do have" (Watson, 113). Moreover, to pick up a lost thread, when these modalities of difference are perceived, they are generally called implausibilities. They are not perceived, or are misperceived, because the scripting of this fantasy does not bring the aesthetic "forepleasure" Freud says fantasy scenarios inevitably bring: pleasure bound to recognition and *identification* (54), the "agrément" Genette assigns to plausible narrative. (Perhaps we shall not have a poetics of women's literature until we have more weak readers.)

In *Les Voleuses de langue,* Claudine Herrmann takes up what I call the politics of dreams, or the ideology of daydreaming, in *The Princess of Clèves:*

> A daydream is perpetuated when it loses all chance of coming true, when the woman dreaming [*la rêveuse*] cannot make it pass into reality. If women did not generally experience the love they desire as a repeated impossibility, they would dream about it less. They would dream of other, perhaps more interesting things. Nevertheless, written in a language of dream, dreamt by Mme de Lafayette, the Princess of Clèves never dreams . . . for she knows that *love as she imagines it* is not realizable. What is realizable is a counterfeit she does not want. Her education permits her to glimpse this fact: men and women exchange feelings that are not equivalent. . . . Woman's "daydreaming" is a function of a world in which nothing comes true on her terms. (77–79)

"Men and women exchange feelings that are not equivalent." Mme de Clèves's brief experience of the court confirms the principle of difference at the heart of her mother's maxims. Mme de Clèves's rejection of Nemours on his terms, however, derives its necessity not only from the logic of maternal discourse (Nemours's love, like his name, is negative and plural: *ne/amours*) but also from the demands of Mme de Lafayette's dream. In this dream nothing can happen to the heroine, because she understands that the power and pleasure of the weak derive from circumventing the laws of contingency and circulation. She withdraws then and confesses not merely to resist possession, as her mother would have wished, but to improve on it: to *rescript* possession.

The plausibility of this novel lies in the structuration of its fantasy. For if, to continue spinning out Herrmann's metaphor, the heroine does not dream, she does daydream. And perhaps the most significant confession in the novel is neither the first (to her husband, that she is vulnerable to desire) nor the third (to Nemours, that she desires him) but the second, which is silent and entirely telling: I refer, of course, to her nocturnal reverie at Coulommiers. Although all three confessions prefigure by their extravagance the heroine's retreat from the eyes of the world, it is this dreamlike event that is least ambiguous in underlining the erotic valence of the ambitious scenario.

At Coulommiers, her country retreat, Mme de Clèves sits one warm evening, secretly observed by Nemours, winding ribbons of his colors around an India cane. (I take her surreptitious acquisition of his cane to be the counterpart of his theft of her miniature, in this crisscrossing of desires by metonymy.) As Michel Butor observes in his famous reading of this scene, "the mind of the princess is operating at this moment in a zone obscure to herself; it is as if she is knotting the ribbons around the cane in a dream, and her dream becomes clear little by little; the one she is thinking of begins to take on a face, and she goes to look for it" (76–77). Thus, having finished her handiwork, she places herself in front of a painting, a historical tableau of members of the court that she has had transported to her retreat, a painting including a likeness of Nemours: "She sat down and gazed at this portrait with an intensity and dreaminess [*rêverie*] that only passion can inspire" (168/155). And Butor comments, "One hardly needs a diploma in psychoanalysis to detect and appreciate the symbolism of this whole scene" (76). Indeed, it is quite clear that the princess is seen here in a moment of solitary pleasure, in a daydream of "fetishistic sublimation" (Grossvogel, 134). This autoeroticism would seem to be the only sexual performance she can afford in an economy regulated by dispossession.

Her retreat to Coulommiers, though, must be thought of not as a flight from sexuality but as a movement *into* it. As Sylvère Lotringer has observed, Mme de Clèves leaves the court not to flee passion but to preserve it (517). To preserve it, moreover, on her own terms. Unlike Nemours—who is not content to possess the object of his desire in representation (the purloined portrait) and who pleads silently after this scene, "Only look at me the way I saw you look at my portrait tonight; how could you look so gently at my portrait and then so cruelly fly from my presence?" (171/157)—the princess chooses "the duke of the portrait, not the man who seeks to step out of the frame" (519). Here she differs from Austen's heroine Elizabeth Bennet, who stands gazing before her lover's portrait and feels "a more gentle sensation towards the original than she had ever felt in the height of their acquaintance" (272). Elizabeth can accept the hand of the man who steps out of the frame; the princess cannot. For if, in the world of *Pride and Prejudice*, "between the picture's eyes and Elizabeth's hangs what will be given shape when the marriage of the lovers is formalized"

(Brownstein, 130–31), in the world of the court the princess's response to Nemours must remain specular. Her desire cannot be
framed by marriage—*à l'anglaise*. If, however, as I believe, the
withdrawal to Coulommiers is homologous to the final withdrawal, then there is no reason to imagine that at a remove from
the world—or, rather, in the company of the world contained by
representation in painting—the princess does not continue to experience her "erotic longings." But the fulfillment of the wish is
to be realized in the daydream itself.

The daydream, then, is both the stuff of fairy tales ("Someday
my prince will come") and their rewriting ("Someday my prince
will come, but we will not live happily ever after"). The princess
refuses to marry the duke, however, not because she doesn't want
to live happily after but because she does. And by choosing not
to act on that desire but to preserve it in and as fantasy, she both
performs maternal discourse and italicizes it as repossession. Her
choice is therefore not the simple reinscription of the seventeenth-
century convention of feminine renunciation, dependent on the logic
of either/or, but the sign of both/and, concretized by her final
dual residence: in the convent *and* at home. "Perverted convention," as Peggy Kamuf names it, writing of another literary fetishist (Saint-Preux in Julie's closet): "The scene of optimal pleasure
is within the prohibition which forms the walls of the house. Just
on this side of the transgressive act, the fetishist's pleasure . . . is
still in the closet" (203–4). This form of possession by metonymy
both acknowledges the law and short-circuits it. Nobody, least of
all the duke of Nemours, believes in her renunciation (just as her
husband never fully believed her confession):

> Do you think that your resolutions can hold against a man
> who adores you and who is fortunate enough to attract you?
> It is more difficult than you think, Madame, to resist the at-
> traction of love. You have done it *by an austere virtue which
> has almost no example;* but that virtue is no longer opposed
> to our feelings and I hope that you will follow them despite
> yourself. (191/174–75; emphasis added)

Mme de Clèves will not be deterred by sheer difficulty, by mere
plausibility, by Nemour's *maxims*. She knows herself to be without a text. "No woman but you in the world," she has been told
earlier in the novel, "would confide everything she knows in her
husband" (123/116). "The singularity of such a confession," the
narrator comments after the fait accompli, "for which she could

find no example, made her see all the danger of it" (134/125). The danger of singularity precisely is sociolinguistic: the attempt to *communicate* in a language, an idiolect, that would nonetheless break with the coded rules of communication. An impossibility, as Jakobson has seen: "Private property, in the domain of language does not exist: everything is socialized. The verbal exchange, like every form of human relation, requires at least two interlocutors; an idiolect, in the final analysis, therefore can only be a *slightly perverse fiction*" (33; emphasis added). Thus in the end Mme de Clèves herself becomes both the impossibility of an example for others "in life" and its possibility in fiction. "Her life," the last line of the novel tells us, which "was rather short, left inimitable examples of virtue" (198/180). The last word in French is the challenge to reiteration—*inimitables,* the mark of the writer's ambitious wish.

I hope it is understood that I am not suggesting we read a heroine as her author's double—a biographical conflation that from the beginning has dominated and distorted the literary criticism of women's writing.[19] Rather, I am arguing that the peculiar shape of a heroine's destiny in novels by women, the implausible twists of plot so common in these novels, is a form of insistence about the relation of women to writing: a comment on the stakes of difference within the theoretical indifference of literature itself.

Woolf begins her essay on Eliot in the *Common Reader* by saying, "To read George Eliot attentively is to become aware how little one knows about her" (166). But then, a few pages later, she comments:

> For long she preferred not to think of herself at all. Then, when the first flush of creative energy was exhausted and self-confidence had come to her, she wrote more and more from the personal standpoint, but she did so without the unhesitating abandonment of the young. *Her self-consciousness is always marked when her heroines say what she herself would have said.* She disguised them in every possible way. She granted them beauty and wealth into the bargain; she invented more improbably, a taste for brandy. The disconcerting and stimulating fact remained that she was compelled by the very power of her genius to step forth in person upon the quiet bucolic scene. (173; emphasis added)

What interests me here is the "marking" Woolf identifies, an underlining of what she later describes as Eliot's heroines' "demand

for something—they scarcely know what—for something that is
perhaps incompatible with the facts of human existence" (175).
This demand of the heroine for something else is in part what I
mean by "italicization": the extravagant wish for a *story* that would
turn out differently.

In the fourth chapter of book 5 of *The Mill on the Floss* Maggie
Tulliver, talking with Philip Wakem in the "Red Deeps," returns
a novel he has lent her:

> "Take back your *Corinne*," said Maggie. . . . "You were
> right in telling me she would do me no good, but you were
> wrong in thinking I should wish to be like her."
>
> "Wouldn't you really like to be a tenth muse, then, Mag-
> gie?" . . .
>
> "Not at all," said Maggie laughing. "The muses were un-
> comfortable goddesses, I think—obliged always to carry rolls
> and musical instruments about with them . . ."
>
> "You agree with me in not liking Corinne, then?"
>
> "I didn't finish the book," said Maggie. "As soon as I came
> to the blond-haired young lady reading in the park, I shut it
> up and determined to read no further. I foresaw that light-
> complexioned girl would win away all the love from Corinne
> and make her miserable. I'm determined to read no more books
> where the blond-haired women carry away all the happiness.
> I should begin to have a prejudice against them. If you could
> give me some story, now, where the dark woman triumphs,
> it would restore the balance. I want to avenge Rebecca, and
> Flora MacIvor, and Minna, and all the rest of the dark un-
> happy ones. . . ."
>
> "Well, perhaps you will avenge the dark women in your
> own person and carry away all the love from your cousin Lucy.
> She is sure to have some handsome young man of St. Ogg's
> at her feet now, and you have only to shine upon him—your
> fair little cousin will be quite quenched in your beams."
>
> "Philip, that is not pretty of you, to apply my nonsense to
> anything real," said Maggie looking hurt. (348–49)

Maggie's literary instincts were correct. True to the laws of genre,
Corinne—despite, or rather because of her genius and exceptionality—is made miserable and the blond Lucile, her half-sister, carries the day, although she is deprived of a perfectly happy end. But
whatever Eliot's, or Maggie's, "prejudices" against the destinies
of Scott's heroines, Maggie no more than Corinne avenges the

dark woman in her own person. Even though, as Philip predicts, Maggie's inner radiance momentarily quenches her fairhaired cousin Lucy, "reality"—that is to say, Eliot's novel—proves to be as hard on darkhaired women as literature is. What is important in this deliberate intertextuality, which has not gone unnoted (Moers, 174), is that both heroines revolt against the text of a certain "happily ever after." As Madelyn Gutwirth observes in her book on Germaine de Staël, Corinne prefers "her genius to the . . . bonds of marriage, but that is not to say she thereby renounces happiness. On the contrary, it is her wish to be happy, that is to be herself *and* to love, that kills her" (225). Maggie Tulliver, too, would be herself and love, but the price for *that* unscriptable wish proves again to be the deferral of conventional erotic longings, what Maggie calls "earthly happiness." Almost two hundred years after the challenge to the maxim wrought by the blond (as it turns out) princess of Clèves, George Eliot, through the scenario of definitive postponement, "imitates" Lafayette.

The last two books of *The Mill on the Floss* are called, respectively, "The Great Temptation" and "The Final Rescue." As the plot moves toward closure, the chapter headings of these books— "First Impressions," "Illustrating the Laws of Attraction," "Borne Along by the Tide," "Waking," "St. Ogg's Passes Judgement," "The Last Conflict"—further emphasize the sexual struggle at the heart of the novel. For, as Philip had anticipated, Maggie dazzles blond Lucy's fiancé, Stephen Guest, in "First Impressions," but then, surely what Philip had not dreamt of, the pair is swept away. Maggie, previously unawakened by her own fiancé, *Wakem*, awakens both to her desire and to what she calls her duty, only to fulfill both by drowning, attaining at last that "wondrous happiness that is one with pain" (545). Though I do some violence to the scope of Eliot's narrative by carving a novel out of a novel, the last two books taken together as they chart the culmination of a heroine's erotic destiny have a plot of their own—a plot, moreover, with elective affinities to the conclusion of *The Princess of Clèves*, and to the conclusion of my argument.

Like Mme de Clèves after her husband's death, Maggie knows herself to be technically free to marry her lover but feels bound, though not for the same reasons, to another script. And Stephen Guest, who like Nemours does not believe in "mere resolution" (499), finds Maggie's refusal to follow her passions "unnatural" and "horrible": "If you loved me as I love you, we should throw everything else to the winds for the sake of belonging to each other"

(447). Maggie does love him, just as the princess loves the duke, passionately; and she is tempted: part of her longs to be transported by the exquisite currents of desire. But her awakening, like that of the princess, though again not for the same reasons, is double. She falls asleep on the boatride down the river. When she awakens and disentangles her mind "from the confused web of dreams" (494), like Mme de Clèves after her own brush with death, Maggie pulls away from the man who has briefly but deeply tempted her. She will not build her happiness on the unhappiness of others:

> It is not force that ought to rule us—this that we feel for each other; it would rend me away from all that my past life has made dear and holy to me. I can't set out on a fresh life and forget that; I must go back to it, and cling to it, else I shall feel as if there were nothing firm beneath my feet. (502)

What is the content of this sacred past? Earlier, before the waking on the river, when Maggie was tempted only by the "fantasy" of a "life filled with all luxuries, with daily incense of adoration near and distant, and with all possibilities of culture at her command," the narrator had commented on the pull of that erotic scenario:

> But there were things in her stronger than vanity—passion, and affection, and long deep memories of early discipline and effort, of early claims on her love and pity; and the stream of vanity was soon swept along and mingled imperceptibly with that wider current which was at its highest force today. . . . (457)

Maggie's renunciation of Stephen Guest, then, is not so simple as I have made it out to be, for the text of these "early claims" this archaic wish has a power both erotic and ambitious in its own right. That "wider current" is, of course, the broken bond with her brother. And the epigraph to the novel, "In their death they were not divided," is the telos toward which the novel tends; for it is also the last line of the novel, the epitaph on the tombstone of the brother and sister who drown in each other's arms.

Maggie, obeying what Stephen called her "perverted notion of right," her passion for a "mere idea" (538), drowns finally in an implausible flood. Maggie, no more than Mme de Clèves, could be *persuaded* (to invoke Jane Austen's last novel); for neither regarded a second chance as an alternative to be embraced. Maggie's return home sans husband is not understood by the community. And the narrator explains that "public opinion in these cases is always of the feminine gender—not the world, but the world's wife" (512–13). Despite the phrase, Eliot does not locate the inadequacy of received social ideas in gender per se; her attack on the notion of a "master-key that will fit all cases" is in fact directed at the "men of maxims": "The mysterious complexity of our life is not to be embraced by maxims" (521). This commentary seeks to justify Maggie's choice, her turning away from the maxim, and thus inscribes an internal "artificial plausibility": the text within the text, as we saw that function in *The Princess of Clèves*. The commentary constitutes another reading, a reading by "reference," as Eliot puts it, to the "special circumstances that mark the individual lot" (521). Like Mme de Clèves, Maggie has been given extraordinary feelings, and those feelings engender another and extravagant narrative logic.

There is a feminist criticism today that laments Eliot's ultimate refusal to satisfy her heroine's longing for that "something . . . incompatible with the facts of human existence":

> Sadly, and it is a radical criticism of George Eliot, she does not commit herself fully to the energies and aspirations she lets loose in these women. Does she not cheat them, and cheat us, ultimately, in allowing them so little? Does she not excite our interest through the breadth and the challenge of the implications of her fiction, and then deftly dam up and fence round the momentum she has so powerfully created? She diagnoses so brilliantly "the common yearning of womanhood," and then cures it, sometimes drastically, as if it were indeed a disease. (Calder, 158)

It is as though these critics, somewhat like Stendhal disbelieving the conviction of Mme de Clèves, would have Maggie live George Eliot's life. The point is, it seems to me, that the plots of women's literature are not about "life" and solutions in any therapeutic sense, nor should they be. They are about the plots of literature itself, about the constraints the maxim places on rendering a female life in fiction. Lafayette quietly, George Eliot less silently, both italicize by the demaximization of their heroines' texts the difficulty of curing plot of life, and life of certain plots.[20]

In her essay "On Women and Fiction," Lynn Sukenick describes the uncomfortable posture of all women writers in our culture, within and without the text: what I would call a posture of imposture. And she says of the role of gender in relation to the literary project: "Like the minority writer, the female writer exists

within an inescapable condition of identity which distances her
from the mainstream of the culture and forces her either to stress
her separation from the masculine literary tradition or to pursue
her resemblance to it" (28). Were she to forget her double bind,
the "phallic critics" (as Mary Ellman named them) would remind
her that she is dreaming: "Lady novelists," Hugh Kenner wrote
not so long ago, "have always claimed the privilege of transcend-
ing *mere plausibilities. It's up to men to arrange such things. . . .
Your bag is sensitivity, which means knowing what to put into
this year's novels*" (in Sukenick, 30; emphasis added). And a re-
viewer (in 1978) of a woman's novel in *Newsweek:*

> Like most feminist novels [this one] represents a triumph of
> sensibility over plot. Why a strong, credible narrative line that
> leads to a satisfactory resolution of conflicts should visit these
> stories so infrequently, I do not know. Because the ability to
> tell a good story is unrelated to gender, I sometimes suspect
> that the authors of these novels are simply indifferent to the
> rigors of narrative. (Prescott, 112)

The second gentleman is slightly more generous than the first. He
at least thinks women capable of telling a good—that is, credi-
ble—story. The fault lies in their *in*difference. The magazine re-
viewer echoes, with curious persistence, the objections of Bussy-
Rabutin's correspondence.

The attack on female plots and plausibilities assume that women
writers cannot or will not obey the rules of fiction. It also assumes
that the truth devolving from *veri*similitude is male. For sensibility,
sensitivity, "extravagance"—so many code words for feminine in
our culture that the attack is in fact tautological—are taken to be
not merely inferior modalities of production but deviations from
some obvious truth. The blind spot here is both political (or philosophical) and literary. It does not see, nor does it want to, that
the fictions of desire behind the desiderata of fiction are masculine
and not universal constructs. It does not see that the maxims that
pass for the truth of human experience and the encoding of that
experience, in literature, are organizations, when they are not fantasies, of the dominant culture. To read women's literature is to
see and hear repeatedly a chafing against the "unsatisfactory reality" contained in the maxim. Everywhere in *The Mill on the Floss*
one can read a protest against the division of labor that grants
men the world and women love. Saying no to Philip Wakem and
then to Stephen Guest, Maggie refuses the hospitality of the happy

end: "But I begin to think there can never come much happiness to me from loving; I have always had so much pain mingled with it. I wish I could make myself a world outside it, as men do" (430). But as in so much women's fiction a world outside love proves to be out of the world altogether. The protest against that topographical imperative is more or less muted from novel to novel. Still, the emphasis is always there to be read, and it points to another text. To continue to deny the credibility of women's literature is to adopt the posture of the philosopher of phallogocentrism's "credulous man who, in support of his testimony, offers truth and his phallus as his own proper credentials" (Derrida, "Becoming Woman," 113). Those credentials are more than suspect.

## NOTES

1. Although what is being pointed to ultimately is an "elsewhere" under the sign of an androgyny I resist, I respond here to the implicit invitation to look again. The quotation should be replaced both in its original context and within Carolyn Heilbrun's concluding argument in *Toward a Recognition of Androgyny*, which is where I found it (again). There is an interesting discussion of this passage in Jane Marcus's *Virginia Woolf and the Languages of Patriarchy* (160–62). Marcus reads the falling of the leaf as a textual maternal legacy, which in my argument oddly refigures the fate of the final daughter in Lafayette's novel.

2. If one must have a less arbitrary origin—and why not?—the properly inaugural fiction would be Hélisenne de Crenne's *Les Angoysses doulou-reuses qui procèdent d'amours*, 1538. But *The Princess of Clèves* has this critical advantage: it also marks the beginning of the modern French novel.

3. Bussy-Rabutin's oft-cited remarks on the novel are most easily found in Maurice Laugaa's volume of critical responses, *Lectures de Mme de Lafayette*, pp. 18–19. The translation is mine unless otherwise indicated.

4. On the function and status of the confession in Mme de Villedieu's novel and on the problems of predecession, see Micheline Cuénin's introduction to her critical edition of *Les Désordres de l'amour*. The best account of the attack on the novel and the problem of *vraisemblance* remains Georges May's *Le Dilemme du roman au XVIII^e siècle*, especially his first chapter.

5. I allude here (playfully) to the first definition of "extravagant" in *Le Petit Robert*: "S'est dit de textes non incorporés dans les recueils canoniques" [Used to refer to texts not included in the canon].

6. In my translation-adaptation of Genette's analysis I have chosen to render *vraisemblance* by "plausibility," a term with a richer semantic field of connotations than "versimilitude."

7. The best overview of the discussion about women's writing in France remains Elaine Marks's 1978 "Women and Literature in France."

8. For Kristeva's (1977) position on a possible specificity to women's writing, see "Questions à Julia Kristeva."

9. The opposition between these positions is, I think, more rhetorical than actual, as Woolf's gloss on Coleridge in *A Room of One's Own* shows.

10. I understate the stakes of an apparently passive indifference. As Edward Said has written in another context: "Any philosophy or critical theory exists and is maintained in order not merely *to be there, passively around everyone and everything,* but in order to be taught and diffused, to be absorbed decisively into the institutions of society or to be instrumental in maintaining or changing or perhaps upsetting these institutions and that society" (682).

11. When I wrote "Emphasis Added" in the fall of 1978, I was unaware of Sandra Gilbert and Susan Gubar's groundbreaking work. Obviously *Madwoman in the Attic* has radically transformed our understanding of women's writing. To the extent that my book records its own history, I have preferred simply to place in a note here my esteem for their accomplishment.

12. See, for instance, Showalter's chapter "The Double Critical Standard and the Feminine Novel," pp. 73–99.

13. Mary Jacobus has written interestingly about Irigaray's and Eliot's metaphorics of women and language in "The Question of Language: Men of Maxims and *The Mill on the Floss.*"

14. Eliot herself has commented on the use of italics by lady novelists: "We imagine the double-refined accent and profusion of chin which are feebly represented by the italics in this lady's sentences!" ("Silly Novels," 315)

15. My translations from *The Princess of Clèves* are deliberately literal; page references to the French are from the readily available Garnier-Flammarion edition (Paris, 1966) and are incorporated within the text. The published English translation is Penguin (New York, 1978) and I have included page references to it.

16. Jules Brody, in "*La Princesse de Clèves* and the Myth of Courtly Love" (1969), Domna C. Stanton, in "The Ideal of *Repos* in Seventeenth-Century French Literature" (1975), and Joan DeJean in "Lafayette's Ellipses" (1984) also interpret the princess's final refusal of Nemours and her renunciation as heroic and self-preserving actions within a certain seventeenth-century discourse.

17. On the content of popular women's literature and its relationship to high culture, see Lillian Robinson's "On Reading Trash."

18. See Elizabeth Janeway's discussion of this notion in her essay "On the Power of the Weak."

19. On this desperately unimaginative hermeneutics, see my discussion of Jean Larnac in "Writing Fictions."

20. I'm playing here with the terms of Peter Brooks's analysis of the relations between "plot" and "life" in his illuminating essay "Freud's Masterplot."

# [ 2 ]

# Writing Fictions: Women's Autobiography in France

Were I a writer and dead, how I would love it if my life, through
the pains of some friendly and detached biographer, were to
reduce itself to a few details, a few preferences, a few inflections, let us say to "biographemes."

Roland Barthes, *Sade, Fourier, Loyola*

Is there, for me, no other haven than this commonplace room?
Must I stay forever before this impenetrable mirror where I
come up against myself, face to face?

Colette, *The Vagabond*

THE OFT-CITED and apparently transparent epigraph to Colette's
*Break of Day*—"Do you imagine in reading my books that I am
drawing my portrait? Patience: it's only my model"[1]—challenges
the reader's competence in distinguishing life from art, nature from
imitation, autobiography from fiction. Although this inaugural
gesture, anticipating both our misreading and our improper la-
beling of the text, will prove to be more than a simple inveighing
against the fallacy of reference, let us, for the moment, proceed as
docile and linear readers. The novel opens with a letter, and the
author's first words ostensibly authenticate the document: "This
note, signed 'Sidonie Colette, née Landoy,' was written by my
mother to one of my husbands, the second. A year later she died
at the age of seventy-seven" (5). The invitation thus extended
to seal the identity gap between the "I" of narration and Sidonie
Gabrielle Colette is reissued in the second chapter. Defending herself against "one of my husband's" claims that she could write
nothing but love stories, the narrator (a novelist) reviews the history of her fictional heroines and the genealogy of her *name*:

In them I called myself Renée Néré or else, prophetically, I
introduced a Léa. So it came about that both legally and fa-
miliarly as well as in my books, I now have only one name,
which is my own. Did it take only thirty years of my life to
reach that point, or rather to get back to it? I shall end by
thinking that it wasn't too high a price to pay.[2] (19)

Who is speaking? And in whose name? The liminary warning operates like a free-floating anxiety, already there at the very threshold of the text to prevent the foreclosure of identification. The "I"
of narration may, like Colette, have "only one name" but her project is no less ambiguous for that symmetry.[3] To bypass the ambiguity would be to assume, for example, that the fiction of *Break
of Day* is a page from Colette's autobiography, and hence to perform a "masculine" reading:

Why do men—writers or so-called writers—still show surprise that a woman should so easily reveal to the public love-
secrets and amorous lies and half-truths? *By divulging these,
she manages to hide other important and obscure secrets which
she herself does not understand very well* . . . Man, my friend,
you willingly make fun of women's writings because they can't
help being autobiographical. On whom then were you relying
to paint women for you? . . . On yourself? (62; emphasis
added)

"Colette" would have her critics not confuse "the illuminated zone"
of the feminine sector, love's brilliant disasters, with the darker,
shadowy text of the female self, "the true intimate life of a woman"
(62–63). But that intimacy, that maskless self, has to do with
"*preference*," and here, we are told, she will "keep silent" (45).
  Shall we take "Colette" at her word then? That what we have
are deliberate *fictions* of self-representation, "rearranged fragments of . . . emotional life" (45) as she calls them, and not autobiography after all? Philippe Lejeune, whose *L'Autobiographie
en France* constitutes the first attempt to define and classify autobiography in the French tradition as a genre, would have it so.
He excludes Colette from his repertory, citing her own reluctance
to talk about herself; but more to the point, the absence of what
he poses as a necessary condition of autobiography: the "autobiographical pact" (72–73). This pact is a declaration of autobiographical intention, an explicit project of sincere truth telling; a
promise to the *reader* that the textual and referential "I" are one.

For Lejeune, however confessional a text may seem, without that covenant of good faith, we remain in the realm of fiction.

It seems, perhaps, perverse that despite the caveat implicit in "Colette's" jibe at the male reader expecting to find autobiography seeping through the pages of women's literature, we so reluctantly accept her exclusion from the French autobiographical canon.[4] This resistance comes not so much from doubts about Lejeune's criteria (as they do or do not apply to Colette) as from a hesitation about embracing wholeheartedly any theoretical model *indifferent* to a problematics of genre as inflected by gender. With this hesitation in mind, let us consider instances of those female autobiographers included by Lejeune—George Sand, Daniel Stern (Marie d'Agoult), and Simone de Beauvoir. Taking his criteria as a point of departure, and moving dialectically between the points of textual production and reception, of authorship and readership, we will return in closing—with some stops along the way—to Colette. Thus by virtue of her undecidable relation to the androcentric paradigm, Colette will serve as the fiction, the pretext really, which allows us to play with the theory.

LEJEUNE'S DEFINITION of autobiography as the "retrospective narrative in prose that someone makes of his existence, when he places the main emphasis on his individual life, especially on the history of his personality" (14), provides a point of departure from which to ask the question: is there a specificity to a female retrospective; how and where in the narrative will it make itself felt? To the extent that autobiography, as Diane Johnson has put it, "requires some strategy of self-dramatization" and "contains, as in fiction, a crisis and a denouement" (19), what conventions govern the production of a female self as *theater*?[5] How does a woman writer perform on the stage of her text?

Historically, the French autobiographer, male or female, has had to come to terms with the exhibitionist performer that is Jean-Jacques Rousseau.[6] Both George Sand and her contemporary Daniel Stern take a certain distance from the *Confessions* because of the inclusive quality of his rememorations. Sand, for example, asks in the "pact" to *Histoire de ma vie*: "Who can forgive him for having confessed Mme de Warens while confessing himself?"[7] (2:13). Daniel Stern takes up the same point in her *Mémoires,* rejecting Rousseau's promiscuous gesture, and concluding that for herself, "I felt neither the right nor the desire, in recalling my own memories, to mix in, inappropriately, those of others" (11). And

both issue warnings that the reader hoping for scandalous revelations will be disappointed; their truth, if not their memory, will
be selective. Now the problem of selectivity is of course not a
problem for women only. Every autobiographer must deal with it.
Chateaubriand, for one, writes in the preface to the *Mémoires
d'outre-tombe* that he will "include no name other than his own
in everything that concerns his private life" (1:547). To some extent, then, this reticence about naming names is a matter of historical context: the nineteenth-century backlash to the tell-all stance
of Rousseau—especially in the area of the sexual connection, the
erogenous zones of the self. But not entirely. The decision to go
public is particularly charged for the woman writer.

In the preface to her second volume of memoirs, *The Prime of
Life,* Simone de Beauvoir too goes back to Rousseau: "It may be
objected that such an inquiry concerns no one but myself. Not so;
if any individual—a Pepys or a Rousseau, an exceptional or a run-
of-the-mill character—reveals himself honestly, everyone, more or
less, becomes involved. It is impossible for him to shed light on
his own life without at some point illuminating the lives of others." (10) But then, following this relative indifference to the inevitable contiguity of other lives, a familiar caveat:

> At the same time I must warn [my readers] that I have no
> intention of telling them everything. I described my childhood
> and adolescence without any omissions. . . . I cannot treat
> the years of my maturity in the same detached way—nor do
> I enjoy a similar freedom when discussing them. I have no
> intention of filling these pages with spiteful gossip about my-
> self and my friends; I lack the instincts of the scandal monger.
> There are many things which I firmly intend to *leave in ob-
> scurity.* (10; emphasis added)

And she adds (in the next sentence): "On the other hand, my life
has been closely linked with that of Jean-Paul Sartre. As he intends
to write his own life story, I shall not attempt to perform the task
for him." It is fair, I think, to assume that while for all autobiographers already figures of public fiction there is a strong sense of
responsibility about speaking out, because being known, they expect their words to have an impact within a clearly defined readers' circle, the female autobiographers know that they are being
read as *women;* women, in the case of Sand, Stern, and Beauvoir
(and this is no less true for Colette), known for (or even through)
their liaisons with famous men. The concern with notoriety, then,

functions as an additional grid or constraint placed upon the truth, upon "the shaping of the past" as truth (Pascal, 5).

Daniel Stern articulates with the greatest insistence the role played by a feminine identity in the autobiographical venture, and the *gender* of sincerity. She asks a friend in 1850, years before actually writing the first volume of her memoirs: "How do you think a work of this sort written by a woman, by a mother, should be composed? . . . I would favor a grave confession, narrow in scope, disengaged from detail, rather moral and intellectual than real. But I am told that that would be without charm" (in Vier, 4:250). And thirteen years later, in a diary entry (but by this time, it would seem, she has already begun writing): "No, my friend, I won't write my *Mémoires*. . . . My instinctive repugnance has conquered . . . I had conceived of a daring book. Feminine confessions as sincere as and consequently more daring (because of public opinion) than those of Jean-Jacques. Once I thought this book was going to come about: *L'Histoire de ma vie* was announced. *I cannot do it*" (in Vier, 4:255).[8] The book does get written, however, and in the preface to *Mes Souvenirs*, Stern traces the logic of her hesitations: "I was a woman, and as such, not bound to a virile sincerity"; but when a woman's life is not governed "by the common rule . . . she becomes responsible, more responsible than a man, in the eyes of all. When this woman, because of some chance or talent, comes out of obscurity she instantly contracts virile duties" (viii–ix). Thus an exceptional woman, by virtue of that exceptionality, becomes subject to a double constraint: masculine responsibilities and feminine sensitivity. For whatever is wrong in the world, Stern contends, "woman has felt it more completely in her whole being"; if a woman is an instrument more sensitive than a man in picking up the "discordances" of society, however, she must nevertheless be more discreet than a man in rendering those vibrations: "My persuasion being . . . that a woman's pen was more constrained than another's by choice within the truth" (*Mémoires*, 11).

Although, as Georges Gusdorf has written in his well-known essay on autobiography, "the man who tells his story . . . is not involved in an objective and disinterested occupation, but in a work of personal justification," and although such self-justification in the eyes of the world may well constitute "the most secret intention" (115) of any autobiographical undertaking, for Stern (as is true in varying degrees of intensity for Sand and Beauvoir) the self being justified is indelibly marked by what Beauvoir calls *féminitude:*

a culturally determined status of difference and oppression (in *L'Arc*, 12). Thus Stern would show (and surely this is the not-so-very-hidden agenda for Sand and Beauvoir) that while a woman may fly in the face of tradition, that is, of traditional expectations for women, particularly in regard to the institution of marriage, she is no less a *human being* of merit; that while on the face of it she is an outlaw, the real fault lies with society and its laws. To justify an unorthodox life by writing about it, however, is to *reinscribe* the original violation, to reviolate masculine turf: hence Stern's defensiveness about the range of her pen. The drama of the self (to return to the histrionic metaphor proposed earlier) is staged in a public theater, and it is *thesis* drama. The autobiographies of these women, to invoke another literary genre, are a defense and illustration, at once a treatise on overcoming received notions of femininity and a poetics calling for another, freer text. These autobiographies, then, belong to that type of women's writing Elaine Showalter in *A Literature of Their Own* has described as "feminist": "*protest* against [the] standards of art and its views of social roles," and "*advocacy* of minority rights and values, including a demand for autonomy" (13). The subject of women's autobiography here is a self both occulted and overexposed by the fact of her femininity as a social reality.

It should come as no surprise that for women determined to go beyond the strictures of convention, conventionally female moments are not assigned privileged status. One does not find even metaphorical traces of what Hélène Cixous calls for in her "feminine future"; "the gestation drive—just like the desire to write: a desire to live self from within, a desire for the swollen belly, for language, for blood" (891). Autobiology is not the subtext of autobiography. It is not, however, entirely repressed. George Sand, for example, who gives birth nine months after her marriage, embraces her pregnancy with pleasure and female solidarity: "I spent the winter of 1822–23 at Nohant, rather ill, but absorbed by the feeling of maternal love that was revealing itself to me through the sweetest dreams and the liveliest aspirations. The transformation that comes about at that moment in the life and thoughts of a woman is, in general, complete and sudden. It was so for me as for the great majority" (2:32). Forced by her doctor to remain in bed and perfectly still for six weeks, Sand comments: "The order . . . was severe, but what wouldn't I have done to maintain the hope of being a mother?" (2:35) And the account of childbirth itself, if abbreviated and discreet, is no less positive: "My son

Maurice came into the world June 30, 1823, without mishap and very hardy. It was the most beautiful moment of my life, that moment when after an hour of deep sleep which followed upon the terrible pains of that paroxysm, I saw, on waking up, that tiny being asleep on my pillow. I had dreamed of him so much ahead of time, and I was so weak, I wasn't sure I wasn't still dreaming" (2:37).

Colette, in that slim volume of reminiscences called *The Evening Star,* also gives pregnancy a few pages of retrospective attention. Colette, taken by surprise at age 40, is, in the beginning, less sanguine and more anxious than (the younger and at that point in her life more conventional) Sand: "I was simply afraid that at my age I would not know how to give a child the proper love and care, devotion and understanding. Love—so I believed—had already hurt me a great deal by monopolizing me for the past twenty years" (in Phelps, 199/132).[9] This concern results in secrecy about her condition, which when finally revealed to a male friend leads him to say: "You're behaving as a man would, you're having a masculine pregnancy!" The "masculine" pregnancy, however, temporarily gives way to a slightly ironic but no less "feminine" text:

> Insidiously, unhurriedly, the beatitude of pregnant females spread through me. I was no longer subject to any discomfort, any unease. This purring contentment, this euphoria—how give a name either scientific or familiar to this state of preservation?—must certainly have penetrated me, since I have not forgotten it and am recalling it now, when life can never again bring me plentitude. . . . One gets tired of keeping to oneself all the unsaid things—in the present case my feeling of pride, of banal magnificence, as I ripened my fruit. (Phelps, 200/132–33)

Despite the euphoria, Colette continued to write: "The 'masculine pregnancy' did not lose all its rights; I was working on the last part of *The Shackle.* The child and the novel were both rushing me, and the *Vie Parisienne,* which was serializing my unfinished novel, was catching up with me. The baby showed signs that it would win the race, and I screwed on the cap of my fountain pen" (Phelps, 203/135). The account of childbirth itself is characterized less by benign irony and humorous reticence than by a brutal distancing from the female lot: "What followed . . . doesn't matter and I will give it no place here. What followed was the prolonged

scream that issues from all women in childbed. . . . What followed was a restorative sleep and selfish appetite" (Phelps, 203/
136). But the anaphora already perceptible in the passage cited above
("What followed"/*la suite*) continues to structure insistently the
narrative of this *hapax,* this unique moment in the writer's life,
connecting an undifferentiating and hence (for Colette) negative
female bond to a singular and bittersweet experience, her post-
partum response to her daughter: "But what followed was also,
once, an effort to crawl toward me made by my bundled up little
larva that had been laid down for a moment on my bed. What
animal perfection! The little creature guessed, she sensed the presence of my forbidden milk, and blindly struggled toward that
blocked source. Never did I cry more brokenheartedly. Dreadful
it is to ask in vain, but small is that hurt when compared with the
pain of not giving . . ." (Phelps, 203–4/136).

Colette accords a few more paragraphs to her passage into
motherhood, but she returns quickly to the "competition between
the book and the birth," the saving grace—for her writing—of
her "jot of virility," to conclude with speculation about her own
mother's probable reaction to this improbable maternity: "When
I was a young girl, if I ever happened to occupy myself with some
needlework, Sido always shook her soothsayer's head and commented, 'You will never look like anything but a boy who is sew-
ing!' She would now have said, 'You will never be anything but
a writer who gave birth to a child,' for she would not have failed
to see the accidental character of my maternity" (Phelps, 205–6/
137).

A writer who gave birth to a child, this *hierarchization* of roles
has everything to do with the shape of the autobiographies under
consideration here: mothers by accident of nature, writers by design. While marriage (and for Beauvoir the decision not to marry),
and childbearing (and again for Beauvoir the decision not to bear
children) sharply punctuate the female retrospective, they are not
self-evidently *signifying* moments. They shape lives rather in counterpoint to the valorized trajectory: the transcendence of the feminine condition through writing. If there is, to return to the language of theatricality invoked earlier, crisis and drama and
denouement in the staging of the autobiographical self, it takes
place around the act of writing. Although Beauvoir is the only
autobiographer of this group to oppose in mutually exclusive categories writing and maternity, her assumption of writing as a vo-

cation and as locus of identity is emblematic: "I knew that in order to become a writer I needed a great measure of time and freedom. I had no rooted objection to playing at long odds, but this was not a game: the whole value and direction of my life lay at stake. The risk of compromising it could only have been justified had I regarded a child as no less vital a creative task than a work of art, which I did not" (67). Mothers or not, maternal or not, destiny is not tributary of anatomy in these texts.[10]

Sand, who is the least ambivalent of the three about her maternity, in the autobiographical account of her apprenticeship to writing in Paris tells (with great relish) the following anecdote about writing and children. As a young woman, already a mother (Sand comes to live in her Parisian mansard with her little daughter), she ponders the ways of the world of letters and wonders whether she has what it takes to make it as a writer in Paris. On the recommendation of a friend, she pays a visit to a certain M. de Kératry, the successful author of *Le Dernier des Beaumanoir* (a story in which a woman, thought to be dead, is raped by the priest whose task it is to bury her), and seeks his advice about her project. The man is terse: "I'm going to be frank with you. A woman shouldn't write." Sand decides to see herself out, but the man suddenly becomes loquacious. He wants to expose his theory on women's inferiority, "on the impossibility for even the most intelligent among them to write a good book." Finally, seeing Sand about to make her exit, he utters his parting shot (that Sand characterizes as an example of Napoleonic wit): "Believe me, don't make books, make babies" (2:150).

The cogito for Sand, Stern, and Beauvoir would seem to be, I write, therefore I am. Writing—for publication—represents entrance into the world of others, and by means of that passage a rebirth: the access through writing to the status of an autonomous subjectivity beyond the limits of feminine propriety established by a Kératry.[11] The meaningful trajectory is thus literary and intellectual.[12] The life of the mind is not, however, coolly cerebral. It is vivid and impassioned. Thus Stern describes her motivation in becoming a writer: "I needed to get outside myself, to put into my life a new interest that was not love for a man, but an intellectual relationship with those who felt, thought, and suffered as I did. I published therefore . . ." (*Mémoires*, 215). The textualization of a female "I" means escape from the sphere inhabited by those "relative beings" (as Beauvoir has characterized women) who experience the world only through the mediation of men. To write is to come out of the wings, and to appear, however briefly, center stage.

It is in those terms that Beauvoir describes the publication of her first novel: "So through the medium of my book I aroused curiosity, irritation, even sympathy: there were people who actually liked it. Now at last I was fulfilling the promises I had made myself when I was fifteen. . . . For a moment it was sufficient that I had crossed the threshold: *She Came to Stay* existed for other people, and I had entered public life" (441). One arrives, then, at this curious but finally not very surprising paradox: these autobiographies are the stories of women who succeeded in becoming more than *just women,* and by their own negative definition of that condition.

Sand, for example, reflecting on Montaigne's exclusion of women from the chapter on friendship by virtue of their inferior moral nature, protests and would exempt herself—at least partially—from that category by virtue of her education:

> I could see that an education rendered somewhat different from that of other women by fortuitous circumstances had modified my being. . . . I was not, therefore, entirely a woman like those whom the moralists censure and mock; in my soul I had enthusiasm for the beautiful, thirst for the true, and yet I was indeed a woman like all the others, sickly, highly strung, dominated by my imagination, childishly vulnerable to the tender emotions and anxieties of maternity. (2:126–27)

While Sand in this reflection concludes that "the heart and the mind have a sex," and that "a woman will always be more of an artist and a poet in her life, a man always more in his work" (but objects to an interpretation of that difference as a definition of "moral inferiority"), she no less aspires to transcendence, dreaming of those "male virtues to which women can raise themselves" (2:127). The question one must now ask is whether the story of a woman who sees conventional female self-definition as a text to be rewritten, who refuses the inscription of her body as the ultimate truth of her self, to become, if not a man, an exceptional woman (hence like a man), is a story significantly different from that of a man who becomes an exceptional man (particularly in this instance of figures who became exceptional by virtue of their writing).[13]

The difference of gender *as genre* is there to be read only if one

accepts the terms of another sort of "pact": the pact of commit-
ment to decipher what women have said (or, more important, left
unsaid) about the pattern of their lives, over and above what any
person might say about his, through genre. I say "his" deliberately.
Not because men in fact lead genderless lives, but because the fact
of their gender is given and received literarily as a mere donnée of
personhood; because the canon of the autobiographical text, like
the literary canon, self-defined as it is by the notion of a human
universal, in general fails to interrogate gender as a meaningful
category of reference or of interpretation. This is not to say, of
course, that the male autobiographer does not inscribe his *sexuality*. And Rousseau is hardly silent on the matter. But when, for
example, Rousseau writes at the beginning of his *Confessions*: "I
want to show my fellow men [*mes semblables*] a man in all nature's truth," he conflates in perfect conformity with the linguistic
economy of the West maleness and humanity, as do most of the
readers of autobiography cited in these pages.

To read for difference, therefore, is to perform a diacritical gesture; to refuse a politics of reading that depends on the fiction of
a neutral (neuter) economy of textual production and reception.
This refusal of a degendered reading fiction is a movement of oscillation which locates difference in the negotiation between writer
and reader. The difference of which I speak here, however, is located in the "I" of the beholder, in the *reader's* perception. I would
propose, then, the notion of gender-marked reading: a practice of
the text that would recognize the status of the reader as a differentiated subject, a reading subject named by gender and committed in a dialectics of identification to deciphering the inscription
of a female subject. (This move is what in "Arachnologies" I will
call "overreading.")

Let us now engage a less docile reading of our autobiographers,
and especially of Colette. Toward the end of the *The Evening Star*,
Colette imagines a publisher asking her: "When will you make up
your mind to give us your memoirs?" And has herself answer:
"Dear Publisher, I will write them neither more, nor better nor
less than today" (141). She thus rejects the specifically autobiographical project in its generic specificity. But then she suddenly
wonders about an earlier female writer and autobiographer:

How the devil did George Sand manage? Robust laborer of
letters that she was, she was able to finish off one novel and
begin another within the hour. She never lost either a lover

or a puff of her hookah by it, produced a twenty volume *His-toire de ma vie* into the bargain and I am completely staggered when I think of it. Pell-mell, and with ferocious energy she piled up her work, her passing griefs, her limited felicities. I could never have done so much, and at the moment when she was thinking forward to her full barns I was still lingering to gaze at the green, flowering wheat. (Phelps, 502/141)

Colette, reading Sand, wonders about that life: the weave of writing, love, happiness, unhappiness. And makes the comparison to her own: she/I. If, as Gusdorf suggests, the "essence of autobiography" is its "anthropological significance" (119), Colette is a good *reader* of autobiography because the text of another's life sends her back to her own (which has been the challenge of autobiography since Augustine). Why Sand, and how does Colette think back to Sand? Having introduced, as we have just seen, the question of memoirs, and having rejected the undertaking, Colette then imagines her image in a publisher's eyes: "God forgive me! They must expect a kind of 'Secret Journal' in the style of the Goncourt brothers!" (141) By ellipsis Colette rejects this negative and implicitly masculine dirty-secrets model. Instead, thinking about how much time and what sacrifices were involved in the elaboration of her own life's work—"It has taken me a great deal of time to scratch out forty or so books. So many hours that could have been used for travel, for idle strolls, for reading, even for indulging a feminine and healthy coquetry" (Phelps, 502/141)—Colette makes a feminist connection: how did Sand manage?[14]

This structure of kinship through which readers as women perceive bonds relating them to writers as women would seem to be a "natural" feature of the autobiographical text. But is it? Are these autobiographies the place par excellence in which the self inscribed and the self deciphering perform the ultimate face to face? I don't think so. Despite the identity between the "I" of authorship and the "I" of narration, and the pacts of sincerity, reading these lives is rather like shaking hands with one's gloves on.[15] Is this decorum a feature of gender? To the extent that autobiography, like any narrative, requires a shaping of the past, a making *sense* of a life, it tends to cast out the parts that don't add up (what we might think of as the flip side of the official, reconstructed personality). Still, autobiography can incorporate what Roy Pascal has called the "cone of darkness at the center"; indeed, as he comments, "it seems to be required of the autobiographer that he should

recognize that there is something unknowable in him" (184–85).
One has the impression reading Stern,[16] Sand, and Beauvoir that
the determination to have their lives make sense and thus be susceptible to *universal* reception blinds them, as it were, to their own
darkness: the "submerged core," "the sexual mystery that would
make a drama" (Kael, 100–1).[17] It is as though the anxiety of gender identity, of a culturally devalued femininity, veiled its inscription in strategies of representation.

But should we give up so easily? We are, after all, given clues
in the autobiographies telling us where to look (or not to look)
for what Colette calls the "unsaid things." When Beauvoir, for
example, describes the stakes of her fiction writing, how she wanted
to be read, she tells us something important about her other self:

> I passionately wanted the public to like my work; therefore
> like George Eliot, who had become identified in my mind with
> Maggie Tulliver, I would myself become an imaginary char-
> acter, endowed with beauty, desirability, and a sort of shim-
> mering transparent loveliness. It was this metamorphosis that
> my ambition sought . . . I dreamed of splitting into two selves,
> and of having a shadowy alter ego that would pierce and haunt
> people's hearts. It would have been no good if this phantom
> had had overt connections with a person of flesh and blood;
> anonymity would have suited me perfectly. (291)

Sand points us in the same direction:

> It was inevitably said that *Indiana* was my person and my
> story. It is nothing of the sort. I have presented many types
> of women, and I think that after reading this account of the
> impressions and reflections of my life, it will be clear that I
> have never portrayed myself [*mise en scène*] as a woman [*sous
> des traits féminins*]. I am too much of a romantic [*trop ro-
> manesque*] to have seen the heroine of a novel in my mirror.
> . . . Even if I had tried to make myself beautiful and dram-
> atize my life, I would never have succeeded. My *self*, con-
> fronting me face to face would have dampened my enthusi-
> asm. (2:160)

By suggesting, as I am, that a *double* reading—of the autobiography with the fiction—would provide a more sensitive measure
for deciphering a female self, I am not proposing a return to the
kind of biographical "hermeneutics" that characterizes a Jean Larnac
(in his 1929 *Histoire de la littérature féminine*). Like Colette's in-

terpellated male reader in *Break of Day,* Larnac reads all women's fiction as autobiography: "In the center of every feminine novel, one discovers the author. . . . Incapable of abstracting a fragment of themselves to constitute a whole, [women writers] have to put all of themselves into their work" (253–54). (It is not, of course, a question of saying, as he does, Indiana is George Sand—in female drag.)

I am proposing instead an intratextual practice of interpretation which, in articulation with the gendered overreading I have just proposed, would privilege neither the autobiography nor the fiction, but take the two writings together in their status as text.[18] Germaine Brée has performed such a reading. In an essay on George Sand entitled "The Fictions of Autobiography," Brée isolates what she calls the "matrix of fabulation" (121) and analyzes its function in both the autobiography and the fiction. The matrix is that structure through which Sand deals with the problem of origins and identity. Brée decodes the Sandian inscription of the self, allowing the "fictional fiction" and the "fictions of autobiography" to illuminate each other (446). Because of the literary protocol and cultural constraints that historically have governed women's writing, and the problems of imagining public female identities, not to perform an expanded reading—in this instance, not to read the fiction *with* the autobiography—is to remain prisoner of a canon that bars women from their own texts.

And Colette?

Let us return briefly to the epigraph from *Break of Day.* Early in the novel, the narrator gives us a portrait of her mother taking stock at the end of her life. The metaphor used for this putting-into-perspective of the past is that of a painter before a canvas: "She stands back, and returns, and stands back again, pushing some scandalous detail into place, bringing into the light of day a memory drowned in shadow. By some unhoped-for art she becomes—equitable. Is anyone imagining as he reads me, that I'm portraying myself? *Have patience: this is merely my model*" (34–35; emphasis added). In context, then, the epigraph seems to narrow its focus. Indeed, it has been taken to mean that the model in question is "the model of the mother," and that this "affiliation, recognized and reclaimed" constitutes the deep structure of the novel (Mercier, 46); painter of her mother, and through her mother, herself. This is no less, however, the portrait of the writer in this same novel as autobiographer: "No other fear, not even that of ridicule, prevents me from writing these lines which I am willing to risk will be published. Why should I stop my hand from gliding over this paper to which for so many years I've confided what I know about myself, what I've tried to hide, what I've invented and what I've guessed?" (62) Every inscription of the self is an approximation and a projection; a matter of details, shadows, adjustment, and proportion—an *arrangement* of truths. Still, does the collection of self-portraits make an autobiography? Robert Phelps tried to construct one in a volume called *Earthly Paradise: An Autobiography* in which he strings together moments in Colette's life through passages from her works in a thematic and roughly chronological continuum. Lejeune rejects Phelps's construction as just that: one does not ghostwrite an autobiography; the "pact" cannot be concluded by a third party.

How then to conclude?

At the end of an article published two years after *L'Autobiographie en France,* Lejeune renounces his previous attempts to find a definition of autobiography that would be coherent and exhaustive. Having decided that autobiography is as much a *mode of reading* as a mode of writing, he looks instead to a history (as yet to be written) of autobiography that would be the history of the way in which autobiography is read. To be sure, Lejeune is not concerned with female autobiography. But his notion of a contractual genre dependent upon codes of transmission and reception joins our purposes, because it relocates the problematics of autobiography as genre in an interaction between reader and text.

And Colette?

To read Colette is not, perhaps, in the final analysis (*pace* Lejeune), to read (generically) a woman's *autobiography.*[19] It is, however, to read the inscription of a female signature: a cultural fabrication that names itself as such, and that we can identify through the patient negotiation we ourselves make with the neither/nor of "memoirs mixed with fiction, fictions compounded of fact" (Gass, 12). Colette's textual "I" is not bound by genre. For Sand, Stern, and Beauvoir, despite their pact, the locus of identification, I would suggest, is no different. The historical truth of a woman writer's life lies in the reader's grasp of her intratext: the body of her writing and not the writing of her body.

NOTES

1. See, for example, Elaine Marks in her critical study *Colette*, p. 213; translation is hers. All future references to *Break of Day*, however, will be drawn from the Enid McLeod translation.

2. Christiane Makward has pointed out the importance of this evolution in her analysis of patronyms and their relationship both to women's writing and the representation of femininity: "not only is the father's name feminized and stripped of its function (to signify descendence) but it takes the place of a first name. 'Colette' is no longer a first name, a patronym or a pseudonym but *the name* that a free woman took fifty years to make for herself." "Le Nom du père: Ecritures féminines d'un siècle à l'autre," paper delivered at the Third Annual Colloquium in Nineteenth-Century French Studies, October 1977, Columbus, Ohio.

3. Elaine Marks comments, citing the same passage: if the narrator is "no longer wearing an obvious mask . . . she is, however, wearing the mask of 'Colette'." And this "Colette" only exposes a self protected by inverted commas. *Colette*, pp. 212–13.

4. It is a nice paradox that Colette is always read biographically, and at the same time excluded from the corpus of autobiographical writing. Perhaps this is a useful way to think about the place of women's writing.

5. In Lejeune's terms, autobiographical writing itself is an act of "staging": *l'écriture y est mise en scène* (73). In a way, the theatricality of female subjectivity is central to feminist writing, thematically autobiographical or not. I deal with this notion more fully in chapters 7 and 9.

6. For Lejeune, French autobiography begins officially with Rousseau; and he dates the genre as beginning around 1760. As for the response to Rousseau, Lejeune writes: "Rousseau is the only one to say aloud what everyone thinks in private. All the autobiographical pacts that follow are written against Rousseau's disastrous frankness" (82).

7. Béatrice Didier, in "Femme/Identité/Ecriture: A propos de *l'Histoire de ma vie* de George Sand," begins her article with an excerpt from Sand's correspondence: "I confess that I am neither humble enough to write confessions like Jean-Jacques nor impertinent enough to praise myself like the literary lights of the century. Furthermore, I don't believe that private life falls within the purview of the critics" (561).

8. Thus Stern distances herself from Sand's *Histoire de ma vie* as well as Rousseau's *Confessions*. Stern comments on Sand's work—based on an incomplete reading—in the following manner: "It seems to me that [the work] is true or not true enough, and that is not how I would conceive of Confessions"; letter to Hortense Allart, dated 1855, cited by Vier, 4:307, n. 727.

9. Colette's *Evening Star* (*L'Etoile Vesper*) has been translated by David LeVay. His translation, however, often misses Colette in spirit and style and I have chosen instead to use those passages cited from this volume of recollections as anthologized by Robert Phelps in *Earthly Paradise*. Phelps's translator, Herma Briffault, seems closer to Colette's rhythms. For those who might wish to consult the passages cited in context, I have provided the page

references to the complete translation; if only one page reference appears, it is to LeVay.

10. The contrast between Sand and Stern is important to note. Sand writes, for example, about maternal feelings: "I wasn't deluded by passion. I had for the artist [Chopin] a kind of very intense, very true maternal adoration, but which could not for an instant compete with maternal love [*l'amour des entrailles*], the only chaste feeling that can be passionate" (2:433). Stern, for her part, reverses the hierarchy: "Let [women] say and repeat that maternal love surpasses all other forms of love, while they cling to it as a last resort [*un pis-aller*], and because they have been too cowardly, too vain, too demanding, to experience love and to understand friendship, those two exceptional feelings which can only germinate in strong souls" (*Mémoires,* 82).

11. This emphasis on intellectual pursuits is not restricted to women writers in France. In "Female Identities," Patricia Spacks comments on the autobiographical works of four eighteenth-century English writers, Mrs. Thrale, Mrs. Pilkington, Mrs. Clarke, and Lady Mary Wortley Montagu: "With an almost mythic insistence all four of these women reiterate a theme common in the century's fiction: the female apology, heavily tinged with resentment, for the life of the mind. Men think, therefore exist; women, who—men believed—hardly think at all, have, therefore, perhaps a questionable hold on their own existences" (78–79).

12. Sand's *Histoire de ma vie,* Béatrice Didier maintains, "is especially and in the end the story of a birth to writing—a difficult birth deferred, sometimes occulted, of which the narrative traverses the entire text . . . this birth becomes . . . the very object of the book" (567–68).

13. Historically, for example, for women writers in France, artistic activity must seem to be economically motivated to be socially justified, to justify the violation of gendered identity. In this sense, Claudine Herrmann argues in *Les Voleuses de langue* that George Sand "sought in every way to convince her readers that she was writing to earn a living." This (alibi?) is placed in the context of Stendhal's discussion of female authorship in *De l'amour.* Stendhal (who, Herrmann comments, audaciously compares women's condition to that of black slaves in nineteenth-century America, and who further observes that "all geniuses born as women are lost to the public good") remarks: "For a woman under the age of fifty to publish a book, is to subject her happiness to the most terrible of lotteries; if she is fortunate enough to have a lover, the first thing that will happen is that she will lose him. I see one exception only: a woman who writes books [*fait des livres*] to feed and raise her family" (31–33).

14. This is oddly close in language to Woolf's remarks on Colette's writing. In a letter to Ethel Smythe about an article of Colette's on Anna de Noailles, Woolf says: "I'm almost floored by the extreme dexterity insight and beauty of Colette. How does she do it? No one in England could do a thing like that. If a copy is ever going I should like to have one—to read it again. and see how its done: or guess. And to think I scarcely know her books! Are they all novels? Is it the great French tradition that lifts her so serenely, and yet with such a flare, down, down to what she's saying? I'm green with envy . . ." June 25, 1936 (49). I am grateful to Brenda Silver for finding this reference for me.

15. I am tempted, though the context is radically different, by the passage

in Morrison's *Sula* where we read this contrast between "that version of herself . . . she sought to reach out to and touch with an ungloved hand" and
"the naked hand" (121) as a way of talking about degrees of intimate contact.

16. I must here, somewhat belatedly, distinguish between Stern's *Mes Souvenirs* (1806–1833) and her *Mémoires* (1833–1854). Both were published posthumously, in 1880 and 1927, respectively. The later text, which is an account
of her love affair with Liszt, is extraordinarily moving. However, the volume
itself is a construction, a compilation made by the editor, Daniel Ollivier. It
includes journal entries (hers and Liszt's), notes, and fragmentary chapters of
the unfinished *Mémoires*. (As one might imagine, the journal is the more passionate, disturbed and disturbing document.) Stern herself seems to have fa-
vored this installment of her life's story. In a letter dated 1867, cited by Vier
(262), Marie d'Agoult writes: "I am just finishing the second volume of the
*Mémoires:* the story of passion that will not be a masterpiece, but *my* masterpiece;" italicized in the text. As I will argue, if one is reading to discover,
uncover, a female self, the corpus must be expanded by breaking down the
barriers of genre; or rather the hierarchies of the canon: fiction, autobiography, correspondence, diaries, and so on. Here, Vier's remarks on reading
the *Mémoires* with the correspondence are very much to the point: "It is
Marie whom the *Mémoires* portray; the letters give us glimpses of the Count-
ess d'Agoult; the former is fragile and passive, the latter chatelaine and suz-
eraine; the former belongs completely to the man she loves and admires, the
latter knows herself to be an original mind and senses in herself a literary
vocation" (1:175).

17. Pauline Kael, reviewing Lillian Hellman's *Julia* with *Pentimento,* the
filmic fiction with the autobiography. Not surprisingly, Hellman's conclusion
to the volume of her memoirs called *An Unfinished Woman* points to the
dangers lurking in the passion for a coherent self: "I do regret that I have
spent too much of my life trying to find what I called 'truth,' trying to find
what I called 'sense'. I never knew what I meant by truth, never made the
sense I hoped for. All I mean is that I left too much of me unfinished because
I wasted too much time. However." (244)

18. Gusdorf himself seems to make a case for a double reading when he
remarks: "There would therefore be two versions, or two instances of autobiography: on the one hand, the confession strictly speaking, on the other,
the entire work of the artist which takes up the same subject matter in complete freedom and with the protection of incognito" (121).

19. Reading this essay over and revising it for this book ten years after I
wrote it, I am struck and slightly dismayed by the dogged way I follow through
and worry about Lejeune's moves. (Particularly since I know how profoundly
irreversible the interest is!) And yet am I today cured of the gesture to revise,
to begin by turning to the male model to see how and where it doesn't work?
When will there be an end to the double work of revision, I wonder.

# II

## *The Subjects of Feminist Criticism*

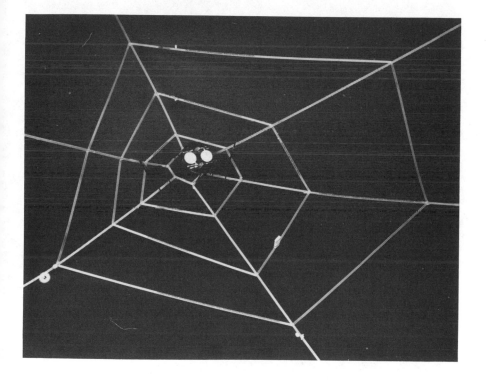

*Arachne & Athena: An Invitation to Dinner*. An installation by Sheila Levrant de Bretteville, 1985. Photo by Lois Gervais.

# [ 3 ]

# The Text's Heroine: A Feminist Critic and Her Fictions

*"The Text's Heroine" was originally written for a Symposium on
Feminist Criticism held at Cornell University in October 1981. The
conference had been conceived, at least in part, as a forum in which
to discuss French and American views on the theory and practice
of feminist criticism. After the event, the editors of* Diacritics *saw
the exchange between Peggy Kamuf and me as a "dialogue" on
the conference's general theme and published it the following year,
labeled as such, in an issue of the journal called "Cherchez la femme:
Feminist Critique/Feminine Text."*

*Since this exchange has generated a certain measure of scrutiny,
I want to comment here on an asymmetry one can read in
the "dialogue" that is only partly circumstantial (I read Peggy
Kamuf's piece before writing my own). To the extent that I had
been following her work for several years and since we often worked
on the same texts, in a sense I was already responding to Kamuf's
position before even reading "Replacing Feminist Criticism." Thus,
"The Text's Heroine" should be read just as much in "dialogue"
with the earlier essay "Writing Like a Woman" as with "Replacing Feminist Criticism" written for the occasion. For her part, Kamuf
"replies" to a certain American feminism. Why I felt the need to
make a case for a feminism from which I myself had already clearly
marked my distance (in "Emphasis Added," for instance) is another matter, but I have come to regret the impasse in feminist
literary theory created by the current sclerosis of "French/Amer-
ican" positions and especially the role the Kamuf/Miller "dialogue" continues to play in keeping this oppositional structure alive
on those terms. Both pieces should be replaced within a very particular historical and critical moment. On the other hand, and for
some of those very reasons, it has seemed impossible for me not*

*to include this moment as such in the self-consciousness of this book's project.*

> I will go so far as to risk this hypothesis: The sex of the ad-
> dressor awaits its determination by or from the other. It is the
> other who will perhaps decide who I am—man or woman.
> Nor is this decided once and for all. It may go one way one
> time and another way another time.
>
> Jacques Derrida, *The Ear of the Other*

> Man has been raised in order to function, in order to address
> the world like a text destined to find its readers, while woman
> was elected to constitute a metaphorical other-world, a repose
> of thought which steps aside in order to dream for an instant.
>
> Claudine Herrmann, *Les Voleuses de langue*

WHEN THE feminist critic institutionalizes the woman writer, what story authorizes her to do so? As I begin to answer that question, I will be locating myself in a discursively polemical (but personally irenic) relation to Peggy Kamuf's questions about what might constitute an "effective feminist practice of criticism" ("Replacing Feminist Criticism," 44), particularly in relation to the epistemological mapping and Foucauldian paradigms she so elegantly outlines. I want to say at the start, however, that I foresee no real agreement on this matter here or elsewhere, because I think that the question of an effective feminist practice is *insoluble*. Or rather, while there indeed exist effective practices—written documents or strategies which by their analyses and accounts move, persuade, even transform—I do not believe it is possible to theorize, to think aloud, the grounds of such a practice in a way that transcends powerful internal contradiction. (This may always be the case when practice and its demands precede theory, which historically has been the case with feminism.)

Before addressing the question of the woman writer—the woman who signs "woman" and the feminist critic who places her in the institution—I want now to map out the territory of the dilemma. It is characterized by the polarities of what might be thought of as metonymies as opposed to metaphors; psychohistorical needs as opposed to epistemological claims; material contingencies as opposed to theoretical urgencies. Those oppositions have also been named by Elaine Marks—in a presentation she described as existing in a zone somewhere between a working paper and a position paper at a Barnard College Women's Issues Luncheon (spring 1981)—as the American, empirical, and social science model of Women's Studies vs. the French ludic endeavor; the latter emerging from the more speculative operations of "les sciences de l'homme" engaged in by decentered subjects of the "feminine" (rather than "feminist") persuasion. This problematic may also be understood in relation to *shoes*: as in the sturdy, sensible sort worn by "American" feminists, and the more frivolous, elegant type worn by Cixous herself. This is in fact a Cixousian exemplum. In the course of an informal presentation, also at Barnard, in the fall of 1979, Hélène Cixous figured the same (American/French) paradigm in shoes in order to make a point about difference and recuperation: the danger of a feminist identification too readily perceived; and the distinction as well between lesbian and "homosexuelle."

I think that these polarizations are unfortunate, if all too accurate, when they separate *effectively* women who (ideally) might otherwise collaborate within a single institution or (more realistically) within the larger project of feminist scholarship, but they do not seem about to go away. And they are not going away, I think, because of a larger problem in the women's movement itself, a problem currently reflected in the debates on the proper place of Women's Studies—in the margins or in the mainstream—that Kamuf alludes to in her paper. The problem has everything to do with sexual identity and the ways in which those two terms should be understood, separately and conjoined. For the purposes of argument, but also because of the scene of my enunciation, I will align myself with those on the side of what Peggy Kamuf in these pages calls "correction"; with those who wish to "rectify or reverse women's exclusion" without, apparently (or at least sufficiently), taking the proper measure of the *epistemological* dangers implicit in such a position.

I will speak as one who believes that "we women" must continue to work for the woman who has been writing, because not to do so will reauthorize our oblivion. Perhaps I can expand upon my conviction that it matters who writes and *signs* woman by an example that in many ways works against me. It is the case of the

*Portuguese Letters.* These are five letters published anonymously in Paris, in 1669, as being the translation of letters written in Portuguese. They were enormously popular, and for some the debate over their origins and authenticity is not over. (Indeed, in a 1979 paperback edition of the *Letters* [*Lettres de la religieuse portugaise*], Yves Florenne rehearses the "evidence" yet again, arguing for the true sound of "a woman's voice" [77], the pained cries of a woman in love; or at least for the possibility that anonymous was a woman.) I believe—as ultimately Kamuf seems to—that the letters were probably written by a man, a Frenchman and literary type (a hack, some say) named Guilleragues, though thought for centuries (by many) to have been written by a *real* Portuguese nun.

Why bother with this slight text, written (perhaps) in the final analysis, by a man? It serves in the French history of the novel not as *the* first novel, as opposed to other forms of prose fiction—for that place is occupied by the anonymously published *Princess of Clèves*—but literally as its pre-text. It prefigures—one might also say, it engenders or at least generates—the production of an epistolary fiction whose fundamental trope, I have argued in " 'I's' in Drag," is that of a *"penultimate* masochism, the always renewable figure of feminine suffering" (56). The nun's last words in the face of her fickle lover's persistent silence are these: "But I wish nothing more of you; I am mad to repeat the same things so often: I must give you up and think no more of you; I even think I will no longer write to you. Am I obliged to give you an exact account of all my various movements?" The *Portuguese Letters* are a rewriting of Ovid's *Heroides.* Ovid famously feminized the epic model of female suffering by scaling it down, casting it in elegiac verses: the imagined love letters, primarily written by abandoned women to their lovers, of which the exemplary case is Virgil's Dido, who made the fatal error of believing the man would stay and respect her in the morning.

It matters to me that the letters from a "Portuguese nun," as the case in point, situate their line of descent in a patrilineal fashion, because I think that the textualization—hence glamorization—of female suffering around the male is an important issue for women, though less simple than some feminists want to imagine, before and after the epistemological rupture Foucault diagnoses (Kamuf, "Replacing Feminist Criticism," 43–44). Indeed, society did not wait for the invention of man to repress "woman" or oppress women, and the "end of man" in no way precludes the reinscription of woman as Other. What bothers me about the metalogically "correct" position is what I take to be its necessary implications for practice: that by glossing "woman" as an archaic signifier, it glosses over the *referential* suffering of women. Moreover, and implicitly, to code as "cosmetic," and to foreclose as untimely, discussions of the author as sexually gendered subject in a socially gendered exchange—who produced, for example, *this* masochistic discourse and for whose benefit?—is to be too confident that nondiscursive practices will respond correctly to the correct theory of discursive practice. It may also be the case that having been killed off along with "man," the author can now be rethought beyond traditional notions of biography, now that through the feminist rewritings of literary history the adequacy of a masculine identity to represent the universal has been radically questioned.

In "Writing Like a Woman," Kamuf, preparing to review the debates over the origins and authorship of the *Portuguese Letters*—written by a man or by a woman—declares (arguing with Patricia Meyer Spacks in *The Female Imagination*):

> If the inaugural gesture of this feminist criticism is the reduction of the literary work to its signature and to the tautological assumption that the feminine "identity" is one which signs itself with a feminine name, then it will be able to produce only tautological statements of dubious value: women's writing is writing signed by women. . . . If these . . . are the grounds of a practice of feminist criticism, then that practice must be prepared to ally itself with the fundamental assumptions of patriarchy which relies on the same principles. If, on the other hand, by "feminist" one understands a way of reading texts that points to the masks of truth with which phallocentrism hides its fictions, then one place to begin such a reading is by looking behind the mask of the proper name, the sign that secures our patriarchal heritage: the father's name and the index of sexual identity. (285–86)

Kamuf concludes, after applying deconstructive pressures to the terms of the debate, that by refusing the tautological and empirical definition of identity (writing as a woman is to be a woman writing) in favor of an attention to the figuration of resemblance (writing as a woman) one has at least staged another kind of *reading*: a reading that by refusing the metaphors of a hegemonic paternity—the signature—allows for the emergence of a less stable rhetoric of maternity; "reading a text . . . *as if,* in other words, it were illegitimate, recognized by its mother who can only give it a borrowed name" (298). But Kamuf—like Kristeva, whose interest in a female practice is related primarily to a more general concern with an avant-garde, dissident, and marginal work in language— would prefer to see "feminist" criticism address itself not to the productions signed by biological woman alone but to all productions that put the "feminine" into play—the feminine then being a modality or process accessible to both men and women. (This might also be said to be the case of Cixous in "The Laugh of the Medusa," where in one of her famous footnotes she lists Genet along with Colette and Marguerite Duras as examples of French writers who have produced inscriptions of femininity.)[1]

More locally, it doesn't matter to Kamuf's reading whether the *Portuguese Letters* were written by a woman or by a man, but it does to mine. Just as I care if *The Story of O* was written by "Pauline Réage" or Jean Paulhan, which is in fact the same example (though for me the pornographics of female submission is no more than—surely no worse than—the rhetoric of sentimental masochism). I prefer to think that this positioning of woman is the writing of a masculine desire attached to the male body. Just as I like to know that the Brontëan writing of female anger, desire, and selfhood issues from a female pen. This preference, as I indicated earlier, is not without its vulnerabilities. It could, I suppose, one day be proven definitively that the heroines of the *Letters* and *The Story of O* were female creations after all. I would then have to start over again. But it would be a different story, since the story of the woman who writes is *always* another story.[2] In "Ad/d Feminam" Catharine Stimpson astutely assesses the political implications of these bodily identities:

> . . . male writers—a Genet—can appropriate the feminine as a stance for the male through which to express receptive subordination before God or a god-like phallus. . . . Still other male writers, like a Henry James, write about women, particularly lovely victims. Self-consciously empathetic, they speak of and for the feminine.
>
> Each of these strategies is limited, if only because of the obvious anatomical differences. . . . A male writer may speak of, for, to and from the feminine. He cannot speak, except fictively, of, for, to and from the female. This inability hardly has the dignity of a tragic fact, but it does have the grittiness of simple fact. (179)

This "grittiness of simple fact" has everything to do with the ways in which the signature of women has functioned historically: in terms of the body, the sexual ideologies that define it; in terms of civil status, the legal restrictions that construct it. I want to invoke briefly Virginia Woolf's speculation about Judith Shakespeare:

> And undoubtedly . . . *her work would have gone unsigned.* That refuge she would have sought certainly. It was the relic of the sense of chastity that dictated anonymity to women even so late as the nineteenth century. Currer Bell, George Eliot, George Sand, all the victims of inner strife as their writings prove, sought ineffectively to veil themselves by using the name of a man. . . . *Anonymity runs in their blood.* The desire to be veiled still possesses them. (52; emphasis added)

The desire to be veiled that unveils the anxiety of a genderized and sexualized body, I would argue, is *not* what runs in the blood of the "Portuguese nun." What is at work there instead, I think, is a male (at least masculine) desire to paper over an anxiety about destination and reception: a sense of powerlessness about writing in a new genre addressed to an unknown "destinataire" that takes the abandoned woman's body—the next best thing to a female corpse—as its pretext. The woman-in-love figured here is the masochist Simone de Beauvoir analyzed in *The Second Sex,* whose passion turns to self-mutilation when it turns out that "no man really is God" (612).

In other words, what I read in the *Portuguese Letters* is an ideology of desire that allows woman to become a subject only upon the condition of her "subordination before . . . a god-like phallus." Just as we read of O:

> O was happy that René had had her whipped and had prostituted her, because her impassioned submission would furnish her lover with the proof that she belonged to him, but also because the pain and shame of the lash, and the outrage inflicted on her by those who compelled her to pleasure when they took her, and at the same time delighted in their own without paying the slightest heed to hers, seemed to be the very redemption of her sins. (93)

"Mariane" the "nun" writes her third letter: "I saw you leave, I can't hope to ever see you return and yet I'm still alive: I've betrayed you, I beg your forgiveness. But don't grant it! Treat me severely! Don't judge that my feelings are violent enough! Be more difficult to satisfy! Tell me that you want me to die of love for you! And I beg you to give me this help so that I can overcome the weakness of my sex. . . ." (80). If "dying of love is a trope," as Kamuf queried during the round table, what is it a trope of? Kate Millett has interrogated the psycho-logics of these feminine investments in pain: "It is ingenious," she writes of Freud's "Femininity," "to describe masochism and suffering as inherently feminine. . . . [I]t justifies any conceivable domination or humiliation forced upon the female as mere food for her nature. To carry such a notion to its logical conclusion, abuse is not only good for woman but the very thing she craves" (194–95).

I arrive here, however, at the end of my "American" posture. For the next step in that agenda typically is to establish reading lists that reflect orthodox feminist positions, and to call for the production of literature with positive role models. To be fair, this prescriptive esthetics represents only one strain of criticism; it does not tell the whole story.[3] Nevertheless, hortatory formulations of this sort, "But women's literature must go beyond the scenarios of compromise, madness and death. Although the reclamation of suffering is the beginning, its purpose is to discover the new world," threaten to erase the ambiguities of the feminist project, unless they are at the same time reproblematized, as is the case here with Elaine Showalter, who goes on, in her review of feminist tropologies, to cite literature, like Adrienne Rich's poetry, that has "gone beyond reclaiming suffering to its re-investment" (134).[4] Nor would I argue that reading works by women because of the signature is an activity *ethically* superior—*because marginal*—to that of reading works by men; or works by women alongside those of men, though I myself *feel* it to be an absolutely compelling project. Indeed, I think that "intersextuality" (to borrow a coinage from Naomi Schor), has much to teach us ("La Pérodie," 85). Sand's reading and rewriting of Rousseau is as important as her reading of Staël; and what would James have done without Eliot? Nevertheless, I do believe in books and courses based on the signature even if, as in the case of the *Portuguese Letters, The Story of O,* and the novels of the Brontës, the signature was not at the time of reception a reliable index of sexual identity. (The exceptions in the final analysis only point to the rules.) Even though such lists and such courses may betray a naïve faith in origins, humanism, and centrality, because they also make visible the marginality, eccentricity, and vulnerability of women, they concretely challenge the confidence of humanistic discourse as *universality.*

Let us turn to Foucault before closing; to Foucault perhaps against Foucault at the end of "What Is an Author?" He imagines what would happen in a society "without need for an author":

> No longer the tiresome repetitions:
> "Who is the real author?"
> "Have we proof of his authenticity and originality?"
> "What has he revealed of his most profound self in his language?'
> New questions will be heard:
> "What are the modes of existence of this discourse?"
> "Where does it come from; how is it circulated; who controls it?"
> "What placements are determined for possible subjects?"
> "Who can fulfill these diverse functions of the subject?"
> Behind all these questions we would hear little more than the murmur of indifference:
> "What matter who's speaking?" (138)

This sovereign indifference, I would argue, is one of the "masks . . . behind which phallocentrism hides its fictions" (138); the authorizing function of its own discourse authorizes the "end of woman" without consulting her. What matter who's speaking? I would answer it matters, for example, to women who have lost and still routinely lose their proper name in marriage, and whose signature—not merely their voice—has not been worth the paper it was written on; women for whom the signature—by virtue of its power in the world of circulation—is *not* immaterial. Only those who have it can play with not having it. We might want to remind ourselves of the status of women's signatures in France before the law of 1965:

> since 1965, a woman can exercise any profession without her husband's permission. She can alone establish a contract which concerns the maintenance of the home and open a personal bank account. Hereafter dual consent is necessary in order to buy, sell, mortgage a building . . . finalize a commercial lease . . . or make purchases on credit. (Albistur and Armogathe, 641–42)

In the place of proper closure, and in the face of insolubility: let us retain a "modern," posthumanistic reading of "literature" that has indeed begun to rethink the very locations of the center and the periphery, and within that fragile topology, the stability of the subject. But at the same time, we must live out (the hortatory always returns) a practical politics within the institution grounded in regional specificities. This is to call for, then, a decentered vision (*theoria*) but a centered action that will not result in a renewed invisibility. If feminists decide that the signature is a matter of indifference, if Women's Studies becomes gender studies, the *real* end of women in the institution will not be far off. The text's heroine will become again no more than a fiction.

What we might wish for instead, perhaps, is a female materialism attentive to the needs of the body as well as the luxuries of the mind. Can we imagine, or should we, a position that speaks in tropes and walks in sensible shoes?[5]

## NOTES

1. Elsewhere in the essay, and in subsequent work as well, Cixous also makes claims for a feminine specificity, attached to a female body and libido.

2. Kaja Silverman, in a complexly argued essay on *The Story of O*, puts the matter well: "I do not intend to enter here into the general speculation about the identity of Pauline Réage. To some degree that speculation is irrelevant, since regardless of who actually wrote the novel, the subjectivity designated by the name 'Pauline Réage' is a pornographic construction" (348).

In this sense, perhaps, the pornographic signature, is always terminally conventional in the gendering of its positions. In *O m'a dit*, a book of "interviews" that Régine Deforges conducts with Pauline Réage, "Réage" describes the context of authorship: "I would never have been tempted to write [the book] if I hadn't met someone who wanted to read it. I would never have written it if there hadn't been this need to write a letter. It's a letter" (100). In an interview with Germaine Brée about erotic writing, Alain Robbe-Grillet talks about men's and women's fantasies, and speculates about Dominique Aury ("Pauline Réage") and Jean Paulhan: "She wrote it for Paulhan. Or perhaps they wrote it together; I don't really know, I'm not familiar enough with it. Perhaps they really did both write it; no one has any idea how it was done. From the start, she's been the one who has collected the royalties, but what was Paulhan's role? *It's a couple's fantasy,* it's not necessarily someone's solitary fantasy" (91; emphasis added).

3. This position is laid out clearly enough in Cherri Register's "American Feminist Literary Criticism: A Bibliographical Introduction," in the Donovan volume Kamuf refers to. But it really seems an easy and early (1975) target.

4. In a later overview, "Feminist Criticism in the Wilderness," Showalter takes a nonprescriptive position which is much closer to my own: "feminist critics," she concludes, must address themselves "to what women actually write, not in relation to a theoretical, political, metaphoric, or visionary ideal of what women ought to write." (205)

5. I would like to thank Sandy Petrey and Christie V. McDonald for their help at several key moments in the development of this essay.

# [ 4 ]

# Arachnologies: The Woman, the Text, and the Critic

*"Arachnologies" had its first incarnation as a paper for the Georgetown Conference on Literary Theory organized by Susan S. Lanser and Michael Ragussis. The theme that year (1984) was "Interpretation." I had been elaborating the concept of "over-reading" as a reading strategy for noncanonical works, and more specifically women's writing. This was a double-sided project, historical and metacritical. Building on Annette Kolodny's "revisionary rereading," I wanted to construct a poetics that could account for the problem of signature posed by the "underread," works excluded from the library of general culture, the volumes of the already read (or the déjà lu). To talk about this I had taken as possible tropes of feminist literary agency examples from antiquity of women's weaving. I was really not interested so much in weaving, however, as in the representation of writing as instances of a textuality hopelessly entangled with questions of its material. Weaving, in that sense, provided me with an irresistible metaphorics: it allowed me to figure a writing identity as grounded and located in a scene of work, thus holding together representation and cultural production. (I had in fact originally conceived the account of Graffigny's knots and Zilia's quipus as part of this discussion.) I saw this concern as being necessarily at odds with a postmodern suspicion about the subject, and in the contrast I establish between Arachne and Ariadne my aim is to make these two embodiments of women in the text display the differences that separate feminist readings from the current rhetorics of indifference and a poetics that imagines itself beyond the effects of gender. In my reading, Arachne is self-positioned as a feminist, Ariadne troped as masculinity's feminine other. This has everything to do with the politics of critical pleasure.*

*With the thematic framework of the conference in mind, however, I emphasized in the earliest version of this chapter the exotic landscape of* Indiana *as an occasion for overreading, for the practice of a feminist hermeneutics. I was at that point particularly attracted to the hieroglyphics that the (young, male) narrator ponders at the end of Sand's novel as an open invitation to a feminist reading: a solicitation to decipher the presence of another text, that in turn points to a* poetics of dissent, a critique *of the dominant culture. In the many revisions this essay has undergone, the hieroglyphics have lost their original centrality, but the practice of reading topographically as a way of making sense of women's plots has remained central to my concerns here and throughout the book.*

*Speaking as a feminist reader at the conference (at which there was only one other woman panelist, Gayatri Spivak) I felt, as I said in discussion then, figured by Arachne. It seemed to me that* the fate of Arachne's text—first discredited, then detached from the cultural record, and finally ignored—*was not entirely unlike that of feminist critics whose writing, like Arachne's tapestry, constitutes a critique of phallomorphic privilege and a certain institutionally authorized violence.*

*It was therefore especially sweet to read the paper again at the Poetics of Gender Colloquium in the fall of 1984. There, in a room I knew well, filled mainly with other feminist critics and students, I felt that I was speaking not so much as Arachne as* for *her. In fact, the performative heroine I invoked then was Lucy Snowe. Like Lucy Snowe, the feminist critic, as I suggest in "Changing the Subject," performs a challenge to the dominant discourse by insisting on the particulars of another subjectivity. As Mary Jacobus remarks in* Reading Woman, *like Lucy Snowe and Charlotte Brontë, the feminist critic is "bound, if she's to gain both a living and a hearing, to install herself within the prevailing conventions of academic literary criticism. To this extent, hers must also be an ex-centric text, a displacement into criticism of . . . hunger, rebellion, and rage" (60). At the Poetics of Gender conference, which transformed an annual colloquium on (dominant) poetics into a feminist event, the tension between feminist critical studies and literary studies, the eccentric and the central modes of their unequal positionings, seemed temporarily suspended (perhaps only reversed). It was an interesting moment. I'm not sure now that it wasn't finally an effect of* Brigadoon, *but it was nice while it lasted.*

O Jack! that such a sweet girl should be a rogue!

Her morning gown was a pale primrose-coloured padu-
asoy: the cuffs and robings curiously embroidered by the fingers of this ever-charming Arachne, in a running pattern of
violets and their leaves; the light in the flowers silver; gold in
the leaves. A pair of diamond snaps in her ears. A white hand-
kerchief, wrought by the same inimitable fingers, concealed—
O Belford! what still more inimitable beauties did it not conceal!

Richardson, *Clarissa*

Most of the reasoning of women and poets is done in parables. Now think of a spider.

Diderot, *D'Alembert's Dream*

IN ONE of the final segments of *The Pleasure of the Text* (1973),
Roland Barthes elaborates a typically etymological definition of
one of the key words in his title:

*Text* means *Tissue;* but whereas hitherto we have always
taken this tissue as a product, a ready-made veil behind which
lies, more or less hidden, meaning (truth), we are now em-
phasizing, in the tissue, the generative idea that the text is made,
is worked out in a perpetual interweaving; lost in this tissue—
this texture—the subject unmakes himself, like a spider dis-
solving in the constructive secretions of [her] web. Were we
fond of neologisms, we might define the theory of the text as
an *hyphology* (*hyphos* is the tissue and the spider's web). (64)

As one may guess from the title of this essay, we too are fond of
neologisms, and in a moment will offer our theory of the text as
an arachnology. But first let us review this fable of metamorphosis.
In the move from product to production, from work to text, as
Barthes puts it in an earlier essay by that name, the emphasis moves
also from the image of a centrally strong or unitary subject to a
more ambiguous and fragile identity dependent upon the indeterminacy of *process*. The subject in this model is not fixed in time
or space but suspended in a continual moment of fabrication.

In the theorizing on the status of the text that has taken place
in this country over the past ten or so years, two of Barthes's tropes
in this passage have become fashionably postmodern: that the textual is the textile; and that the text maker, previously known as

the author, to the extent that he is still figurable, paradoxically owes his representation to an undoing: a destabilization of the terms of identity itself brought about by a breakdown in the boundaries between inside and outside (and other well-known binary oppositions). At issue for me, however, is not so much the "Death of the Author" himself—in so many ways, long overdue—but the effect the argument has had of killing off by delegitimating other discussions of the writing (and reading) subject.[1] This suppression is not simply the result of an arbitrary shift of emphasis: when a theory of the text called "hyphology" chooses the spider's *web* over the spider; and the concept of textuality called the "writerly" chooses the threads of lace over the lacemaker (Barthes, *S/Z*, 160), the subject is self-consciously erased by a model of text production which acts to foreclose the question of agency itself.[2]

The recasting of the text as texture—the better to bring about the dissolution of the subject—has other important, if ironic, implications for feminist critics (who themselves often favor the tropology of the loom) that parallel the effacement of the spider and the lacemaker. For one thing (and I will return to the question in some detail at the end of this chapter), the language of textiles tends to engender in the dominant discursive strategies of much contemporary literary criticism a metaphorics of femininity deeply marked by Freud's account of women and weaving.[3] For another, the discourse of the male weavers stages "woman" without in any way addressing women. This "masculine recuperation" of the feminine (Schor, *Breaking the Chain*, 5)[4] is a variant of the phenomenon Alice Jardine has named *gynesis*—"the putting into discourse of 'woman'"(*Gynesis*, 25)—and Gayatri Spivak has described, somewhat differently, as the "double displacement."[5]

In other words, if Barthes had been less fond of neologisms, and a feminist, he might have named his theory of text production an "arachnology." In English, the word exists to describe the study of spiders, so we would have had not a neologism but a catachresis;[6] or a "gynocritics" (Showalter, "Toward a Feminist Poetics," 185). We will want to remember that Arachne, the spider artist, began as a woman weaver of texts. By arachnology, then, I mean a critical positioning which reads *against* the weave of indifferentiation to discover the embodiment in writing of a gendered subjectivity; to recover within representation the emblems of its construction. It is from that perspective that I propose now to read Arachne's story: both as a figuration of woman's relation of production to the dominant culture, and as a possible parable (or critical modeling) of a feminist poetics.[7] Arachnologies, thus, involve more broadly the interpretation and reappropriation of a story, like many in the history of Western literature, that deploys the interwoven structures of power, gender, and identity inherent in the production of mimetic art.

## ARACHNE'S TAPESTRY

IN BOOK 6 of the *Metamorphoses,* we learn the story of the motherless daughter of a wool dyer, Arachne, who, though "lowborn" had "gained fame [*nomen memorabile*] for her skill [*studio*]." In fact her accomplishments in the "art of spinning and weaving wool" [*artis*] made those who came to see her "finished work," or "watch her as she worked" assume that Pallas Athena (Minerva) had taught her (289) (despite the Latin origins of the tale, the Greek name has become the more familiar one). But Arachne refuses this implicit hierarchy of talents and claims equality in artistic skill with the goddess. Disguised as an old woman, Athena comes to warn Arachne against defiance of the gods, but Arachne persists in her daring, and the two engage in a contest of representation: "They weave in pliant threads of gold, and trace in the weft some ancient tale" (293). Athena "pictures [*pingit*] the hills of Mars . . . and that old dispute over the naming of the land. There sit twelve heavenly gods on lofty thrones in awful majesty, Jove in their midst; each god she pictures [*inscribit*] with his own familiar features" (293). Athena also represents herself separately armed and victorious. The central display of Olympian power is restaged in the margins: "she weaves in the four corners of the web four scenes of contest, each clear in its own colours, and in miniature design." In each of these "pictured warnings," a mortal is punished by transformation out of human identity for having challenged the gods. These embedded mininarratives may, I think, also be seen as self-reflexive, internal commentaries on the authority of representation itself. Thus, when she finishes her work at the loom, and in a final gesture of authorization, the goddess signs her text by a self-referring metonymy, with a "border of peaceful olive wreath . . . [from] her own tree" (295).

Against the classically theocentric balance of Athena's tapestry, Arachne constructs a feminocentric protest: Europa, Leda, Antiope, are the more familiar names of women carried off against their will by the "heavenly crimes" of divine desire, whose stories

she weaves; Medusa, and more obscurely Erigone, who in one account, deceived by Bacchus, "later hangs herself on a nearby tree."[8]
When Arachne completes her "realistic" figuration of the ancient
heroines of the oldest western stories of seduction and betrayal,
like Athena she too frames the finished product, but the legibility
of her signature is more ambiguous: "The edge of the web with
its narrow border is filled with flowers and clinging ivy intertwined" [*intertextos*].[9]

As the exempla in the corners of Athena's tapestry had anticipated, this is not a contest for a mortal to win. And thus though
the product is judged flawless in the signifiers of its art—the *ver-
isimilitude* of its representation—"real bull and real waves you
would think them"—its producer must be punished for its signified. Thus, outwomaned, and in phallic identification with
Olympian authority, the goddess destroys the woman's counter-
cultural account: she "rent the embroidered web with its heavenly
crimes" (297). Symptomatically (we recall that Athena identifies
not only with the gods but with godhead, the cerebral male identity that bypasses the female) she goes on not only to mutilate the
text, but to destroy its author by beating her over the head with
the shuttle—their shared emblem.[10] Arachne, in indignation, tries
to hang herself, at which point Athena both pities and transforms
her; she is to hang and yet to live: her head shrinks, her legs become "slender fingers" and, virtually all body—the antithesis of
the goddess—she continues the act of spinning: "and now a spider, she exercises her old-time weaver art."

In the neologism of the text as hyphology, the mode of production is privileged over the subject, whose supervising identity
is dissolved in the work of the web. But Arachne's story, as we
have just seen, is not only the tale of a text as tissue: it evokes a
bodily substance and a violence to the teller that is not adequately
accounted for by an attention to a torn web. Represented in Ovid's
writing re-presenting the stories of sexual difference as a matter
of interpretation, Arachne is punished for her point of view. For
this, she is restricted to spinning outside representation, to a reproduction that turns back on itself. Cut off from the work of art,
she spins like a woman.

Barthes maintains in *S/Z* that "there is no *first* reading"; that
if we act as though "there were a beginning of reading, as if everything were not already read," we are "obliged to read the same
story everywhere" (16). I want to suggest here that the poetics of
the "already read" depends upon the same logic as that of the

"subject lost in the tissue": in both cases the animating assumption of the critical model depends upon the confident posture of mastery that a post-Cartesian subject enjoys in relation to the texts of his culture. As Annette Kolodny argues in "Dancing Through the Minefield," "we read well, and with pleasure, what we *already know* how to read; and what we know how to read is to a large extent dependent upon what we have already read (works from which we've developed our expectations and learned our interpretive strategies)" (154; emphasis added). Only the subject who is both self-possessed and possesses access to the library of the already read has the luxury of flirting with the escape from identity—like the loss of Arachne's "head"—promised by an aesthetics of the decentered (decapitated, really) body.

What I want to propose instead as a counterweight to this story of the deconstructed subject, restless with what he already knows, is a poetics of the *underread* and a practice of "overreading." The aim of this practice is double. It aims first to unsettle the interpretive model which thinks that it knows *when* it is rereading, and what is in the library, confronting its claims with Kolodny's counterclaim that *"what we engage are not texts but paradigms"* (153). In a second, parallel gesture, this practice, like Kolodny's "revisionary rereading" ("A Map," 59), constructs a new object of reading, women's writing. Specifically, the latter project involves reading women's writing not "as if it had already been read," but as if it had never been read; *as if* for the first time. (This assumption has the added advantage of being generally true.) Overreading also involves a focus on the moments in the narrative which by their representation of writing itself might be said to figure the production of the female artist. This might mean a scene like Arachne's that thematizes explicitly the conditions of text production under the classical sex/gender arrangements of Western culture, or more coded representations of female signature of a sort we will consider in a moment.

To overread is also to wonder, as Woolf puts it famously in *A Room of One's Own*, about the conditions for the production of literature: "fiction," she writes, "is like a spider's web, attached ever so lightly perhaps, but still attached to life at all four corners. . . . When the web is pulled askew, hooked up at the edge, torn in the middle, one remembers that these webs are not spun in mid-air by incorporeal creatures, but are the work of suffering human beings, and are attached to grossly material things, like health and money and the houses we live in" (43–44).[11] When we tear the web of women's texts we discover in the representations of writing itself the marks of the grossly material, the sometimes brutal traces of the culture of gender; the inscriptions of its political structures.


## REPRESENTING WRITING: OPHELIA DROWNS

[Prosper Mérimée] once opened his eyes, in the raw winter dawn, to see his companion, in a dressing gown, on her knees before the domestic hearth, a candlestick beside her and a red *madras* round her head, making bravely, with her own hands, the fire that was to enable her to sit down betimes to urgent pen and paper. The story represents him as having felt that the spectacle chilled his ardour and tried his taste; her appearance was unfortunate, her occupation an inconsequence, and her industry a reproof—the result of all which was a lively irritation and an early rupture.

Henry James, "Notes on Novelists"


IN HIS 1893 essay on George Sand in *French Poets and Novelists*, Henry James considers "what makes things classical" and contrasts Sand's novels to Balzac's. He concludes that Balzac will last longer: "We cannot easily imagine posterity travelling with 'Valentine' or 'Mauprat,' 'Consuelo,' or the 'Marquis de Villemer' in its trunk." But he also imagines that "if these admirable tales fall out of fashion, such of our descendants as stray upon them in the dusty corners of old libraries will sit down on the bookcase ladder with the open volume and turn it over with surprise and enchantment. What a beautiful mind! they will say; what an extraordinary style! Why have we not known more about these things?" (180–81).[12] It is against that question that I propose a novel of George Sand for an exercise in overreading. Taking more specifically the closural moves of her "signature" novel *Indiana* (1832), I want to suggest the ways in which, by an internal figuration of its own ambivalent relationship to the dominant literature and its critics, the narrative itself stages the difficulty of reading women's writing.

Because the novel has remained largely unread, it may be useful to provide a brief account of its major events here.[13] Indiana is a young, beautiful creole from the Ile Bourbon married to a much older and thoroughly unpleasant man, the retired Colonel Delmare. Living with her husband and cousin in seclusion on a country estate in France, she meets Raymon, a handsome, aristocratic rake from a neighboring estate, who has already seduced her maid and foster sister, Noun. When Noun, who is pregnant, realizes that Raymon is falling in love with her mistress, she drowns herself. Indiana blindly continues to believe in Raymon and fantasize about love, but when Colonel Delmare's business fails, and he decides to return to the Ile Bourbon, Indiana suddenly throws caution to the winds and comes alone to Raymon's rooms. Appalled by the implications of her gesture of self-sacrifice, Raymon sends Indiana away, and in despair, she heads for the Seine. She is saved from drowning by her faithful cousin Ralph (led to her by her dog Ophélia). Ralph returns to the island with the unhappy couple, and continues to watch over Indiana, who continues to dream of Raymon and of another life. Then, in a repetition of the earlier episode, Indiana, encouraged by Raymon's rhetoric of love— he writes a letter of regret for having failed to value her love— returns to France alone, overcoming enormous physical difficulties (in a particularly brutal scene, Ophélia is killed trying to follow her) only to find that he has married a rich woman, Laure de Nangy, and taken over her former property. Rejected once again, she is found and saved by Ralph, and the two return to the Ile Bourbon, this time making a joint suicide pact. (The husband has died during Indiana's trip to France.) In the penultimate scene of the novel Ralph confesses his love to Indiana, then taking her in his arms in a final embrace they poise to plunge to their death into the ravine below.

The novel was an overnight success and "made" George Sand. But the ending Sand chose for her "signature" novel, the first novel she published without the collaboration of Jules Sandeau, then and now posed problems for its readers. In his review of the novel, reprinted in *Portraits contemporains* (1870), Sainte-Beuve refers to "les étranges invraisemblances vers la fin" (471), the "strange implausibilities [that occur] toward the end of the novel"; and Pierre Salomon, in his introduction to the Garnier edition, speculates: "The . . . epilogue might have been added for purely opportunistic reasons. It is not absurd to imagine that the end volume was considered too slim and that to have the right number of pages, the publisher proposed the addition of a commercially satisfying conclusion, not exactly a happy marriage, but something equivalent" (vi). I don't want to argue here all the ways in which ideology leads and misleads that interpretation of the conclusion, and the closure of women's fiction in general. I would like instead to consider briefly the metacritical function of the final volume. What might it tell us about *how to read* the novel it integrally frames? And, more generally, as I have asked elsewhere, what does the "strange" and implausible ending tell us about reading for the plot of women's fiction?[14]

In the pages often referred to as the epilogue, and which bear a separate address (to A. J. Néraud), the narrator, whom the reader meets for the first time, finds himself on the island, and meets the couple who in fact did not fall into the abyss; they are living together in their "Indian cottage" on the island, freeing the slaves, and caring for the poor. And we learn that it is from Ralph himself that the narrator has heard the story we have just read. The narrator, we are told in the preface, is a young man who "abstains from weaving into the woof of his narrative preconceived opinions, judgments all formed" (np/78). What are we now to make of this male "weaver" who wanders into the wilderness and tries to decipher the mysteries of its landscape?

> I halted at the foot of a crystallized basaltic monument, about sixty feet high and cut with facets as if by a lapidary. At the top of this strange object an inscription seemed to have been traced in bold characters by an immortal hand . . . curious hieroglyphics, mysterious characters which seem to have been stamped there like the seal of some supernatural being, written in cabalistic letters.
>
> I stood there a long time, detained by a foolish idea that I might find a meaning for those ciphers. This profitless search caused me to fall into a profound meditation, during which I forgot that time was flying. (316/341)

Hieroglyphs are of course a commonplace of Romantic writing, and constitute by their semiotic protocol an automatic appeal to interpretation. But in the pause, during which the narrator contemplates nature's messages and tries to decipher the meaning of its "mysterious characters," the reader, I think, ponders more locally the fate of the lovers left on the "threshold of another life" and the meaning of their suspended narrative. In other words, I want to suggest that, coming after a certain narratological flamboyance, a literal cliffhanger marked by the (. . .) punctuation of suspense (deleted in the English translation), this sudden staging of the hermeneutic act forces us to pay particular attention to its operations. At stake here is what amounts to a *mise en abyme,* as it were (the pun is not only terrible and irresistible but important), of a signature, the delineation of a writer's territory. For the "female landscape" is not only, as Ellen Moers has shown, a scene within which to read metaphors of sexuality (255), it is also the iconography of a desire for a revision of story, and in particular a revision of closure. This desire for another logic of plot which by definition cannot be narrated looks elsewhere for expression: in the authorization provided by the novel's *discours* and in descriptive emblems tied to the representation of writing itself. A practice of overreading self-consciously responds to the appeal of the abyss.[15]

Gilbert and Gubar have argued that the story of female authorship, its mode of self-division, may often be read as a "palimpsest" (73) through the script of the dominant narrative. In *Indiana* that story is figured by this canonical representation of the romantic artist who measures his creativity against divine (or diabolical) makers. Thus the narrator speculates about the creators of this awesome scene, and wonders who could have "toyed with mountains as with grains of sand, and strewn, amid creations which man has tried to copy, these grand conceptions of art, these sublime contrasts impossible of realization which seem to defy the audacity of the artist and to say to him derisively: 'Try it again' " (316/341). Against what model can a *female* artist measure herself in nineteenth-century France? Like the young male narrator who meditates upon nature's blueprint, Indiana perceives the poetic structures of landscape. But when she wanders over the island and contemplates the sails on the horizon, her vision does not translate into acts of representation. Instead, the woman is immobilized by her own imagination; she dreams not of making art, but of being in love in Paris (24:229–30/254).

And she writes. Like the heroine of an eighteenth-century epistolary novel prevented from acting in the world, Indiana writes as a way of establishing control over her lack of control. Indiana "had adopted the depressing habit of writing down every evening a narrative of the sorrowful thoughts of the day. This journal of her sufferings was addressed to Raymon, and, although she had no intention of sending it to him, she talked with him, sometimes passionately, sometimes bitterly, of the misery of her life and of the sentiments which she could not overcome" (26:248/268). That the construction of such a text is a gesture of potentially transgressive self-empowerment can be seen in her husband's response to discovering its existence. Having broken open the box that contained her papers—which included Raymon's letters—the hus-

band, in his rage, "unable to utter a word . . . seized her by the
hair, threw her down, and stamped on her forehead with his heel"
(26:249/269). This marking—what we might think of as the dominant signature—generates the final sequences of the novel, and
Indiana's heroinism.

To be sure, Indiana's writing by itself cannot produce effective
forms of protest against the powers of the social text, but Sand
grants her heroine a literary victory of sorts. Thus, when Raymon
panics at the social implications of Indiana's decision to live for
love and beyond convention, and mocks her for having studied
society in novels "written for the entertainment of lady's-maids"
(20:191/210), Sand in *her* novel challenges that literary judgment
by returning it to him. Indiana writes from the island: "You see
I was mad; according to your cynical expression I had acquired
my knowledge of life from novels written for lady's-maids, from
those gay, childish works of fiction in which the heart is interested
in the success of wild enterprises and in impossible felicities" (23:222/
240). Indiana's writing is incorporated within a critique of the love
narrative itself, which in turn becomes the frame for a different
social realism. It is, after all, the dog named Ophélia who drowns.
And unlike the victim of female plot, the darker double, Noun, in
the end the heroine of these "strange implausibilities," does not
die of unrequited love; indeed, she may, with Ralph, live the "impossible felicities" she had read about.[16]

In *L'Histoire de ma vie*, Sand explains that writing *Indiana* also
marked the end of a collaboration characterized by its inefficiency:
one of them would spend the day unwriting what the other one
had written the day before. This double authorship [*ce remanie-
ment successif*], she explains, "made of our work an embroidery
like Penelope's" [*faisait de notre ouvrage la broderie de Pénélope*
(2:174)]. In *Indiana* the traces of a certain doubling seem to remain. A contemporary critic, thinking Sandeau was still on the
scene, imagined that he saw what we might call today a "bisexual"
origin in the authorship of *Indiana*: "One would say that this brilliant but unharmonious material [*cette étoffe brillante mais sans
harmonie*] is the work [*oeuvre*] of two very different workers [*ouv-
riers*]; the hands of a young man stretched the strong, sturdy fabric
and the hands of a woman embroidered flowers of silk and gold"
(2:1343, n. 4). In a way, it is true that the novel offers a dual model
of authorship, but the division of labor is not marked simply along
the fault lines of sexual difference. If we read the feminine hand
in Indiana's embroidery work, "the flowers that had bloomed be-

neath the breath of fever, watered by her daily tears," we might also read the "masculine" identity figured in a less docile female figure, in Sand's other portrait of the female artist cast in the body of a woman who paints: Laure, a rich aristocratic young woman who appears fleetingly at the beginning of the novel long enough to label Raymon a ladies' man, a Lovelace. Sitting at the place formerly occupied by the worktable where Indiana embroidered, Laure, at the novel's close, to amuse herself copies the wall hangings of the chateau in watercolor. She parodies the rococo pastoral "fictions" of eighteenth-century France—which are already historical commentaries—and marks the ambiguous status of her signature in the corner of her painting: in the place of her name she writes the word "pastiche" (28:266–67/288).[17]

Like Arachne at her loom, Laure at her easel offers a representation of the female signature of protest. An ironic nineteenth-century female artist refuses the pathos and limits of the woman who embroiders her way through the plot of her life: eighteenth-century woman, whose *proper* activity according to Laure is "paint[ing] fans and produc[ing] masterpieces of threadwork." Like Myth under Arachne's threads, History under Laure's satirical brush derides the pastoral, the Boucher-like landscape in which the "costumes of the boudoir and the shepherd's hut [are] curiously identical" (28:267/288). But like "the engravings representing the pastoral attachment of Paul and Virginia" (7:59/82) that decorate Indiana's virginal bedroom, recontained by women's writing, pastoral comes back to indict history. Thus it is not so surprising that in the end Sand relocates Indiana on the island of her beginnings. The novel moves backward from France to its colonies, and at that distance points to the limits of the dominant narrative. Sand's nostalgic preromanticism—like George Eliot's insistence on the daisy fields of childhood in another watery text—is itself a mode of critique.

Pastiche is a term particularly charged for Sand, since it is the word with which her mentor Latouche measures her progress as a writer. As she tells the tale in her autobiography, his first reaction (flipping through the pages) to *Indiana* is not flattering: "Come now, this is a pastiche! School of Balzac! Pastiche! What do you mean by it?" (2:173). Latouche comes to regret his hasty evaluation, and writes the following morning: "Your book is a masterpiece. I stayed up all night to read it. No woman alive can sustain the insolence of a comparison with you. Successes like those of Lamartine await you. . . . Balzac and Mérimée lie dead under *Indiana*" (2:1342, n. 1). Literary history has not borne out Latouche's judgment, but that is another story. The pleasure of the text is also a critical politics.

Toward the end of his 1893 essay on Sand, James claims that he has been trying to "read . . . over" the "author's romances," but that he must "frankly confess that we have found it impossible" (180). George Sand, he writes, "invites reperusal less than any mind of equal eminence," and wonders whether this is "because after all she was a woman, and the laxity of the female intellect could not fail to claim its part in her?" (181). The question, being after all rhetorical, is left without an answer. Although earlier in the essay James accepts the objection to the novels that they "contain no living figures . . . who like so many of the creations of other novelists, have become part of the public fund of allusion and quotation" (156), the invocation of sexual logic here suggests that the grounds of citational difference in fact derive from an older poetics of gender. It is precisely the persistence of that move in critical discourse that overreading seeks to challenge.


## THE ARIADNE COMPLEX

> I could not have been Ariadne: it's all right that she gives herself out of love. But to whom? Theseus doesn't tremble, doesn't adore, doesn't desire; following his own destiny, he goes over bodies that are never even idealized. Every woman is a means. I see that clearly.
>
> Hélène Cixous, *The Newly Born Woman*


IN AN ESSAY called "The Voice of the Shuttle Is Ours," Patricia Joplin reviews Geoffrey Hartman's "The Voice of the Shuttle: Language from the Point of View of Literature," which turns on a gloss of Aristotle's recording of a phrase from a lost play of Sophocles based on Philomela's story: "As you know," Hartman explains, "Tereus, having raped Philomela, cut out her tongue to prevent discovery. But she weaves a tell-tale account of her violation into a tapestry (or robe) which Sophocles calls 'the voice of the shuttle.' If metaphors as well as plots or myths could be archetypal, I would nominate Sophocles' voice of the shuttle for that distinction" (25).

Joplin argues, as does Jane Marcus in "Liberty, Sorority, Mis-

ogyny" (88), that when Hartman interrogates the power of the
metaphor he "celebrates Language and not the violated woman's
emergence from silence. He celebrates Literature and the male poet's
trope, not the woman's elevation of her safe, feminine, domestic
craft—weaving—into a new means of resistance. . . . When
Hartman exuberantly analyzes the structure of the trope for voice,
he makes an all too familiar elision of gender" (26). "The specific
nature of the woman's double violation," she comments further,
"disappears behind the apparently genderless (but actually male)
language of 'us,' the 'I,' and the 'you'," who in Hartman's account
"attest to that which violates, deprives, silences only as a mysterious unnamed 'something.' For the feminist unwilling to let
Philomela become universal before she has been met as female, this
is the primary evasion" (30). Joplin's attention to the universalizing moves in Hartman's discourse away from the details of
Philomela's silencing, and her reappropriation of the Philomela story,
forcefully raise the question of a more specifically *"feminist poetics"* (28) that would reclaim the voice of the shuttle from the
myth of a poetics beyond gender.

I would like to turn now to an essay of J. Hillis Miller's which,
I will argue, like Geoffrey Hartman's, fails to "meet" the female;
in this case, the female in Arachne. The essay, which many of you
will know, is entitled "Ariachne's Broken Woof." It takes as its
pretext a passage from Shakespeare's *Troilus and Cressida* (Miller
quotes from the Variorum):

> . . . This is and is not *Cressid:*
> Within my soule, there doth conduce a fight
> Of this strange nature, that a thing inseperate,
> Divides more wider than the skie and earth:
> And yet the spacious bredth of this division,
> Admits no Orifex for a point as subtle,
> As *Ariachnes* broken woofe to enter. . . . (45)

Much is at stake here, since to make sense of or merely to decipher
the phrase 'Ariachne's broken woof'—is it a "slip of the tongue
or of the pen?" (45)—for Miller involves nothing less than a gloss
on the relations between the sexes and a theory of the text. At
stake as well in my choice of this essay is a look at the relations
between deconstruction and feminism as practiced in the United
States, two critical movements which like Arachne and Ariadne
are both "alike and different" (57). The question through which I
will more specifically address the problem of that relationship in

these final pages is this: what grounds allow one to link or separate the two names Arachne and Ariadne, which conflated in "a
single word, Ariachne, mime the mode of relationship between two
myths which exist side by side in a culture, and are similar without
being identical"? (55)[18]

Miller comments on the sexual transpositions imaged in these
ambiguous lines: "Ariachne's broken woof, figure of a torn or deflowered virginity, becomes, in a mind-twisting reversal of the sexes,
itself a 'point' which might tear, though it can find in this case no
orifex to penetrate. . . . Tearer and torn here change places, as
Ariachne's broken woof both is and is not male and is and is not
female, as the stories of Ariadne and Arachne are both alike and
different" (57). But does the inversion of penetration, the blurring
of the lines of sexual difference that Miller enlists to "justify"
the yoking of the two women's names in the lines of *Troilus and
Cressida*, also inhabit their stories *outside* the Shakespearean context? Are all differences created equal?

Put another way, if viewed from a position which presumes the
indeterminacy of meaning and the insecurity of all identity, tearer
and torn trade places in a linguistic play of indifference, does it
follow that no significant difference inhabits the two *stories*? Putting the matter politically, if we can't tell the difference between
the stories, what are our chances of identifying the material differences between and among women that for feminist theory remain crucial? If Arachne and Ariadne change places in the threads
of the loom, is nothing lost in the translation? In a way this is also
to worry whether we can, at least in critical practice, preserve women
from the fate of "woman."

As a way into and, by the logic of the labyrinth, out of these
questions, let us briefly review Ariadne's story. In the *Metamorphoses,* Ariadne is never *named* in an account which figures a
trajectory and an engagement that take place essentially between
men. Minos, the father/king, to hide the monster produced by his
wife and a sacrificial bull, commissions Daedalus, the architect/
Artist, to build an enclosure; a space designed to provide no exit.
Theseus, the adventurer (and ladies' man), arrives to press his claim
to fame. This heroic gesture brings death to the Minotaur "when,
by the virgin Ariadne's help" (the Latin reads, *ope virginea; ops*
also means might and power) the difficult entrance, which no former adventurer had ever returned to, was found by winding up
the thread (419). Having provided the thread that unravels the maze,
Ariadne, madly in love, is carried off, seduced and abandoned on

the island of Naxos by the faithless hero. In alternate endings of
the story, she is then either rescued and consoled by Dionysos,
who marries her and offers her a crown of stars which he sends
up to the skies; or disconsolate, like Arachne, hangs herself with
her own thread.

What then is figured by Ariadne's thread, the woman or the
thread? the agency of her desire or the process of solution she authorizes? When the critic suffering from an "Ariadne complex"
(Schor, *Breaking the Chain,* 3) follows the thread of a reading practice common to the post-structuralist models of Barthes,
Derrida, Deleuze—and more locally, of Hillis Miller—that by its
metaphors and metonymies associates itself with the feminine, whose
story is it? When the critic follows the thread handed to him by
the "woman in the text," the thread that enables him to weave his
way back through the meanders of the path already taken, whose
powers do we admire?[19] The man who entered to kill, or the woman
who allowed him to exit alive? Or is this a case, like the minotaur,
and the mermaid troped by Dorothy Dinnerstein, of an uneasy but
no less powerful heterosexual arrangement founded on the deadly
inseparable ("inseperate") relation between the two?

"Ariadne's thread," Miller writes in the essay by that name, "is
both the labyrinth and a means of safely retracing the labyrinth"
(156). Thus, in his textural metaphorics, within its reversible fabric
Ariadne's story, like Arachne's, figures sexual difference only to
undo it:

> The stories turn on enigmatic oppositions: making/solving,
> hiding/revealing, male/female, or is it female/male, united in
> ambiguous or androgynous figures, like Dionysus himself,
> or like Ariadne, who is perhaps too aggressive to be purely
> "feminine" in the male chauvinist sense of the word, or like
> Arachne, devouring phallic mother, weaver of a web, *erion* in
> Greek, which also, as Jacques Derrida observes in *Glas,* means
> wool, fleece, the ring of pubic hair. (154)

Philology makes odd bedfellows: how shall we square our account
of Ariadne as the epitome of the resolutely feminine with Miller's
"aggressive" type?[20] Or Arachne as "devouring phallic mother"
with Joplin's reading of the woman artist battered into silence by
the phallic woman (49)?

As the fixed expression "Ariadne's thread" confirms, Ariadne
remains tied to her gift as a kind of package deal. Confident in
her knowledge of the figures of the text, her feel for its turns, she

rewards the seeker who makes his way to her with a way out. She is that which allows the male adventurer, the legislator, the ladies' man, the critic who fancies himself all of the above, to penetrate the space of the great artist like Daedalus (or Ovid himself) without the risk of getting stuck there. In this sense Ariadne is but the pretext for the homosocial bond Eve Sedgwick has described that links and separates men in western culture.[21] Ariadne is thus the "woman in the text" the critic takes into the abyss of discourse that constructs his identity. Domesticated, female desire becomes the enabling fiction of a male need for mastery. Or, more perversely, as Nietzsche's Dionysos sings to Ariadne's lament: "I am your Labyrinth."

Ovid in the *Heroides* represents Ariadne as an abandoned woman. Alone on the island where Theseus has forgotten her, "abandoned on a solitary shore," Ariadne, like Indiana writing in her journal of lamentations, writes to Theseus and pleads not to "be stolen from the record of [his] honours," when he tells "gloriously" of "the death of the man-and-bull, and of the halls of rock cut out in winding ways" (10:131). Lost or found, dead or married to the figure who represents the eternal return of male narcissistic desire, Ariadne's letter is written for the record of the already read; the question of her desire circulates only as repetition of the trope: the abandoned woman. Ovid in fact repeats Catullus, who in *his* poem (64) details Ariadne's sufferings on "an embroidered . . . coverlet."

In a note to the title of "Ariachne's Broken Woof," Miller explains that his "essay is a segment cut from a work in progress . . . to be called *Ariadne's Thread*" (44). The choice of title for the forthcoming book—"on linear imagery and narrative form"—I think confirms a preference for the Ariadne matrix already at work in the body of both texts. In the choice between proper names, Miller takes the name of the woman who leaves the classical metaphors of representation intact.[22]

## OVID'S SISTER[23]

I SAID at the beginning that we might want to read Arachne's story as a parable of women's writing, a model for understanding how it has classically been read. As in the standard library references, the dictionaries, and the encyclopedias—the cultural text James called the "public fund of allusion and quotation"—in Hillis Miller's account of Arachne reference is not made to the representations of Arachne's tapestry, to *what* she has been weaving.[24] Miller thus elides what I take to be the critical difference that sep- arates, finally, Arachne from Ariadne: the making of a text. The image of Arachne Miller offers, the "arachnid who devours her mate, weaver of a web which is herself, and which both hides and reveals an absence, the abyss" (161) is the image of the spider Arachne the spinner *becomes*. When Miller moves from the abyss to Arachne's "text as *mise en abyme*" he installs a vacancy her tapestry refuses. Arachne in fact recontains the iconography of Ariadne's tale: according to Graves's etymologies, Ariadne is also known in antiquity as Erigone, one of the despairing female bodies we saw earlier portrayed in Arachne's tapestry.

Athena's punishment returns Arachne to the limits of femininity, to the eternal reproduction of female labor, to precisely the secre- tion of the spider, subject of Barthes's neologism, to the threads in the hands of the lacemaker he invokes in *S/Z* as a figure of text production. Despite the recognition Arachne's art is granted within the narrative of its production—after all (and this is not the case of the mortals in Athena's exempla) she does *not* lose the con- test—her posterity as an artist is cut off by the female guardian of the law.[25] In a move analogous to Barthes's invention, then, of the spider and her web, Ovid tells a story in which a female desire to produce art is staged, but no sooner does he textualize that agency than he deauthorizes the story that motivated its produc- tion in the first place. The artist is returned to "woman"; to the domain of the natural in which, as Joplin observes, she weaves only "literal webs, sticky, incomprehensible designs" (50–51).

In the aftermath of her tale, the spider woman seems to block completely the woman weaver of golden threads: it is as though Athena's punishment had destroyed not only the figures of a wom- an's text, but Ovid's. Or rather, Ovid has succeeded only too well, since his "intention," he writes in his opening lines, was to tell of "bodies changed to different forms." That we remember the spider and not the woman is in part a function of the poet's project: good readers, we retain the metamorphosis, the metaphors of the trope as turn. But it is Ovid's legacy and its effects that I am putting in question here, not his mastery: how *in history* the portrait of the *artist* becomes (spider) woman. In the many revisions of the *Me- tamorphoses* the images of Arachne's tapestry have been consis- tently reappropriated by interpretive gestures that dematerialize the gender of cultural productions, and in the process of displacement allegorize the referential claims of the female body in representation *to* representation.[26] It is thus also the task of feminist criticism to read for Arachne, which is to say not only for her, for the "other woman," but for emblems of a female signature elsewhere and otherwise, as I have tried to in this book for a tradition of feminist writers.

In a gesture of recognition Gilbert and Gubar have described, the eighteenth-century poet Anne Finch remembers nostalgically Arachne's contest with Athena as an earlier assertion of female agency and ambition. In the *"Tapestry* of old," Finch writes, Arachne "Whilst sharing in the Toil . . . shar'd the Fame, / And with the *Heroes* mixt her interwoven *Name.* No longer, *Females* to such Praise aspire, / And serfdom now we rightly do admire" ("A Description of One of the Pieces of Tapestry at Long-Heat," in *Madwoman,* 525). It is not so much the lament that interests me here, however, as the rendering of the signature: "The edge of the web with its narrow border is filled with flowers and clinging ivy intertwined" was the way, we remember, Arachne finished off her representation. The line in Latin ends on the word *intertextos.* Reinscribing the "interwoven *Name,*" the woman poet recognizes the signature of the female precursor and restores her to her text.

Curiously, however, Finch doesn't seem to remember the content of the representations that brought Arachne fame as a weaver. Pamela White Hadas does, though, in a poem called "Arachne"; she remembers the grounds of her protest as well (*Designing Women,* 20–21):

> My craft unwinds
> confabula beyond
> self-portrait: dense
>
> sublimities of rape: it takes all kinds
>
> to teach defeat.
> I won,
> so lost my head
> by blow and henbane,
> hanged me
> by my thread.

To remember Arachne only as the spider, or through the dangers of her web alone, is to retain the archetype and dismember, once again, with Athena, the subject of its history: to underread. The goal of overreading, of reading for the signature, is to put one's finger—figuratively—on the place of production that marks the spinner's attachment to her web. This is also, of course, to come closer to the spider's art itself: in the end, the material of arachnologies may allow us to refuse and refigure the very opposition of subject and text, spider and web.

This move, then, to recover the figurations of Arachne's tapestry—like the gold and silk flowers of Indiana's embroidery and the pastoral landscape of Laure's watercolors—is meant not only to retrieve those texts from the indifference of the aesthetic universal, but to identify the act of this reading as the enabling subjectivity of *another* poetics, a poetics attached to gendered bodies that may have lived in history.

## NOTES

1. "The Death of the Author" (1968) and "From Work to Text" (1971) appeared in English in 1977 in a volume of essays translated by Stephen Heath, *Image/Text/Music*. "La mort de l'auteur" and "De l'oeuvre au texte" were collected in France in *Essais Critiques IV: Le Bruissement de la langue*, 1984. I think it is important to keep these dates in mind as markers of a powerful disjunction between French rhythms and contexts of production, and American cadences and frameworks of reception and consumption. The time lag and difference between institutional structures are perhaps more important to understanding Franco-American critical relations than the linguistic problems of translation.

I take on the more specifically political relations between the deconstructive resonances of the "Death of the Author" and the reconstructive project of the feminist critic in "Changing the Subject." I argue there that in the wake of the Dead Author we might usefully distinguish between the discussions around patriarchal texts that move to dismantle the originating powers of authorship, and the readings of women's writing that seek to establish the material and figurative grounds for elaborating a history of female authorship.

2. It might also be noted in passing that both models bear the "mark of gender": the spinning spider is after all female, as is the lacemaker. In both cases a female subject is bound to the mindless work now performed by women, overwhelmingly of the Third World, in what has come to be known as the "integrated circuit." See Haraway, 84–85.

3. Freud in the essay on "Femininity," described weaving as women's unique contribution to civilization, an invention symbolically bound up with their "genital deficiency" (132). In weaving, the argument goes, women reenact nature's art of concealment by which pubic hair comes to hide what is said to be missing. In his essay, "The Clarification of Clara Middleton," J. Hillis Miller reads the weaving as a "metaphor claiming the existence of what is not there [a "mock phallus"] so covering the fact that the phallus is not there" (109). It is this second degree of metaphor, I think, that leads him to argue so readily for the interchangeability of male and female: "The phallic thicket becomes a vaginal gap" (109), etc.

4. In the essay "For a Restricted Thematics," written in 1975 and re-printed in her book *Breaking the Chain* (1985), Naomi Schor, citing the passage from Barthes with which I began, and the quotation from Freud, describes the persistent relationship between the "textural" and the textile as an "Ariadne Complex" (3–5).

5. Spivak focuses more specifically on Derrida in "Displacement and the Discourse of Woman."

6. Barthes writes interestingly of catachresis in his "Conclusions" to the Colloquium at Cerisy, 1977, of which he was the "pretext": "You remember that catachresis occurs when one says, for example: *the arms of a chair* . . .; it's a way of speaking which produces an obvious effect of metaphor (arms), and yet behind these images there is no word in the language which allows one to denote the figure's referent; to designate the arms of the chair there are no other words than 'the arms of the chair.' Modern discourse is 'catachretic' because it produces a continuous effect of metaphorization, but on the other hand, because there is no possibility of saying things otherwise except by metaphor" (438–39). This has everything to do with current feminist attempts to describe women's writing.

7. Early in the elaboration of this material, which then included a discussion of the figures of Philomela and Penelope, I discovered Patricia Joplin's important work on Philomela and feminist poetics. My work on Arachne has been informed by hers, as the subsequent acknowledgments in this essay should make clear.

Book 6 of the *Metamorphoses* opens on Arachne's story and ends on Philomela's; the young women's stories frame the central moment of Niobe's text of maternal agony.

8. In "Ariadne's Thread" (150) Hillis Miller, by an associative logic that I will refer to later, connects Erigone to the story of Theseus and Ariadne via Dionysos.

9. In his commentary on the *Metamorphoses*, William Anderson suggests that Ovid seems generally (if ambivalently) to be attracted to Arachne's "kind of composition: freer, more mannered, more dramatic and distorted, less specifically didactic" (160). He specifically reads the "rhetorically ordered repetition [*verum taurum* . . . *freta vera*]" as both an "editorial note on the realism" of her representation of Europa's fate, and "an appeal to the audience for agreement" (165).

At the Bunting Institute (Spring 1984), I learned from Blair Tate, who is a weaver, that Ovid, who gets most of the other details of the mechanisms of weaving right, misrepresents the framing of the border which produces the effect of a "signing." Since a tapestry moves up on the loom from the bottom, the border would be integrated from the beginning. I've taken the risk of drawing the inference that Ovid here insists on the mark of the signature as the emblem of a writing identity.

10. Athena herself raises problems of identity and identification—whose side is she on?—that I have not tried to answer in this paper. Nor have I addressed the ways in which this is a story (clearly) that takes place between women: in a context generated by women tellers and spinners. We learn in book 4 that Athena is worshipped by spinners, the daughters of Minyas, who prefer to tell stories than worship Bacchus. For this they will be transformed into bats. More generally, in addition to the emblems of a masculine warlike

identity—the shield, helmet, etc.—Athena is also associated with the domestic signs of the distaff and the spindle. On the ambivalences attached to
these instruments for the female spinner who also wants to write, see Ann
Jones's discussion of Renaissance women poets in *The Poetics of Gender*. On
the relations between woven and written texts embedded *through* the figure
of Athena herself, see also François Rigolot's discussion of the role played by
the Arachne/Athena story in the work of Louise Labé.

11. This passage from Woolf provides the epigraph to Susan Sniader
Lanser's important book *The Narrative Act: Point of View in Prose Fiction*.
I'm grateful to her for her exceptionally helpful comments on the essay in its
earliest form.

12. James wrote several essays on Sand. Patricia Thompson's study, *George
Sand and the Victorians*, discusses the evolution of his complex attitude toward her work in some detail (216–44).

13. Although the long out-of-print 1962 text of *Indiana* in the Classiques
Garnier was reissued in 1983, the novel like most of Sand's fiction, despite
the enormous impact it had on her contemporaries, has only recently received
any serious critical attention. This neglect has begun to be repaired by the
general interest in women's writing produced by feminist scholarship, and by
a more specific interest in Sand herself stimulated in part by the centenary of
her death in 1976 and largely sustained by a small committed group of scholars in France. Nonetheless, because Sand's work, unlike Balzac's, does not
belong to the French canon of the nineteenth-century novel—which is essentially the realist tradition and its legacy—virtually no critical tradition of
Sandian readings exists. The "underread" therefore has important implications for the history of literary history. To what extent do we continue to
read, and teach, and write about the already read because it *has already been
written about?* Some recent contributions to a new point of departure for
readings of *Indiana* include Françoise van Rossum-Guyom's "Les Enjeux
d'*Indiana* I," in the collection of papers (1983) from the George Sand Colloquium at Cerisy held in 1981; and Naomi Schor's "Portrait of a Gentleman."

14. James writes perversely: "We believe Balzac, we believe Gustave
Flaubert, we believe Dickens and Thackeray and Miss Austen. Dickens is far
more incredible than George Sand, and yet he produces more illusion. In spite
of her plausibility, the author of 'Consuelo' always appears to be telling a
fairy-tale. We say in spite of her plausibility, but we might rather say that
her excessive plausibility is the reason of our want of faith" ("Notes on Novelists," 156). See also Arlette Béteille's "Où finit *Indiana?* Problématique d'un
dénouement," and my "Emphasis Added."

15. The abyss here is not infinitely (i.e., deconstructively) regressive. Mieke
Bal argues both that the *mise en abyme* always *interrupts* the linearity and
the chronology of the text, and that we should therefore see its "effect . . . as a general mode of reading" (*Lethal Love*). See also Bal's "Mise
en abyme et Iconicité." Nancy Goulder, a recent Columbia Ph.D. in English,
has done interesting work on the ways in which iconography in the novel
carries its own (often disruptive) narrative.

16. The literariness of the critique of the love plot is doubled in the novel
by Noun's letter to Raymon, a pleading love letter the reader is not given to
read, a letter Raymon never finishes reading: "It was a masterpiece of in-
genuous and graceful passion; it is doubtful if Virginia wrote Paul a more

charming one after she left her native land." But the power of the pastoral model (see also below) is without effect in Raymon's economy: "Poor girl! That was the last stroke. A letter from a lady's maid! Yet she had taken satin finished paper and perfumed wax from Madame Delmare's desk, and her style from her heart" (4:32–33). Style is not enough, without class. On the woman who allows woman to write, see also Jane Gallop, "Annie Leclerc, Writing a Love Letter."

In "George Sand and the Myth of Femininity" Leslie Rabine argues that "the use of Noun in the novel demonstrates how the prostitution of lower class women was necessary to preserve the chastity of bourgeoise women for the sake of bourgeois men, and their system of property inheritance" (14). But Sand's rewriting of Bernardin de Saint-Pierre's drowning of the pure Virginia is still more complex, I think, and participates in the irony of pastiche.

17. Ives's English translation, "copy," misses the painterly origins of the word, which appears in France for the first time at the end of the eighteenth century.

I want to thank Gina Kovarsky, a graduate student in Slavic at Columbia, for her analysis of the double figure, romantic and ironic, of the artist, and for her attention to the notion of pastiche (Seminar, French Women Writers and the Novel, Fall 1984). P. Salomon, editor of the Garnier edition, also connects the use of the term "pastiche" to Latouche's language (288, n. 1).

18. In a feminist poetics the two names begin the alphabet of female precursors. "Like Ariadne, Penelope, and Philomela, women have used their loom, thread and needles both to defend themselves and silently to speak of themselves" (*Madwoman*, 642). Curiously, Arachne is not named in this discussion of Dickinson's "spider artist." Hillis Miller also, though to different ends, connects these women weavers and wonders "how to stop the widening circle of contextual echoes" (58).

19. I'm adapting the phrase to my purposes from Mary Jacobus's analysis of the relations between women and theory, women and writing, in "Is There a Woman in This Text?"

20. I'm thinking of George Eliot's use of Ariadne (*Madwoman*, 526–28; and in those pages Eliot's use of the web). See also on Ariadne and Eliot, U. C. Knoeplflmacher's "Fusing Fact and Myth: The New Reality of Middlemarch." On Miller's version of the web and the "adventure of critical feminism," see Teresa de Lauretis in *Alice Doesn't* (2 and 187, n. 5).

21. See especially the "Introduction" to *Between Men* (1–20). Like the little boy in Freud's fable who practices mastery by casting a reel out of his crib and pulling it back, thus dominating his passive anxiety about maternal absence; like Theseus rising to the challenge of the monster, the masculist critic uses Ariadne to negotiate his encounter with the woman perhaps in himself, the monstrous self the male critic might meet at the heart of the maze of heterosexuality.

22. That is, Miller embraces a Freudian poetics. On the appeal of the labyrinth as abyss in critical discourse, see Frank Lentricchia's account of recent critical history, in particular the chapter, "History or the Abyss: Poststructuralism," which begins with Georges Poulet's metaphorics, and the latter's influential invocation of the "threshold of the labyrinth" (158).

Taking an altogether different perspective on the implications of Ariadne's fate, Carolyn Heilbrun, in "James Joyce and Virginia Woolf: Ariadne and the Labyrinth," argues for a positive or at least less relentlessly "feminine" reading of Ariadne's destiny as metaphor after the labyrinth: "Theseus betrayed Ariadne, leaving her open to the world of female myth and female possibility. It was that world into which Woolf would follow Ariadne." Jane Marcus in *Virginia Woolf: A Feminist Slant,* describes the new feminist criticism on Woolf as an "Ariadne's thread . . . a braided narrative with three separate strands of thought" that offers ways out of Woolf's fictional mazes (2).

23. By the title "Ovid's Sister" I refer of course to Woolf's tale of Shakespeare's sister. But I also want to invoke Ariadne's sister Phaedra, who offers a whole other network of associations for the French tradition of this myth. Lawrence Lipking has offered his provocative but finally problematic notion of a feminist poetics in "Aristole's Sister." In "Fictions of Sappho," Joan DeJean takes on Lipking's claims and rereads both Ovid and Racine's treatment of Phaedra. She questions the "recurrent critical desire to consign prominent literary women to abandonment" (787).

24. A typical example reads: "In Greek mythology, woman of Lydia who challenged Athena to a trial of skill in weaving. Angered at such presumption, the goddess destroyed Arachne's work, whereupon the woman hanged herself. Athena then turned her into a spider." *The New Columbia Encyclopedia,* 1975 (132). In *Le Dictionnaire des antiquités grecques et romaines,* Arachne's story appears only as a subset of Athena's (1915).

25. What is at stake in having a woman stand in for the law? To what extent could we read the destruction of Arachne's text by Athena as a Bloomian symptom: the poet's need to vanquish the precursor? Is it completely far-fetched to argue that Ovid stages here *through women* his own "anxiety of influence"? (For a feminist reading of the male paradigm, see Gilbert and Gubar, *Madwoman,* 46 ff.) On Athena as an alibi or pseudo woman, "the Law (giving) daughter," see Spivak, "The Double Displacement" (187); see also 174, 179.

26. It is the tendency to read allegorically, reading woman out—aren't these just stories of *human* overreaching, Apollo and Marsyas, etc.—that over-reading works self-consciously against: reading woman back in. My example here is the only visual representation of Arachne *as artist* I have encountered, Velazquez's *Fable of Arachne* (1644–68). I am grateful to Marcia Welles for bringing this painting to my attention. Although it was "long thought to be a realistic view of the Royal Tapestry Factory of Santa Isabel of Madrid," the work is now typically read as an "allegory of the arts." It is of no small interest to my case that in the Velazquez painting Arachne's tapestry is *re-figured,* in fact *replaced* by Titian's *Rape of Europa,* which then functions as a pictorial intertext. Arachne appears as an artist only to disappear, transformed back into a woman in the text.

On the complicated intertextual relations between the *Rape of Europa* and the fate of Arachne's tapestry in the Renaissance, see David Rosand's "'Ut Pictor Poeta': Meaning in Titian's *Poesie,*" especially 540–46. Rosand's analysis of Velazquez's reading of Titian demonstrates (though this is not of course its aim) the ways in which male artists pay tribute to each other through the figuration of a rape. In "Muiopotomos: or the Fate of the Butterflie," in which Spenser rewrites Ovid's account of Arachne's text, emphasis also falls on the representation (in detail) of the rape of Europa.

# [ 5 ]

# Changing the Subject: Authorship, Writing, and the Reader

*In the spring of 1985 I wrote "Changing the Subject" for two conferences that provided me with an occasion after "Arachnologies" to elaborate my thinking about the woman writer and her feminist reader in relation both to questions of feminist theory and to the various post-structuralist discussions of writing and sexual difference. The first of these events was held at the Pembroke Center, Brown University in March 1985; its agenda was flagged in the punctuation of its title, "Feminism/Theory/Politics"; the second, held at the Center for Twentieth-Century Studies of the University of Wisconsin-Milwaukee in April 1985, was entitled "Feminist Studies: Reconstituting Knowledge."*

*The session at which I spoke at the Pembroke conference was called "The Feminist Politics of Interpretation," and the panelists were asked to reflect upon a crux of issues very similar to the general charge of the Milwaukee conference as Teresa de Lauretis described it in her opening remarks (now the introduction to* Feminist Studies/Critical Studies). *Both call for an interrogation of the current state of feminist projects: "What is specifically feminist about the varieties of feminist critical practice? Are feminist strategies of reading written and visual texts transferable to the study of such things as social and political institutions?" (Pembroke conference, emphasis added). In de Lauretis's letter to participants: "there are a general uncertainty, and among feminists, serious differences as to what the specific concerns, values and methods of feminist critical work are, or ought to be. . . . Speakers will seek to identify the* specificity of feminism *as a critical theory" (Milwaukee conference, emphasis added).*

*These are not easy questions, and in this essay I have not attempted to describe the specificity of feminist theory and practice*

*directly. Instead I have chosen to rehearse a certain number of*
*positions against, from, and through which feminist critical theory*
*might define itself as it emerges within the discourse of literary*
*studies. This rehearsal identifies two chronologies, post-structur-*
*alist and feminist; two rhetorics, dilatory and hortatory; and, to*
*return to the figure of the "exquisite dance of textual priorities"*
*named by Hortense Spillers and evoked by de Lauretis at the open-*
*ing of the conference (13), two moves, or rather a hesitation be-*
*tween, say, the calls of a square dance and the ritual of a minuet,*
*as the dance searches for the right steps and rhythm, perhaps the*
*waltz satirized by Dorothy Parker, or as one of the participants*
*suggested after the conference, the fox trot (which has interesting*
*possibilities).[1]*

*Though I may indeed be looking for a third tropology (in the*
*feminist spirit of always mapping the territory of future perspec-*
*tives), I want just as strongly to leave the hesitation in place, and*
*refuse the temptation of a synthesis, because the question forming*
*before us is none other than the question of female subjectivity,*
*the formation of female critical subjects. And this, in face of the*
*current trend toward the massive deconstitution of subjectivity, is*
*finally the figure I'm looking for.*

## AUTHORSHIP, WRITING, AND THE READER

THE QUESTION of authorship has been on the agenda of intel-
lectuals and literary critics in France since at least 1968, a date that
also marks a certain theoretical repositioning in political and social chronologies. In 1968, for example, Roland Barthes contended
in "The Death of the Author" that the author, as we have known
him, has lost what was thought to be a "natural" authority over
his work. The author gives way to *writing*, a theory and practice
of textuality which, Barthes argued then, "substitutes language itself for the person who until then had been supposed to be its
owner" (143). From such a perspective, the emergence of this disembodied and ownerless *écriture* in fact requires the author's
suppression.[2] In the structuralist and post-structuralist debates about
subjectivity, authority, and the status of the text that continue to
occupy and preoccupy the critical marketplace, the story of the
Author's disappearance has remained standard currency.

Now, to the extent that the Author, in this discourse, stands as
a kind of shorthand for a whole series of beliefs about the function

of the work of art as (paternally authorized) monument in our culture, feminist criticism in its own negotiations with mainstream hegemonies might have found its positions joined by the language of those claims. It is, after all, the Author anthologized and institutionalized who by his (canonical) presence excludes the less-known works of women and minority writers and who by his authority justifies the exclusion. By the same token, feminist criticism's insistence on the importance of the reader—on positing the hypothesis of her existence—might have found affinities with a position that understands the Birth of the Reader as the necessary counterpoint to the Death of the Author. (Barthes actually puts it a good deal more apocalyptically: "the birth of the reader must be at the cost of the death of the Author" [148].)

The political potential of such an alliance, however, has yet to be realized. The removal of the Author has not so much made room for a revision of the concept of authorship as it has, through a variety of rhetorical moves, repressed and inhibited discussion of any writing identity in favor of the (new) monolith of anonymous textuality or, in Foucault's phrase, "transcendental anonymity" (120). If "writing," then, as Barthes describes it, "is that neutral, composite, oblique space where our subject slips away, the negative where all identity is lost, starting with the very identity of the body writing" (142), it matters not *who* writes. In the same way, the shift that moves the critical emphasis from author to reader, from the text's origin to its destination, far from producing a multiplicity of addressees, seems to have reduced the possibility of differentiating among readers altogether: "the reader," Barthes declares, "is without history, biography, psychology" (148). What matters who reads? The reader is a space and a process. The reader is only *"someone"* written *on.* (I also think that the failure of an effective critical alliance is more generally due to the fact that the relationship between mainstream feminism and the practices and positions that have come to be grouped together under the label of deconstruction or post-structuralism in U.S. academic scenes has not been one of a *working* complicity: of fighting the same institutional battles. But this deserves a discussion of its own.)

*I want nonetheless to make a distinction between the asymmetrical demands generated by different writing identities—male and female, or more perhaps more usefully, hegemonic and marginal. It is inarguable that the destabilization of the paternal—patriarchal, really—authority of authorship (Milton's for example) brought about through deconstruction has been an enabling move for feminist critics. But it does not address the problem of his "bogey" at the level of subjectivity formation. The effect of his identity and authority on a female writing identity remains another matter and calls for other critical strategies. The psychological stress of that negotiation in literature for the nineteenth-century woman writer has been formulated dramatically by Gilbert and Gubar in* Madwoman in the Attic. *Here I am trying to resituate that question at the level of theory itself, or rather theory's discourse about its own project.*

So why remember Barthes, if this model of reading and writing by definition excludes the question of an identity crucial to feminist critical theory? Well, for one thing because Barthes's interest in the semiotics of literary and cultural activity—its pleasures, dangers, zones, and codes of reference—intersects thematically with a feminist emphasis on the need to situate, socially and symbolically, the practices of reading and writing. Like the feminist critic, Barthes maneuvers in the spaces of the tricky relations that bridge the personal and the political, the personal and the critical, the interpersonal and the institutional (his seminar, for example). Barthes translates seductively from within French thought the more arduous writings of Derrida, Lacan, Kristeva, for or into literature; and in the same gesture represents metonymically outside the Parisian scene (or in North American literature departments) most of the concepts that animate feminist (and other) literary critics not hostile to Theory's stories: currently, the post-structuralist epistemologies of the subject and the text, the linguistic construction of sexual identity.

In the preface to *Sade, Fourier, Loyola* (1971) Barthes returns to the problem of authorship: "For if," he writes, "through a twisted dialectic, the Text, destroyer of all subjects, contains a subject to love—*un sujet à aimer*—that subject is dispersed, somewhat like the ashes we strew into the wind after death" (8). And he continues poignantly in the same sentence, "were I a writer, and dead [*si j'étais écrivain, et mort*] how I would love it if my life, through the pains of some friendly and detached biographer, were to reduce itself to a few details, a few preferences, a few inflections, let us say: to 'biographemes' " (9). What interests me here, more than yet another nomination, another code, is Barthes's acknowledgment of the persistence of the subject as the presence in the text of perhaps not some*one* to love in person, but the mark of the need to be loved, the persistence of a peculiarly human(ist?) desire for connection. It is as though thinking of a writer's life—a "life" of Sade, a "life" of Fourier appended to a reading of their writing—generated a thinking of self: for Barthes then imagines himself "a writer."[3] But we have just seen the writer is already dead, his ashes scattered to the winds; and the self fatally dispersed. Thus no sooner is the subject restored metaphorically to a body through love, than he is dispersed figuratively through death. If one is to find the subject, he will not be in one place, but modernly multiple and atopic.

Will *she*?

The postmodernist decision that the Author is Dead and the subject along with him does not, I will argue, necessarily hold for women, and prematurely forecloses the question of agency for them. Because women have not had the same historical relation of identity to origin, institution, production that men have had, they have not, I think, (collectively) felt burdened by *too much* Self, Ego, Cogito, etc. Because the female subject has juridically been excluded from the polis, hence decentered, "disoriginated," deinstitutionalized, etc., her relation to integrity and textuality, desire and authority, displays structurally important differences from that universal position.

*In* Breaking the Chain, *Naomi Schor takes up Barthes's analysis in* S/Z *of the cultural discourse on "femininity," which he locates for the sake of argument in a passage from Balzac's* Sarrasine. *Curiously, this is also the passage that serves as the opening citation of "The Death of the Author": "This was woman herself. . . ." (etc.) Following Schor's lead, it is interesting to puzzle the connections that for Barthes join* écriture *and "woman" in a definition of textuality that refuses a coherent subjectivity.*

*In "Mapping the Postmodern" Andreas Huyssen asks: "Isn't the 'death of the subject/author' position tied by mere reversal to the very ideology that invariably glorifies the artist as genius, whether for marketing purposes or out of conviction and habit? . . . [D]oesn't poststructuralism, where it simply denies the subject altogether, jettison the chance of challenging the ideology of the subject (as male, white, and middle-class) by developing alternative and different notions of subjectivity? (44).*

*In "Women Who Write Are Women," Elaine Showalter, arguing against Cynthia Ozick's belief (subsequently rearticulated by Gail Godwin in the same publication) that "writing transcends sexual identity, that it takes place outside of the social order,"* pointedly observes that in the gender asymmetry of dominant culture *"the female witness, sensitive or not, is still not accepted as first-person universal" (33)*.

It seems to me, therefore, that when the so-called crisis of the subject is staged, as it generally is, within a textual model, that performance must then be recomplicated by the historical, political, and figurative body of the woman writer. (That is, of course, if we accept as a working metaphor the location of women's subjectivity in female authorship.) Because the discourse of the universal historically has failed to include the testimony of its others, it seems imperative to question the new doxa of subjectivity at this juncture of its formation.

Feminist critics in the United States have on the whole resisted the fable of the author's demise on the grounds that stories of textuality which trade in universals—the Author or the Reader—in fact articulate marked and differentiated structures of what Gayatri Spivak has called masculine "regulative psychobiography." Feminist critics, I argue in "The Text's Heroine," have looked to the material of the female authorial project as the scene of perhaps a different staging of the drama of the writing subject. But what does it mean to read (for) the woman writer when the Author is Dead? Or, how can "reading as a woman"—a deconstructionist phrasing of a reconstructionist feminist project—help us rethink the act of reading as a politics? I'd like to see a more self-conscious and deliberate move away from what I think remains in dominant critical modes, a *metaphysics* of reading. As Foucault asks in "What Is an Author": "In granting a primordial status to writing (*écriture*), do we not, in effect, simply reinscribe in transcendental terms the theological affirmation of its sacred origin?" (120).

*In her presentations at both the Pembroke and the Milwaukee conferences, Spivak contrasted the psychobiography of a male subjectivity based on naturalized access to dominant forms of power with that of the "postmodern female subject" created under late capitalism (emblematized by the hegemony of the computer chip): women of color whom imperialism constructs as a permanent casual labor force doing high-tech work for the multinationals. Her relation to networks of power is best understood through the concept of "women in the integrated circuit," which Donna Haraway describes as "the situation of women in a world . . . intimately*

*restructured through the social relations of science and technol-*
*ogy" (84–85). It is not self-evident what form testimony would*
*take in such an economy.*

*Speaking from within a certain "new French feminism," Hélène*
*Cixous makes a homologous argument for the need to recognize*
*a deuniversalized subjectivity: "until now, far more extensively and*
*repressively than is ever suspected or admitted, writing has been*
*run by a libidinal and cultural—hence political, typically mascu-*
*line—economy" (879). This definition of a sexually "marked writ-*
*ing" that expresses and valorizes masculine access to power emerges*
*from the critique of phallogocentrism, but because of its place in*
*the network of Derridean operations, it remains at odds with the*
*reconstructive impulses of much feminist literary criticism in the*
*United States: the analysis of canon formation and reformation*
*through the study and valorization of women's writing.*

*Thus, in his concluding remarks to the section of* On Deconstruction *devoted to feminist criticism, Jonathan Culler builds on*
*Peggy Kamuf's troping of signature and identity in "Writing as a*
*Woman": "For a woman to read as a woman is not to repeat an*
*identity or an experience that is given but to play a role she con-*
*structs with reference to her identity as a woman, which is also a*
*construct, so that the series can continue: a woman reading as a*
*woman reading as a woman" (64). The question for feminist crit-*
*ical theory is how to imagine a relation between this logic of de-*
*ferral and the immediate complexities of what Adrienne Rich calls*
*"a politics of location" (*Blood, Bread, and Poetry, 215*).*

I want to offer one kind of political reading with a passage from
a famous account of a female "psychobiography." I take it as an
example of what has been characterized as the "first moment" or
first stage of feminist criticism, a criticism Jonathan Culler describes as "based on the presumption of continuity between the
reader's experience and a woman's experience" (46). The account
is Adrienne Rich's "When We Dead Awaken: Writing as Re-Vision," which, she explains in a retrospective frame, was originally
given as a talk on "The Woman Writer in the Twentieth Century"
in a forum sponsored by the Commission on the Status of Women
in the Profession at the MLA in 1971. I cite Rich's return to the
context of her talk by way of suggesting that we review these issues *both* in "women's time" and in men's, the Eastern Standard
Time of mainstream events. (I'm referring here to Elaine Showalter's personal take on the history of feminist criticism.)[4]

Rich notes:

A lot is being said today about the influence that the myths and images of women have on all of us who are products of culture. I think it has been a peculiar confusion to the girl or woman who tries to write because she is peculiarly susceptible to language. She goes to poetry or fiction looking for *her* way of being in the world, since she is looking eagerly for guides, maps, possibilities; and over and over . . . she comes up against something that negates everything she is about: she meets the image of Woman in books written by men. She finds a terror and a dream, she finds a beautiful pale face, she finds La Belle Dame Sans Merci, she finds Juliet or Tess or Salomé, but precisely what she does not find is that absorbed, drudging, puzzled, sometimes inspired creature, herself, who sits at a desk trying to put words together. (39)

Rich's woman "susceptible to language," like Roland Barthes, goes to literature as a *writing subject:* she does not, however, find there "un sujet à aimer." She finds instead, a terror and a dream. To find "somebody to love," as the song goes, Rich, like Barthes, would have to find someone somehow *like her* in her desire for a place in the discourse of art and identity from which to imagine and image a writing self—"absorbed, drudging, puzzled"—at a desk. For the girl "susceptible to language" the words have established a split she cannot overcome: Woman whose image, whose "beautiful pale face" has installed in her place a regime of the specular and excluded her from production.[5] Woman leaves the woman poet in exile.

In her 1983 essay, "Blood, Bread, and Poetry: The Location of the Poet" (where she outlines the borders of scenes of writing in North America and in Central America), Rich returns to the biography of her reading, or the history of its subject, to develop in more explicitly political terms the implications of the split between the girl and the poet, "the girl who wrote poems, who defined herself in writing poems, and the girl who was to define herself by her relationships with men" (40). To close "the gap between poet and woman," Rich argues here, the fragmentation within the writing subject requires the context of a "political community" (536). For Rich, on *this* side of identity, the condition of dispersal and fragmentation Barthes valorizes (and fetishizes) is not to be achieved, but overcome:

I write for the still-fragmented parts in me, trying to bring them together. Whoever can read and use any of this, I write for them as well. I write in full knowledge that the majority of the world's illiterates are women, that I live in a technologically advanced country where forty per cent of the people can barely read and twenty per cent are functionally illiterate. I believe that these facts are directly connected to the fragmentations I suffer in myself, that we are all in this together. (540)

In "Blood, Bread, and Poetry," Rich maps the geopolitics of a poetics of gender. This vision of a global context for women's writing emerges from a program of text production as a collective project. In the sixties, under the logic of "the personal is the political," the communication with the community involved writing "directly and overtly as a woman, out of a woman's experience," taking "women's existence seriously as theme and source for art" (535). In "When We Dead Awaken," Rich had contrasted this euphoric turn to feminocentric production—a more prosaic, or rather less lyrical account of the agenda valorized by Cixous (in "The Laugh of the Medusa")—with the anxieties of the fifties where, she writes, "I began to feel that my fragments and scraps had a common consciousness and a common theme, one which I would have been very unwilling to put on paper at an earlier time because I had been taught that poetry should be 'universal,' which meant, of course, nonfemale" (44). Now, in the eighties, the formula "the personal is the political" requires a redefinition of the personal to include most immediately an interrogation of ethnocentrism; a poetics of identity that engages with the "other woman."[6] If for Rich in 1971 the act of women's reading as a critique of the dominant literature was seen not merely as "a chapter in cultural history" (135) but as "an act of survival," in 1983 the act of women's writing becomes inseparable from an expanded definition of, and expanded attention to, the social field in which the practices of reading and writing are located and grounded. Now the question arises, if the ethics of feminist writing involve writing for the woman who doesn't read—to push this model to its limits—then what would be required of a responsive, responsible feminist reading?

The question will remain open and generate other questions. Does the specificity of feminist theory entail reading for the other woman? Would this mean reading *as* the other woman? In her place? Wouldn't this assumption reinstate a universal or an interchangeability of women under the name of woman and thereby "collapse," as Denise Riley put it to me at the Pembroke conference, "the different temporalities of 'women'" which she glosses as "the uneven histories of the different formations of different categories of 'women' from the side of politics"? In more strictly literary terms, I would now say that we must think carefully about the reading effects that derive from a <u>poetics of transparence—writing directly from one's own experience, especially when doubled by an ethics of wholeness—joining the fragments.</u>

*Rich speaks in this essay of her discovery of the work of contemporary Cuban women poets in a book edited by Margaret Randall called* Breaking the Silences. *And it is in part because of reading this book (her* tolle e lege*) that she decides to go to Nicaragua (a decision which provides the occasion for "Blood, Bread, and Poetry"). To what extent does this active/activist model of reading establish the grounds for a prescriptive esthetics—a "politically correct" program of representation—of the sort that shaped the arguments of Barbara Smith and Sondra O'Neale at the Milwaukee conference?*[7]

Against the necessarily utopian rhetoric of an unalienated art that Rich reads in Cuban women poets ("the affirmation of an organic relation between poetry and social transformation" [537]) I want now to juxtapose the discourse with which I began this discussion of critical strategies. On the back jacket to *Sade, Fourier, Loyola* Barthes states the "theoretical intention" of his project. It is a kind of self-referential challenge: to discover "how far one can go with a text speaking only of its writing [*écriture*]; how to suspend its signified in order to liberate its materialist deployment." "Isn't the social intervention achieved by a text," he asks rhetorically, located in the "transport" of its writing, rather than in the "message of its content"? In the pages of the preface, Barthes addresses the problem of the "social responsibility of the text," maintaining that since there is "today no language site outside bourgeois ideology," "the only possible rejoinder" to, say, the establishment, is "neither confrontation, nor destruction, but only theft: fragment the old text of culture, science, literature, and change its features according to formulae of disguise, as one disguises [*maquille*] stolen goods" (10). We see here the double move we saw earlier in "Death of the Author": on the one hand disperse the subject, on the other, fragment the text, and repackage it for another mode of circulation and reception.

<u>Dispersion and fragmentation, the theft of language and the subversion of the stereotype attract Barthes as critical styles of desire and deconstruction, rupture and protest.</u> Certain women writers

in France like Hélène Cixous, Luce Irigaray, and I would argue, paradoxically, Monique Wittig, have also been attracted to this model of relation: placing oneself at a deliberately oblique (or textual) angle to intervention. Troped as a subversion—a political intertextuality—this positionality remains in the end, I think, a form of negotiation within the dominant social text, and ultimately, a local operation.

Because it is also my sense that the reappropriation of culture from within its own arenas of dissemination is still a political urgency, I will recast my earlier question about the female subject in feminist theory to ask more narrowly now: what does it mean to read and write as a woman *within* the institutions that authorize and regulate most reading and writing in the university?

## "OUBLIEZ LES PROFESSEURS"

IN CHARLOTTE BRONTË'S *Villette* acute attention is paid to the construction of female subjectivity, and in particular to the way in which female desire as quest aligns itself uneasily with the question of mastery (including, importantly, mastery of the French language), mastery and knowledge within an academy necessarily, in 1853, a female one. In the scene I will review here, the heroine, Lucy Snowe, is dragged off to be examined by two professors, "Messieurs Boissec and Rochemorte" (the etymology is of course motivated). This examination perceived by Lucy as a "show-trial" set up to prove that she indeed was the author of a remarkable essay the men suspected their colleague M. Emmanuel, Lucy's professor/friend, of having written for her (forging her signature in order to document his pedagogical agency) provides us with a vivid account of the institutional power arrangements that historically have constructed female experience. These two specimens of deadwood interrogate Lucy:

> They began with classics. A dead blank. They went on to French history. I hardly knew Mérovée from Pharamond. They tried me in various 'ologies, and still only got a shake of the head, and an unchanging 'Je n'en sais rien.' (493)

Unwilling or unable to reply, Lucy asks permission to leave the room.

> They would not let me go: I must sit down and write before
> them. As I dipped my pen in the ink with a shaking hand, and
> surveyed the white paper with eyes half-blinded and over-
> flowing, one of my judges began mincingly to apologize for
> the pain he caused. (494)

They name their theme: "Human Justice."

> Human Justice! What was I to make of it? Blank, cold ab-
> straction, unsuggestive to me of one inspiring idea. . . . (495)

Lucy remains blocked until she remembers that the two examiners
were in fact known to her; "the very heroes" who had "half fright-
ened [her] to death" (495) on the night of her arrival in Villette.
And suddenly, thinking how little these men deserved their current
status as judges and enforcers of the law, Lucy falls, as she puts
it, "to work."

> 'Human Justice' rushed before me in novel guise, a red, ran-
> dom beldame with arms akimbo. I saw her in her house, the
> den of confusion: servants called to her for orders or help which
> she did not give; beggars stood at her door waiting and starv-
> ing unnoticed; a swarm of children, sick and quarrelsome,
> crawled round her feet and yelled in her ears appeals for no-
> tice, sympathy, cure, redress. The honest woman cared for none
> of these things. She had a warm seat of her own by the fire,
> she had her own solace in a short black pipe, and a bottle of
> Mrs Sweeny's soothing syrup; she smoked and she sipped and
> she enjoyed her paradise, and whenever a cry of the suffering
> souls about her pierced her ears too keenly—my jolly dame
> seized the poker or the hearth-brush. . . . (495–96)

Writing "as a woman," Lucy Snowe domesticates the public al-
legories of Human Justice. Her justice is not blind (hence serenely
fair), but deaf to the pathetic cries that invade her private space:
arbitrary and visibly self-interested, marked not by the sword and
scales of neoclassical iconography, Lucy's "red, random beldame,"
smokes her pipe and sips her syrup.

However perversely, I am tempted to take this scene in which
a woman is brought forcibly to writing as a parable of—which is
not to say a recommendation for—the conditions of production
for female authorship (or for the practice of feminist criticism).
Because she reappropriates the allegory of timeless indifference
particularized through the identification of the men and fiction-

alized through the imagined body of an aging woman, Lucy both overcomes the terror of the blank page and undermines the regime of a universal self-reference.

I should perhaps have mentioned that the chapter in which this writing out takes place opens with a line rich in implications for the conclusion of my argument: "Oubliez les professeurs." Now in context, this imperative is a warning issued by Mme Beck that Lucy not think of M. Paul for herself. But clearly in this collegial psychodrama the relation to *him* is not only a question of female rivalry and the love plot. As I have just suggested, the scene asks more generally the question of women's relation to the arbitrariness of male authority, to the grounds of their power and their laws.

Lucy, we know, can't forget her particular professor, for she is moved more than she will say by his offer of friendship. But in her apprenticeship to the world of work, she has learned to make distinctions. To accept M. Paul does not mean that she accepts the system of institutional authorization in which their relation is inscribed. Nor is the point of her essay, its style, lost on M. Paul who, having read the exam paper, calls her "une petite moqueuse et sans coeur" (496). Lucy's mockery, which is the flip side of her pathos, could also be figured as irony, which is, I think, a trope that by its status as the marker of a certain distance to the truth, suits the rhetorical strategies of the feminist critic.[8]

The chapter in which the scene of writing is staged is called "Fraternity," for it is here that M. Paul asks Lucy to be the "sister of a very poor, fettered, burdened, encumbered man." His offer of "true friendship" (501), of a "fraternal alliance" (503), while not exempt from its own ironies, nonetheless announces a less depressing mode of relations between women and institutional authorities than that of the "daughter's seduction" diagnosed by Jane Gallop, for it figures a working ground of parity.[9] At the end of Brontë's novel, through the enabling terms of the alliance, Lucy Snowe has not only her own seat by the fire but her own house and school for girls. Within that space, she makes Paul a "little library"; he whose mind, she had said earlier, was her library, through which she "entered bliss" (472). And of course, in his absence, and in his place, she writes the narrative of *Villette*.

This being said, one might, in the final analysis, do better to restore to the fraternal its historical dimensions. Women writers' idealization of fraternity belongs to a long and vexed tradition of feminist discourse about equality and difference that in 1949 provided Simone de Beauvoir with the last words of *The Second Sex:* "To gain the supreme victory, it is necessary . . . that by and through their natural differentiation men and women unequivocally affirm their brotherhood" [*fraternité*] (814).

## SUBJECT TO CHANGE

IN 1973, in an essay called "Toward a Woman-Centered University," Adrienne Rich described her vision of a future for feminist studies. In it we read: "The university I have been trying to imagine does not seem to me utopian, though the problems and contradictions to be faced in its actual transformations are of course real and severe" (153). Yet looking back over the past ten to fifteen years of Women's Studies, can we say that "masculine resistance to women's claims for full humanity" (as Rich defines the project) has been overcome in any serious way? Nothing could be less sure.

In fact, I think that though we may have our Women's Studies programs, our centers, journals, and conferences, feminist scholars have not succeeded in instituting the transformative claims we articulated in the heady days of the midseventies. Supported by the likes of William Bennett, Rochemorte and Boissec are going strong: they continue to resist, and to attack, feminism's fundamental understanding that the deployment of the universal is inherently, if paradoxically, partial and political. And the M. Pauls, who like Terry Eagleton et al. offer friendship and the promise of "fraternal alliance," seem to be saying at the same time: "feminism is theoretically thin, or separatist. Girls, shape up!" (Spivak, "The Politics of Interpretations," 277). More serious, perhaps, because it is supported by the prestige of philosophy, the ultimate purveyor of universals, is the general failure on the part of most male theorists, even those most interested in "feminine identity," to articulate sufficiently in the terms of their own enunciation what Rosi Braidotti calls "the radical consciousness of one's own complicity with the very power one is trying to deconstruct" (Ms.). Like the humanists, they have not begun to question the grounds on which they stand, their own relation to the "sexual differential" that inhabits "*every* voice" (Spivak, 277); their own difference from the universal, from the institution which houses them and from which they speak.

But we have of course participated in our own failure to challenge the " 'ologies" and their authorities in a significant way. Our

greatest strength in the seventies, I would argue, was our experience, through consciousness raising, of the possibility of a collective identity resistant to but intimately bound up with Woman—
in fact our account, analysis, and valorization of experience itself
(de Lauretis makes the point forcefully at the end of *Alice Doesn't*).
For reasons I cannot fully articulate here, but which have to do
on the one hand with the difficulty of constructing theoretically
the discourse of women's experience, a difficulty derived in part
from the feminist bugaboo about essentialism—which can only be
understood in relation to a massively theorized "antiessentialism"
(Russo, 228); and on the other, particularly for those of us working
in things French, with the prestige of a regime of accounts of post-
gendered subjectivities, we seem to have have gotten stuck between two varieties of self-censorship.

In the face of a prevailing institutional indifference to the question of women, conjoined with a prevailing critical ideology of the
subject which celebrates or longs for a mode beyond difference,
where and how to move? On what grounds can we remodel the
relations of female subjects to the social text? In the issue of *Tulsa
Studies* devoted to the current state of feminist criticism (republished in *Feminist Issues in Literary Scholarship*) there is at least
one pressing call to forget the professors, theorists masculine and
feminine, to "reject male formalist models for criticism" in the
belief, Jane Marcus writes, that "the practice of formalism pro-
fessionalizes the feminist critic and makes her safe for academe"
("Still Practice," 90). We must, I think, see this as too simple. Not
only because, as Nina Auerbach argues in the same issue, "whether
we like it or not, we live in one world, one country . . . one university department with men" (155), but because we don't. If
Women's Studies is to effect institutional change through critical
interventions, we cannot afford to proceed by a wholesale dis-
missal of "male" models. Rather, like Lucy in the school play (in
another forced performance), who refuses to play a man's part
dressed in men's clothes and instead assumes "*in addition*" to her
"woman's garb" the signifiers of masculinity (209; emphasis added),
the effectiveness of future feminist intervention calls for an ironic
manipulation of the semiotics of performance.[10]

Earlier in *Villette,* Ginevra pressed Lucy to explain herself, to
reveal some deeper truth that seems to elude her grasp: "Who *are*
you, Miss Snowe?" And Lucy, "amused at her mystification," replies, "Who am I indeed? Perhaps a personage in disguise. Pity I
don't look the character" (392–93). But Ginevra is not satisfied

with this flip account: "But *are* you anybody?" This time Lucy is
slightly more forthcoming, supplying information, at least, about
her social insertion: "Yes . . . I am a rising character: once an
old lady's companion, then a nursery-governess, now a school-
teacher" (394). Ginevra persists in thinking there is more to Lucy
than Lucy will say, but Lucy will offer nothing more. If we take
Lucy Snowe's account of herself at face value, not persisting like
Ginevra in a hermeneutics of revelation that is structured, Barthes
has taught us, on oedipal narratologies, we begin to take the measure of Brontë's radical achievement in this novel: creating a heroine whose identity is modulated through the cadences of work;
through the effects of institutions. This is not to suggest that Lucy's
subjectivity is recontained by a work history, circumscribed by its
hierarchies of class. On the contrary, we have seen Ginevra's conviction that despite the institutional inscription, Lucy somehow
continues to escape her, not only because Ginevra is looking for
a social language she can understand—"a name, a pedigree"—
but because in some palpable and troubling way, Lucy, like the
Lacanian subject she anticipates, also resides elsewhere in the "field
of language" which constitutes her otherness to herself (Mitchell,
241).

I want to float the suggestion, then, and by way of a gesture
toward closure, that any definition of the female writing subject
not universalized as Woman that we try to theorize now must include Lucy Snowe's ambiguities: in work, in language. This is a
process that recognizes what Elizabeth Weed describes as the "impossible . . . relation of women to Woman" (74) and acknowledges our ongoing contradictions, the gap and (and perhaps permanent) internal split that makes a collective identity always a
horizon, but a necessary one.[11] It is a fragmentation we can, however, as feminist readers work with and through. This is the move
of resistance and production that allows Lucy to find language "as
a woman" despite the power of the " 'ologies," despite the allegory of *human* justice.

*At the end of "Femininity, Narrative, and Psychoanalysis" (1982),
an essay in which she takes as her example Emily Brontë's* Wuth-
ering Heights, *Juliet Mitchell outlines a question by way of providing herself with a solution of closure to her discussion of the
female (writing) subject and a critique of Kristeva's valorization
of the semiotic, the heterogeneous space of the subject-in-process.
To her own question of what identity and text might mean construed along the lines of such a theoretical model—"in the process*

of becoming what?"—*Mitchell responds: "I do not think that we can live as human subjects without in some sense taking on a history; for us, it is mainly the history of being men or women under bourgeois capitalism. In deconstructing that history, we can only construct other histories. What are we in the process of becoming?" (294).*

*Mitchell shrewdly leaves the question open, but since this is my essay and not hers, I have felt it important to risk a reply. At the Pembroke conference, I ended by saying: I hope we are becoming women. Because such a reply proved too ironic to occupy the privileged place of the last word, I will now say: I hope we are becoming feminists. In both phrases, however, the hope I express for a female future is a desire for all that we don't know about what it might mean to be women beyond the always already provided identity of Women with which we can only struggle; the hope for a negotiation that would produce through feminism a new "social subject," as de Lauretis puts it in* Alice Doesn't *(186), and that I have figured here as the work of female critical subjects.*

## NOTES

WITH THE EXCEPTION of the introductory remarks, which I read in slightly different form at Milwaukee, the material that appears in italics was written after the events of the paper as discursive endnotes; not so much as side issues, as asides pointing to the limits of the essay's rhetorical space. Its place here in dialogic relation to the main body of the text is the result of an experiment brought about by the always imaginative critical judgment of the editor of the volume in which it first appeared, *Feminist Studies/Critical Studies*, Teresa de Lauretis. Once I saw it in print, I decided to reproduce it here in that form, with a few editorial changes of my own.

1. The foxtrot is defined in Webster's Third as "a ballroom dance in duple time that includes slow walking steps, quick running steps, and two steps." What appeals to me here is the change of pace, the doubleness of moves within the shape of the dance, and the collaborative requirement. The latter will reemerge at the end of this paper, but really runs through the argument: the deadendedness of the one-way street that bears the traffic (to mix a few metaphors) between feminist and dominant critics.

This figuration of the problem bears a certain resemblance to my discussion of shoes and tropes in "The Text's Heroine." My current position has been reformulated for me by Biddy Martin, who said at the Milwaukee conference that indeterminacy (what I am thematizing here as the denegation and denigration of identity) is no excuse for not acting; that we must find a way to ground indeterminacy so that we can make political interventions. The question before us then becomes how to locate and allow for particularities within the collective.

2. Barthes's essay should be situated within the discussion of changing definitions of art in conjunction with the laws governing authorship in France, in particular a 1957 law which attempted to account for new kinds of artistic and authorial production not covered by the copyright law (*droits d'auteur*) of 1793. I am indebted to Molly Nesbit's "What is an Author," for an illuminating explanation of this material. Nesbit points out that the death of the author for Barthes seems to have meant "really the imprinting author of 1793"; she also describes the original occasion for the essay: "in 1967 in America for *Aspen* magazine, nos. 5+6 . . . dedicated to Stéphane Mallarmé." It is boxed (literally) along with all kinds of "authorial work, much of it technologically based" (241–43). See also "Le Droit d'auteur s'adapte à la nouvelle économie de la création," in *Le Monde*, August 3, 1985. These are pieces of a more contextual history of criticism.

3. At the Cerisy colloquium of which he was the "prétexte," this phrase drew a certain amount of attention. In his comments on the meaning of the phrase Barthes situated his own relation to the historical context of writing *Sade/Fourier/Loyola*: "It was the heyday of modernity and the text; we talked about the death of the author (I talked about it myself). We didn't use the word writer [*écrivain*]: writers were slightly ridiculous people like Gide, Claudel, Valéry, Malraux" (413–13).

4. In "Women's Time, Women's Space: Writing the History of Feminist Criticism," Showalter adopts Julia Kristeva's "genealogy" of subjectivity; of a *space* of generation which is both "European *and* trans–European" (15). In writing the history of American feminist criticism, she wants "to emphasize its specificity by narrating its development in terms of the internal relationships, continuities, friendships, and institutions that shaped the thinking and writing of the last fifteen years" (30). As examples of asymmetrical events in these nonparallel chronologies, Showalter contrasts the 1966 conference on "the Structuralist Controversy and the Sciences of Man" (Johns Hopkins University) with "the first feminist literary session at the Chicago MLA in 1970" (32), neither of which I attended. In 1971 I was reading Roland Barthes, not Adrienne Rich. The discovery of Rich, for me a belated one, comes from being involved with a Women's Studies Program; this trajectory, I think, figures an inverse relation to the reading habits of much mainstream American feminist criticism, while remaining outside the classical reading patterns of women in French; which may or may not explain the feeling people have had that I am mixing things—Barthes and Rich—that somehow don't belong together. What is worrisome to me is the way in which conferences in literary studies continue to follow their separate paths: though women are invited to English Institute (for which Showalter wrote this essay), Georgetown, etc. and men to Pembroke and Milwaukee, there is no evidence yet that feminist critical theory has affected dominant organizations and theorizations.

5. The stories of readers and writers emerge in both Rich and Barthes from a gendered poetics of sexual difference and family romances. For Barthes, like Rich, the Author is male, and in his effects, patriarchal: "As an institution, the author is dead: . . . dispossesed, his [identity] no longer exerts the formidable paternity over his work that literary history, teaching, opinion had the responsibility of establishing . . . but in the text, in a certain way *I*

*desire the author*: I need his figure (which is neither his representation, nor his projection)" (45–46). In Barthes's model of desire the reader and the writer participate in a system of associations that poses the masculine experience as central and universal. This "I" who desires the author, and desires to be desired by him, who worries about the return of the father (having banished him), who takes his pleasure in a fragmented subjectivity, desires, worries, enjoys within an economy as (he of course says it himself) a son. The failure to differentiate (the question, for example, of the daughter's desire) becomes more than a matter of philosophy or style when allied with the authority—of the intellectual, writer, teacher—that supports the concept of indifference in the first place. On the politics of indifference, see Naomi Schor's "Dreaming Dissymmetry: Barthes, Foucault and Sexual Difference."

6. This move corresponds to Gayatri Spivak's insistence on "a simultaneous other focus: not merely who am I? but who is the other woman? How am I naming her? How does she name me?" "French Feminism in an International Frame," 179. On the "other woman," see also Jane Gallop's "Annie Leclerc Writing a Letter, with Vermeer."

7. Smith wrote in her 1977 essay, "Toward a Black Feminist Criticism," from which she read at the Milwaukee conference: "I finally want to express how much easier both my waking and sleeping hours would be if there were one book in existence that would tell me something specific about my life. One book based in Black feminist and Black lesbian experience, fiction or nonfiction. Just one work to reflect the reality that I and the Black women who I love are trying to create. When such a book exists then each of us will not only know better how to live, but how to dream" (184). For O'Neale's position, see her "Inhibiting Midwives, Usurping Creators: The Struggling Emergence of Black Women in American Fiction."

In the *New York Times Book Review*, June 2, 1985, Gloria Naylor, in a survey of writers' favorite opening passages, comments on the beginning of Toni Morrison's *The Bluest Eye*. Naylor writes: "While the novel handles a weighty subject—the demoralization of black female beauty in a racist society [also the subject of O'Neale's paper]—it *whispers* in the mode of minimalist poetry, thus resulting in the least common denominator for all classics: the ability to haunt. It alerts my students to the fact that fiction should be about storytelling, the 'why' of things is best left to the sociologists, the 'how' is more than enough for writers to tackle . . ." (52). It seems to me that we are in desperate need of a specifically text-based discussion between black and white feminist critics and writers on the relations between the why and the how, between reference and representation. Without it we run the risk of a devastating repolarization of the sort that at times during the Milwaukee conference resulted in bitter asides and accusations of racism.

8. At the Milwaukee conference Jane Gallop asked about the implicit risk one runs that irony can misfire. In *A Handlist of Rhetorical Terms* Richard Lanham describes this problem under the rubric of "rhetorical irony" (61). He points out that the "relationship of persuader and persuaded is almost always self-conscious to some degree," and goes on to make the claim that "every rhetorical posture except the most naive involves an ironical coloration, of some kind or another of the speaker's *Ethos*." To the extent that the ethos (character, disposition) of feminism historically has refused the doubleness of "saying one thing while it tries to do another" (the mark of clas-

sical femininity one might argue), it may be that an ironic feminist discourse finds itself at odds both with itself (its identity to itself), and with the expectations its audience has of its position. If this is true, then irony, in the final analysis, may be a figure of limited effectiveness. On the other hand, since nonironic, single, sincere, hortatory feminism is becoming ineffectual, it may be worth the risk of trying out this kind of duplicity on the road.

In "A Manifesto for Cyborgs," Donna Haraway, calling for a greater use of irony "within socialist feminism," argues: "Irony is about contradictions that do not resolve into larger wholes, even dialectically, about the tension of holding incompatible things together because both or all are necessary and true" (65).

9. The task of "dephallicizing the father," as Gallop puts it in *The Daughter's Seduction*, to succeed must break out of the limits of the family circle (xv).

10. If Lucy in the classroom writes her way out of humiliation and into agency, on stage the use of language becomes a question of voice. The difficulty, Lucy discovers, once she begins to speak, lies not in the audience but in her performance: "When my tongue got free, and my voice took its true pitch, and found its natural tone, I thought of nothing but the personage I represented" (210). In both instances, Lucy's performative subjectivity is structured through a text and in another language. I have a more sustained analysis of this phenomenon in the chapters on *Corinne* and *The Vagabond*.

11. In "A Man's Place," a talk she gave at the 1984 MLA sesion on "Men in Feminism," which has been published in the volume *Men in Feminism*, Elizabeth Weed brilliantly outlined many of the issues with which I struggle here.

# III

## *Feminist Signatures: Coming to Writing in France, 1747–1910*

*Paris Boulevard, 1910.* T. T. Swann. Color lithograph. Private collection, New York.

# [ 6 ]

## *The Knot, the Letter, and the Book:*
## *Graffigny's* Peruvian Letters

Faire des noeuds c'est ne rien
faire, et il faut tout autant
de soin pour amuser une femme qui
fait des noeuds que celle qui
tient les bras croisés.

Jean-Jacques Rousseau, *Les Confessions*

In fact, it wasn't me my brother told about going to Los Angeles; one of my sisters told me what he'd told her. His version
of the story may be better than mine because of its bareness,
not twisted into designs. The hearer can carry it tucked away
without it taking up much room. Long ago in China, knot-
makers tied string into buttons and frogs, and rope into bell
pulls. There was one knot so complicated that it blinded the
knot-maker. Finally an emperor outlawed this cruel knot, and
the nobles could not order it anymore. If I had lived in China,
I would have been an outlaw knot-maker.

Maxine Hong Kingston, *The Woman Warrior*

IN ONE of the most remarked upon scenes in the history of the
French novel, the heroine sits alone at night in her country estate
making knots. In the secluded forest pavilion she has had constructed for her personal use, the princess of Clèves daydreams
about the man whose cane she decorates with knots and bows,
and who, unbeknownst to her, watches her work. The man and
the woman, fixed in representation, framed by its laws, might be
said to figure the perfect erotic relation between the sexes in the
feminine fictions of seventeenth-century France: she gazes at his
portrait; he tries to capture her gaze; apart together, they fantasize
possession at a distance.[1] This elegant standoff is a moment of
tension the narrative must find a way to resolve; an "involvement"
[*le noeud de l'intrigue*]—to invoke the language of Aristotle's dis-

course on plot—a knot of desire that requires a *dénouement,* an untying of the knot.[2]

In the end, we know, the novel does not unite these lovers. When the princess is freed by her husband's death to marry the most desirable man at the court, she chooses instead to remain alone, spending part of the year in the convent, part of the year at home. We saw in "Emphasis Added" that this choice, which by failing to retie the knot through marriage has come to be known as "the refusal of love," continues to divide the critics of the novel who debate whether the ending represents the death of desire or its victory. I want, then, to bracket that question here but, leaving it in place, consider the ways in which a female subject may be constituted in the *displacement* of desire; a displacement that literally and metaphorically relocates the scene of its operations in a fashioning of closure outside the conventions of marriage. This movement may, I think, be read emblematically as a *coming to writing,* even though this is not the language of its articulation in Lafayette's novel; for by coming to writing I include the psychological and symbolic gestures that authorize a writing subject.[3]

Almost fifty years later, Françoise de Graffigny's *Lettres d'une Péruvienne* (1747) rewrites that passage from knot to denouement in a way that thematically and materially *grounds* the seventeenth-century account of a subjectivity constituted through the refusal of the love story and retreat from its places. By its insistence on the material processes of coming to writing, on the apprenticeship to the act of writing itself, the eighteenth-century text explicitly stages the move beyond female plot as a repositioning of feminine desire through authorship. But in neither case does the denouement undo the originary knot. Both strategies of closure bear the mark of the irreducible ambiguity of woman's desire, but more pointedly of her ambivalent relation to its expression in a social world: to the writing of fictions and to the authority of readers that interpret them and adjudicate their place in the library.

In "Emphasis Added" I showed that from the time of its publication readers of *The Princess of Clèves* have somehow not believed in or accepted the refusal that engenders the novel's ending. We will see a similar resistance on the part of readers and critics to the decision that shapes the ending of the *Peruvian Letters.* This resistance comes, I think, from the reading effect of what Rachel DuPlessis calls "writing beyond the ending": "Writing beyond the ending," she argues, "produces a narrative that denies or reconstructs seductive patterns of feeling that are culturally mandated,

internally policed, hegemonically poised" (5). Such narratives refuse what I have described as the alternatives of the "heroine's
text": the "choice" constructed for the female protagonist between
death and marriage. That formulation about the textual politics
of closure emerged from a reflection on male-authored fiction in
eighteenth-century France and England. It seems to me now, looking at the question in the context of a reflection on the tradition
of women's writing (the possibility of establishing that tradition),
that from the beginning of women's fiction in France, another kind
of plot has in fact been put in place by female authors; and at the
same time, that sometimes even the "old plot" rewritten by women
also supplies a critique of the available cultural solutions.[4] As I
argue in "Arachnologies," we may read these female fictions as
parables that reenact the fables of Arachne's tapestry: both as figures of the artist who protests woman's place in the dominant narrative and as metaphorical modelings of a feminist poetics.

## THE GAZE OF THE OTHER

> On peut être tranquille, je viens parler ici ni du drame de *Cénie,*
> ni même des *Lettres péruviennes,* de ces ouvrages plus ou moins
> agréables à leur moment, et aujourd'hui tout à fait passés.
>
> Sainte-Beuve, *Causeries du lundi*

LIKE MOST women's writing in France the *Peruvian Letters* enjoyed tremendous popularity when it was published, and in this
case even a certain posterity: thirty editions, including ten in English
and Italian, until 1777, and then continuous publication until 1835.
Nonetheless, despite its contemporary popular and critical recognition (it was one of the most widely read novels in the eighteenth century), like most women's fiction, the novel does not figure seriously in the standard accounts of the eighteenth-century
novel, nor even the more recent literary histories.[5] Unlike many
female-authored novels, however, the *Peruvian Letters* have had
a reprieve of sorts. In 1967 an Italian scholar, Gianni Nicoletti,
brought out a critical edition of the novel which had not been
republished since the early nineteenth century. And in 1983, Garnier-
Flammarion issued a paperback edition based on Nicoletti's work
in a collection of love-letter novels. This volume has made it possible for the first time to teach the novel as a matter of course.

Will this be the case? Despite the material availability of the text, without a rethinking of the criteria that consigned the novel to oblivion in the first part of the nineteenth century, without a critical reflection about the act of women's writing as a type of cultural intervention, it is not at all clear that the *Peruvian Letters* will emerge from the margins to be read alongside, for example, the Persian ones. I want to offer a brief digression to illustrate the problem. This is the story of a footnote, a real one and a metaphorical one.[6]

About six hundred pages into Burney's nine-hundred page novel, *Camilla,* the heroine receives the visit of the ebullient Mrs. Mittin. Mrs. Mittin eagerly tells Camilla the story of her getting to know Mrs. Berlinton; a story, we might say, about the status of women's writing in the canon.

> I happened to be in the book shop[1] when she came in, and asked for a book; the Peruvan Letters[2] she called it; and it was not at home, and she looked quite vexed, for she said she had looked the catalogue up and down, and saw nothing she'd a mind to; so I thought it would be a good opportunity to oblige her, and be a way to make a prodigious genteel acquaintance besides; so I took down the name, and I found out the lady that had got the book, and I made her a visit, and I told her it was particular wanted by a lady that had a reason; so she let me have it, and I took it to my pretty lady, who was so pleased, she did not know how to thank me. . . . (606)

Frances [Fanny] Burney's 1796 novel was republished by Oxford University Press in 1983 in an annotated edition established by Edward A. Bloom and Lillian D. Bloom. The editors' footnotes are abundant, informative and useful, authoritative in tone, and, on the face of it, scrupulously documented. Thus on this passage, for "book shop" they offer: "obviously a circulating library. In *The Southampton Guide* (6th ed., c. 1801, pp. 74–75) [the story takes place in Southampton] there is a description of such a library: 'T. Baker's Library, in the High street, contains a well chosen selection of nearly seven thousand volumes, forming a more general collection of useful and polite literature than is usually found in circulating libraries. The books are lent to read, at 15s. the year, 4s. 6d. the quarter, and 5s. for the season.'" As someone who rarely does this kind of research herself, I love having access to information provided with such detail. The precision of it—"4s. 6d. the quarter"—feeds the fantasy (which I occasionally entertain) that one might be able to reconstruct the true past of reading; the material history of letters.

Despite the seductions of its information, however, this is not the footnote I just referred to; merely its context. The note in question comes (next in sequence) to explain the title of the volume requested, the "Peruvan Letters." The editors write: "Mrs. Mittin meant either Charles de Secondat Montesquieu's *Persian Letters* (tr., 1722) or George Lyttleton's *Letters from a Persian in England to his Friend in Ispahan* (1735). In her ignorance she failed to distinguish between Persia and Peru" (949–50). The failure to distinguish between Persia and Peru, however, is neither securely nor uniquely a matter of Mrs. Mittin's ignorance. The editors themselves fail to distinguish between Montesquieu and Graffigny. Françoise d'Issembourg d'Happoncourt Graffigny's *Lettres d'une Péruvienne* were translated in England in 1771, 1774, and 1782.[7] Gestures like these, born less of prejudice, I imagine, than oversight and happenstance—after all, why Burney and *not* Graffigny?— have come nevertheless *collectively* to constitute the set of references that through its exclusions—the either/or's—form the canon.

The literal failure to read women's writing has other theoretical implications. Unlike the reading of the "classics" which almost always includes the frame of interpretations that have been elaborated over generations of critical activity, reading women's writing has had to compensate for the absent structure of critical commonplaces.[8] In this perspective the deconstructive injunction to *re*-read, i.e., to read "as if everything were . . . already read" (*S/Z*, 16) must be seen to depend and build on the library of canonical texts. The reconstructive project of reading women's writing, as I argue in "Arachnologies," necessarily involves different textual strategies, since its materials have been cut off from the kind of historical and metacritical life that characterizes the works of majority French literature, the volumes of the *déjà lu*. In the presence of the underread, the *sous lu*, one overreads.

At stake in overreading, I have shown, is first a reading (intratextually) for the signature of a gendered subject. By this I mean more narrowly an icon or emblem within the fiction itself that obliquely figures the symbolic and material process entailed in becoming a (woman) writer. But it must also involve what I will call here, reading outward (intertextually) toward the literature it engages through its own writing; or reading "in pairs": reading at the gendered intersections of literary production to suggest the lines of another history of the novel, a history more like the one that

actually took place: of male and female writers.[9] In the pages that
follow, I will trace out the thematics of writing and authorship
that structure the *Peruvian Letters* as an example of overreading
in this double sense.

Because the novel still is not generally known, I will provide the
briefest idea of its plot.

Zilia, the heroine, is an Inca princess. When abducted by Spanish
invaders from the Temple of the Sun, from which she was to emerge
married to Aza, prince of the Sun, and transported against her will
from sixteenth-century Peru to France, Zilia becomes the subject
of an eighteenth-century epistolary novel. She writes incessantly to
her fiancé, Aza (who is carried off to Spain) even though she cannot be sure she will ever be able to send or that he will receive
this record of her thoughts. Despite the violence of this radical
alienation, Zilia manages to describe her innermost feelings of passion and distress, analyze the contradictions of European behaviors, and comment in detail on native customs. Not merely a heroine, then, Zilia becomes a *philosophe*.

Déterville, an honorable Frenchman of noble birth, who super-
vises Zilia's transfer to civilization and oversees her progress in it,
becomes so devoted to her happiness that he tracks down and recovers both fiancé and her lost Inca treasures. The novel (which
is brief—about 100 pages) seems to build toward a happy end: the
reunion and marriage of the lovers cruelly separated by fate. But
the narrative a second time swerves violently away from the euphoric denouement, when a faithless Aza betrays Zilia's expectations of perfect union. Déterville, long enamored of the Inca princess, declares his love and devotion. But Zilia replies that her heart
will not "consent to wear new chains," and offers friendship in
love's place as she imagines for herself instead a life outside the
limits of the heroine's text and the plausibilities of heterosexual
plot. Against those familiar teleologies, but in dialogue with them,
she invents the figure of a woman alone installed in a house of her
own at a calculated distance from the city, and from the man whose
name motivates the deflection from it, Déterville *(détour-ville)*.

Even without benefit of a plot summary, the workings of the
already read would probably have conjured at least two textual
models for Graffigny's title in the minds of most readers of eighteenth-century novels: Montesquieu's *Persian Letters* (1721), and
Guilleragues's *Portuguese Letters* (1669).[10] Indeed, to the extent
that the *Peruvian Letters* appear at all in histories of the French
novel, they are typically situated in reference to these texts, to the

witty standard of the *philosophe*, to the passionate rhetoric of the
woman in love. The relation to the dominant predecessor is normally cast invidiously: Montesquieu did it better, at least, the
"philosophical part" (Coulet, 383). My concern will be to read the
novel not in those evaluative terms but nonetheless through the
concept of derivation, in order to consider what the derivation, or
the structure of belatedness, might be able to tell us about the posture of the woman writer in eighteenth-century France.[11]

Graffigny's apparent reinscription of the precursors' projects
signals a complex project of its own. To invoke the genre of the
*philosophe* may be read as a desire to be counted if not among
the philosophers—at least among the authors who count; a producer, then, not merely of novels—a genre abundantly associated
with women in the eighteenth century—but of knowledge, of cultural information. But if to rewrite the story of the dominant gaze
by changing the subject—making the classical object of human
science and letters their beholder—is a challenge to Enlightenment
assumptions about female identity and authorship, by the same
token, choosing to organize a love story around a female subject
who will abandon the model of writing put in place by the (male
in female drag) precursor's tropes, *ironizes* the story of the abandoned woman told in the *Portuguese Letters*. I see these two pieces
as intertwined authorial strategies. The aim of our reading is therefore also double: first, to replace the *Peruvian Letters* in literary
history as a feminist commentary from the margins on the central
age-of-reason preoccupation with custom, law, and the nature of
the human subject. And second, at the same time to understand
the novel's recasting of the "female" precursor's narrative as part
of a same anxiety about originality and derivation, identity and
posterity, about writing as a woman intellectual in a man's Enlightenment (this is how I read the novel's ending). Put another
way, as I have argued about *The Princess of Clèves*, the *Peruvian
Letters* is a novel structured by both an erotic and an ambitious
wish.

The *avertissement*, or prefatory note, that frames the novel begins with a brief allegory of reading: "If the truth strays from ver-
isimilitude and loses its credibility in reason's eyes, it is not a lost
cause. But if the truth goes against prejudice, it rarely gains ac-
ceptance before its tribunal" (249). The discourse on truth articulates two eighteenth-century lines: the Enlightenment's commit-
ment to cultural relativism and the novel's negotiation with reality.
It also codes the woman writer's particularly vulnerable relation

to the culture's central notions of plausibility. The difficulty of that relation (which at the very least may be read here as an authorial anxiety about the ending of the novel) continues to find expression in the next paragraph, which more specifically addresses the question of audience and reception:

> What hasn't the publisher of this work to fear in presenting the public with the letters of a young Peruvian woman, whose style and thoughts bear so little relation to the not very flattering idea [*médiocrement avantageuse*] that an unjust prejudice has given us of her nation? (249)

If we produce a shift from "publisher" to "woman writer" and "nation" to "sex," the question slightly recast provides an emblem of the female anxiety of going public in the age of Enlightenment:

> What hasn't a *woman writer* to fear in presenting the public with the letters of a young Peruvian woman, whose style and thoughts bear so little relation to the not very flattering idea that an unjust prejudice has given us of her *sex*?

The overlap in semantic territory shared by "sex" and "nation" (contiguity, if not interchangeability), is expressed in praise for the novel by a contemporary critic. Fréron writes, in 1749: "Madame de G*** has contributed to the glory of her sex & her nation" (80). But as the editor/publisher of the *Peruvian Letters,* Graffigny speaks only in the universalizing plural of degendered origins: *nous,* we, *on,* one/they. In the preface to this anonymously published work, Graffigny addresses not the matter of female subjectivity but the letters' relation to the authorial intertexts that might be seen to situate this collection of "original" material. In the familiar ironic style of eighteenth-century philosophical discourse, she regrets the power of prejudice that leads "us" (the French) to scorn other nations, notably the Indians, "except to the extent that their customs imitate ours, that their language resembles our idiom" (249). "We" might today as feminist critics interpret this statement as bearing on the Other of sexual difference, as a gloss on the status of women's writing in the dominant culture. "We recognize only what mirrors and mimes us" also says: the canon retains what it knows how to read only when it recognizes its own language.

The critique of self-reference is directly followed by the incorporation of probably the most famous line from Montesquieu's letters: "Comment peut-on être Persan?" How can one be Persian? What does it mean to be Persian, or rather, what does it mean to be French? This is the pithy sentence that gives both the measure of hegemonic discourse—the Same determines the truth of the Other—and the basic trope of Montesquieu's prose in the letters, irony. Graffigny leaves the citation without commentary (or quotation marks), but the source is given its due: the first of the annotations in the novel reads, "Lettres persanes" (249).

This notion of imitation in which they (Peruvians) constitute (and play) the other to our self-identity (French) also embodies Luce Irigaray's notion that women's relation to language is one of mimeticism. Imitation, but also within her model, subversiveness through reappropriation. The woman writer reenacts in narrative that relation to the dominant discourse: she plays with her cultural subordination in the symbolic order by replicating herself in the syntax of its familiar grammar, but always as a commentary on it. From within literature's commonplaces, she performs an operation of displacement. Like Lafayette, Graffigny pushes against the limits established by the maxims of the collective doxa. But if subversion from within here receives increased political resonance by the structure of colonial relations, Graffigny's choice of the *female* colonized "savage" as the central consciousness of her work is not without problems of its own. If the gaze of the female Other allows Graffigny to point to an important blindspot in the Enlightenment's project to reorganize knowledge—its failure to take the measure of female subjectivity—it also runs the risk of effacing "the other woman" by writing in her place.[12]

Graffigny then goes on to lament the fact that the history of the Incas, "these unfortunate peoples," is both already there to be read—"in everybody's hands," and yet unread. The ignorance prevails despite the fact that "one of our greatest poets," she writes, referring to Voltaire (whose text "Alzire" is also identified in a note), "has sketched Indian customs in a dramatic poem, which must have helped make them known" (249). The strategic function of these references to the literature of the "already read" seems to prepare the reflection that follows: "with so much light shed on the character of these peoples, one shouldn't have to fear seeing original letters taken for a fiction" (26). This "fear" of course belongs to the generic staging of the epistolary mode (according to which all published letters are authentic). But I want to suggest that this move may disguise another, perhaps more interesting one: the fear the "original letters" will seem a "fiction" is no less a coding of an ambitious wish for the work to be appreciated for its singularity (the last words of the preface refer to this "singular work") despite and because of its belatedness; coming after Montesquieu and Voltaire, but also writing with them at the intersections of philosophical reflection.[13]

The letters, we learn, "needless to say" were "translated by Zilia herself: one can easily guess that being composed in a language and traced in a manner that are equally unknown to us, the collection would never have reached us if the same hand hadn't written them in our language." The insistence upon the coincidence of author and translator is worth reflecting upon. Both the anonymously published *Persian Letters* and the Portuguese ones are explicitly announced as translations (yet another topos). From the *au lecteur* on the title page of the anonymously published *Portuguese Letters* we learn that not only Mariane but the person to whom the letters were sent and the person who translated them are unknown. This triply anonymous text, however, is to pass for original letters: unlike the Persian product, this is "an exact copy of the translation [*une copie correcte*]" the better to preserve the authenticity of the fiction of female passion.[14] For his part, Montesquieu explains that he merely copied the letters, which were written by the Persians who lived with him during their stay in Paris (some of the letters without their permission): "My function, therefore, has been merely that of a translator; all I have taken the trouble to do is adapt the work to our own habits" (39). The adaptation has taken the form of editing: he has "relieved the reader of oriental turns of phrase," and "preserved him from countless lofty expressions which would have bored him sublimely." But if, as we shall see, Graffigny reinscribes the aggressive, hence ironically undercut ethnocentrism, in her publishing position she does not take on the bravado of his stance. Montesquieu writes: "I'm not asking anyone's protection for this book. People will read it if it is good, and if it is bad I do not care whether they read it or not." Though Montesquieu plays with anonymity—he might publish other letters if the public likes these, but only if he can remain "unidentified"—"if my name were to become known I should keep silent from that moment on. I know a woman who walks quite gracefully," he writes, but, he adds, following out the logic of his posture, "she limps as soon as anyone looks at her" (39). Montesquieu writes from the position of the beholder.

What are we to make, then, in Graffigny's break with convention, of the unusual continuity of same to same? Does the work of "identity"—the same hand—erase the play of difference between the before and after of her story, between the Indian and the French? Without the self-authorized translation, the story would never have passed into the community of French readers. But the insistence on Zilia's agency in her own translation is not merely a matter of transmission. The translation becomes the text's metaphor for its own bilingualism. By this I mean that the embedded presence of the other, maternal language, at the level of both the sentence and the plot structure, points to a project of writing through difference. The account of the editorial intervention that like the translation preceded publication, I think must be interpreted in the same spirit. Some judicious cutting (Montesquieu's "adaptation") has taken place. Graffigny/Editor explains: "We [*on*] limited ourselves to suppressing a great number of figures no longer used [*hors d'usage*] in our style: we only left in what was necessary to demonstrate the necessity of cutting them out." Suppressed, then, is that which doesn't fit the dominant discourse, the figures not current in our collective style.

Fréron, reviewing the novel when it appeared, comments on this passage as it then stood:

> "We limited ourselves," they say, "to suppressing a great number of *Oriental terms and comparisons* that had escaped from Zilia." . . . If by *Oriental comparison* one means the figurative, on what grounds was one persuaded that Peruvian style and eloquence were in what we call oriental taste? It seems to me, therefore, that it would have been better to say that Zilia let escape not terms, but expressions, turns of phrase in conformity with the genius of her language, even though she knew French perfectly. (81)

But "Oriental" or Peruvian, what do these figures figure? What key to identity lies in the *turn of phrase*? I want to suggest that in the account of suppression—we eliminated just enough to let you know there was a complete original version—Graffigny reconstructs the question of woman's identity as a problem of figuration. Put another way, the Enlightenment allegory of *cultural difference* is no less a feminist fable of sexual identity *in language*. In "Sexual Linguistics," Gilbert and Gubar argue suggestively that Woolf's famous discussion of a "woman's sentence" may be read as a "*fantasy* about a utopian linguistic structure," a desire to "revise *not woman's language but woman's relation to language*" (523). In this sense, we might want to think about Zilia's access to and mastery of two languages—both the *materna lingua* of the "original" and the *patrius sermo* of its version for the library—as a fantasy of woman's empowerment (539) in eighteenth-century dress. How can one be "une péruvienne," a Peruvian woman, a French woman, a women, a woman writing? To write "as a woman" is to write at a remove from one's represented identity, but in dialogue with it, with that self as Other. In these framing gestures, then, Graffigny refuses, or at least declines to name, the writing model critics have generally provided for her—that of another foreign woman in translation, Mariane, the Portuguese nun, whose desperate discourse reembodies the letters of Ovid's abandoned women in the *Heroides,* and thus launches, it has been argued, the great vogue of the epistolary novel in eighteenth-century France. But unlike Montesquieu (and the great poet Voltaire), the impersonated female precursor is neither named nor alluded to in Graffigny's text.

Graffigny's silence on the fiction of the abandoned woman would seem to situate her book outside the expectations of female authorship. By casting herself instead in the role of the Editor of the dominant culture, Graffigny performs what we might call (after Gayatri Spivak) "a double displacement." On the one hand, by not acknowledging the emblematic heroine of epistolary desire, the quintessential woman-in-love-as-text (the woman her heroine nonetheless is in part), Graffigny takes her distance from a glamorized "feminine" suffering.[15] On the other, by situating woman in the observer's place, she implicitly interrogates the universalizing ground of the male precursor whose text inaugurates the anticonventional literature of the Enlightenment. Through her radical revision of the flow of power in the anthropological gesture— the politics of the gaze that structures subject/object relations— Graffigny's text both rereads critically the model of authority that organizes high Enlightenment prose, revealing the desires of its reasons, and stages a productive, performative subjectivity.

By imagining a female ethnographer in love, Graffigny tests the limits of gender, identity, and generic constraint. Combining what in the century tended to remain separate, the *roman sentimental* and the *roman philosophique* (Coulet, 382–83), and locating her subject of difference in writing and language—as opposed to the ceremonies of the seraglio—she provides a figure of what female Enlightenment might mean. Writing as a woman, Graffigny produces not so much minor fiction as a minority literature of protest, which of necessity demands to be read in majority context, against what we have learned to see as the monuments of the dominant culture. As Myra Jehlen has argued: "the work of a woman—

whose proposal to be a writer in itself reveals that female identity is not naturally what it has been assumed to be—may be used comparatively as an external ground for seeing the dominant literature whole" (585). Thus, we might also claim that when Zilia translates her own letters, she enacts and reproduces through her "double-voiced discourse" (to borrow Susan Lanser's important formulation in "[Why] Are There No Great Women Critics?" 86) the peculiar situation of the female critical subject: writing from the "wild zone," perhaps, but trained to negotiate the spaces of the dominant structures (Showalter, "Feminist Criticism in the Wilderness," 200 ff.), Zilia produces feminist writing.

## KNOTS

Each civilization insisted in its own way before it went away.

Gertrude Stein, *The Making of Americans*

IN THE 1752 edition of the novel, which has become the basis for modern editions, the narrative is doubly framed. A "Historical Introduction" follows the *avertissement,* and in a few impassioned pages Graffigny reviews the unfortunate destiny of the Inca peoples with an emphasis on the ultimate decimation of their culture by the Spanish. (She ends with a quotation from Montaigne—"On Vehicles"—attesting to the extreme violence of this devastation.) Graffigny's invocation of human suffering is followed by a summary of Inca customs at the end of which she observes: "Although the Peruvians were a people less enlightened than ours, and possessed fewer arts, they had sufficient to supply every want" (19) [*pour ne manquer d'aucune chose nécessaire* (255)]. This self-sufficiency in the face of what might seem to be a culture of lack is precisely the organization of another economy that will allow Zilia finally to refuse European closure (lack being located in the eye of the beholder).

The novel begins against this text of what takes itself for a self-conscious ethnography, but its story is placed under the sign of the sentimental with a heroine's apostrophe to her beloved fiancé: "Aza, mon cher Aza!" The palindrome of his identity imperfectly mirrors the heroine's name itself: anagrams of each other (both marked *as other* for the European reader by the "Z"),[16] their names embody the plenitude of self-identity (from A to Z and Z to A).

On the threshold of conjugal life, the bride has conceived a project of representation, a text of the couple:

> eager to perform what my fondness had inspired during the night, I ran to my *Quipos,* and availing myself of the silence that still reigned throughout the temple, hastened to knot them, in the hope, with their assistance, to immortalize the history of our love and felicity. As I advanced in my work, the undertaking appeared to me less difficult; till, by degrees, this immense clew of threads became under my fingers a faithful representation of our sentiments and our actions, as it was formerly the interpreter of our thoughts during long intervals of absence. (1:28/258)

A footnote explains *quipo:* "a great number of little strings of different colours, which the Indians used instead of writing [*au défaut de l'écriture*], to reckon the pay of the troops, and the number of people. Some authors assert that they likewise served to transmit to posterity the memorable actions of their *Incas*" (1:28/258). Quipus (or quipos as they alternatively are spelled) are knots, a system of knotting, to be more precise, used throughout the Inca empire. Quipus were used for all the record keeping requirements of the bureaucracy—which were elaborate—and have been characterized by anthropologists as the emblem of Inca culture (see Ascher and Ascher, 48 ff.).

Graffigny relied heavily, almost exclusively, on the work of the sixteenth-century historian, Garcilaso de la Vega, for her information about quipus and other features of Indian life. His history of the Incas was extremely popular in eighteenth-century France, and had been reprinted in 1744.

The Inca knots, as Garcilaso describes them, were primarily an accounting instrument for maintaining inventories of arms, stocks of foodstuff, regional demographics, etc. They were also used as a kind of aide-mémoire: knots were placed at different points in the strings as reminders of dates or other things one might want to remember (like tying a string around one's finger). Although official scribes—called *quipucamayus*—used quipus to record the shape of historical event, technically speaking they could not be used to write words. Fréron's criticism of Zilia's use of "figures" (which Graffigny seems to have heeded in the 1752 edition) points indirectly, I think, to what interested Graffigny in the Incas as Other:

the quipus as the mark of Inca specificity. Without that material detail she could have chosen any non-Western Other—since the referent of difference tends to disappear under the wash of Orientalism. The detail of the knot, I will argue, guarantees her signature as a feminist writer.

Garcilaso explains that the *quipucamayus* were "imperial accountants" whose task it appropriately was to *totalize:* "everything that could be counted, was counted in this way, even to . . . royal speeches" (159). The quipus thus *play* writing to speech, and not surprisingly, *as writing* they articulate what Derrida has described as a "genealogical anxiety" (*Of Grammatology,* 124). One could argue that the anxiety here works in two directions: reaching into the past, of course, but also looking into the future with an eye to preserving the *present as past.* Thus Garcilaso specifies that the transmission of historical information passes from *father to son:* as historians, "they never let their quipus out of their hands . . . so as not to forget the tradition behind all these accounts" (159). In these public acts of rememoration, the "authors" are male. So when Graffigny maintains that "some authors" claim that quipus could store information for posterity, we must be careful to understand what "memorable actions" are involved and who performed the recording. Garcilaso is attracted by the analogy that links knotting to writing, and tempted to elide the distance between the noting of "numbers, places and dates" in the recording of historical detail, and the writing of history as text: "the Incas used a form of messages," he observes of the quipus, "that *might almost be said to have been written*" (158; emphasis added). The temptation to blur the distinction despite his own statement that it "was only possible to record numbers in this manner, not words," is not lost on Graffigny.

What then of the knotting *woman*? A recent edition of Garcilaso's *Royal Commentaries* includes illustrations by the contemporary artist, Guamán Poma de Ayala. Of particular interest to us is his own commentary on a series of drawings, "The Ages of Woman": "the widows and old women wove coarse wool for the common people; they also served as chambermaids and cooks and kept the quipus for the household accounts" (165). In her work on Graffigny, Charlotte Hogsett also describes the quipus by virtue of their status as *textile* as "a typically female form in which to work." It is perhaps because of the *domestic limits* of female access to quipus that Graffigny does not address the issue of *woman as scribe,* the improbability of a female composition in knots destined to private writerly ends.[17] Instead she flaunts its impossibility by making it her master trope.

By not raising the issue of the two kinds of knotting and its two spheres—for history and for the household—Graffigny appears to elide this problem of female signature under the attention to cultural difference, leaving the unsaid of female subjectivity—despite the feminine inflection of identity in the book's title—to the work of the plot. Or so it would seem. It is perhaps precisely the question of sexual difference in the material structures of symbolic language that the preface with its attention to style and syntax figures. In the same way, Graffigny's choice of knots, which in eighteenth-century France, are, as my epigraph suggests, an emblem of feminine *handiwork as leisure* calls attention to the complex status of women's social and cultural work.

In Zilia's project of representation, as we have seen, the knots are to become a *public text:* a representation (in her words, *"une peinture fidèle"*) for others unknown to her to admire. In this desire to immortalize the story of love that ties her to Aza, however, Zilia must abandon temporarily the "epistolary" fiction she has been writing *with* him for a different form—the memoir novel— though the basic material of course remains the same. In this sense, we might argue that Graffigny stages here, obliquely to be sure, the question of the gender of genre and the gender of writing.[18]

Writing "like a woman," in an exchange of letters, Zilia dwells on the private and ephemeral realm of feeling "to the moment": writing "like a man" for a reading public, she accedes to the territory of the *memorable.* But the ambitious project to create a *text* for posterity is cut off when the movement that was to mark the climax of the erotic plot is also cut off by the violent invasion of the virginal female space. The doors to the temple are thrown open, and soldiers take Zilia prisoner. The knots (which, with Pamela-like reflexes, Zilia thinks to hide under her dress) again become the intermediary of a private communication. Zilia must stop memorializing their happiness as text in order to retrieve her own identity in the epistolary novel over which she has suddenly lost narrative control. Though fatal to the story she inhabits, this double swerve from genre is utterly generative of the story whose heroine she is to become. In the original model, she weaves the narratology of the couple. Indeed, the process of knotting and unknotting articulates the terms of the lovers' relationship: "the same knots that shall apprize you of my existence, by assuming a change of form under your hands, will likewise acquaint me with your lot" (2:31/260). Quipus literally embody the metaphor of their relation, the inseparability of self and other.

Torn from the web of union, Zilia will end by constructing a singular self. But this new fabulation necessarily passes through a demystification of the dream of symmetry figured in their names and that overdetermines their destiny in the old plot. Thus Zilia writes of the first knotting/unknotting exchange: "As I unravel [*en dénouant*] the secrets of your heart, mine is bathed in a sea of perfumes. You live! and the bonds [*chaînes*] that ought to have united us are not broken" (2:33–34/261). Is this identification— heart to heart—a delusion? Are they links in the same chain (Altman, 15)?

In a feminist rhetoric which inevitably conjures, perhaps self-consciously, the rebellious discourse of Roxane in the *Persian Letters*,[19] Zilia praises Aza for having crossed the barriers of custom to raise her to his level:

> Had you been like other men, I might have continued in that darkness which my sex is condemned to; but your soul, superior to vulgar prejudices; your soul, greatly disclaiming the distinctions of custom, prostrated its barriers, in order to exalt me to your own importance. You could not suffer a being like your own to be confined to *the humiliating advantage of merely giving life to your posterity*. It was your pleasure that our divine *Amautas* should adorn my mind with their sublime philosophy. Yet, oh light of my life! without the desire of pleasing you, could I have reconciled myself to quit my careless ignorance for the laborious pursuit of science [*étude*]? (2:34–35/261; emphasis added)

It is important, I think, to see the extent to which the representation of the classical (European) model of female destiny is undermined from inside the terms of its "primitive" arrangements. Thus, though overdetermined by union with the superior Other through an education in philosophy, Zilia's fate has nonetheless already been moved beyond the limits of (mere) patriarchal reproduction—*his* posterity—thereby displacing and challenging the confident regime of signs from within. In Graffigny's fable, Zilia will develop from a destiny of love, union, and domestication to symbolic "individuation" through a mastery of cultural semiotics.

The shape of the book articulates that passage through the apprenticeship of languages, to the poetics of her own production: *writing* for her own posterity.[20]

### THE WRITING CURE

> *Memoirs*
> When I began to fill the pages of this notebook, I wrote hurriedly, expecting to bare in haste what normally lies hidden under the courtesies and constraints which make human beings bearable to live with: I mean the unique conjunction of feeling and event which, I presumed, forms the matrix of our histories like the memory knots on an Incan *quipu*. Somehow I expected to peel off the mask of my everyday self, revealing half-forgotten mysteries and surprising meanings.
>
> Caroline Richardson, *Sweet Country*

IN THE first moments of her captivity, Zilia struggles to maintain her identity despite the loss of an interlocutor; her privileged *destinataire*.

> These knots, which strike my senses, seem to give more reality to my thoughts. A kind of resemblance, I imagine them to have with words, creates an illusion that beguiles my pain. I fancy myself speaking to you; telling you of my love, assuring you of my vows, and my fidelity. This sweet deception is the comfort of my life. If my work is interrupted by the fulness of my heart, I sigh at your absence. Thus wholly dedicated to my tenderness, there is not one of my moments, that belongs not to you. (4:54–55/270)

Like words, knots figure presence; they stand in for the power of the voice. The woman in love (mis)takes the illusion of presence for life itself. As it turns out, only when the contract of identity that abolishes the difference between self and other is broken will the heroine of the old plot perceive the possibility of living another life story. The affective logic that Simone de Beauvoir analyzed in her portrait of the *grande amoureuse* is the model of feminine desire incarnated in the Portuguese nun so admired in the first part of the eighteenth century (*The Second Sex*, 605 ff.). ("The Portuguese nun," she writes, "could only be abandoned" [*Le deuxième sexe*, 2:577].)[21] Of course, as I have suggested, it is also *against* this organization of female identity that Graffigny writes, with *and* against in the play of intertextualities. At stake in Graffigny's novel is the possibility of repositioning the figure of (masochistic) desire, who "fascinated by [her] own status as object, through the agency of others" seeks to abolish boundaries in a dream of "ecstatic union" (Beauvoir, *The Second Sex,* 611).

Though the movement from identification to singularity, the translation from knotting to writing, of which we read the results after the fact, in the end deconstructs the illusion of presence and voice and lays bare the loneliness of writing in absence, it is nonetheless an apprenticeship that must pass through the acquisition of language and the valorization of phonology. The first French words Zilia deciphers are "Déterville," the word for the "floating house" which is ship, and the land of their destination, which is France. Thus her first words articulate a primitive form of female plot: the story of a being brought to destination. In Zilia's characteristic trope, the passage from Peru to France takes place in a "floating house." It could be argued further, as Melinda Sansone has suggested, that this floating house, with its "perpetual balance" (3:45/266), is a metaphor as well for the hesitation between plots and strategies of closure that will be resolved only at the end of the novel, just as Zilia advances from periphrasis to proper names through an understanding of metaphor itself.[22]

Missing at this point from Zilia's first attempts at French is a verb. It is soon supplied by the man whose plan it is to relocate her within a European version of the marriage plot (the Indian version now suspended). Zilia learns literally by repetition. But the pedagogical stakes of this spoken French lesson, "*yes, I love you . . . I promise to be yours*" (9:74/278), will attain its final implications only when the pupil will explicate in writing to the master's mortification the difference between love and friendship, between the verbs to love and to like.

The movement of the novel itself seems to hesitate between fear of premature closure and the desire for the end, for revelation and proper closure. This hesitation, which prefigures the valorization of intransitive writing at the end of the novel, finds expression near the middle of the narrative when Zilia confronts a crisis in the material grounds of communication:

I have so few *Quipos* left, my dear Aza, that I am almost afraid to use them. When I fain would proceed to knot them, the dread of seeing them exhausted stops me, as if by sparing

I could multiply them. I am going to lose the pleasure of my soul, the support of my life. No resource will then be left me to relieve the weight of your absence: I shall sink under it. (16:109/295)

Writing is the central, lifegiving activity which maintains the proper balance between conserving and spending. Zilia derives pleasure from *taking in,* monitoring internal and external events; she finds sensual enjoyment in analyzing private reactions and identifying public quiddities: "I tasted an exquisite delight in preserving the remembrance of the most secret movements of my heart to offer you its homage. I wished to preserve the memory of the principal customs of this singular nation, to amuse your leisure in more happy days" (16:109/295). But in her economy, this pleasure is incomplete without its conversion into instrumentality: the point of remembering, of recording is to offer it to the beloved, absent other. Like the representation of the couple's actions and feelings undertaken in the temple, these knots are being tied for Aza to read in a happier time. Making knots compensates for absence: to lose the power to communicate is to lose a central definition of self. The importance of the quipus, then, would seem to be exclusively relational: Zilia "writes" to preserve history for the other. This, of course, is not the whole story. On the one hand, we might think of the account of the "principal customs of this singular nation" as a plan for a third book, a book like, say, the *Persian Letters;* a book for the others, for the public that is not Aza. On the other, I would like to suggest—but this will be the burden of the rest of my argument—that Zilia also, even primarily, writes for herself, to preserve the "exquisite delight" [*volupté délicate*] (16:109/295) *within* herself. But perhaps we should not separate the project of critique—subjecting the other to the gaze of judgment and knowledge—from a pleasure of the text located in the act of production. Taken together, they articulate a poetics of dissent that in turn offers at least a working description of feminist writing.

## THE WRITING LESSON

A LOCAL "savage" is hired to give Zilia lessons in writing: "a method in use here," Zilia explains to Aza, "of rendering a sort of existence to ideas." In this, indeed, writing is a lot like making knots, except that one uses other instruments: "This is done by drawing with a feather certain small figures, which are called *letters,* upon a white and thin substance, they term *paper.* These figures have names, which being put together represent the sounds of words." The learning process, Zilia insists, is difficult: "These names and sounds seem to differ so little from each other [*si peu distincts*], that if one day I succeed in learning them, I am sure it will cost me a great deal of trouble" [*beaucoup de peines*]. The apprenticeship is doubly arduous: "This poor savage takes incredible pains to instruct me, and I take much more to learn" (16:110/295).

Zilia's desire to penetrate the mysteries of the dominant culture—a desire legitimated and euphemized in the fiction by her need to reconnect with Aza—seems to explain the insistence on the regime of pain. In light of the pleasure associated with the quipus, however, this regime of pain is worth dwelling upon briefly. Thus Zilia claims she would give up the writing lessons completely if another means of enlightenment were available. But when she laments that since there is no other, and that her "only pleasure, therefore, consists in this new and singular study" (16:111/296), we want to linger a moment over the place pleasure takes in the new economy: "I would willingly be alone" [*vivre seule*], Zilia goes on to explain, "in order to pursue it without interruption" [*m'y livrer sans relâche*] (16:110/296). In the wish to live alone and give herself over to study we can also read a wish that cannot be named directly; a desire, I want to claim, for authorship, which will be put in place only by the undoing of the old plot of identity through love: "alas! my *Quipos* are just finished; I am come to the last thread; I am tying the last knots. Those very knots, which appeared to me a chain of communication between my heart and yours, are now only the melancholy objects of my regret" (16:117/299). Despite this nostalgia for originary knots, the chain letter attaching Zilia to systems of the past, the apprenticeship to writing on paper comes to console Zilia for the loss of material that seems to threaten her identity.

As her mastery increases, Zilia expresses the extravagant impulse to "inscribe" (*tracer*) her love for Aza "upon the hardest metal, upon the walls of my chamber, upon my garments, upon every thing that surrounds me, and to proclaim it in all languages" (18:120/300). The desire to go public is not only a figuration in sentimental codes of the overpowering feelings that today we call romantic. As I argued earlier for the authorial choice of the quipu as emblem of difference, the heroine's wish here is, I think, rather clearly the desire for authorship: to inscribe one's feelings *in all languages* is to move not only from the intimacy of the epistolary to the public judgment of audience, but beyond the naturalized writing of epistolary relations to the guilty pleasures of publishing and transmission, dissemination and translation.

Graffigny's graffiti are the signature of a minority writer with fantasies of majority status, and the anxiety that must attend such a wish expresses itself here in an emphasis on material difficulty: Zilia has trouble forming the letters themselves, she cannot always read her own handwriting, reconstruct her train of thought. In the same way, she thinks the problems of composition would vanish if the objects of representation were feelings, if all she had to paint were the "expressions of tenderness": if at stake was only the writing of letters. But this, clearly, is not the case: at stake is the authorship of a *book*.

The *Portuguese Letters* end with a question: "Am I obliged to give you an exact account of all my various movements?" The question remains unanswered, for poignantly, pointedly, the absent other is beyond any sort of reply. The rhetorical conventions of these famous letters inhabit Zilia's lover's discourse as well. Like the Portuguese nun, Zilia writes love letters from within an ideology of feminine writing that enjoins woman to tell all—without discrimination to a privileged interlocutor. But at the same time she writes with a feminist awareness that "woman's experience" does not of itself take narrative form. Zilia wants more. She wants to account for everything that has happened, everything she has done: "I would not have you ignorant of any of my actions. They have been of late, however, so uninteresting and so uniform, that it were impossible to distinguish one from another" (19:123/301). Like the names and sounds Zilia had trouble telling apart in the writing lessons, the condition of narratability lies precisely in the act of differentiation.

To be sure, the problem here is not simply a matter of being able to make distinctions. At work as well is the ideology of literary categories themselves. The story of feelings is also the literature George Eliot will call "silly novels by lady novelists." Zilia brackets this literature (or rather, implicitly restricts it to the original function of the quipus). The story of actions, on the other hand, the relation of events is a way to deal with information, knowledge, history. The difference between writing letters about the self and writing a book about the world has been enacted by the formations of the canon. Zilia would have been chagrined to learn that Graffigny's *Peruvian Letters* in the standard reference are grouped under the rubric, the novel of feeling [*le roman sentimental*] and published as a "love-letter novel," while Montesquieu's Persian ones count as philosophy. This distinction is in part traceable to the hierarchy of tropes and the vicissitudes of esthetic modes: Montesquieu, it is said, manipulates irony: Graffigny, pathos. But if it is true that Graffigny represents feelings in a style that in the chronologies of literary history (Coulet, 378) bridges the gap between Lafayette's (classical) *Princess of Clèves* and of Rousseau's (preromantic) *New Heloise,* in the *Peruvian Letters* she also *rewrites* pathos by revising its final figures.

## CODA (TO THE WRITING LESSON)

Le "pli" disparaît, il faudra en trouver d'autres, mais ce sera à la fois l'empire sans limite d'une cartepostalisation qui commence avec le trait même, avant ce qu'ils appellent l'écriture (avant même le courrier des *sticks-messages* et des *quippos*), *et* la décadence de la carte postale au "sens étroit," celle qui, depuis à peine plus d'un siècle mais comme un des derniers phénomènes, un signe d'accélération vers la fin, fait partie du système postal "classique," de la "*posta*," de la *station* dans l'acheminement du courrier, du "document" à transmettre, support et message.

Jacques Derrida, *La Carte postale*

WE CAN perhaps take a more interesting measure of Graffigny's revisions if we retain their indebtedness to dominant Enlightenment strategies. In this sense I want to juxtapose rapidly Graffigny's account of Zilia's "coming to writing" with Lévi-Strauss's "Writing Lesson," and more specifically, the writing lesson revisited (critically) by Derrida in *Grammatology*.[23] Lévi-Strauss, we recall, describes in *Tristes Tropiques* a scene in which the Nambikwara, who do not know how to write (or draw), learn what writing is, what it can do, from the anthropologist, by imitation: "Without understanding [the] meaning or [end] of writing, they make 'wavy lines' in their calabashes and they call the act of writing, 'drawing lines'" (in *Grammatology,* 123). Derrida writes:

It is quite evident that a literal translation of the words that mean "to write" in the languages of peoples with writing would also reduce that word to a rather poor gestural signification. It is as if one said that such a language has no word designating writing—and that therefore those who practice it do not know how to write—just because they use a word meaning "to scratch," "to engrave," "to scribble," "to scrape," "to incise," "to trace," "to imprint," etc. As if "to write" in its metaphoric kernel, meant something else. Is not ethnocentrism always betrayed by the haste with which it is satisfied by certain translations or certain domestic equivalents? (123)

I want to suggest that in Graffigny's account, which makes the "native" the anthropologist but maintains (ethnocentrically) the passage to writing in the classical (properly anthropological) order—from quipu to handwriting—we have nonetheless the possibility of seeing a powerful example of a feminist ethnography that consistently refuses the "domestic equivalents." Does Graffigny's internal miming of the writing process challenge Derrida's general critique of translation? Yes and no. Derrida writes, "If it is true as I in fact believe, that writing cannot be thought outside of the horizon of intersubjective violence, is there anything, even science, that radically escapes it?" (127). If in the instances we have seen, Graffigny, in "thinking" writing, thematically locates its production along that horizon of violence (Zilia is torn away from her originary text, physically debilitated when she cannot communicate by the writing "lessons," etc.), it is no less true that her fantasies of authorship attest to the desire for writing to be produced *outside* the "intersubjective violence" of its precincts; as though graffiti weren't always a form of social aggression.

### FIGURES OF SELF-AUTHORIZATION

ZILIA CONTINUES to justify her desire to master the language of her French captors in terms of her quest for information about how to find Aza, her need to place their story within the European landscape. This pretext is necessary given the conventions of the novel: how else to create a heroine—but not a "précieuse ridicule"—who would become superior to her lover and yet remain "guided by the light of [his] mind" (25:162) [*soumise à tes lumières* (319)]? It is again an issue of translation: Zilia will explain to Aza everything she learns in *their* language; keep nothing for herself. The account of Zilia's discovery of books, however, suggests that this desire to know is not simply a desire to locate Aza, to put an end to her anxiety about him, but a desire to find something else. "I am indebted for a part of this information," she explains, "to a kind of writing, which they call *books*" (20:131/305). In Zilia's taxonomy, the books are of two sorts: some teach of what men have done, others what they have thought. Zilia experiences a passion for books. But their importance for her is not entirely a matter of desire in language. Books as a source of pleasure and knowledge are also the scene—or screen—of authorship. "I cannot express to you, my dear Aza, the infinite pleasure I should take in reading them, if I understood them better, nor the extreme desire I feel to be acquainted with some of their divine authors" (20:131/305). If Zilia does not move to distinguish the divinities of male authorship from female, she does distinguish herself as a *female reading subject* from Déterville's sister Céline: "she has scarcely given it a thought that books were composed by men: she knows nothing of their names, nor even whether they are still living" (20:132/305). Unlike the unenlightened Céline, Zilia longs to meet the authors so that she might further learn from them; of this she despairs.

Zilia's own desires for authorship (her relation to the *book*) until the final turn of the plot, remain identified with the knot of her connection to Aza; for the act of writing itself is isomorphic with that relation, whether the writing is in knots or on paper. This representation of the writing self emerges from the constructions of classical feminine identity; the metaphysics of the writing woman requires the enabling fiction of the masculine other as interlocutor. Thus Zilia's definition of existence is articulated only within the terms of the couple; the founding doubt she seeks to erase through writing is that of not being known to Aza. How can she be sure she exists, if he doesn't know where she is, *that* she is: "you will never know where I am, whether I love you, whether I exist" (6:62/273). Necessarily, then, when the structure of destination seems to collapse, feminine writing solipsistically turns on itself: "my letter is finished and the characters are traced only for myself" (23:152/314). The consolation of writing to the other as a promised end to anxiety thus proves illusory. What the novel will work out is the transformation of this model from transitivity to intransitivity, from "writing *to*" to writing.[24] The terms of closure make it possible for the pleasure of solitude experienced in writing *to* the other to be transformed into the pleasure of writing as an act of self-reference—or rather, self to the world, neither authorized nor mediated by the fiction of the unique masculine other.

Until that point, however, the move toward denouement within the space of the novel follows the logic of a lovers' reunion that typically organizes the erotic plots of epistolary fiction. Zilia writes:

> Be it as it may, my heart is subject to your laws. Guided by the light of your mind, I will implicitly adopt everything that may render us inseparable. What have I to fear? Shortly reunited to my comfort, to my being, to my all, my every thought shall emanate from you. I will live only for your sake. (25:162/319)

One is struck by the neat way in which the rhetoric of passion as subordination to the other maps onto the language of enlightenment as liberation: literally, "submissive to your lights, I will blindly adopt." Love for the woman writer is thus also ironically wedded to the hierarchy of phallic arrangements. The novel's task will be to remap these symmetries.

## MISE EN ABYME

ONCE AZA has been found, a second, more classically epistolary period of expectation is inscribed (intercalated, really) within the fiction. As Zilia waits for her letters to reach Aza in Spain, and then for him to come to France, chests that the devoted Déterville has located arrive, bearing the "sacred remains" of the couple's Inca existence. Zilia's personal choice of objects is animated by the rules of affective metonymy: "All that comes from you, all that is nearly connected with your remembrance, I preserve in my own hands" (27:176/325). And in her room, she reconstructs in miniature [*en raccourci*] "[the image] of those magnificent gardens, where I have so often indulged in the idea of you" (27:177/326). Thus Zilia reconstructs metaphorically as a representation the scene of her old relation of love and worship. An authorial note explains that in Peru "the gardens of the Temple and those of the royal palaces, were filled with all sorts of imitations in gold and silver" (27:177/326). Thus it is that imitation in the *second degree* relocates Zilia in the liminal posture of her past: the golden chair, emblem of patrilineal descent, "placed on one side of [her] chamber in the form of a throne," represents Aza's greatness and rank; and Zilia prostrates herself before the *image* of the sun suspended above her head (26:176/325). This is the figuration of the heroine fixed in repetition. In order for Zilia to become the heroine (and translator) of the *Peruvian Letters,* this miniaturization itself has to be recontained. In letter 35 (out of 41 letters) Zilia's room of her own (in the convent where she briefly resides with Céline) will become a house of her own, and in that positioning of the "precious monuments of the past" Graffigny both grounds securely the final gestures of closure and installs the conditions for its "aftertext": "the perspective envisaged beyond the termination of writing" (Berg, 214).

THE CONDITIONS of Zilia's authorship, like her voyage to France, are not sought but thrust upon her: she is made the heroine of a scenario her French benefactors, Déterville and Céline, brother and sister, imagine, stage, and enact for her. On a country estate outside Paris, and in the mysterious absence of the mistress of the house, Zilia has been charged, they announce, to "do the honors of the house" (39:2:36/347). She willingly consents to the game, but the festivities, it seems, require legal authentification as well. Zilia must sign her consent to the role "in writing." Then without reading the document placed before her, and thinking she had entered a fairy tale, Zilia appends her signature to "a paper already written on" (35:2:36/347). After a day spent in various pastoral events—young virgins dressed in white, with flowers in their hair, sing Zilia's praises; peasants arrive bearing greetings, etc.—Céline explains that the house and the grounds belong not to a friend away on a visit, but to Zilia. The brother and sister had wanted to provide the displaced princess with "at all events, a dwelling that took [her] fancy, and for rendering [her] life, in future, comfortable and independent." Zilia thus learns that she had signed not a play document but "the authentic instrument, that makes [her] mistress of both" (35:2:40/349). This metaphorics of entitlement now so familiar from *A Room of One's Own,* like the coming to writing that begins with the quipus, seems to guarantee the authority of female signature within the novel. We must also see, however, the limits that structure the fantasy of entitlement.[25]

The woman writer's claim to a place in the world, and the parallel desire to have her writing assure her a life of independence, are cast in the wish-fulfillment patterns of fairytales and daydreams, just as the impulse to write is itself cast in the erotics of the love story. We will want also to think about the ways in which the signature, here bound to the possession of independence through property, is also bound up with the desire property houses: what

story is to be written from within this protected space, a space
that maintains sociality at a distance, and that figures the ideal
social relation as heterosexual friendship within a female-controlled space, but a space nonetheless designed by a complicity
with hierarchies of power? What *new* story can be written upon
"paper already written on"? (This is always the question of wom-
en's writing in its contradictory relation to the traditions of the
novel as representation.)[26]

Let us then consider in detail two crucial aspects to this unusual
act of female empowerment: its financing and its primary symbolic
valences. To an amazed Zilia, Déterville explains that he has taken
the throne from the original temple of the sun, and through a
"magical operation" converted the golden chair (which we saw
earlier in Zilia's room) into "a house, a garden, and domain"
(35:2:44/351). Inside the house Déterville has had the games and
ceremonies of the Inca city reproduced in painting on the walls of
a special room. This "new temple of the Sun" reintegrates within
the domain of the "enchanted palace" (36:2:47/352) the objects
of her past Zilia had arranged worshipfully in her convent room.
No longer the entire sphere of her existence, "the wonderful closet"
as miniature becomes a discrete secular space she can open and
close at will with a golden key, and that coexists under the same
roof with a library and cupboards filled (by Céline) with women's
things [*tout ce qui est à l'usage des femmes* (35:2:45/351)]; contiguities of masculine and feminine.

The fairytale princess imagines she will inhabit the "enchanted
palace" with the "being like [her] own" whose identity has shaped
her story from the beginning. But when the prince proves to be
unfaithful—not the matchless (br)other—he is abruptly removed
from her plot: Aza arrives in France only to return Zilia's letters,
and returns himself to Spain to marry another woman. Zilia suffers greatly, wishes to die, but survives the betrayal.[27] After this
brief flirtation with the destiny of the abandoned woman, her first
desire on recovery is to withdraw to the solitude the French brother
and sister have constructed for her (40:2:63/359). From within that
European space, regulated by servants under her authority, Zilia
turns to the supply of books in her library, reads to overcome her
unhappiness, and writes in the final letter of the novel her refusal
to belong to Déterville on his terms. She offers instead the fidelity
of friendship and a program of exchange: he will increase her
knowledge of arts and sciences, she will help him develop the virtues of the heart.

Despite the conventional division of labor these gender arrangements present—his brains vs. her heart—Zilia's proposal radically breaks with masculine traditions of female destiny as love or death. Occupied in the library and studying nature, Zilia proposes a nonrelational and intellectual ideal: "the pleasure of being" (41:2:69/362). This pleasure requires only the self-conscious thought of one's existence—"I am, I live, I exist" (41:2:70/362)—and not the dependent attachment to the lover as interlocutor whose validation alone gives meaning to those verbs. In this revised ontology, the verb "to love" critically falls out of the definitions of identity and existence. Thus, against Déterville's claims of love and devotion, Zilia asserts the counterclaims of independence and solitude: alone in her château, she may imagine the beginning of another kind of life, an anti-story, perhaps, but like the retreat of the princess of Clèves, it remains unfigured by plot, and historically unfinishable.

## A LIBRARY OF ONE'S OWN

ALTHOUGH Graffigny's imaging of closure as a solitary refuge from "turbulent passions" (2:70/362) is perfectly consistent with an ideal of retirement common to the fiction and the philosophical discourse of the period (particularly the memoir novels of the 1730's), to many readers this "female utopian fantasy" seemed unsatisfactory because it felt like "an unfinished story" (Showalter, "*Lettres*," 16). Thus, despite the enormous popularity of the novel, readers actively resisted the grounds of the denouement: sequels appeared, the most famous of which (1749) reprinted in many editions along with the original (as was the case with the *Portuguese Letters*), has the story end with the marriage between Aza and Zilia. This solution, which English Showalter has shown appealed to male readers, pleased women readers less: women would have preferred to see Zilia marry Déterville. Graffigny rejects both masculine and feminine preference for the couple; and the signed 1752 edition of the novel, with its addition of letters addressing the social relations between the sexes, confirms the logic of the original solution. Showalter suggests that the public's desire (as manifested in the sequels) for the more conventional closure—marriage, with either of the two men; or death, Zilia's—indicated that the novel was not judged by Enlightenment standards for *philosophical* texts— i.e., a frame of mind predisposed to the iconoclastic, the unconventional—but as "escape literature." Like *The Princess of Clèves*, Graffigny's novel was read as "women's fiction."[28]

Another way of looking at this problem—readers' desire for the happy ending—would be to examine the overtly feminist discourse of the novel; and in particular letter 34, one of three letters added to the signed edition of 1752, in which Zilia wonders, for instance, about the range of masculine power: "When you know that here authority is entirely on the side of the men, you will see my dear Aza, that they are accountable for all the disorders which happen in society" (2:30/345). And having determined that the injustice of the laws is of a piece with this authority, Zilia expresses her doubts about marriage à la française: "In short, my dear Aza, it seems that in France, the ties of marriage are reciprocal only at the moment of its celebration, and from that hour the women alone are bound to observe them" (34:2:31/345). This letter directly precedes the description of the "charming retreat" [*charmante solitude* (35:2:43/351)] offered to Zilia by Déterville and Céline, and thus functions as a prelude to Zilia's refusal to marry, to tie the knot. But it might also be argued that the attack on marriage comes *after* the fact, to underwrite explicitly the refusal of marriage that frustrated the readers of the first edition more comfortable with the predictability of the "heroine's text."

In the transfer that takes Zilia from the temple of pure contemplation to the library as the scene of translation, we can read Graffigny's attempt to locate female textuality outside patriarchal plausibilities. But like the contemporary audience, some modern readers see this move instead as a defeat for the heroine. Nicoletti, for example, ends his introduction to the critical edition of the novel with a description of Zilia at the novel's close: "a foreigner, a virgin, and unhappy" [*straniera, vergine e infelice* (44)]. Isabelle Landy-Houillon, one of the two Garnier-Flammarion editors, drawing on a different lexicon, draws similar conclusions: "the repose so vaunted by Zilia in 1747 bears a very strong resemblance, despite the Rousseauian enthusiasm [*élans*], to the Augustinian dreariness [*grisaille*] of Mme de Lafayette" (18). And in the introduction to the novel itself, the editors, reviewing the "ideological perspectives" opened by the novel, have this to say of the text's feminism: one can point to "the feminist indictment firmly launched by [Graffigny whom] her friends, always fond of nicknames, called "la Grosse," and who certainly was unhappy in many aspects of her life as a woman" (246). It is the dreariness of this kind of reasoning about female destiny (and feminism)—the *grisaille* of a (pleasantly plump) feminist's life outside plot—that overreading reads against.

For example, early in the novel, Zilia describes a dream to Aza I think we can interpret as a fantasy of the powers of powerlessness from which to understand the stakes of female authorship in Graffigny's novel. At death's door, Zilia writes:

> I fancied myself transported into the interior of your palace; I arrived here just as they were telling you the news of my death. My imagination painted in such lively colours what would indeed have happened, that the truth itself could not have made on me a more sensible impression. I saw you, my dear Aza, pale, disfigured, deprived of your senses, like a lily parched by the burning heat of noon. Is love therefore sometimes cruel? Yes, I triumphed [*jouissais de*] in your grief, I rejoiced to excite it by sorrowful adieus; I found a sweetness, perhaps a pleasure in spreading over your days the poison of regret; and yet that same love which made me so barbarous, harrowed my heart with the horror of your pain. (3:48–49/ 267–68)

In the dream, Zilia (like Pamela before her) excites herself by picturing herself dead to the beloved other. She thrills to imagine his perpetual suffering; this will be her legacy, as opposed to the production of his progeny. In the fiction Graffigny subsequently imagines for her heroine, the ecstasy of this fantasy is transmuted: the sexual valences of passive desire are converted to active textual operations. Alive in her leisure, Zilia calmly translates her quipus, resubmitting to her control the material emblem of her place in the knot. Beyond the constraints of female denouement, Zilia replaces her story within a system of exchange in which readers (not fathers) determine the rules of circulation. Although Zilia's book, we learned in the preface, bore the marks of an editor's hand— that *left in* some "grammar mistakes" and "stylistic lapses" [*négligences de style*] for local color—it is not, like the letters its heroine writes, subject to the reception of an absolute arbiter (as Zilia used to name Aza). Rather, this "singular work" has been freely communicated to Déterville, who, as the interpreter between private and public spaces, brings the text to the judgment of readers in the marketplace.

Françoise de Graffigny, we know, was abandoned by a man with whom she was passionately in love. She claims in a letter (to Panpan, her privileged interlocutor) that the letters published in the novel were merely "reminiscences" of her own letters to the lover (English Showalter, 18). In this sense, we could perhaps say that the original letters, like the quipus, were "translated" by Graffigny herself. By this I mean that when the woman in love goes public on her own terms (as Riccoboni will ten years later) the letters become a book, and by that transformation, the poetics of abandonment becomes a politics of reclamation.[29]

But if the staging of a coming to writing entails the rejection of classical female destinies—Dido on the pyre; the figure of Ariadne, abandoned, writing to Theseus, rewritten as the Portuguese nun; if it rewrites instead the more austere desires of the princess of Clèves; to the extent that at stake in female authorship is a negotiation with the real, this novel, unlike its more purely aristocratic precursor, situates the material conditions of authorship *within* the fantasy of empowerment itself.

Thus, despite the ironic restructuration of patriarchal space achieved in the "enchanted palace," that masterpiece of feminist *bricolage,* as readers we are not allowed to overvalue the disappearance of the paternal throne. Indeed, the signifier of paternal authority has merely been dispersed, not erased. The remainder of the conversion—the "ruins" or "debris" of the chair—has been cleverly transformed into pieces of gold for use in the French system of exchange: "This you must know is not the least necessary article," Déterville explains to Zilia (35:2:44/351). Like the figures of speech retained from the original version of Zilia's correspondence through the intervention of her own translation, the house with its perfect replications of the past—"the image of the Sun suspended from the middle of a ceiling" (35:2:43/351)—displays the ambiguity of the woman writer's always mediated relation to the patriarchal narrative, the absent but no less present model of the circulation of meaning and goods, books and money.

If Zilia writes originally from the zones of a radically female discourse—the virgins' space within the temple—the transmission of her writing depends finally upon her negotiations with a man of the world: as I have just suggested, it is only through the intermediary of Déterville, we learn in the preface to her text, that her correspondence has reached us. It is no less his manipulation of the rules of currency and circulation that enables Zilia to translate "in her leisure," and read the "prodigious number of books" in her library. For if Zilia writes in her leisure, we also see that the leisure has been purchased, that she writes from within an economy. As she had wondered earlier: "I have neither gold, nor lands, nor industry, and yet necessarily compose a part of the citizens of this place. Oh heaven! in what class ought I to be ranked?" (20:130/304). Puzzling over the status of "those wonderful men who compose books," Zilia wonders what "rank they held in the world . . . what honours or triumphs they were decreed for so many advantages they afford to society" (32:138–39/308). She is shocked to learn that despite their superiority these men are often "obliged to sell their thoughts, as people sell, to get a livelihood, the meanest productions of the earth" (32:139/308).[30]

On the title page of the 1747 edition of the novel, the words "A Peine" stand as a placename in the place of Paris. Critics have read the substitution biographically, seeing in Zilia's critique of life in France reflections of Graffigny's unhappy days in Paris (Bray and Landy-Houillon, 246). We might also imagine that to mark the place of a book's authorship under the sign of "Peine" is to signal the difficulty of that production, its trouble and cost; and its contingency—"A peine"; like the apprenticeship to writing: "This poor savage takes incredible pains to instruct me," she explained to Aza, "and I take much more to learn." Françoise de Graffigny had to pay men to correct the spelling and grammar of the *Peruvian Letters,* and put in proper punctuation. An agent, of course, was required to sell the manuscript she wanted to circulate as a book in Paris.

Graffigny wrote over two thousand letters to her friend Panpan. The *Peruvian Letters* was her only novel. In letters to her friend she describes her need as a writer for solitude, the freedom to be alone. Paradoxically, the literary success she finally achieved deprived her of the time she required to write, and by 1752 (the second edition of the novel), sociability overtook the literary career. As it turned out, then, the dream of knowing authors that stimulated Zilia when she discovered the existence of books proved to be incompatible in Graffigny's world with the demands of authorship as a working condition (Showalter, 21). Alone in the house designed for her authority, beyond the surveillance of the gaze, Zilia in fiction controls precisely that which escapes control in a woman's life.

## NOTES

1. On the recontainment of the princess's gaze by the masculine scopic power arrangements that structure this novel, see Michael Danahy's "Social,

Sexual, and Human Spaces in *La Princesse de Clèves*," especially his discussion of the construction of Coulommiers as an attempt to establish a scene under feminine control (218–19).

2. In "Autre étude de femme," Balzac connects the feminine, seduction, the laws of novelistic closure and the truth through the semantics of the knot: "Cette réponse était une de celles que les juges et les avoués nomment *dilatoires*. Rosalie me paraissait située dans cette histoire romanesque comme la case qui se trouve au milieu d'un damier; elle était au centre même de l'intérêt de la vérité; elle me semblait nouée dans le noeud. Ce ne fut plus une séduction ordinaire à tenter; il y avait dans cette fille le dernier chapitre d'un roman . . ." (106; emphasis added).

3. The phrase, "coming to writing," to describe a possible specificity of a woman's relation to language belongs to Hélène Cixous (in *La Venue à l'écriture*). Joan DeJean makes suggestive use of Cixous's concept in a recent essay, "Staël's *Corinne:* The Novel's Other Dilemma." Myra Jehlen analyzes the process (minus Cixous) in "Archimedes and the Paradox of Feminist Criticism" as, "the *anterior act* by which women writers create their creativity . . .; a conceptual and linguistic act: the construction of an enabling relationship with a language that of itself would deny [women] the ability to use it creatively. This act is part of their work . . . and organic to the literature that results" (583; emphasis added). This problematics of authorship as a movement toward writing (in more psychological terms) is of course also at the heart of Sandra Gilbert and Susan Gubar's *Madwoman in the Attic*.

4. Joan DeJean, Charlotte Hogsett, Susan Lanser, and Melinda Sansone have begun to document this tradition of critique in seventeenth and eighteenth-century women's writing.

5. For a case in point, see the volumes devoted to the eighteenth century published by Arthaud in 1984.

6. I am indebted to my friend and colleague Rachel Brownstein for this reference, which I might otherwise have missed.

7. I rely here on Nicoletti's history of publication. English Showalter tells me that Nicoletti has missed a few translations himself.

8. The situation has begun to change for a small number of texts where several feminist readings are currently available. *The Princess of Clèves* clearly is one, *Indiana* is becoming another; in English, the list of obvious candidates is much longer, *The Mill on the Floss, Villette, Frankenstein*, etc. In fact some would argue that a feminist canon of critical writing on these texts has already been installed. But I think my argument remains widely true, and especially in French studies.

9. Georges May's *Le Dilemme du roman au XVIIIᵉ siècle* (1963) shows this importantly. More recently, Myra Jehlen has called for a gendered literary history—"a radical comparativism"—and Naomi Schor has identified instances of "intersextuality" in nineteenth-century France. Using Elaine Showalter's paradigms in "Feminist Criticism in the Wilderness" (262 ff.), we could say that the novels of women writers, while written in part from the "wild zone" of female experience, also and necessarily pass through the *symbolic* economy of the dominant culture embodied in the structure of its language. Thus women's texts connect in a tradition to women's writing, *and* to a tradition of men's literary texts. One might even want to argue that this double intertextuality is the mark of women's writing, a specificity based

not on essence but on complex relations of language, power and space. (In her recent work on black women writers, "Black Women Writers: Speaking in Tongues," Mae Henderson doubles that intertextuality.)

10. I should note here that the English title of the translation I am using, (by R. L. Whitehead, Esq., Hatchard, Bookseller to Her Majesty, London, 1805) has two distinct drawbacks. The first is that it shifts the emphasis from a singular producing female subject—"d'une Péruvienne"—to a national product, or artifact; the second is that it supports a false symmetry between Graffigny's and Montesquieu's texts. There are some translations of the title that maintain the French construction, *Letters of a Peruvian Princess* (1818), and *Letters Written by a Peruvian Princess* (1748, 1771), but they in turn introduce an insistence absent from the French title.

The history of the titles of the *Portuguese Letters* is equally mixed. Current editions vary in the French: *Lettres portugaises* (the original title) published by Garnier-Flammarion, and *Lettres d'une religieuse portugaise*, Librairie Générale Française, 1979. The English translations also vary.

11. This line of thinking slightly modifies Gilbert and Gubar's revision of Bloom's theories about the relations of struggle that obtain between male poets (*Madwoman in the Attic*, 45 ff.). I think what we see here is a mixed structure: on the one hand, Graffigny looks to the female precursor in Lafayette for authorization to write "beyond the ending"; but on the other, she is attracted to a form of writing associated with men who belong to a tradition of moral comment—Montesquieu, Voltaire, Montaigne, etc. (See also Elaine Showalter on double parenting for women writers [265]). I don't yet know to what extent this double allegiance—not necessarily in a line of descent, however—is characteristic of other women writers in the eighteenth century, or in other periods; though George Sand comes immediately to mind—her sense of competitiveness with the male writers, Balzac and Hugo, who are her contemporaries (*Histoire de ma vie*, 2:4:15, 154 ff.). The study of this "horizontal" interaction between male and female writers is crucial to canon re-formation, but becomes possible only when the vertical continuities of women's writing have been put in place.

12. On dominant white (French) feminists' blindness to "the other woman," see Gayatri Spivak (1981) and Jane Gallop (1986).

13. Graffigny's sense of the importance of *The Persian Letters* may have been shaped by the invidious remarks as reported in her *Lettres de Cirey:* "I heard yesterday that the *Lettres persanes* were puerile: it's mediocre, a light-weight book . . . I don't know why yet, but I'll try to find out a little later" (quoted in Fernando Cipriani, 171). On Graffigny's anxiety of originality, see English Showalter, 17–18.

14. On the general trafficking in female passion in seventeenth-century France, see DeJean's "Lafayette's Ellipses."

15. As I argue in "The Text's Heroine," it is important to understand the power of this trope as a fantasy of a certain type of imagination. Jane Marcus calls Lawrence Lipking's reflection on a "poetics of abandonment," a "poetics of need," a "tragic essentialism [that] focuses on eternal victimization," and writes: "The suffering posture of the abandoned woman is appealing to the phallic feminist because the absent male is at the center of the woman writer's text . . ." (82). See also my "'I's' in Drag."

16. Starobinski writes of the "Z" in the eighteenth century: "'Z' is the

exotic letter of our alphabet" (*L'Invention de la liberté*, 23). And Fréron, at length: "The names Zilia and Aza remind me that over the years the 'Z's have become very fashionable in the names of heroes of novels or tragedies. One sees almost no names without 'Z.' Zaïre, Zaïde, Zelisca, Zulime, Alzire, Zamore, Zolinder, Zirphé, Zirphile, Zaïs, Zulmis, Zelmaïde, Alzaïde, Althazaïde. I could cite thousands of others. There are philosophers so stiff-necked that they make an argument against our customs based on this soft and effeminate pronunciation" (82). I'm especially struck by the contiguities of "A" and "Z." And then there is of course Barthes on "Z" in *S/Z*, especially, p. 113, as a letter of mutilation and sexual ambiguity.

17. Fréron takes up the matter of the knots' plausibility as a means of letter writing. "But the quipus were used only to help [*soulager*] the memory and not to write letters. The Peruvians did not possess the art of writing to those far away: they had couriers in relays from distance to distance, who often passed on orally [*de vive voix*] the orders of the rulers from one province to another; which proves that quipus were normally insufficient. . . . Zilia therefore could not have made the quipus the interpreters of her passion. But you would legitimately accuse me of injustice and bad temper if I picked out the *defects of implausibility in novels. We read [novels] with the same eyes that we see our Operas. To enjoy either one, one must necessarily admit certain presuppositions*" (84; emphasis added) (1749).

18. I owe the notion of generic modeling *within* Graffigny's novel here and later in the chapter to Charlotte Hogsett.

19. Although some critics see Montesquieu's narrative decision to end his fiction with Roxane's suicide as a feminist protest, a protest, precisely, over the question of female identity and the subjugation of women's desire, I'm less convinced that his thematics of freedom and independence problematize the question of female subjectivity itself, the central point of Graffigny's fiction. In Montesquieu's Enlightenment text, imprisonment becomes a metaphor for humanity, but for Graffigny woman is not substitute to herself.

20. The originating marriage plot, thus, is interrupted and displaced by a quest structure of female *Bildung* which culminates in the reappropriation of a place in the world. In DuPlessis's terms, a "quest plot may be any progressive, goal-oriented search with stages, obstacles, and 'battles,' which in general involves self-realization, mastery, and the expression of energy, where this may be at the service of a larger ideology (e.g., in *Pilgrim's Progress* or in *Parcival*)." She contrasts this structure to the "romance or marriage plot" in which "conjugal love [is] a telos" (200, n. 22). In Graffigny's novel the marriage plot is displaced by the quest for knowledge. In this sense, the belief that *knowledge as instrumentality* brings access to the truth, and syllogistically, happiness, a basic Enlightenment cliché, could be described as the "larger ideology." But as it turns out, in this feminization of the period's topoi— only "an acquaintance . . . with the language of this country will satisfy me of the truth, and put an end to my anxiety" (11:80/281)—truth and illumination will bring a kind of pain which with an end to anxiety will put an end to the desire for story altogether.

21. The sentence, mysteriously, does not appear in the English translation. I am grateful to Elizabeth Houlding for having brought this to my attention.

22. Sansone reads the boat that takes Zilia from Peru to France as a metaphor for literary innovation, the hesitation that marks the invention of new

strategies of representation, notably the construction of an autonomous female subject. On the general use of periphrasis in the novel, see the introduction to the Garnier-Flammarion edition (47).

23. Barbara Babcock sent me back to these pages in Lévi-Strauss. On the writing stakes in Derrida's reading of Lévi-Strauss, see Christie V. McDonald's "Writing," 22–24.

24. This transformation is what makes it possible for me to read Zilia's apprenticeship to writing as the portrait of the artist as young woman; as opposed, for example, to the dysphoric trajectory of Emma Bovary. See Naomi Schor's analysis of Emma, for whom, as is the case for the heroines of male-authored eighteenth-century novels, "coming to writing" is linked with renunciation and death (*Breaking the Chain*, 15–20).

25. One might want to think here about the historical status of woman's signature in France, Valentine's signing away—without taking time to read the paper put before her by her husband—all rights to her "patrimony," for example. For the seventeenth century, see DeJean's analysis of signature in its symbolic and material valences, in "Lafayette's Ellipses."

26. I am suggesting that the creation of privileged spaces for women—the princess's and Valentine's pavilions, Indiana's island, Corinne's Italy, the vagabond's landscapes—offers grounds that constitute *non-narrative solutions* to the requirements of the dominant plot.

27. In dialogue with Zilia's amorous discourse, Aza's infidelity can be read as authorial need to prevent the solution the novel's narratological desires naturalize. (Graffigny here probably rewrites Valville's "French" infidelity in *La Vie de Marianne*.)

28. The escape from the agitation and temptations of city life, the desire for the country retreat is an old mainstream desire and dream. Since Horace's *beatus vir*, it generally embodies an androcentric poetics—Des Grieux's library, the count's at the end of Duclos's *Les Confessions du Comte de ***.* Nonetheless, women writers, particularly seventeenth- and eighteenth-century memorialists, have often been attracted to the pastoral retreat as a form of protest: protest against the rules of circulation that make women victims of love and marriage plots; Graffigny's choice of the library sharpens the focus of her resistance: in the library Zilia does not merely read novels "like a woman." She becomes a subject of knowledge.

On problems of closure and women's writing in the eighteenth century, including Graffigny's novel, see Elizabeth MacArthur's insightful essay, "Devious Narratives." MacArthur argues that to some extent openendedness was built into the epistolary form itself.

29. I'm thinking especially of Riccoboni's *Fanni Butlerd*. Charlotte Hogsett has interestingly contrasted the two acts of publication and female publicity.

30. I give Fréron the last word: "The Peruvian finds it strange that Authors sell their thoughts; if she had been a little more frenchified, she would have scarcely admired those who give them for nothing" (99).

# Performances of the Gaze:
## Staël's Corinne, or Italy

What then of the look for the woman, of woman subjects in
seeing? The reply given by psychoanalysis is from the phallus.
If the woman looks, the spectacle provokes, castration is in
the air, the Medusa's head is not far off; thus, she must not
look, is absorbed on the side of the seen, seeing herself seeing
herself, Lacan's femininity.

Stephen Heath, "Difference"

### "WHAT IS CORINNE, FATHER?"

AT THE BEGINNING of the novel that is to bear her married name
as its title, Mademoiselle de Chartres, shortly after her arrival at
court, goes alone to a jeweler's: "she went to match some precious
stones [*assortir des pierreries*] at the house of an Italian who did
a world-wide traffic in such things. . . . While she was there the
Prince de Clèves arrived. . . . [He] gazed at her with admiration,
unable to believe that such a beauty and of the highest rank (as
he saw by her manner and her attendants) could exist without his
knowing who she was" (37/42). In her suggestive reading of this
passage, Peggy Kamuf argues that the question raised by their encounter is not, like the prince's, bound to the enigma of identity—
"Who is this woman?"—but rather to the mystery of a woman's
desire:

"What does this woman want that she does not already
have?" The precious stones that she brings with her, that part
of her inheritance that she carries out of the maternal home,
is brought to the stranger so that he might supply their mate,
the jewel missing from the set her mother gave her. The missing piece of the puzzle is not Mlle de Chartres's name, the

value of the stones already in her possession, but the name of another, in its hard brilliance, its perfect shape, and its inestimable worth.

Thus the motive for Mlle de Chartres's visit to the jeweler's repeats and *displaces* the motive for her mother's return to court, a return which is prompted by the desire to find a *match of equal value for the young woman*. (*Fictions of Feminine Desire*, 72–73; emphasis added)

Like the matter of identity, the question of the mother's match is quickly resolved: the prince marries the beautiful girl with whom he had fallen in love at first sight, and names her.[1] But the daughter's question is less simply settled. Beyond the mother's motive, what the daughter is looking for that would go with what she already has, what she might hope to find that she does not already have, remains for the novel and its readers to worry about and work through.

If we approach the plot as a logic of events, however, what *seems* to be an answer comes in the form of the man as missing piece: when the duke of Nemours, the most handsome man at court, "nature's masterpiece" (31/37), dances with the princess when they meet for the first time shortly after her marriage, "a murmur of applause ran around the ballroom" (52/54) as if to confirm collectively and publicly acknowledge the perfection of the match. In this sense, then, we might be tempted to say the match is that which though perfect *as* representation fails to work in narrative and thus does the work of narrative. But is this failure simply a case of bad timing, or does the prohibition of woman's desire always precede her in the literature of its representation? Put another way, in the daughter's displacement of the mother's matchmaking, we may also read another story: the need for something that would suit might articulate not just the marital symmetry of a perfect couple (*un couple bien assorti*) but another, less classical, less closural form of desire: a suitor perhaps, as distinct from a partner in marriage (*un parti*).[2]

On the face of things, in Germaine de Staël's enigmatically entitled *Corinne, or Italy*,[3] Lafayette's exquisitely crafted novel of a daughter's desire and a mother's match would seem to be radically refigured through what might properly be called an epic of female vocation:[4] the extravagant staging of a woman's performance (demonstration) of what she wants. Is this the case, or has the problem merely shifted territory from a matching prohibited by a previous marriage, and then inhibited by the maxims of maternal discourse, to a matching inhibited but not precluded by a prior engagement and the will of a dead father? Do the displacements from a scene of social identity to a scene of cross-cultural conflict produce a critical difference or do we remain, in the end, within the troubled economy of the missing piece, with the unfinished business of a woman writer's fantasy?

I want to ground this question by a return to the scene at the jeweler's with which we began and in which the trope of the "male gaze" (the lover's discourse as vision) comes to delimit the field of woman's quest. Astonished by Mademoiselle de Chartres's beauty, the prince can't help staring; he keeps looking at the woman as though this act could reveal an answer to the enigma of his desire: how could she exist without his *knowing* who she was? His admiration disturbs the object of his look: "he noticed that whereas most young people enjoy seeing the effects of their beauty upon others his glances [*ses regards*] embarrassed her" (38/42). Unlike other women, Mademoiselle de Chartres becomes impatient under the constraints of this scopic tribute, and her reaction, here as throughout the novel, is to withdraw from the arenas of surveillance. This scene thus both exposes the basic model of the look of sexual difference as articulated famously by John Berger in *Ways of Seeing*—the man surveys the woman who is constituted within that glance—and supplies a gesture of critique: a woman's resistance to being mapped within its precincts. In this interaction, the woman's awareness of that scrutiny becomes an integral part of feminine identity: of woman's sense of herself as sighted and sited in a dialectics of power. Reviewing Laura Mulvey's now classic positions on the subject from a similar position, film theorist E. Ann Kaplan argues in "Is the Gaze Male?": "To begin with, men do not simply look; their gaze carries with it the power of action and of possession which is lacking in the female gaze. Women receive and return a gaze, but cannot act upon it" (31).

Because the gaze is not simply an act of vision, but a site of crisscrossing meanings in which the effects of power relations are boldly (and baldly) deployed, it is not surprising that feminist theorists and writers should take it up as a central scene in their critique of patriarchal authority. Given Beauvoir's analysis in *The Second Sex* of subjectivity as a way of looking at the world, Irigaray's theoretical work on the politics of visibility in the formation of sexual identity, and the recent work in feminist film theory and art history on the look as a central piece in the production of ideologies of desire, it seems somehow inevitable that feminist readings of literary texts would also focus, as I do in this chapter, on the gaze in representation. But should this shift be articulated more carefully? Does the literal or material medium of the visual—film, for instance—entail a specificity distinct from a metaphorics of seeing in literature? It seems to me that in the larger project of theorizing the social, cultural, and political context in which the elaboration of women's subjectivity takes place, the collapse of differences I operate here between the categories of the visual and the literary would have to be taken on as a subject of theorization itself. But I want to run the risk of proceeding according to a certain Barthesian overconfidence in semiotics, for it also seems to me that in reading the culture for the signs in which woman is figured, the regimes of the visual and the literary relay each other in complicated ways; that love at first sight, for instance, is as much a figure in speech as a figure of speech, or an appeal to a text that would embody the visual surprise.

To what extent, then, I will be asking, does Staël's novel as a feminist text engaged with issues of subjectivity as process support or unsettle the claim that woman's place in culture is constructed by man's view of her, by a look that emanating from his position of self-identity seeks to circumscribe hers? Can the gaze of a woman writer "speak" the body differently in images that don't "fix her in the frame" (Doane, 34)?

In *Corinne* where as a performer the object of the gaze takes pleasure in being admired and is at the same time in her own right the producing *subject* of a gaze, one would expect the lines of sight to complicate the structuring effects of the dominant gaze. In the same way, since Corinne's identity as a woman takes place, so to speak, in scenes foreign to its privileged witness, Oswald (and presumably to its French readers), paradigms of sight in the novel are articulated with codes of cultural reference that, already intertwined, map on to the constructions of sexual difference. The text both dramatizes the power of the gaze to delimit the proper sphere of femininity and offers a powerful resistance to it. Put another way, Staël's novel engages the possibility of an authoritative vision within femininity that refuses the legitimacy of a permanent patriarchal construction. The novel, in this sense, is a book about the fathers as an authorizing, all powerful location and body of intention; about the name of the father, about the fatherland, about the organization of separate spheres in which the letter of the father's law compels the son's desire, and the daughter's seeks to inhabit another, perhaps maternal space. With all this in mind, I want now to track the power of the gaze *elicited by performance,* produced by its effects, and perhaps reopen the question of its sex, or at least of its gender.[5]

## LOVE AT FIRST SIGHT?

IF, then, in Lafayette's novel both the prince and the duke first lay eyes on the princess within a world in which all the parties know each other—or will—and where the behaviors of desire are strictly regulated according to the rules of a self-perpetuating social discourse, Lord Nelvil's first sight of Corinne occurs in a context organized by an economy of radical otherness. Although in the seventeenth-century fiction both the prince and the duke register amazement at their first glimpse of the blond beauty who appears unexpectedly in their midst, when in Staël's novel Oswald awakens, his first day in Rome, to the sound of church bells and cannons announcing the crowning at the Capitol of "the most celebrated woman in Italy . . . Corinne, poet, writer, *improvisatrice,* and one of the most beautiful women in Rome," he must negotiate a surprise of a rather different order (2:1:19/49). It does not necessarily follow, moreover, that such hyperbolic distinction in a woman would predispose him to fall in love at all. On the contrary, the narrator underlines the fact that "focusing the public eye on a woman's fortune" [*cette grande publicité*] ran counter to "an Englishman's customs and opinions" (2:1:19/49) and explains that "the combination of mystery and public notice" would be harshly judged by Oswald in England as a violation of social protocols through which femininity becomes a public riddle, a circulating text to be glossed: "Her last name was not known; her first work had come out five years earlier signed only *Corinne.* No one knew where she had lived before or what kind of person she had been" (2:1:20/50). But the Englishman is in Italy. Out of place, observer of a scene to which by definition he does not belong, Oswald suspends the conventional rules that regulate social life in England and becomes a fascinated spectator who anticipates the coronation as though it were a work of poetic imagination (2:1:20/50). He is indeed dazzled by the performance and when he meets Corinne privately, enchanted by her, but is this a match? What do they see in each other?

The work of the gaze as a gendered and (gendering) asymmetrical operation of looks from the beginning structures the relations of power and desire between Corinne and Oswald. Oswald sees Corinne for the first time before she begins to speak, while she is still an object of discourse and admiration, and in that moment it is *her look* that inaugurates their exchange: "her expression, her eyes, her smile, spoke in her favor, and one look [*le premier regard*] made Lord Nelvil her friend even before any stronger feeling brought him into subjection" (2:1:21/50). Despite the power of Corinne's self construction as a visible public object—a woman pleased to be admired; despite the extraordinary context of Oswald's first sight; Corinne, in white, dressed like Domenichino's Sibyl, seated in an antique chariot drawn by four white horses—and the "electrifying" effect of this sight on his imagination (2:1:22/52), when Oswald then watches Corinne at the crowning itself, on the stage of the Capitol, he sees only the woman in the performance. Corinne's performing gaze offers the spectacle of genius located in a woman's body, but as spectator Oswald insists on separating the genius from the woman: "in the very midst of all the splendor and all her success, Corinne's eyes [*par ses regards*] pleaded for the protection of a friend, a protection no woman can ever do without, however superior she may be. And he felt that it would be gratifying to be the sustaining strength of a person whose sensibility alone made sustenance necessary" (2:2:22/54). This flagrant gesture of interpretation as self-reference by which the man reads the woman's unexpressed needs in her eyes because she is a woman instantly privatizes the public meanings of a woman's gaze, and installs the couple firmly within the regime of what Monique Wittig in "The Straight Mind" calls "the heterosexual contract" (110).

Oswald's resistance to stepping outside his own categories leaves him fixed in his identity as the judge of woman. This inability to see except *as a man* is, I think, the central piece in Staël's critique of patriarchy, a critique, I should emphasize, attentive to the damage done to its sons as well as its daughters.[6] I will make the further claim that the narrator's insistence on the limits of Oswald's vision of Corinne as a performer is part of what makes the book feminist, or rather makes the question of representation for a feminist reader inseparable from a politics of the gaze. If Oswald watches Corinne like a man, through a legacy of patriarchal looks, the reader, authorized by the narrator's feminist writing, reframes his gaze, rereading as a woman.[7] We might wonder who owns the gaze here?[8]

In every way, the three brief chapters of book 2, "Corinne at the Capitol," provide an emblematic figuration of the complex lines of force that structure Staël's novel. Through this *mise en abyme* the crowning will become both the catalytic moment in the narrative of Corinne and Oswald's erotic relation, and the central event of Corinne's trajectory as an artist: the moment of glory fantasmatically rewarded. It seems worth underscoring the fact that this crucial point of reference is intimately bound up with the valences of the gaze as a constitutive effect of power and heterosexual plot. Thus, in his introduction to Corinne's performance, during which he invites foreigners to "gaze on [Corinne as] the image of our beautiful Italy," Castel-Forte uncannily catches the look in Oswald's eye: "'Yes,' he continued, his gaze happening to fall on Oswald just then, 'look on Corinne if you can spend your life with her, if the double existence she will give you can go on for a long time. But if you are condemned to leave her, then do not look upon her: so long as you lived, you would seek in vain the creative soul that shared and multiplied your feelings and your thoughts, for you would never find it again'" (2:2:24–25/57). What does the Italian see in the foreigner's look?

Before Corinne improvises at the crowning, she is described in a recital of sonnets and odes.[9] The poets in their portrayal of her genius are properly respectful, but Oswald is "impatient": "he thought that just by looking at her, he could have done a portrait of her more accurate, true, and detailed, a portrait that would fit no one but Corinne" (1:1:23/20). What besides his position as the subject of desire, perception, and knowledge (a conflation of agencies which rolled up into one constitute a unitary subject in power), entitles Oswald to believe in the power of his "regard," to believe that he has access to woman's truth merely by looking at her? In part, Corinne's signs of regard for him. During the ceremony of the crowning, Oswald separates himself from the crowd with the intention of speaking privately to Corinne. Corinne notices his moves but is careful not to reveal her attention: she doesn't want him to notice that she notices. But as she leaves the scene of her triumph, she turns back to see the melancholy man she has picked out of the crowd of admiring faces. Like the heroines of feminocentric novels who precede hers, in taking notice of the man the woman makes a misstep—a *mouvement en arrière*; or rather the movement causes her crown to fall. She does not fall, sprain her ankle, or make a faux pas that catches her gown. But displaced upward from the foot to the head, the gesture of feminine vulnerability produces the same sequences of masculine plot: when the woman's need to see *as a woman* causes her crown to fall and the man gallantly picks it up for her, their relation is detheatricalized and conventionally regendered. The text of their interactions throughout the novel is structured by this oscillation in the narrative between a public display designed for spectators in which Corinne is a powerful figure of female genius who takes pleasure in her performance and a private exchange in which she is brought (and brings herself) back into the ordinary fictions of femininity. Every spectacular scene is closed down by a domestication that brings it all back home.

Immediately after this exchange, for example, Oswald, in a state of dreamy reflection, finds his thoughts wandering back to his father. He removes the miniature portrait of his father he wears around his neck and guiltily consults what will later in the novel be described as its "silent gaze" [*regard muet*] (8:1:131/201). Here and throughout the text, as the gesture is repeated, it is as though the father's look, concretized in a visible emblem of security, functioned as an apotraic device or talisman designed to ward off woman's power of enchantment, to counter the petrification her laughing gaze threatens (and the father's severity guarantees).[10] If the power of patriarchy is thus fetishized, what does this tell us about its sons' desire? At the very least, it suggests that Oswald as the son of a father identified with an originary authority is not only the *producer* of the desiring gaze that in heterosexual topoi fixes its object, but also the vulnerable object of patriarchal judgments. In this sense, Staël might also have called her novel, *Oswald, or England.*

At the scene of the crowning, I argued, Oswald's views on separate spheres prevented him from submitting to the regime of excitement offered by Corinne's public self-display. I did not, however, emphasize the ways in which that judgment is grounded in a discourse of national difference. Oswald sustains his position on sexual difference by his allegiance to national codes: the codes of behavior that in England govern domestic and public life, what historian Joan Kelly calls "the social relations of the sexes" (809–24). It is perhaps the constant elaboration of the claims of national identity in the text that leads Ellen Moers in her pioneering work on women writers to make the claim that *Corinne* "is not in any polemical sense a feminist work. Indeed [Staël's] point," she writes, "is to show that regional or national or what we call cultural values determine female destiny even more rigidly than male. . . ." She goes on to conclude with a leap directly into the next para-

graph: "Oswald's father is quite right. Corinne really is not a proper
wife for Nelvil, or for anyone else" (207). What interests me here
is the way in which despite herself Moers hits on the very piece
of Staël's fiction that in my view makes the novel classically, even
polemically feminist. And this is precisely the role of Oswald's father, indeed we might say of patriarchal authority given as a syn-
onym for England. What motivates Moers's apparent non sequi-
tur, then, is that she follows the logic of the fathers that in woman
see only wife: the match of equal value; the laws of propriety that
make woman—even a national heroine—finally subject to the laws
of patriarchy. In another vein, it strikes me as worth remarking
that Moers here gives a vivid demonstration of what it means to
read "as a man" (the literary equivalent of the male gaze). Like
the keepers of the nineteenth-century French canon who retain, for
their reading lists, the Staël of *De L'Allemagne* while disdaining
the novels, *Corinne* and *Delphine,* Moers is embarrassed by the
woman who, by "making a spectacle of herself," threatens a reversal of social power arrangements that turns the fathers off (Russo,
216–17).

At the same time, of course, it is perfectly true, as Moers maintains, that the novel is about the ways in which human lives are
shaped by national values. What a feminist analysis that takes the
personal and the political, the private and the public *together* as
concatenated scenes of operation can provide, however, is an account of the deeply imbricated nature of these relations. In that
sense, for instance, both Corinne's and Oswald's lover's discourse
is inseparable from the figurations of Italy and England. Corinne's
offer of a guided tour is both a demand for love and a cultural
intervention.


## SHOWING

WHAT CORINNE wants Oswald to love in Italy is another time,
another economy, another set of values. She also wants him to stay
in Italy, so that he will love her. Provoked by her friend and ad-
visor Castel-Forte's skeptical view of the couple's future as a problem of taste—"you know to what extent the English are slaves to
the customs and habits of their country" (4:1:49/90)—Corinne
looks on the tour as a way of *keeping* the Englishman in Italy. The
verb in French is *fixer,* a verb rich in associations for readers of
the eighteenth-century novels *Corinne* revises. To take a case in

point, in Laclos's *Liaisons dangereuses,* both the virtuous Mme de Tourvel and the canny Mme de Merteuil fear that they would not be able to "fix" Valmont in the name of love—to stop the machine of libertine sequence that requires the masculinist hero to keep moving on down the list—and hold onto him. In Staël's novel, Corinne's desire to keep Oswald (though to be sure Oswald is no Valmont) transforms the feminine yearning for a pause, a metaphorical space of feeling, by grounding it *as space* and as such, an alternative to plot.

In Staël's novel, a woman's space, like Coulommiers and Valentine's pavilion, has a story of its own. Space suspends the masculine plot (Oswald's anxiety about closure and destination) by an insistence on description that puts plot itself into question.[11] Not surprisingly, however, given a canon that "keeps" *Adolphe,* the formal experiment here—the travelogue, the "interpolated" descriptions of Italy which embody the resistance to conventional plots—seems to have resulted in the novel's emargination, its exclusion from the very tradition of patriarchal writing the novel maps from its edges. In this reading of *Corinne* I want to evoke both the critique of men's writing and the creation of a new writing for women I am calling feminist that Staël puts in place through the play of cultural tropes. We might also think of this review or revision of earlier literature as the work of a feminist gaze.

A great deal, then, is at stake in the Italian material.[12] The first place Corinne has chosen for their visit of Rome is the Pantheon. As they enter the building, Corinne tries to define what makes this monument Italian. She explains to Oswald that because the destruction of the Caesars' empire destroyed the possibility of political independence it is not the figures of statesmen or military men that have come to replace the pagan gods; rather "the genius of imagination" (4:2:54/96). Thus, "the busts of our most famous artists . . . decorate the niches where the gods of antiquity once sat" (4:2:54/996). Corinne argues that a country that values the talents of its people deserves "a nobler destiny." (Oswald is hard on nations: they get what they deserve. If Corinne is [like] a nation, does she get what she deserves? to be a beautiful victim?) She goes on to embrace that destiny by identifying with the spirit of Italy's people, "the artists among us who love glory," whose goal it is to "win a place here. I have already marked out mine" (4:2:54/96). The niche Corinne has claimed for herself is empty (an editorial note in the new French edition informs us that it still is!).

In claiming her place among the artists of Italy, her place in the

Pantheon of greatness, Corinne, we might say, signs Staël's work: its ambitious plot. But we must also see that the wish for recognition as an artist is never in this novel entirely separable from an *erotics of acknowledgment* bound up with other desires. Indeed, having identified herself with the love of glory, Corinne attaches the man to the scene of its fulfillment. She imagines Oswald returning to the Pantheon after her death and seeing her bust placed within its walls. Thus with the signature of a female artist's posterity, Corinne creates at the same time the classical figure of the male mourner (poetically) in love with a dead woman. (Or rather she revises the trope already put in place by the reference to Petrarch whose poetry provides the epigraph to the novel and by the paternal death that frames her story with Oswald.) In the move that refigures the female artist as a beloved dead woman, Corinne's character articulates a contradiction the narrative never undoes; this is a necessary effect of the coexistence and incompatibility between public and private desires. The story of the novel plays itself out within the knots of this double bind, the competing differences within feminist desires.

Against the brilliance of Corinne's improvisation—the poetry that would earn her a place in the Pantheon—works the prose of domestic life: Oswald's sense of destination—England, his fatherland; the woman the father has chosen. But in a characteristic instance of the ideological conflict that inhabits this text, despite her passionate attachment to Italy—which I read here as the maternal landscape of her desire—throughout the guided tour, Corinne herself recurs to the cultural values of the patriarchal text which separate her from Oswald. Thus, when Corinne and Oswald visit the cemetery outside Rome, the grave Corinne chooses to stop over and contemplate monumentalizes a form of exemplarity radically opposed to that of the niche in the Pantheon. The gravestone, "the one tomb still almost intact" is that of a daughter, a young girl; the monument was erected by her father (5:1:79–80/131). For different reasons, the two "orphans" (as Corinne and Oswald see themselves) are moved by this reversal of nature's logic. The presence of arms on the tombstone—even though it is the grave of a woman, the daughter participates in her father's trophies—leads Corinne to remember an elegy of Propertius that provides her with an invidious intertext for her own life: the model of Roman femininity, Cornelia. She repeats the lines of Cornelia's heroinism: *"from marriage to the funeral pyre, no spot has stained my life; pure I have lived between the two flaming torches."* What Corinne finds sublime in this image is the integrity of the life it embodies: "How enviable the fate of a woman who has managed to retain the most perfect oneness in her destiny, and who carries only one memory off to the grave! That is enough for a life" (5:1:80/130). Corinne thus articulates her attractions to the two aspects of the ideal female life (purity and unity), against which measures her own necessarily will seem inadequate.

If we understand the ascription of her place in the Pantheon of talent and genius *as a woman* as the emblem of the text's feminist project in the novel, an iconographic representation that supplies and images an oblique commentary on the negative inevitabilities of female plot (a critique of essentialism), we must now reread Corinne's gloss on Roman patristics in the cemetery (monuments to what Engels will call the "perfect type" of paternal power in the family), as the fate of that commentary in narrative. As we will see, the novel's dissenting relation to the familiar structures of fiction that conflate narrative resolution and female destiny as a matter of marriage or death entails a disruption of story.

Corinne's explication of the Italian text through its monuments constitutes a strategy of deferral the narrator compares to the famous storytelling of Scherehezade (5:1:81/133). The narrator's analogy points to Corinne's fear of Oswald's power to decide her fate, but it also points more generally to the workings of male authority within literature and its judgments about women's texts: Corinne fears Oswald's attachment to patriarchal plots, and like her precursor she tries to forestall their closure through the elaborate show and tell she performs as a guide to Italy (staying alive by keeping Oswald in Italy).

The stakes of narration—what will Oswald think and do when Corinne tells him her story—are knotted up with the plots of abandonment that operate in the novel as a kind of anxious intertext; as though the act of revelation, following the rules of oedipal narratology, necessarily entailed punishment. Thus, when Corinne decides to accompany Oswald to Naples—to delay further and at the same time to give him a "proof of love" (10:6:187/277)—the count Erfeuil, who as a Frenchman is given the most conventional discourse in the novel, warns Corinne about the consequences of such a decision: "What! You really intend to set off with Lord Nelvil even though he is not your husband, even though he has not promised to marry you! *And what will become of you if he leaves you?*" [*que deviendrez-vous s'il vous abandonne?*] (10:6:187/278; emphasis added).[13] Corinne's reply that she would be miserable only if Oswald ceased loving her, that her idea of love transcends reputation, does not deter Erfeuil from sketching out the logic of seduction and betrayal that is the stuff of French eighteenth-century novels and that echoes Castel-Forte's earlier warnings about the power of English plot: "Lord Nelvil is a man like any other . . . he will go back to his country, pursue his career: in a word, he will be reasonable" (10:6:188/279). Although Corinne scoffs at the count's predictions, placing herself and her love outside "the usual broad categories for which ready-made precepts [*maximes toutes faites*] exist" (10:6:188/280), before presenting her story of origins to Oswald, she organizes an improvisation at Cape Miseno so that he might hear her once more *as* "Corinne," "as she had been that day at the Capitol, with all the talent she had received from heaven" (8:4:240/348), as though "Corinne" could protect her from the fate of woman. The theme requested by the audience this time is *"the memories recalled by these places"* (8:4:241/348), and Corinne ends the improvisation with what we might think of as her own *Heroides*—"Some memories of the heart, some names of women, also lay claim to your tears"—as she evokes not the heroes of antiquity, but the women left behind, silent heroines attached to the pain of absence (8:4:244/353).


TELLING

THE DAY at Cape Miseno marked by Corinne's verbal brilliance ends, however, with an instance of Oswald's physical heroism. On returning to Naples from Vesuvius, Oswald dives into the water to save an old man from drowning.[14] That the gesture is, of course, tied to Oswald's guilt about his father is signaled by the consequences of taking the plunge: water damages the father's portrait. The effaced image was barely recognizable, but a few days later Corinne returns the portrait to Oswald "repaired"—and "with a much more striking likeness than before" (8:7:249/359). We might want to think about this restoration of the image as an emblem of the central gamble at the heart of the novel.

Corinne's docility here as a brilliant copyist does not produce the ironic twist of feminist signature Laure's manipulation of artistic tradition through *pastiche* figures in *Indiana*, but we may perhaps overread it as a troubled figuration of the ways in which a woman artist re-presents ideology. More specifically, we might also wonder to what extent the very gesture of restoring the image by definition reinforces the regime of the specular (concretized in the gaze) that Corinne struggles against throughout the text. Put another way, it may be that this *adding* to the conventions of representation, of resemblance and identity, is a symptom of the text's self-contradictions: its challenge to representation's hegemony (through performance, lyric, discontinuity, spatialization—emphasis added); and at the same time, its obsessive need for representation's support: Corinne's unerring choice of the man most likely to *replace* her, precisely, in the feminine identity required and created by patriarchal plots.

Oswald interprets Corinne's uncanny ability to reproduce the father's image as a sign that she should reign over his life forever. And as if breaking with his own principles of deferral, in a gesture of good faith, he removes his father's ring from his finger (the ring his mother wore), to give it to Corinne *before* she delivers her story. Thus Corinne's long-delayed account of *her* "secrets" is doubly framed by emblems of the father's rule. In book 14 (there are twenty books in this epic novel), we are finally given to read Corinne's written account of her name and origins. Born in Italy of an Italian mother and an English father, Corinne rejoins her father in England at age fifteen, five years after her mother's death, and after an education in letters in Florence. The first-person narrative of her six years in England makes clear the interdigitated relations between gender and culture, and the crucial role played by a father's will in their articulation: her father and his. If Corinne, who is unhappy in England, senses she could not conform to the model of life her own father has embraced by his return to it, she is no less subject to its law as long as she lives under the paternal roof: "I was almost twenty when my father decided it was time for me to marry, and it was then that my appointed destiny started to unfold" [*c'est ici que toute la fatalité de mon sort va se déployer*] (14:2:259/247).

The particular fatality that regulates a woman's lot in fiction is always bound up with fathers. Here that configuration becomes inseparable from the tropes of performance and the patriarchal gaze that judges the performing woman. Corinne's father, having picked out Oswald as her future husband, invites Oswald's father to visit with the family. Corinne is flattered by this choice, since she has heard much about Oswald and awaits the arrival in a state of anxiety [*une véritable anxiété*] (14:2:260/373)]. Wanting passionately to please Lord Nelvil, Corinne shows everything she can do—singing, dancing, improvising—and fears that in this astonishing performance she has somehow gone too far. That she has indeed been too much for this father—*une personne trop vive* (14:2:373)—will be confirmed in writing. Later in the novel, Oswald is given to read posthumously a letter exchanged by the fathers in which Lord Nelvil senior locates Corinne's unsuitability as a wife for his son in her desire *to be seen:* "she has a great need to please, to captivate, to attract attention . . . and I do not know what theater would be broad enough for the active mind, the impetuous imagination—for the passionate character, in short, perceptible in her every word" (16:8:329/466). Corinne's need for a theater—a scene in which to display herself—is also pointed to by the stepmother's discourse (in bitter remarks to Oswald) as the origin of Corinne's undesirability: "she needs a theater where she can display all those gifts you prize so highly, and that make her life so difficult" (16:6:325/461). The geographical conclusions such a need to be seen entails are self-evident: this kind of spectacle belongs to Italy "In even the smallest Italian towns," Corinne observes, "there is a theater, music, actors" (14:1:257/369). In England "a perfected mechanical doll" (258/369) might as well live in her place.

With the death of her father, and the inheritance at her majority from her father and her mother, the question of Corinne's marriage—the father's desire—becomes instead of one of destiny, what renamed as Corinne she might become; and then more simply, of destination as geography: the return to Italy. But Corinne does not construe the return as the simple refusal of all English cultural values. Rather, in her account, she imagines a more complicated form of existence for herself; beyond the exclusive, either/or models of the fathers: "Thanks to the rare combination of circumstances that had given me a dual education and if you will, two nationalities, I could think myself destined for special privileges" (14:3:264–5/379). I think the doubleness, or marks of "differences within" that Corinne identifies as a positive grounding for a productive subjectivity, may also be read metaphorically as Staël's way of accounting for a more radical idea of femininity than her plot can handle, and that takes form in the performances the text embodies: the exphrasis of the travelogues and the lyrical improvisations.

At the same time, therefore, despite the cited advantages of different maternal and paternal heritages, the condition of Corinne's return to Italy requires a suppression of the English difference as patriarchy at the crucial level of the proper name: rather than hurt her (English, half-) sister's chance of a future "establishment" by the reputation of her own (Italian) "extraordinariness," "Miss Edgermond," following her stepmother's instructions, disappears.

But Corinne also goes beyond the erasure of the name of the father. She completely refigures an identity. She takes a single name: "I took only the name of Corinne, after the poet and friend of Pindar I had come to love when I learned her story" (14:4:269/386).[15] What I want to emphasize here beyond the relationship to a female poet of antiquity as precursor, is the textual impact *for the reader* produced by the suppression of not only the troublesome patronymic that could bring shame on the Edgermond family, but Corinne's given first name. Plausibly, this would have been a name chosen by the mother, an Italian name, perhaps, but a name the narrative never discloses. I will discuss the implications of this silence later in the chapter. For the moment, let us retain the evacuation of all originary identity in the gesture of self-naming.

When Oswald finishes reading Corinne's account, he thinks he still loves the woman, but feels hurt by her story. The effect of Corinne's critique of English life, her acknowledgment of *other* stories and desires, moreover, is to bring Oswald back to the question of paternal authority, to the authorized version. Thus the woman's testimony, far from challenging the son's view of things, confirms, as Corinne suspected, the father's vision: the epitaph in the Roman cemetery. The aftertext of Corinne's history moves the narrative closer to the plot of abandonment whose tropes, of course, have been in place from the beginning. For the return to Italy, where theaters and music do exist for Corinne's fulfillment, does not, as we have already seen, resolve the issue of feminine identity for a female poet and performer.

## PARADOXES OF THE COMEDIENNE

ALTHOUGH in the representation of Corinne's glory the crowning is the event the narrator and Corinne return to as the ultimate euphoric reference of her existence—the moment, in the terms of my argument, in which the performance of an identity creates a productive female gaze—the scene in which Corinne plays Juliet shows more complexly the stakes involved in what Naomi Schor in "Portrait of a Gentleman" has called "the battle of the gazes" in this novel, the struggle between the judgments of patriarchy and the desires of a feminist subject. The performance of Shakespeare's tragedy of paternal prohibitions and fatal visions (translated by Corinne and returned as it seems to the audience to "its native tongue" [*sa langue maternelle*] (8:3:126/194), dramatizes, we might say, both Corinne's need for a theater in which to be seen and Oswald's desire to replace that scene with himself. He will tolerate the praise of the world Corinne elicits only if "the look of love, more heavenly still than [her] genius," is directed uniquely at him (7:3:125/193). Once again, as in the scene at the Capitol, the man needs to separate the woman from the genius in order to consolidate his own identity.

Corinne's perspective involves a different kind of separation. On stage she knows she is acting. She can *see* the effect her acting has upon Oswald, and she splits herself from Juliet within the act of performance itself: "How happy Corinne felt on the day she played that noble tragedy for her chosen friend! How many years, how many lives would be dull after such a day!" (7:3:125/197) In this public moment we see the work of Corinne's *performing* gaze, the field of its mastery, and the scene of her ultimate pleasure: "living for a moment in the sweetest of the heart's dreams." This pleasure—*la jouissance pure*—is not, however, and this has its importance, an erotics cut off from her private feelings for Oswald. On the contrary, if "for the authority of art" Corinne would not want Oswald to play a part on the stage in the play with her, she does want him in the audience: she wants him there to see the extraordinary power of her emotional range: "See what capacity I have for love!" (7:3:128/198). The narrator analyzes the complex nature of Corinne's pleasure in performance: it is to experience "all the charm of emotion with none of reality's agonizing distress" (128/198) and at the same time the reality of emotion's effects: both the pleasure of public recognition—applause, etc.— *and* the satisfaction of laying all that "through the look in her eyes" (129/198) at Oswald's feet. This economy of pleasure resembles the calculus of fantasy that adds the erotic to the ambitious wish Freud assigns to men in the essay on creativity, "The Poet and Daydreaming" (48). I want simply to note here the way in which the fantasy is undermined from within by the narrator's discourse, as it goes on to characterize the object of Corinne's desire: at the feet of the one object whose approval "was more precious to her than glory" (129/198). This internal subversion is part of the contradiction—the ideological muddle—that inhabits Staël's novel from beginning to end. For like Oswald, Corinne is also tempted by the look of love, and that gaze like the look that judges is embedded in patriarchal plots; not the ecstasy of stasis, the perfect *jouissance* of the moment Corinne exalts in. Thus, the problem here is not simply the sex of the gaze, but its literature.

By its intertext Corinne's gaze *as* Juliet is bound to a pleasure in death: Juliet's lines upon learning Romeo's name, lines reproduced in English in the novel: "Too early seen unknown and known too late!" Like Juliet Corinne comes to learn that a body is not easily parted from its name under patriarchy's eye even if her own renaming has tried to undo those continuities; she learns very exactly "what's in a name." In the same way, when after the play, staggered by Corinne's performance as Juliet and no longer able to distinguish truth from fiction, Oswald comes backstage, he finds himself speaking Romeo's lines in English: "Eyes look your last! arms take your last embrace"; they also suggest that vision under the paternal regime is deadly.

The problem the excess of Corinne's public presence causes the fathers may also be traced to the intimacies of etymological derivations: theater and theory (in Greek) share a root—*thea*—to see: both theater and theory are, then, in this sense scenes of spectating, beholding, contemplating. Now spectators at the various theaters of ancient Greek life (including the events of the polis) were predominantly if not exclusively male; so were the spectators of representation (also known as philosophers).[16] When Corinne is viewed *as theater* by the father and the son their look articulates and regrounds the position of authority occupied by the figure of that privileged spectator of Greek life.[17] Put another way, the gaze is male when its act of seeing cannot separate itself from these dominant powers; seeing enacts ideology. "The privilege of sight over other senses, oculocentrism," Jane Gallop has argued in her reading of Irigaray's revision of Freud's "old dream of symmetry" through his "blind spot," supports and unifies phallocentric, sexual theory." "Every . . . viewing of the subject," she continues, "will have always been according to phallomorphic standards" (*The Daughter's Seduction*, 58).

Staël's production of Corinne's performing gaze wants to unsettle that conflation of contemplation, theory, maleness, phallic authority by showing the political investments of spectating, the limits of its vision from father to son, and by complicating the notion of spectacle. This double move in fact connects the two problematics: of a woman's performance as theater—what she by *her* gaze might give to be seen, *otherwise;* and what it would take for it to be received. We might usefully borrow here from Mary

Ann Doane's discussion of Irigaray's project to "provide the woman with an autonomous symbolic representation" (31). In her development of the notion of a feminine specificity that would not be an essentialism, Doane points to the distinction (drawn from Plato) that Irigaray makes between mimesis as "specularization" and an earlier "productive" mimesis: this first repressed mimesis, Irigaray writes, "would lie more in the realm of music" (*This Sex,* 131/129). In an analysis oddly reminiscent of Kristeva's formulation of the semiotic as a space of rhythm and music that "precedes and underlies figuration and thus specularization" (*Revolution,* 26), Irigaray imagines the possibility of "a woman's writing" "in the direction of, and on the basis of, that first mimesis" (131/129). Throughout the novel, Staël shows the productive, transformative power of this mode, a mode systematically repressed by a discourse of what Irigaray calls "adequation," the commensurability of word and thing. The relation between the two modes, the realm of "music" and the severe zones of the gaze will be rehearsed or placed in representation by the figuration of the tension between Italian and English paradigms. Corinne's dancing of the Tarentella offers an exemplary case:

> It was in no way French dance, so remarkable for its elegance and the difficulty of its steps; rather it was a talent much closer to imagination and feeling. The quality of the music was expressed by movements that were in turn precise and languorous. As if she were improvising, as if she were playing the lyre or sketching faces, Corinne communicated her feelings directly to the souls of the spectators through her dance: everything was language to her. Looking at her, the musicians were moved to make the essence of their music felt more strongly. It is impossible to explain the impassioned joy, the imaginative sensitivity that electrified everyone watching that magical dance, transporting them into an ideal existence where happiness not of this world is dreamed. (6:2:92–93/148)

The explosive potential of this physical improvisation, this body language of immediacy that emerges from a woman's imagination, provides a challenge to the old patriarchal order very much in the spirit of Cixous's celebrated call, that I have evoked elsewhere in this book, for an "écriture féminine," a women's writing that would bring women "into the world and into history by her own movement" (245). Staël's text in fact embodies another, poetic libidinal economy that writes *"the very possibility of change,* the space that can serve as a springboard for subversive thought, the precursory movement of a transformation of social and cultural structures" (249). But the novel also tells the fate of that gesture when it is read by the representatives of the old order.

If the Italians, as men who are moved by women, are transported by dance and music into the ideal, Oswald, the Englishman, remains fixed on the threshold of his real: "Trying to hide his distress, his fascination, and his suffering, he managed to say: 'Well Corinne, what homage, what success! But among all those men who worship you so enthusiastically, is there one brave and reliable friend? Is there a lifelong protector? And should the vain uproar of applause be enough for a soul like yours?'" (6:2:93/149–50). In the end, it seems Staël's (Romantic) recovery of another mimesis, of a modality of dance and poetry, ecstasy and transport fails to achieve its transformative aims because in the writing of a novel Staël necessarily comes up against genre; narrative's need for the linear metonymies of story, for the realities of representation— the demands of Oswald's plot, for instance. (Corinne's persistently somatic relation to performance is a symptom of that inevitable failure.) It would be a mistake, however, to conclude too quickly. For in the posterity of the text that is *Corinne, or Italy* and that contains the story of Corinne and Oswald, the image that remains attached to Corinne's body, that we might say becomes the iconography of her representation (reproduced notably on the cover of the Folio edition), she is figured as a transforming presence with her lyre.

Corinne appears on stage a last time in Venice in a production of Gozzi's comic opera, the *Figlia dell'aria*. At the end of the performance, the character Corinne plays sits on a throne from which she commands her subjects: the audience rises spontaneously to applaud Corinne as though she were a real queen (16:2:306/435). But when the curtain falls, Corinne learns the news she has dreaded since the backstage theatrics of *Romeo and Juliet*: Oswald must leave for England. In the emotional violence of their exchange, Corinne faints, and falling hits her head against the ground. When she comes back to herself, she measures the distance that separates this from their first meeting: "Oswald, Oswald, I was not like this the day you met me at the Capitol. On my forehead I wore the crown of hope and glory, now it is stained with blood and dust" (16:3:308/438). Although Oswald swears on *her* father's portrait, on a "father's name" that their love will continue, the narrator strikes a somber note: "In point of fact, to vanquish love once marks a solemn step in the progress of love: the illusion of its omnipotence is finished" (16:4:315/447). Thus the discourse of the novel comes to elaborate the power of the maxim to shape and regulate behavior.

## SUFFERING AND THE SPECULAR

THE STORY of Oswald and Corinne shows that as long as woman is on display, however sublime her performance, she will be subject to the rigors of patriarchy; the letter of the father's law Bakhtin calls "the dead quotation" (345). But, as we will see now, paradoxically, it is only in the unfolding of the abjection that Corinne endures when she *stops* performing that we finally take the measure of patriarchy's indictment in this text.

Once Oswald returns to England we witness the figural decrowning of Corinne, her insertion as object into the regime of the male gaze as the support of representation; and it is precisely at this point in the narrative that Maggie Tulliver, we recall, in *The Mill on the Floss* stopped reading Staël's novel: "As soon as I came to the blond-haired young lady reading in the park, I shut it up and determined to read no further. I foresaw that that light complexioned girl would win away all the love from Corinne and make her miserable" (432–33). Maggie was a good, stage one resisting feminist reader, who knew enough about images of women in literature to feel sure that this book would not end well for Corinne; and she wishes for "some story . . . where the dark woman triumphs" (433). Was Maggie right to stop reading?

The last five books of the novel display the "miserabilization" of the dark woman Maggie predicted. The reader tracks the fall from the exaltation produced by the tropes of public admiration into the abjection of the woman who now unseen becomes the spectator of staged events in which she does not perform; indeed has no place except that of witness to her own exclusion. The internal insistence on the dysphoric symmetry of these scenes, however, produces a complex reading effect: for paradoxically, the melodramatic moments of intense pathos caused by Corinne's "invisibility" give her in the reader's eye and her own the "theater" she needs by representing her peripeteia *as* theater: as scenes of beholding.

At home in England, Oswald reads his dead father's letter of judgment about Corinne and hesitates about what to do. As

Corinne waits in anguished paralysis for Oswald to write, she receives the visit of a woman who bears in her body the image of Corinne's internal crisis: "The person entering her room was totally deformed, her face disfigured by a dreadful illness; she was dressed in black and covered by a veil meant to conceal the sight of her from those she came near." The woman, who is seeking charity not for herself, but for the poor, is stunned by Corinne's appearance, and the narrator underlines the irony of their relations: "the poor woman, long since resigned to her own fate, looked at this beautiful person with astonishment . . . Italy's most brilliant person who was succumbing to despair!" (17:2:336/475). This figuration of Corinne brought down from the heights of a performing brilliance to the obscure zones of an object of pity will limn the final stages of the novel in which we read the destiny of the dark woman, as she becomes the woman in black who hides herself from view.

Corinne finally decides to come to England herself. In London, she goes see Mrs. Siddons perform in *Isabella, or the Fatal Marriage*. Not knowing that Oswald has returned to England, but not wanting to "attract the attention of some Englishman who might have known her in Italy," Corinne arrives at the theater veiled. She chooses a small box for herself "from which she could see everything without being seen" and follows both the play and the actress (who Oswald has said is like her) with absorption (17:2:340/ 480). But during the intermission she notices "all eyes [*tous les regards*] turning toward a box" (340/481). In a flourish of hyperbole that echoes the description of the effects produced by the appearance of the princess of Clèves at the court—"even in England where women are so beautiful, it had been a long time since anyone so remarkable had appeared"—Lucile (her own half-sister) is posed as the specular ideal. But it is not enough for Corinne to compare herself to the *image* of youth and find herself lacking; the degradation of the fall into specular suffering requires another turn of the spiral. Corinne suddenly sees Oswald, and seeing him for the first time since their separation, follows his gaze, which like the others' attaches itself to her sister's body. When the play is over, Corinne again hides herself from the crowd, and from an opening in her box watches Oswald escorting the young beauty from the theater, "the most beautiful person in England through the countless admirers following in her footsteps" (17:4:342/483). Normally an acute, even paranoid, reader of the slightest fluctuation in Oswald's feelings, suddenly faced with the new configurations of desire, Corinne resists interpretation and reserves judgment. Postponing the privacy of the *tête-à-tête*, she chooses instead a scene of public display—the review of Oswald's regiment in Hyde Park—as a theater in which to determine with "her own eyes" the status of his true feelings for Lucile.

In a reversal of positions which makes Corinne the spectator and Oswald the spectacle, as she prepares to go and watch the man on parade, Corinne now worries about her appearance. She hesitates about how to present herself, what to wear; and then suddenly, looking at herself in the mirror and seeing in its reflection her *sister's* face "light as air" decides against display and dresses in black, draping herself in a mantle, Venetian style (17:4:346/488). When Corinne, who is accustomed to being viewed as the *figure* of "Corinne," poet and improviser, and not simply *as a woman*, observes Lucile being seen *as a woman*, she immediately experiences her subjection to the law of the male gaze by seeing herself through it, or mirrored in it. In John Berger's analysis of this effect of vision: "Men look at women. Women watch themselves being looked at. This determines not only most relations between men and women but also the relation of women to themselves. The surveyor of woman in herself is male: the surveyed female. Thus she turns herself into an object—and most particularly an object of vision: a sight" (47). Once Corinne becomes this sight she enters a realm of acute suffering. Cut off from the mobile *jouissance* of performance, through which she defies the conventional inscription of woman's body, Corinne seems to enter the borderline zones of an identity in crisis; the state, neither subject nor object, that Kristeva describes as abjection.[18]

Like the disfigured woman dressed in black who had come to beg for charity, Corinne, in turn, her face protected from sight by the depth of a carriage, watches Oswald. Prancing on horseback, he performs like the hero of a ninetenth-century novel, in honor of the remarkably blond Lucile toward whom once again all admiring gazes turn: "Oswald gazed at her with looks that pierced Corinne's heart; the unfortunate woman knew those looks; they had been turned upon her" (17:6:346/489). The narrator thus underscores in discourse the repetition in plot of the general structure of reversal which organizes the last movements of the novel; emphasis reiterated on still a third level of the text in the narrator's rendering of Corinne's thoughts: " 'Ah,' Corinne thought, 'it was not like this, no, that I made my way to the Capitol the first time I met him; he has hurled me from the triumphal chariot into the

unfathomable depths of sorrow' " (347/489). We may understand
the fall from the height of art, from the triumph of Corinne's public, even national performance, to the depths of individual suffering as Corinne's descent into the privatized spheres of femininity.
The political economy of this reversal is based in the regime of the
look that constitutes Corinne as Woman.[19]

When Corinne returns to Italy this time, it is not to Rome but
to Florence, the scene of her education and her earliest literary
efforts: "I remembered how my first attempts at poetry had won
praise from a very few but well-qualified judges in Florence. I ex-
ulted in the successes I might win one day . . ." (14:3:265/379).
Now, far from those youthful illusions, bereft and lonely, she wanders through the streets and galleries of Florence; she is suddenly
drawn to a statue of Niobe clasping her "daughter to her breast
with heartbreaking anxiety" (18:3:368/519), and it is her powerful
reaction to this figure that engenders for the first time since the
separation from Oswald a desire to write. The choice of Niobe,
who as a figure of a ruined female destiny, is both a plausible and
paradoxical embodiment of Corinne's grief.[20]

What of Corinne's maternity? And why the choice of the final
daughter, the "littlest one" (*Metamorphoses,* 6:295–303)? The text
does not answer those questions directly here, for what follows
the description of the statues is instead an account—and then a
demonstration by incorporation—of Corinne's attempt to return
to writing. But I think the final pages of the novel show clearly
enough that Corinne suffers from an anxiety about transmission—
an anxiety of influence about what is to follow—in which writing
(as posterity) and maternal descent are intimately bound up with
each other.

Here, reflecting on the works of art she has just seen, tortured
by a wandering mind that stops her hand at every page, Corinne
measures the distance she has come: "How far she was now from
the gift of improvisation!" (18:4:368/519). The violence of her
emotions compels her to portray her own feelings. But the personal poetry that results is judged as a kind of *negative poetics:*

> But no longer were there any general ideas or the universal
> feelings that correspond to all men's hearts; it was the cry of
> grief, ultimately monotonous as the cry of birds in the night
> too fervent in expression, too vehement, lacking in subtlety.
> . . . Good writing requires a base of genuine—but not har-
> rowing [*déchirante*]—emotion. (18:3:368/519)

Unlike Niobe's "heartbreaking anxiety" that has been transfigured to make art, the repetitious rhythms of Corinne's pain seem to require a transformation beyond the (Romantic) powers of art.

As if to figure Corinne's trauma and the difficulty of her recovery, the novel includes several pages of her attempts at writing from this period. Like Clarissa's "mad papers" written after the rape, Corinne's "reflections" both rehearse the violence she has undergone and obsessively embody its aftermath. Entitled "Fragments of Corinne's Thoughts" they tell the story of a double, if circular failure: a suffering that *undoes* talent; and the collapse of the erotic plot. The first stanza reads: "My talent no longer exists, and I mourn for it. I would have liked my name to reach him with some glory attached; I would have wished that as he read some piece of mine, he felt in it some empathy with him" (18:3:369/520). In her book on Staël, Madelyn Gutwirth argues that Corinne generally suffers from a "terror of invisibility," and needs Oswald "to be witness to her success" (206). Here, then, Gutwirth continues, as in other "scenes of despair . . . it is nonrecognition of the heroine *as herself* by the beloved and through him by the world, that is the cause of the trauma" (207). But what would it take for Oswald (or England) to recognize Corinne "as herself"?

If we now return to the reflection with which we began this chapter—what is this woman looking for that she does not already have—the fragments offer a *mise en abyme* of the quest in that question. Corinne wants, I think, not so much a match in marriage as the perfect *destinataire:* the addressee basic to the transactions of narrative communication; a privileged interlocutor and reader in the form of a friend and lover. As she explains to Oswald at the beginning of the tour of Rome: "I did not imagine the coronation at the Capitol would win me a friend, but all the while I sought glory, I have hoped it would make me loved. What use would it be without that hope, for women at least!" (4:3:55/98). In Corinne's need for someone who will know how to read her—what she writes, what she feels—and who will at the same time authorize her glory, she describes what might be seen as a feminist fantasy: to recapture the unconditional love of the mother, the dead mother who named her and who mapped out her destiny by locating her education in Italy with a woman amidst art; she perhaps wants to be loved as the daughter whose name has been erased in this text: for herself. But can a man love like a mother? Is he the "brother," who in Adrienne Rich's language becomes the "man-who-would-understand"?[21] Not if he positions himself in the line of the patriarchal gaze which surveys, judges, and regulates; not if he also occupies the place of the father: not if *as a woman* she also wants him to love her *as a man*.

This, then, is the text's feminist knot, or one of them. For Corinne needs not only an interlocutor and a reader, she requires what in Colette's discourse about women and love in *The Vagabond* is called "the eager spectator to [one's] life and [one's] person" (111/147–48); and this perforce generates the deadly specular logic of representation; for that spectator tends to believe only what he sees: the woman as sight; or as Woolf has shown, his mirror. The witness who looks and sees without a mirror seems to inhabit a lost maternal plenitude. The novel embodies the conflicted attempt to construct (perhaps *re*construct) a female subjectivity through work *and* desire without a maternal support and *against* the power of the paternal gaze to circumscribe that project within the identity of Woman. Staël's fiction challenges the legitimacy of that power in writing—the narrator's and Corinne's; but at the same time, we are also given to see the cost of protest as it is lived out in a somatic body, the vulnerability of its text subjected to the prerogatives of the canon.

## FEMINIST WRITING / FEMALE AUTHORSHIP

> Public opinion seems to release men from any obligation toward a woman acknowledged as having a superior mind: with her you can be ungrateful, faithless, cruel. . . . *Isn't she an extraordinary woman?* That says it all. She is abandoned to her own resources, left all alone to struggle with her sorrow.
>
> Germaine de Staël, "Des Femmes qui cultivent les Lettres"

IN A NOVEL of dissent that places women and literature in social context, the private and privatized tropes of the unhappy love story (the plots of abandonment)—the woman alone ("dying of grief") cannot be separated from its effects in the public and publicized agora of writing. Thus when Oswald returns to Italy and inquires about Corinne, he learns that she has withdrawn from the public eye: "that she had published nothing in the past five years, and lived in the deepest seclusion" (19:6:394/554); "he was told . . . that no one knew anything about her since she had stopped seeing anyone and did not write anymore. Oh! this was not the way

Corinne's name was heralded once; and could the man who had destroyed her happiness and her brilliance forgive himself?" (19:7:398/559). Like Corinne's posthumously published fragments, the discourse of public opinion itself here, as it has done throughout the narrative, interweaves the end of writing—the production of the name—with the consequences of female plot. Thus, although the novel is framed by Oswald's story, the matter of (his) blame and forgiveness remains finally for the reader a matter bound to the text of Corinne's destiny. Although to the question the narrator asks in the concluding paragraph—"but did he forgive himself for his past behavior?"—the answer is evasive—"I do not know, and on this score I wish neither to blame him nor to grant him absolution"—the reader gets the point. Moments before her death Corinne replies to her sister's plea that she see Oswald that she has forgiven him: "I forgive him . . . for breaking my heart. . . . Men do not know the harm they do, and society persuades them that it is a game to fill a heart with happiness, only to follow up with despair" (20:5:418/585). But her forgiveness is followed by a powerful indictment of male advantage.

Thus Castel-Forte, who had predicted that Oswald would succumb to the plausibilities of English plot, does not now hesitate (using Corinne's own language) to condemn Oswald to his face: "A dagger thrust is punished by law, and breaking a sensitive heart simply occasions a joke, so we would do better to choose the dagger thrust" (20:2:404/566–67).[22] The novel indeed makes clear on several levels that Oswald cannot possibly forgive himself; and provides him with a punishment that Corinne herself finally recovers her talent to write. In this sense, I want to argue that while the ambitious wish Corinne embodies in her performances and improvisations is shown repeatedly to be a vulnerable, or rather dangerous one for a woman who wishes also to love, in the end it does not remain without a subversive, or at least critical force.[23] Put another way, although Corinne's final performance demonstrates the heavy price involved in producing female subjectivity within a field of social relations that constitute men as men and women as women, at the same time it does so, precisely, through the production of a text that by its difficulty, the failure of its excess, is *Corinne*.

Oswald's reappearance in Italy at the end of the novel both engenders the final stages of the plot, the outcome of the knot of his impossible relation to Corinne, and revives the question of the power of the gaze. We might say that he returns in order to complete the

framing with which the novel began. Unlike the episodes of the
first part of the novel, however, which deal with Corinne's production in performance and Oswald's role as spectator (the semiotics of intersubjectivity), here (except for the final scene) the
narrative focuses more specifically on the stakes of representation
as a *mimetic* act because they deal with the image of woman fixed
in painting.

In the move that locates Corinne in painting we take the full
measure of the gaze as the support of the dominant ideology—
the discourse that identifies woman's place—and that move as a
crucial one in the feminist polemic that animates this text. Thus,
when Oswald goes to see Castel-Forte with the hope of speaking to Corinne, he is allowed to see her only in representation.[24]
Castel-Forte shows Oswald two paintings. The first is a portrait
of Corinne as Juliet. The narrator reminds the reader of the happiness of that moment, indeed of the day Oswald "had felt most
swept away by her" (20:2:404/566). The reader may, however, remember that day otherwise: as the scene of Corinne's ultimate
*jouissance* (7:3:128/198), performing tragedy for the delectation of
the beloved; and after the play, her terror that Oswald would
abandon her. Juxtaposed to that portrait of Corinne playing Juliet
is one of Corinne as the woman in black: "pale as death, her eyes
half closed, her long eyelids veiling her gaze and casting a shadow
over colorless cheeks." Across the bottom of the portrait was written this line from *The Faithful Shepherd*: "*A pena si può dir: questa
fu rosa* [Scarcely can one say: she was a rose]" (20:2:404/566–67).
The *sight* of what Corinne has become plunges Oswald into a panic
over what he has lost and he writes to ask to *see* Corinne again,
and to be seen by her. This gesture engenders a final exchange of
stories. Oswald invokes destiny and the will of a dead father;
Corinne's reply marks not the reopening of epistolary desire, but
its burial.

As she comes to *incarnate* the trope of the woman dying of grief,
Corinne gathers meaning from the tradition and revises it for the
final twist of the novel: what we might think of as Dido's revenge;
or epic rewritten from the woman's point of view, another, *performative* sort of *Heroides* (not unlike the improvisations at Cape
Miseno). Corinne imagines Oswald as the male mourner to her
fading gaze: a classic trope. But this is not all. The conclusion of
Corinne's letter also turns to her sister and her daughter with
Oswald in a mode that not only insists on the reversals we have
already seen in the structure of the novel but also points to a re-

fusal. In her fantasy for the final performance of her life as a spectacle that she will not witness, Corinne first places Oswald at her funeral as her "brother"—her brother-in-law; and having thus legitimately placed him at the scene, she then imagines herself passing in a coffin along the route she had traveled in her "triumphal chariot" and Oswald returned to the very spot at which he had picked up her crown (20:3:409–10/573). But if she then pulls back from the simple gratification of orchestrated regret over the violence inherent in the thematics of "then" and "now" (like the inscription under the portrait of the woman in black), it is also to produce another form, but a much more complicated one, of posthumous testimony. Against the predictable destinies generated by the authorizing wills of the dead fathers, Staël imagines an open-ended or at least ambiguous aftermath to Corinne's suffering as the abandoned woman, sacrificed like Dido on the altar of national vocation. Although she will place herself through a self-conscious gesture of final mastery in that figuration of authorized violence, it is only after a living legacy is put in place; a legacy that seeks to subvert and challenge patriarchal rule.

When Oswald returns to England after the war and discovers his three-year old daughter, he is struck by the resemblance she bears to Corinne, especially her hair and eyes (19:4:386/542). This dark child, then, has been named Juliette, presumably by Lucile alone in Oswald's absence. The lack of comment about or explanation for this name in a novel that operates through redundancy, repetition, and even authorial footnotes is curious; and I think this silence might usefully be put into relation with the blank we draw about Corinne's first name. What maternal wish, or anxiety, is expressed here in the choice of a name that famously evokes a literature that thrives on, indeed requires, exquisite cadavers, victims of a fatal bad timing? What might be at stake in Lucile's unwitting and uncanny participation in the emblem of performance and bliss that bonds and binds Oswald and Corinne? To what extent does naming the child of the future with the name of the past, literary or familial, paradoxically (or rather, perversely) challenge the inevitability of patriarchal descent?[25]

After her first visit to Corinne, Juliette describes by way of reply to her father's questions her aunt's pedagogical project: "She promised to teach me everything she knows. She says she wants me to be like Corinne. What is Corinne, father? [*Qu'est-ce que c'est que Corinne, mon père?*] The lady didn't want to tell me" (20:4:411/(575). What would it mean to be like Corinne? Unlike the restrictions imposed by her step-mother Lady Edgermond on Corinne's instruction of Lucile in England, Juliette's curriculum pointedly includes music (in addition to Italian). But to resemble Corinne is not only a question of lessons; it is also a question of performance. Thus, Oswald is given to see as a "spectacle" his daughter holding a "lyre-shaped harp made for her size, in the same way that Corinne held it, and her little arms and pretty expression [*ses jolis regards*] imitated Corinne perfectly. It was like seeing a beautiful painting in miniature . . ." (20:4:411/575). Lucile understands and mutely accepts Corinne's desire to pass on her talents as "a legacy she was pleased to bequeath while she was still alive" (20:4:411/575). But as she watches Oswald watch his daughter play a Scottish air on her little harp, Lucile takes the measure of Corinne's writing for the future. The melody Juliette plays, the narrator reminds us, is the one Corinne sang to Oswald in her gallery at Tivoli as he contemplated a painting of Ossian that "retraced" in his mind his father's grave and the paternal landscape of Scotland. Corinne underscored the poignancy of the iconography for Oswald through the words of the song which describe leaving one's country and which are concretized in the signifiers *"no more"* (the words are in English in the text). They wept then, as Oswald weeps now alone at the question implicit in the insistence upon the memorial:[26] "Would you be the worthy companion of my life, just as you are its charm and enchantment?" (8:4:158/238). At that point in the narrative, the question of the relation between those two modes of attachment was seen to depend on the revelation of Corinne's long-delayed story, the hidden truth of her past, the enigma of a woman's identity. But if in the novel the disclosure seems to engender the inevitable narratology of truth and consequence, it is perhaps more important to observe the ways in which the impossibility of a simple (i.e., positive) answer to the formulation has throughout been inscribed in the text; and in the language of Oswald's gaze; in his view of woman's place.

If Oswald is stricken as little Juliette brings back to him the time of enchantment, he weeps when the rest of Corinne's message is delivered. Juliette's teacher has made her promise to play the song for her father every year: on November 17, the anniversary of Oswald's fatal departure from Corinne and Italy (like the warrior in the song who leaves his country and his mistress). The living heritage, therefore, must be seen to authorize the complex and contradictory agendas of the text: the legacy of the exceptional

woman; the posterity of the woman as writer; the bypassing of
reproduction and the inheritance of patrimony through an oblique
form of maternal descent: thinking back through the mothers. But
at the same time, of course, this line is not simply jubilant. To
embody the heritage in the daughter of patriarchy within its very
bosom, so to speak, is also to operate an ambivalent dialogue within
the terms of its desire.

Corinne's punishing forgiveness rereads the literature Oswald's
masculinity crisis enacts as a question of genre. In her final performance, not surprisingly, we are returned to Dido. In the scene
at Tivoli referred to above, Corinne shows Oswald other paintings
in her collection, notably, for our purposes here, a representation
of Dido and Aeneas as they meet in the underworld. Corinne's
exphrasis is brief, but to our point: "The indignant shade moves
off, pleased that she no longer bears in her breast a heart that
might still beat with love at the sight of the guilty man" (8:4:155/
234).[27] When Corinne settles in for the final performance and looks
for Oswald in the audience, the iconography of Virgil's poem reappears. In an involuntary movement, Corinne reaches out to
Oswald, but then immediately pulls back, "turning her face away
like Dido when she meets Aeneas in a world where human passions may no longer penetrate" (20:4:415/581). As was the case
when Corinne played Juliet, Oswald must be restrained from making a spectacle of himself in front of the audience. Unlike Virgil's
Dido who shows only by her anger and flight that human passions
still animate her (*Aeneid* 6:1:617–23), Corinne reveals her continuing engagement with the man who like Aeneas knows he is
guilty and blames fate. More important still, Corinne, unlike Dido,
is not the heroine of an epic of male destiny, but the heroine of a
novel that puts that destination into question as it produces, or
tries to, another kind of female subject (Peterson, 57–58). Corinne,
finally, watches Oswald from the distanced gaze of the Author.

Thus Corinne stages the context in which the final meeting with
Oswald will take place, and the narrator underscores her motivation: "she wanted the ungrateful man who had deserted her to
feel once more that he had given the death blow to the woman
who in her time knew best how to love and how to think. . . .
Perhaps she wanted to remind him of her talent and her success
before she died, indeed of everything she was losing through unhappiness and through love" (20:5:414/580). In a double gesture,
the last chapter of the novel's conclusion insists melodramatically
on the violence that constructs the trope of abandonment: on the

one hand we have the reinscription of the metaphor—the woman "dying of grief"; on the other its rewriting as an indictment of the transparency of the grounds of substitution. We may then ask whether revisited in fiction the figure leaves the nostalgia of poetry in place. Put another way, two questions arise here about the outcome of Staël's project: is the Corinne destroyed *as a woman* in the love plot also destroyed *as a writer* in the ambitious plot? (Is her talent all gone?) Or is there a way in which the operatic devastation of Corinne, emblematized in the recurrent figure of the broken heart, constitutes a *critique* of the love plot and an inscription for posterity of Corinne the poet: poetic justice? This is also by way of asking whether Corinne's legacy to and in Juliette for the women writers who follow comes to challenge the inheritance of patriarchal plots.[28]

## LAST WORDS

OMPHALE CORINNE ELFREDA
LU-HOU MEI-FEI VICVAVARA
QI-JI VIJAYA BHATITARIKA
LUDGARDE GERTRUDE DIANE
ROGNEDE MALAN CLÉOPÂTRE
AMÉRIZ BETHASABÉE CLAUDE

Monique Wittig, *Les Guérillères*

ELLEN MOERS introduces her discussion of Staël's novel by commenting that "*Corinne* is one of the very few works by women which is trivialized rather than honored by being read as a woman's work" (182). By this she seems to have meant that to read the work as being about "female genius" as opposed to the contemporary reception of the novel as a "celebration of the rights of spiritual genius and intellectual freedom" is seriously to miss Staël's "principal intention" which was to "politiciz[e] . . . genius."[29] Since Moers then goes on to show (interestingly) the impact the novel—and the crowning as the emblem of its ambitious wish—subsequently had on women writers as *readers* and their (reading) heroines (like George Eliot and Maggie Tulliver), we might more usefully rework the analysis by refusing its implicit and hierarchical distinctions: political vs. feminist. Whatever Staël's intention may have been, her gesture in *feminizing* genius in a *public* forum is from a feminist perspective politicizing. To see this, however, would require Moers to take woman as the ground of critique, rather than its metaphor, or its effect.

Moers makes the point that "as a woman writer concerned with the theme of fame, Mme de Staël was impelled to bring her heroine's genius out of the study and into the public eye, where she could be shown in the act of swaying the multitude; and as a novelist, Mme de Staël was perhaps the first to discover that book-writing is an anti-novelistic subject" (185). I think we can go further here to argue that if Staël was indeed concerned with "literary genius," it is not simply the problem of representing the act of writing that has Staël bring Corinne into the public eye, but the problem of representing *woman* writing. Indeed, the very public nature of Corinne's identity as a writer is bound up with three separate but related issues for a woman writer's representation of a writing subject: the ways in which female subjectivity is construed in the public sphere; the vulnerability of the exceptional woman to the regulatory power of the male gaze (public opinion); the reception of a woman's text by the male spectator/critic/reader.[30]

By choosing to make Corinne a performing artist, an improviser, Staël deals not only with the (Romantic) question of genius and fame, but with a woman's control or mastery over artistic authority, and the matter of female posterity.[31] So when at the end of the novel, in the splitting off of writing from performing (improvising) Staël returns her heroine to the regime of signature, much is at stake. Since her withdrawal from the world, Corinne, we learn, "no longer had the strength to improvise, but in her solitude she still wrote verse, and she seemed to take a livelier interest in writing since Oswald had come" (20:5:414/580). What seems particularly important about the status of this writing in private is its separation from Corinne's body.

Too weak to perform, Corinne arranges to have her "swan song" read by a girl dressed in white, "crowned with flowers" (20:5:415/581), while she herself, veiled, plans to watch Oswald (*destinataire* and betrayer) without being seen. Thus, in Corinne's final production, we have a radical shift away from talent (or genius) as as physical activity inseparable from other physical qualities—like beauty, or charm, or charisma. In this sense, one could argue that separating the signature from the body of the performer grounds female textual authority.[32] Others have argued that this is after all a high price to pay for authorship, the name on the bound volume, the place in the library, the niche in the Pantheon of talent.[33] But

I have literary support for the line I am taking here that I find telling.

As a woman writer preoccupied with a writer's public identity, George Sand returns interestingly to this moment in *Lélia*. Lélia, described as having the "serious gaze of a long-ago poet" (29/45) is likened by Trenmor to a type: like the poets Tasso and Dante, Shakespeare's heroes—Romeo, Hamlet, "Juliet half-dead, hiding the poison and the memory of a broken love in her heart. . . . Corinne, dying, must have been plunged into mournful attention when she listened to her last poems being spoken at the Capitol by a young girl" (20/46). In Sand's misrepresentation, her transposition of the recital from the academy in Florence to the Capitol in Rome, we have a woman reader's tribute to the public authority of the precursor's text. By rewriting the last performance as the first, Sand marks the power of the female poet Staël created. Through her revision, Sand enacts the possibility of a different sort of literary community/continuity of women.[34] Not the biological and murderous simplicity that appeals so much to the father and son teams of our cultural paradigms (Harold Bloom, Sigmund Freud), but a more complex legacy that like Corinne's passes on its values in life to another generation through reading women's writings and their performatives (Berg, 214). Thus, I want to suggest, it is paradoxically when she is no longer performing that Corinne becomes the figure of the woman writer; that she comes, finally, we might say, to writing.

After Corinne's public farewell to life, Oswald faints and this sight marks the decisive turn in Corinne's fading into death. But there will be yet a final moment. In the presence of a priest, Castel-Forte, Oswald, and Lucile, Corinne has the last word; or rather, in this melodramatic universe, where gestures punctuate the scenes with meanings that cannot be put into words, the last gesture.[35] As Corinne looks out the window at the sky, she points to a moon covered with a cloud. Once again, the narrator supplies the interpretation: this was the same cloud Corinne had pointed out to Oswald on their trip to Naples; the night they had spent together, Oswald's desire "immolated" to Corinne's "virtue." She had then found the cloud "deathly": "I have always known the sky to look paternal or angry and I tell you, Oswald, tonight it condemned our love" (11:1:196/289). That night Oswald had dismissed the omen's implications; faced now with the uncanny return of Corinne's dying gesture he becomes wild with grief. But faithful to her desire for his behavior after her death, he follows the fu-

nereal march in Rome and then returns alone to the gardens at
Tivoli where her ashes are buried. Despite the resemblances to
Adolphe's fate, this solitary seclusion is not to be Oswald's lot.
More like Des Grieux and the eighteenth-century heroes who pre-
cede him, Oswald in the end returns home.

At the very end of the novel, with a twist that irresistibly calls
up the last lines of *The Princess of Clèves,* the narrator comments:
"The order and purity of Lord Nelvil's domestic life were exemplary" (20:5:419/587). But unlike Lafayette, Staël is not satisfied
to close the scene on the understatement of the unreadable (De-
Jean, "Lafayette's Ellipses," 900); and because her subject is not
that which might escape representation (Corinne's Italian first name)
but that which founds it (the bracketed English patronym), the last
words become the question and answer about the framing subject
we referred to earlier; of his forgiveness of himself, or his consol-
ability, of the meaning of his destiny as a man: "But did he forgive
himself for his past behavior? . . . Was he satisfied with an ordinary lot after what he had lost? I do not know, and on this score
I wish neither to blame him nor to grant him absolution" (20:5:419/
587). This "I" of partial knowledge makes its only appearance here
in the narrative, and in its rhetoric of ignorance and negation, invites the reader to admire the ironies of omniscience that have
framed the novel. That it can decline the authority of phallic conviction at the end is no less a "mark of gender,"[36] for like Corinne's
hand pointing to the paternal irritation that animates the sky, it
knows—at whatever cost—it has had in this story the last word.


## AFTERWORDS

THE QUESTION remains, nevertheless, of the cost, on the one hand,
and its secondary gains. Put another way, like the retouching of
the father's portrait meant to console Oswald for his loss, but that
can't help but supplement the authority of paternal desires, does
the gamble of an exceptional woman that she is beyond convention arrest or sustain the inevitabilities of male plots? Or should
we perhaps conclude that it is fatal to construct a feminist poetics
(of performance) dependent on the gaze, on the assent of the spectator? *Corinne* demonstrates vividly the ways in which the singular
challenge to the grounds of representation posed by the woman
of genius is defeated by the limits of social reality. For performance
to be performative, transformative, it requires a collective assent.

Despite the spectacular nature of her final performance, in the end Corinne still points to the paternal horizon; and Oswald wanders guiltily through its landscape.

## NOTES

ELLEN MOERS in her *Literary Women: The Great Writers* (1976), Madelyn Gutwirth in *Madame de Staël, Novelist: The Emergence of the Artist as Woman* (1978), and Carla L. Peterson in *The Determined Reader: Gender and Culture in the Novel from Napoleon to Victoria* (1986) all provide rich and provocative analyses of *Corinne* that students of the novel will pursue with profit. My notes may not indicate the full extent of my debt or my agreement with these earlier studies. This is not a mark of ingratitude, but an effect of intertextuality and absorption.

Staël has also been the subject of important new translations, which should allow a broader public to have access to her writing. Avriel H. Goldberger's *Corinne or Italy* (1987) and Vivian Folkenflik's Staël reader, *An Extraordinary Woman: Selected Writings of Germaine de Staël* (1987). I want to thank Leslie Mitchner, Senior Editor at Rutgers University Press, for allowing me to consult the *Corinne* in page proof.

As this book goes to press, I note two further contributions to the renewal of interest in Staël: Charlotte Hogsett's *The Literary Existence of Germaine de Staël*, and Marie-Claire Vallois's *Fictions féminines: Mme de Staël et les voix de la Sibylle*.

1. The novel thus begins with a clear-cut example of the circulation of women at the heart of dominant sex/gender systems famously analyzed by Gayle Rubin in "The Traffic in Women: Notes on the 'Political Economy' of Sex."

2. Putting this scene in which the princess looks around for a partner and is assigned by the king to dance with Nemours in relation with the encounter at the jeweler's, Kamuf argues interestingly that Nemours becomes the name for "the desire that separates the mother's 'unattainable woman' from this other self" (78). I take off from this to make the claim that what the princess is looking for belongs to but finally escapes from any heterosexual couple she might form. In its most extreme representation this permanent gap or internal fissure becomes the deliberately aimless wandering of Lol V. Stein. When asked what she is looking for, Lol, pretexting vague household errands, replies guiltily: "Oh, some pieces of china impossible to match [*des assiettes dépareillées, pour toujours*], for one thing. You keep hoping some store in the suburbs will have the pattern you want" (85). What I want to contrast here is the notion of endlessly filling in a pattern by definition, or by design, impossible to maintain intact, and the binary set of the couple, which fetishizes the match, totalizes identity. (Duras also provides here a parody of the domestic ideal and the meaning of privatized spheres for women.)

3. In Staël's novel, the impossibility of assembling what a woman wants

in one place is given in the title, *Corinne, or Italy.* The disjunction, or rather the ambiguity bound to valences of the conjunction "or"—which equates or differentiates—becomes more striking when seen against eighteenth-century feminocentric titles: *Julie or The New Eloise, Clarissa or the History of a Young Lady, Evelina or the History of a Young Lady's Entrance into the World, Maria or the Wrongs of Woman.* In this tradition, what is joined to a woman's name functions as a form of redundancy: the woman's name stands in for, or is redoubled by more of the same—an illustrious precursor; any woman—Mary; the "sex" at large. But more important for our purposes is that typically in these titles of fiction, the question of identity implicit in the woman's name (who she is whose story this will be) becomes by its subtitle narrativized through structures of time, exemplified in plot (what's her story?). The oddity of the place name in a novel title raises the possibility of a plotless identity (neither a history, nor adventures) and establishes a dialogical model for its invention in the play between its terms. On the title as an emblem of Staël's project, see Marie-Claire Vallois's "Voice as Fossil, Madame de Staël's *Corinne or Italy:* An Archaeology of Feminine Discourse."

4. Carla Peterson suggests: "Staël's novel may be seen as a repetition of the plot of the *Aeneid*, the central text of Corinne's second improvisation; indeed, we may even say that *Corinne* constitutes a female revision of this founding myth of patriarchy in which the heroine plays at least three parts: the Cumaean sibyl, the tragic queen Dido, and, finally, the questing hero Aeneas" (55).

5. It also seems worth stressing the point that most discussions of the gaze and its sex assume a heterosexual paradigm of white male dominance. The question of the female gaze within this economy (and outside its politics) is now beginning to be elaborated. This reading of *Corinne* is one piece of a possible reworking of the concept. Joan DeJean has proposed a modeling of the female gaze as an act of memorialization beginning with Sappho. See also the work of Mary Ann Doane and the collection of essays by German feminists, *Feminist Aesthetics* (1985), several of which address this issue.

6. Like Charrière writing at the end of the century (*Caliste*, 1788, *Mistress Henley*, 1784), Staël builds here on a line of problematic men in the novels of eighteenth-century women writers. Oswald joins Riccoboni's Alfred, Ossery and Marquis de Cressy, Tencin's Barbasan and Comminge, as a man insufficiently aware of the superiority of the woman in love with him; and blind to his own flaws. This double blindness sometimes reverses itself in the end, but more typically, recognition of what has been lost comes too late. At the same time, Oswald belongs to the heroes of his own generation, that of the *mal du siècle;* Adolphe, of course, and most famously, René. He is, in Margaret Waller's apt phrase, a "mâle du siècle," whose malady has as crucial sympton the inability to assume the life plot set out for him by the paternal maxims; an anguished impotence in the face of the requirements to form a couple and take his legitimate place in the social text.

7. This framing vision of the man's refusal to be moved by a spectacular performance that leaves him instead fixed as the judge of woman is rewritten in Charlotte Brontë's *Villette*. When Lucy Snowe and Dr. John ("that cool young Briton!") watch at the theater in Brussels the "marvellous sight: a mighty revelation," a "spectacle, low, horrible, immoral" of Vashti (Brontë's translation of the French actress Rachel), Lucy in ecstacy at the performance dis-

covers that the doctor is really a man: " 'How did he like Vashti?' I wished to know. 'Hm-m-m' was the first scarce articulate answer. . . . In a few terse phrases he told me his opinion of and feeling towards, the actress: he judged her as a woman, not an artist: it was a branding judgment" (399/442).

8. There is a homologous effect in *The Princess of Clèves* when by the narrator's perspective the reader is given to see the "chain of three men" watching the princess contemplate Nemours's portrait (Danahy, 219).

9. This scene is a rewriting of Scudéry's novel *Cyrus* (see Borowitz, 42) and hence another way of figuring the relation between women writers in the French tradition.

10. Thus in his early "captivated" reaction to the power of Corinne's presence, Oswald worries about Corinne's gaze: "he wondered whether it were possible to be loved by her, to have concentrated on oneself alone such diverse beams of light." Is the plural, excessive gaze of a woman—its diverse beams [*tant de rayons*]—too much for one man? Is one man enough for her? And he puzzles over the paternal rule: " '"Oh father,' wondered Oswald, 'if you had known Corinne, what would you have thought of her?' " (3:39/77).

11. I am grateful to Rachel Krantz, a student in my seminar on French women writers at Columbia (1983) for her illuminating reading of space and plot in Stael's novel (ms.).

12. On the function of the Italian material in the novel see Marie-Claire Vallois's "Voice as Fossil."

13. The count plays a similar role with Oswald: "Marry Corinne! . . . Believe me, my dear Nelvil, if you want to do something foolish, do something that can be set right, but where marriage is concerned, we must look to social convention" (3:3:46/87).

It must also be said that the trip to Naples, which will be the scene of mutual revelations, is framed by several levels of negative anticipation regardless of the outcome: abandoned *or* married. Corinne worries: "If her destined happiness was to have Oswald as husband, he would have to take her away to England, and what would they think of her there?" (10:6:190/282). Castel-Forte, echoing these sentiments, recasts the question not in the language of love but in terms of admiration: "But if you marry Lord Nelvil, you shall have to leave Italy . . . where you are so warmly admired! . . . Where will you be loved as you are here?" (10:6:191/282).

14. Oswald manifests here and throughout the novel many of the elements of a behavior Freud describes in "A Special Type of Choice of Object Made By Men" (1910); a choice that reveals the effort to "reconcile the demands expressed in . . . phantasy with the exigencies of real life" (162): a type of object choice "effected by men" that Freud calls in this essay, "love for a harlot" (164). What Freud finds "astonishing" in this type is not that a man should love such a woman, but that he desires to " 'rescue' the beloved. The man is convinced that the loved woman has need of him . . . that [he] saves her from her fate, therefore, by not letting her go . . ." (165). Freud connects the impulse to rescue with the child's sense that he "owes his life to his parents" which leads him to form the fantasy to repay them by "saving" them. This might mean "weav[ing]" a phantasy of saving his father's life on some dangerous occasion by which he becomes quit with him" (170). In conclusion, Freud adds that "various significations of 'saving' in dreams and phantasies are especially clearly recognizable when they occur in some connection with

water" (172). It seems to me that this matrix of elements is curiously central to the structure of Oswald's motivation as a character in Staël's novel.

15. In her well-documented essay, "The Unconfessed Précieuse: Madame de Staël's Debt to Mademoiselle de Scudéry," Helen Borowitz argues that the choice of "Corinne" was mediated for Staël by Scudéry's Greek pseudonym (44).

In an authorial footnote, Staël explains: "The name Corinne is not to be confused with that of Corilla, an Italian *improvatrice* everyone has heard of. Corinne was a Greek woman well known for her lyric poetry; Pindar himself studied with her" (Notes, 431/592).

16. In her sharp and witty introduction to a special feminist issue of *Paragraph* (Autumn 1986) Diana Knight reviews Geoff Bennington's play on the derivations of theory and the procession as the "locus of theory" through Woolf's speculation on the "procession of educated men" in *Three Guineas.* I am grateful to Helene Foley for her remarks on theory and theater.

17. Thus as Oswald—in Rome—contemplates the production of *Romeo and Juliet,* he worries about loving a superior woman. Like his father, he fears her excess: "she was too remarkable in every domain" (7:3:125/192). Like Staël's novel, the text of a woman's excess overflows (literary) categories: "elle était trop remarquable *en tout genre.*"

18. For a discussion of Kristeva's model of abjection and its relation to the maternal—its potential and danger for feminist theory—see Mary Russo's "Female Grotesques: Carnival and Theory" (219–21) and Gayatri Spivak's critical response to Kristeva's work on the subject in "The Politics of Interpretations" (278).

19. As Staël writes in the chapter on love in *De l'influence des passions* (1796): "Oh women! you the victims of the temple where they say you are worshipped, listen to me. It is true the love that women inspire gives them a moment of absolute power; but in life taken as a whole, even in the development of a feeling, their wretched fate reclaims its ineluctable dominion" (169). The novel charts the taking back of the power that Corinne had exercised in her person. As Castel-Forte, Erfeuil, and Corinne herself had foreseen, returned to England, Oswald is released from the claims of the adored woman's charms.

The topography of the abyss [*l'abîme des douleurs*] is reminiscent of the metaphorics of *The New Eloise,* a novel central to Staël's remapping of eighteenth-century fiction. Her rewriting of the male precursor will be clearer in the invention of Julie-tte we will discuss at the end of the chapter. The metaphors of the fall of course also recall "the romantic image of the artist" Maurice Shroder has emblematized in the figure of Icarus. But what happens when "the revolt of the son against his father" (Shroder, 56) is carried out by a daughter?

20. In "From *Patria* to *Matria:* Elizabeth Barrett Browning's Risorgimento," Sandra Gilbert cites Byron's images of Rome as the "Lone mother of dead Empires," "The Niobe of Nations!" (195). But I am less here interested in the "tropes of Italy" that proliferate, as Gilbert nicely remarks, "like flowers in Fiesole," than in Corinne's gesture of identification with Niobe (she has a copy of the statue in her gallery in Rome). Here when she contrasts the statues of Niobe and Alexander, Corinne distinguishes Alexander's indignation at not having conquered nature, a male posture of heroism, from

Niobe's specifically female, maternal anguish (18:4:368/518). Niobe, then, figures Corinne *as* Italy through loss and fatality; as a punished maternity.

21. In an illuminating analysis of the "consequences of maternal absence and paternal alliance" in the novels of nineteenth-century women writers, Marianne Hirsch in "Female Family Romances" argues: "Predictably, perhaps, the woman writer does not simply hand her heroine from mother to father; she attempts to compensate for the loss of the mother by replacing the father with another man who would offer an alternative to patriarchal power and dominance. The female fantasy which emerges from this will to difference can perhaps be understood in Adrienne Rich's terms as the fantasy of 'the-man-who-would-understand,' the man who, unlike the father, would combine maternal nurturance with paternal power. In this transformation of the marriage plot, the husband takes the form of a 'brother' who can be nurturing even as he provides access to the issues of legitimacy and authority central to plotting. Most importantly, perhaps, he can protect the heroine from becoming a mother and thereby he can help her, in spite of the closure of marriage, to remain a subject, not to disappear from plot as the object of her child's fantasy" (40).

On the maternal man, another twentieth-century fantasy, Cixous's in *La Venue à l'écriture:* "If everything is metaphor, nothing is metaphor. A man is your mother. If he is your mother, is he a man? Ask yourself instead: is there a man who could be my mother? Is a maternal man a woman?" (55).

22. This is exactly the eighteenth-century language Staël herself uses in *De l'influence des passions* (1798) to describe the unequal relations between the sexes and the double standard that fails to take the measure of violence to women. In the earlier writing Staël's discourse is unambiguous in its feminist analysis: "reputation, honor, esteem, all depend on the conduct women have displayed in that respect; whereas according to the public opinion of an unjust world, the laws of morality itself seem suspended in the case of relations between men and women; men can have an honorable reputation and yet have caused women the most atrocious pain that the strength of human emotion can produce in another soul" (170).

23. Gutwirth writes: "*We* [as readers] are invited to rebel against what has crushed Corinne: the terror of a woman's partner before the idea of her superiority" (256).

24. This scene takes place after a viewing of two paintings that "represent" Corinne and her sister in the novel's imaginary. In that discussion, the novel's discourse on the paintings, like the narrative that generates it (but what here is cause, what effect?) requires splitting woman in two. Oswald on his second Italian tour (this time wife in tow) contemplates in sequence, but comparatively, the Madonna and the Sibyl, the angelic mother and child, and the woman as oracle, genius, talent (19:7:400/562). The Sibyl is not so much described for the reader (like the Madonna's veiled gaze, she is pure enigma) but prejudged: her time has passed—"her genius, her talent are all finished now." Gutwirth, who has a developed analysis of the paintings, sees the representation of the sisters as an "internal schism, aspects of a woman's nature seen as a diptych, the divided parts of what ought to be a unity" (241). I think I would want to push a little further to suggest that if the division between the women records the split in Oswald's desire (the mother and the "harlot" in Freud's scenario), it more importantly represents the permanent fractures

in Corinne's singular economy, an economy of desire that seeks to connect public and private, Italy and England.

25. According to Simone Balayé, "Juliette [as a name] refers equally to Shakespeare's heroine as to the first name of Mme Récamier" (21) (Juliette Récamier was a very close friend of Staël's). The child's name thus remains equally attached to public performance and legendary beauty.

26. As if the representation of separation as death were not sufficiently coded, at the end of the scene in her gallery in Tivoli, Corinne tells Oswald that her ashes will be returned to her garden and instructs him (as in the scene at the Pantheon which constitutes him as the male mourner) to return there after her death.

27. Staël wrongly but interestingly places Dido and Aeneas in the Elysian Fields. They in fact meet in the Field of Mourning which is home to those who died of grief. Would this suggest that for Staël's imagination of the couple, the only place to be happy—i.e., the Elysian Fields—necessarily is a scene of death? Like the utopian pavilion in Sand's *Valentine?*

28. If Sand in *Valentine* rewrites the maternal bypass leaving the little girl who is not the heroine's daughter as a liminal figure in a graveyard of the past, Staël here rewrites the end of *The New Eloise* in which Julie's niece Henriette startles the assembled company by her physical and moral resemblance to the dead woman. I am indebted to Joan DeJean's analysis of the intertext and of Staël's novel as a critical gloss on Rousseau's patriarchal tale ("Staël's *Corinne:* The Novel's Other Dilemma"). I return to this issue in "Writing from the Pavilion."

29. Madelyn Gutwirth offers a sharp reading of Moers's position in "*Corinne,* or the Appropriation of Allegory," a paper presented at the Berkshire Conference, Smith College, 1985. Gutwirth comments: "But what Moers does not seem to recognize is that the novel is claiming the 'defense of spiritual genius and intellectual freedom' as *woman's work*" (ms; emphasis added).

30. On the tension between public and private that structures a woman's "coming to writing" in France, see "Writing Fictions."

31. For a powerful discussion of the ways in which in "Renaissance gender ideology, fame was not *for* women," see Ann Rosalind Jones's "Surprising Fame: Renaissance Gender Ideology and Women's Lyric" (74). Her analysis of prohibitions against fame for women in early modern Europe remains oddly pertinent for early nineteenth-century France—under Napoleon.

32. I am taking off from Joan DeJean's analysis of the suppression of authorial signature as a way of maintaining authority for the text ("Lafayette's Ellipses," 899–900). DeJean, however (see below), does not read the return to the written (that I take as the valorization of signature in Staël's novel) as empowering.

33. Like DeJean, Peterson sees the end of the oral as a defeat for Corinne and for the feminine. "After all, Corinne's claim to fame is the uniqueness of her performance," and "her oral improvisations, by nature flexible, unfixed, impermanent, are for the most part lost to posterity" (59).

34. It is not absolutely clear to me what Sand made of her illustrious precursor. In the introduction to Sand's *Lettres d'un voyageur*, Georges Lubin comments on the "rather curious coincidence" that Staël had written a story Sand had to know, "Mirza ou Lettres d'un voyageur" that was collected in a volume along with *Réflexions sur le suicide*, a work of Staël's that greatly

interested Sand (2:635). We find a few remarks on Staël, in addition to confirmation that *Corinne* was one of the books in her girlhood library (2:1471). In a discussion of *Réflexions,* Sand writes, "I read [this work] out of curiosity, wanting to see how this man/woman understood life" (2:752). The expression "man/woman" so often used to account for Sand's own "difference" from and superiority to other women strikes me as a crucial piece in Sand's sense of Staël's accomplishment and her relation to it. (For an account of the history of Staël's literary reputation as an obsession with Staël's "virility," see Noreen J. Swallow's "The Weapon of Personality: A Review of Sexist Criticism of Mme de Staël, 1785–1975.") In that same letter (4), Sand notes her agreement with Staël's reading of Julie's deathbed letter in *The New Eloise* as the text through which Julie "once again becomes dear to the reader," describing Staël affectionately here in these terms: "logical, argumentative [*raisonneuse*], useful" (2:756) (these are very much the terms in which Saint-Preux in the novel refers to Julie). Finally, on the pleasures of reading and losing track of time: "Happy times! oh my Black Valley! oh *Corinne!* oh Bernardin de Saint-Pierre! . . ." (2:826).

35. On the role of gesture in melodrama see Peter Brooks's chapter "The Text of Muteness," in *The Melodramatic Imagination.*

36. I had wanted to use Wittig's phrase "the mark of gender" as a shorthand to suggest the gender of the narrator as a woman. I remain quite seduced by Peterson's discussion of *her* role in the novel, her *discours* as the ultimate female genius (60–61). When I gave part of this chapter as a lecture at Duke (Spring 1987), Wittig, who was in the audience, said that she regretted my gendering of the narrator, feeling that as a space of language narration should be imagined as neutral. It seems to me finally that what we have in Staël's novel is a *feminist* narrative voice. The question then becomes whether it is more useful to see feminist voice as an effect of language or of gender.

# [ 8 ]

# Writing from the Pavilion: George Sand and the Novel of Female Pastoral

*The first version of this essay, "Writing (from) the Feminine: George Sand and the Novel of Female Pastoral," was written for the 1981 meetings of the English Institute at Cambridge. Patricia Spacks invited me to participate in a session entitled "The Representation of Women in Fiction," a panel that included Susan Gubar and Elizabeth Ermath. This was the first program specifically devoted to feminist criticism, which if not an agenda, at least established a not entirely innocuous focus for the audience of this event which brought with it a certain collectively gendered history (on this see Carolyn Heilbrun's introduction to the volume of papers that emerged from the meetings). As it turned out all three papers dealt with the novel, two with the nineteenth century, two with women's writing.*

*My decision to present work on Sand, like the decision in "Arachnologies" to "overread" a Sand novel as an exemplary instance of women's writing, was to some extent a strategic one responsive to the contexts of this event. I was, after all, someone "in French" speaking at the English Institute. In choosing Sand, I felt I was referring to a name that would be recognized by an audience of people "in English," and even better, the name of an author people might feel they ought to have read (in what I take to have been a similar move, Leo Bersani had spoken the previous year on Sade). At the same time, Sand provided me with an unobscure feminist reference (even though the nature of Sand's feminism is in fact the subject of some debate). Sand also offered the advantage of being a nineteenth-century writer who was read by many well-known writers, male and female, and influential in their development. Sand's canonically intertextual relations, which made her, I thought, of some interest to a non-French, nonfeminist audience, of course also* coincided with my own project to elaborate the weave of a feminist writing tradition.

The essay on Valentine *represented my first efforts to block out the pieces of a feminist literary history of novels that "continued"* The Princess of Clèves. *I began with the question of what had been figured in the space of the precursor's pavilion, how this fragile room of one's own came to impede the relentless deployment of patriarchal plot, or at least to postpone its most familiar operations and to house provisionally another scene of desire. Unlike the seventeenth-century text, however, the nineteenth-century novel also stages the wish to make that space a scene of production. Here I call this particular intersection of literary and social modalities female pastoral. Female pastoral as a critique of plot thus becomes a variant of feminist utopianism. By this I mean an attempt to relocate woman's story outside the conventions of linear narrative and by that move, paradoxically, to suggest the tensions of history: a resistance through which a woman would not merely be, but do (this is also Sand's attempt to articulate the complex relations between gender and class identities). In that sense,* Valentine, *like the* Peruvian Letters, Corinne, *and* The Vagabond, *participates in the "poetics of critique" that characterizes feminist writing.*

*Nonetheless, when I look now at the chapters of the readings in this section on Graffigny, Staël, and Colette that I wrote three years after the Sand, it is clear that in several important ways Sand is "different" and that the shape and style of the chapter on* Valentine *reflect another emphasis. Sand's novel does not in the turns of its plot (especially in the lines of closure) conform to the critical narrative of the "coming to writing" of the feminist author that I see as crucial to the French tradition. At the same time, however, it seems to me that in the narrative of Sand's coming to writing* Valentine *has its place. By reading the fiction intratextually with the autobiography, as I suggest in "Writing Fictions," it becomes possible to see the ways in which* Valentine's self-conscious positioning as an artist in the pavilion and the coding of the pavilion as a scene of work are also figurations of Sand's early struggle. *In the change in titles from "Writing (from) the Feminine" to "Writing from the Pavilion," I am marking a shift in emphasis from the gender of authorship as an inflection of authority to the scene of writing; a scene for women writers necessarily located in an intimate relation to patriarchy's discursive domains, but also at a distance, at a remove from the powers of its gaze.*

*In the margins, then, of my central argument, I want to suggest
that* Valentine *represents emblematically the story of Sand's coming to writing in Paris (the actual writing at Nohant notwithstanding). This movement into authorship that we read in the autobiography does not name itself in fiction, but it is decipherable to
us as readers in the appropriation of pastoral.*

Valentine *is the second of the novels signed by George Sand
alone under the pseudonym G. Sand that was to assure her livelihood and eventually her place in literary history. Between
the overnight success of* Indiana *(May 1832) and the violent critical response occasioned by the publication of* Lélia *(July 1833),*
Valentine *(November 1832) marks a kind of pause or space of interrogation in Sand's elaboration of an identity as a writer and a
public figure: "I would like to have lived in obscurity," she writes
in her autobiography, "and since, from the publication of* Indiana
*until that of* Valentine *I had succeeded in remaining sufficiently
incognito for the newspapers always to refer to me as* monsieur,
*I flattered myself that this little success wouldn't change my se-
dentary habits and an intimate circle composed of people as unknown as myself." By the time* Lélia *was published, Sand's "retreat" and "solitude" (Histoire de ma vie, 2:182) were lost, as was
the fantasized protection of an ambiguously virile identity.*

*We might conclude for now that part of Sand's difference from
the women writers I discuss in this book, but also many of
the writers I would have liked to take up — Villedieu, Tencin,
Riccoboni, Charrière, Claire de Duras — who came to writing "as
women" before Sand and who constitute her pre-texts, is bound
up in the fantasy embodied in the signature G. Sand: a woman
writer who like Lafayette did not want to be read "as a woman,"
but who also dreamt of writing "as a man."*[1]

They were all about love, lovers, sweethearts, persecuted ladies fainting in lonely pavilions, postilions killed at every relay, horses ridden to death on every page, sombre forests, heart-
aches, vows, sobs, tears and kisses, little boatrides in the
moonlight, nightingales in shady groves, gentlemen as brave
as lions, gentle as lambs, virtuous as no one ever was, always
well-dressed, and weeping like fountains.

Flaubert, *Madame Bovary*

*Valentine* opens, as do many French nineteenth-century novels, with the fiction of a traveler arriving from Paris who, as a stand-in for the reader, is invited to ponder the semiotics of a provincial topography. But the intertextual power of that ironizing convention fades after this inaugural move, for the fictional world of the Black Valley, unlike Stendhal's Verrières or Balzac's Saumur, is located not under the sign of history and its agitations but under that of pastoral—"the absolute repose of . . . unknown regions" (1:3/2).[2] "Luxury has not found its way thither, nor the arts, nor the mania for scientific investigation, nor the hundred-armed monster called industry. Revolutions are hardly perceptible there. . . . The principal virtue of that race of tillers of the soil is heedlessness in the matter of antiquities" (1:4/2). And yet, despite the narrator's insistence upon a profound, peasant indifference to revolution and historical event, the story of the novel is not located in a timeless moment. This "delicious pastoral scene" [*nature suave et pastorale*] (1:3/1) is grounded precisely in the history of a domain sold "as national property during the Revolution, and redeemed under the Empire" (9:73/78). Indeed, the *before* of the novel is constructed by a marriage uniting "ancient names"—Raimbault—with "newly made fortunes" (9:74/79), and its *after* is posited on a chiastic reinscription of that same formula: "It was worth but little to be a landowner if one were not a noble" (39:335/361). Nor can the lovers whose destiny is plotted in the novel properly be identified outside this space in time: Valentine is the rightful heiress of the Château de Raimbault; Bénédict, who becomes her lover in the novel, is a peasant whose uncle leases the farm Grangeneuve from the aristocratic owners of the château.

I want to consider here the specific ways in which these places, the château and the farm, are (a) originally opposed as materially and symbolically discrete spaces; (b) subsequently mediated by an architectural construction—a third real and fantasmatic place— a pavilion; and (c) finally collapsed into a single signifying space, the château. At the same time, because the pavilion in *Valentine*, as a place which is meant to fix desire outside possession, penultimately locates the plot of Sand's novel of adultery as a fiction of female sublimation, we will want to see to what extent this particular topographical organization of an erotics can tell us something not only about the representation of female pleasure in the French novel but also about how to read *what else* that representation figures. What might women want beyond what can be figured as desire? What story cannot be told? If, for example, the pavilion in *Valentine* must be read intertextually with the pavilion in *The Princess of Clèves*—by way of a detour through Julie's garden in Rousseau's *The New Eloise*—what can these privileged places tell us about reading for female plot?

By female plot I mean quite simply that organization of narrative event which delimits a heroine's psychological, moral, and social development within a sexual fate (a fate I linked in "Emphasis Added" to maxims about the inevitable "truths" of heterosexuality). Female plot thus is both what the culture has always already inscribed for woman and its reinscription in the linear time of fiction. It is generally mapped by the heroine's engagement with the codes of the dominant ideology, her obligatory insertion within the institutions which in society and in novels name her—marriage, for example. These are the bare bones of a narratology that is most commonly plotted in scenarios of courtship leading (at least in theory) to marriage in the eighteenth-century novel, and stories of marriage gone wrong in the nineteenth. It comes to us, of course, from male as well as from female imaginations—*Pamela,* say, or *Madame Bovary.* But female-authored literature generally questions the costs and overdetermination of this particular narrative economy with an insistence such that the fictions engendered provide an internal, dissenting commentary on female plot itself. They thereby solicit a reading that takes into account the ideology at work in this map of female experience. (This is also what I describe throughout the book as the grounds of "female signature.")

*Valentine* begins with a double-courtship plot. Under the heterogenous and comedic emblem of a *fête champêtre,* two entirely appropriate marriages are announced. Both assure homogeneity and the proper transmission of property. Valentine, whose dowry includes both the Château de Raimbault and eventually the farm at Grangeneuve, is betrothed to a count. Bénédict is engaged to marry the heiress to the farm. Betrothed to others, Valentine and Bénédict meet at the ball on the first of May. The ritual of the local dance—the *bourrée*—requires and authorizes Bénédict to kiss his partner Valentine under public scrutiny. But despite the blushing and laughter that punctuate the event, what matters in this scene is not so much the predictable erotics of social difference as an insistence on the heroine's refusal of the erotic plot: "Valentine did not dream of passion. . . . She promised herself that she would steer clear of those ardent fantasies which made other women miserable before her eyes." More like the Princess of Clèves on the eve of her marriage, Valentine fully embraces that woman's destiny "which society imposed upon her like a duty." Although Valentine does not perceive this "reserve" "as a law," the law comes nevertheless to consolidate her identity within its discourse (5:41/42).

In the weeks before the marriages, however, Valentine and Bénédict, while playing innocent games on the banks of the river, become subject to the laws of female plot. Valentine gazes at Bénédict gazing with rapt admiration at her image in the water: "Absorbed herself in a reverie which had no definite subject she yielded to that hazardous curiosity which analyzes and compares. She discovered that there was a vast difference between Bénédict and Monsieur de Lansac. . . . Bénédict at that moment was a man: a man of the fields and a man of nature" (13:111/118). But the discovery through the lure of the male gaze of that difference—the awakening, essentially, to desire as a differentiation *within* what was all the same—does not lead Valentine directly to a heroine's fiction. Rather, in what will become a characteristic gesture of deferral, Valentine *postpones* the consequences of her new knowledge. Thus, though in the name of true love Bénédict will break his engagement to the farmer's daughter, at the end of the second part of this novel in four parts two marriages are nevertheless celebrated. Valentine marries the count of Lansac; Bénédict's former betrothed, Athénaïs, despite her very real disappointment, weds another suitor from the village. When the peasant wedding party comes to the grounds of the château for a joint celebration, the novel again flirts with the possibilities of a comedic equivalence between (the) brides. But the euphoric poetics of celebration cannot resist the dysphoric tension that underwrites the two contracts: the proper circulation of women breaks down, revealing the price—or the ideology—of that economy.[3]

Thus, between the public, verbal consecration of the marriages and the private ritual of the wedding night, Sand opens a gap by revising the expected chronotope,[4] and the novel breaks with the familiar conventions of representation. Pamela, for example, married in the morning, is still writing in her closet at eleven o'clock that night. She anxiously asks her husband for permission to continue for another quarter-hour. She writes, "two glasses of champaign, and, afterwards, a glass of sack . . . kindly forced upon [her]": "so sweetly terrible did he appear to my apprehensions"; and in her very last virginal inscription to her parents, trusting herself to God, she invokes "this happy, yet awful moment" (371–

72). The denouement is announced in the next entry, dated the following evening: "O how this dear excellent man indulges me in every thing!" Pamela's rhetoric of elision comes to undo the oxymorons of her feminine anguish (thus giving rise to the maxim, which Richardson later attempted to refute, that a reformed rake makes the best husband—if his wife, of course, like Pamela, vows to "obey . . . in every thing").

If we look in the French nineteenth-century novel for an intertext to this rhetoric of elision which figures respect for the sacred unsaid of marriage, we find this silence in *Madame Bovary:*

> Charles, who was anything but quick-witted, did not shine at the wedding. He answered feebly to the puns, *doubles entendres,* compliments and the customary pleasantries that were dutifully aimed at him as soon as the soup appeared.
>
> The next day, on the other hand, he seemed another man. It was he who might rather have been taken for the virgin of the evening before, whilst she gave no sign that revealed anything. The shrewdest did not know what to make of it, and they looked at her when she passed near them with an unbounded concentration of mind. But Charles concealed nothing. He called her "my wife," addressed her by the familiar "tu," asked for her of everyone, looked for her everywhere. . . . (21)

Although here in the elision that takes us from the soup course to the morning after, Flaubert on the whole respects what I take to be an unwritten law of the dominant narratology until the twentieth century (where it reverses itself, at least in popular fiction), that the sacred penetration remains sacred by virtue of its ineffability, he also unsettles it slightly by reversing the gender of the performers: the transformation implicit in penetration is incarnated in the male; Charles, deflowered, as it were, becomes a new man. Emma, however, remains *no less woman* in that unknowable. Emma's "self-control" lets nothing show. By showing nothing, Flaubert leaves the enigma intact. Thus it is curious to note that in this novel—and in Emma's body—where the institution of marriage is relentlessly desacralized to the point where even adultery can't save it, this founding physical moment of the social contract which makes two people "man and wife" is left veiled. We might usefully recall here Terry Eagleton's remark that "ideology is not simply a matter of plentiude but also of elision" (153–54).

What, then, does Sand do with the representation of an event that even in Flaubert turns away from representation? To begin with, the novel insists that we witness the acts of the night through the perspective of a male gaze. In Sand's female plot, the heroine, having been allowed to postpone her husband's enjoyment of the first night, spends it "a lifeless statue" (22:191/205), drugged with opium according to her wishes. She is not, however, alone. Bénédict has managed to lock himself into the room with his beloved in order to deliver her, as he puts it, from "this legitimate degradation . . . the vilest degradation inflicted on woman . . . rape" (22:184/198). The wedding night begins with Bénédict's fascinated contemplation of Valentine, and in this sense seems simply to reinscribe the specular economy of desire whose power we saw in the mirroring that took place on the banks of the river. There Bénédict had earlier "adored [Valentine's] reflection in the water" [*son image répétée dans l'eau*] (23:193/208). Though now in the absence of witnesses the gaze could with impunity become an act of carnal knowledge, the modality of desire valorized in this scene will be that of a renewed deferral.

This is the time of stasis (of ecstasy); the moment of sublimated perfection toward which the novel strains and which necessarily it never maintains: "Bénédict imagined that the night would never end, that Valentine would never wake, and that he would live out his eternity of happiness in that room" (23:194/209). This longing for a state of bliss that would defy change and therefore bypass all negotiations with reality is a model typically associated with the heroine for whom happily-ever-after has no form, no shape in time, only an intensity of affect. We could then ask whether by this inversion—like the one undergone by Charles—Sand renews the cliché in a feminist script.

Literarily the case is complicated, for this lover's discourse has indeed been written from the masculine. By Rousseau, for example. And for the reader familiar with *The New Eloise* (as the French nineteenth-century reader would have been), it is difficult to enter Sand's staging of hysterical adoration without feeling interference from the Rousseauist intertext.[5]

Saint-Preux, before Bénédict, writes his fetishistic pleasure from a place whose doors open and close within patriarchal authority. "Writing to the moment," from within Julie's closet, he records and, as he says, "moderates his ecstasy by describing it." As he awaits Julie's arrival in the flesh (a reunion planned under the sign of danger, the death that might result from the legitimate double penetration of the father from his entrance into the room and the thrust of his sword), Saint-Preux both anticipates the fulfillment of his desires and fulfills them in anticipation. For the privilege of living out an hour—the hour of possession—he willingly "gives up the rest of his life to nature's severity." Now the hour of possession, unlike the hour of anticipation, necessarily can be accounted for only after the fact. (Even Valmont must take a break from writing to perform with the "woman as desk.")[6] And in the aftermath, a reevaluation of pleasure takes place. Although Saint-Preux, from whose perspective "that inconceivable night" is recounted, begins the next letter in the correspondence with an insistence on the plenitude of the experience—"Oh let us die, my sweet friend! Let us die, beloved of my heart! What shall we do henceforward with an insipid youth now that we have exhausted all of its delights?"—when he reviews the events of the night, he revises their hierarchy of pleasure. Indeed, what he wants to preserve, what he wants *returned* to him after the fact (of consummation), is what Julie had earlier claimed in *her* economy to be superior to possession: "Come to swear, even in the midst of pleasures, that from the union of hearts they draw their greatest charm." Saint-Preux now accedes to her language, a discourse of desire which *dematerializes* possession: "Give me back that intimate union of souls you had told me of and which you have made me enjoy so well [*si bien goûter*]." By revising in this sense, Saint-Preux condemns his previous (masculinist) difference from Julie—"I wish to enjoy [*jouir*] and you wish to love; I have ecstasies and you have passions"—and laments his distance from the other's self-sufficiency: "that charming state which is enough in itself!" "The charm of possession," Saint-Preux now writes, "was in the soul, no longer momentary but eternal." The key to the revalorized temporality thus is a time of feminized permanence that preserves pleasure from history: "il durait toujours."

But how to fix *jouissance*? How to make the fleeting monumental? Saint-Preux selects the hour *after* possession as the privileged moment: "It is of all the hours of my life the one which is most dear to me, and the only one I should have wished to prolong eternally." This crucial lesson was acquired, however, through the fullness of temporal possession. An authorial footnote—glossing the word *eternally*—makes the point: "Too compliant woman, do you wish to know if you are loved? Examine your lover as he leaves your arms. Oh love! If I miss the age at which you are enjoyed [*goûter*] it is not for the hour of possession: it is for the hour which follows it."

This passage permits us, I think, to differentiate among three chronotopic modes of desire in a sexual and textual economy: masculinist (in its extreme, libertine) discourse, which prizes the time of possession (and possession as penetration); feminizing discourse, which seeks a loving negotiation with the feminine (Saint-Preux enamored in the hour after; ultimately, Roland Barthes); and finally a feminist discourse which in these novels indirectly or directly valorizes the hour that precedes and essentially *precludes* possession (though not enjoyment, which then becomes *jouissance* minus penetration). This last figure is the timing of desire achieved in *The Princess of Clèves* and ultimately muffed in *Valentine*.

In Valentine's chamber, Bénédict contemplates his sleeping beauty, who suddenly stirring from a euphoric, opium-induced dream and "hovering between reality and illusion . . . innocently revealed all her secrets to him" (23:195/210). Her secret is a variant of Julie's fantasy before "that inconceivable night": pursued by her husband, "with drawn sword, she threw herself on Bénédict's breast and exclaimed as she put her arms about his neck: 'Let us both die!'" Bénédict, like Saint-Preux, welcomes such a death but inserts a condition: "Be mine and let us die!" But Valentine returns to her dreams, and Bénédict struggles against his desire to make Valentine his: "He raised her thick tresses and filled his mouth with them to prevent himself from crying out; he wept with love and frenzy. At last in a moment of indescribable anguish, he bit the round, white shoulder which she uncovered before him" (23:196/211). This last has the effect of arousing Valentine: she deliriously imagines that Bénédict is her husband and welcomes him as such to her bed. The wedding night in its representation thus becomes the scene of its own subversion through the fantasized substitution of the violation for the law, the forbidden for the contractual. Bénédict (whose fantasy this also is) in response "threw himself upon her in desperation and, on the point of yielding to the violence of agonizing desires, . . . uttered nervous, heart rending cries" (23:197/212). The *literal* violation of the marriage bed, however, is here postponed a *second* time—neither the husband nor the lover—by a key turning in the lock and an opening of the door.

Returned to his senses, so to speak, Bénédict determines to leave and kill himself, but not before supplying a text of his passage in a letter to Valentine. He explains the contradiction of her position after this exceptional wedding night: on the one hand, she is still, he assures her, "pure and unprofaned": on the other, and not only by virtue of his timing, Valentine is "more entirely in his power than [she] ever will be in [her] husband's." Bénédict has taken her virginity symbolically; he has glued his lips to the "unsubstantial garment which hardly covers [her]" and thus *possessed her in his thoughts*" (23:199–200/214; emphasis added). Thus in a way he has had what he wanted, but not quite. In her dreams, Valentine has only almost returned his caresses (23:199/214).[7] The novel will struggle with the status of this *almost*—the story of Bénédict's "lack" and Valentine's submerged desire—until the plot finds the terms of its closure.[8] In these romantic representations of a contradictory feminine "desire to be blindly ravished, to melt, and the desire to be spiritually adored, saved from the humiliation of dependence and sexual passivity through the agency of a protective male who will somehow make reparation to the woman he loves for her powerlessness" (Snitow, 261), Sand, we might say, is writing nineteenth-century mass-market romance.

Let us return to our earlier question, what does Sand bring to the traditional representations of the wedding night? Most simply, she insists that marriage is always irreducibly referential for women.[9] "Woman," for the feminist writer is more than a site for elaborating the signifiers of Otherness; woman's body, as I argue in the "Text's Heroine," is also a grounded space of material implications. When Sand fleshes out the elision that masks and respects the ineffability of the marriage transaction, she literalizes the phantasmagoria of penetration.[10]

At this point in Sand's novel, however, the rights of possession and their place in a narrative economy remain unchallenged. For Bénédict, we have just seen, believes that Valentine *belongs to him;* and at the same time according to the law, the husband through *his* possession is nonetheless entitled to the orderly transfer of property to his name.[11] What thus remains subject to resolution and remains so until the quirky twists of Sand's ending is the matter of inheritance. It is in this displacement *within* marriage, this deferral which beyond the inscription of a nonconsummated union (a topos of feminist protest in itself) threatens the simplicities of legitimate descent—that a rewriting of the marriage plot in the novel should be located.

This emphasis in Sand's novel upon the material grounds of marriage takes the form of what we might call deictic elision: a "supplied," or supplemented ellipsis which adds emphasis to the plenitude of its own unsaid with such insistence that ellipsis turns to periphrasis.[12] A more familiar example of this figure might be the remarkable wedding night scene in *Daniel Deronda:* Gwendolen Grandcourt's fit of "hysterical violence" on the threshold of her wifely career. Ellen Moers comments on the metaphorical power of the diamonds that have come to commemorate this liminal moment: "There is . . . nothing that could remotely be called pornographic in George Eliot's treatment of Gwendolen's deflowering by her husband . . .; the matter is not even mentioned, directly. But indirectly, by means of the jewel case . . . Eliot conveys all that need be told about Gwendolen's hysterical, virginal frigidity; about Grandcourt's sadistic tastes; and about, in addition, mercenary marriages, wedding night customs, and sexual hypocrisy" (253) in the nineteenth-century thinking about women.

The wedding night (and its ornaments) is of course not the only locus for the woman novelist's protest against the hegemony of male desire supported by the law. I want to turn now to a topical attempt to erect an alternative to the house of marriage and its grounds in fiction: a literal space that would in its own metaphors of representation exist outside the law and outside history, Valentine's pavilion.

When the count leaves the château for his embassy appointment in Russia, Valentine becomes, we are told, the "sovereign mistress of her château of Raimbault" (26:222/240). This ostensible freedom and authority, however, are in fact restricted in several important ways, since the objects of her affection—Bénédict and Valentine's sister Louise—literally are *out of place* in the château. Louise, the mother of an illegitimate fifteen-year-old adolescent boy named Valentin, who has been banished from the family grounds as a consequence of *her* female plot, refuses to enter the château as an intruder bearing her father's name—which is also to say her own. In response, Valentine takes over the pavilion in the park—originally designed to serve as a guesthouse (indeed Lansac had his room there during the engagement period)—and converts it into a space in theory subject to her authority alone.[13] She brings her books and easel to the pavilion, which is thus legitimized as a "sort of study" (26:223/241). A piano soon follows. Louise brings Bénédict to the pavilion in the evenings. (Louise has been nursing Bénédict—after his suicide attempt—in his hermitage, as it is called, his "hut in the ravine," situated in the space separating the farm from the Château de Raimbault). They make music: "During the summer evenings Valentine adopted the custom of having no light, so that Bénédict might not detect the violent emotion which often took possession of her" (27:231/249). Like the princess of Clèves before her, Valentine entertains the illusion that if her desire remains invisible, if her lover remains, precisely, in the dark as to the power of her feeling, the maxims of sexual plot can be eluded indefinitely. But the music melts the lovers, and once Bénédict sees her by her tears that Valentine is "yielding to one of the most irresistible fascinations that ever woman faced" (27:232/250), the next step becomes inevitable. The danger of the relation, already in place, plays itself out in the familiar topographical codes of moral disaster inherited from eighteenth-century fiction: "Valentine felt that she was on the brink of the abyss into which her sister had fallen" (28:239/257).

At this point in the narrative, as the novel begins to move toward closure, the plot seems to find its moral and psychological center. In much the way that Julie's garden, Elysium, can be read as the emblem of virtue in *The New Eloise,* Valentine's pavilion becomes the novel's repository of value. As an effect of its presence, the relations among the characters are reorganized spatially in relation first to the pavilion and second to Bénédict's cottage. Symbolically, economically, and in the play of signifiers, the cottage should be opposed to the château *(chaumière/château).* But that polarization, like the original one opposing the farm to the château, is mediated and displaced by the pavilion. Though the pavilion claims for itself an identity which supersedes origins and social difference, because it is in fact an aristocratic space, its claims are always vulnerable to the hegemony of the château:

> Valentine caused a fence to be built around that part of the park where the pavilion stood. That little reservation was very thickly planted and very dark. On its borders they planted clumps of climbing plants, ramparts of wild vine and birthwort, and hedges of young cypresses of the sort that are trimmed like a curtain and form a barrier impenetrable to the eye. Amid all this verdure, and behind those trustworthy barriers of shade, the pavilion stood in a delightful situation, near a spring, from which a bubbling stream escaped among the rocks, maintaining an incessant cool murmur about that mysterious and dreamy retreat. . . .
>
> Thus the pavilion was a place of rest and pleasure to all at the close of day. Valentine admitted no profane interloper to the sanctuary, and allowed no communication with the people

of the château. Catherine alone was allowed to enter, to take care of the place. It was Valentine's Elysium, the world of her poetic fancy, her golden life. At the château all was ennui, slavery, depression; her invalid grandmother, unwelcome visitors, painful reflections, and her oratory with its remorse-laden atmosphere; at the pavilion, happiness, friends, pleasant reveries, fears forgotten, and the pure delights of a chaste love. It was like an enchanted island in the midst of real life, like an oasis in the desert (29:249–52/268–71).

The repetitions that mark the end of the description—"like an enchanted island in the midst of real life, like an oasis in the desert"—underline by their metaphorics the contiguity of the two spaces. The pavilion, moreover, is totally dependent upon the financial viability of the château for its right to exist as property—an exclusive property—and this dependence is crucial to the status of the fantasy. But if like the pavilion in Lafayette's novel and the garden in Rousseau's, Valentine's pavilion is the fantasized space of an u-topic retreat within privilege, it is also, in its desire for a sublimated ideal, opposed to the license of privilege and the "law of conventionalities and prejudices" (29:249/268). This desire to figure a place that would guarantee happiness against the penetration of history, the attempt to withdraw from the sphere of the public gaze, can also be read as a variant of the topographical model Tony Tanner has described as housing the play of desire in the novel of adultery: the polarization of fictional places that maps the split occasioned by the irruption of forbidden desires.

The attempt to exclude the social in the name of the natural (or rather the natural supervised by virtue) is of course at work in the eighteenth-century intertext. And the reader of *The New Eloise* will not wonder long whether Sand's rewriting will also reinscribe the earlier failure to sustain what Tanner calls a "genuine outside" (23). For if in antiquity the Elysian fields derive their tranquil beauty from their intimate relation to death, this is no less true of Rousseau's self-conscious quotation. Julie explains to Saint-Preux: "In truth, my friend . . . days spent this way suggest the happiness of the next life, and it is not without reason that in thinking of it I have given the name Elysium to this place."[14] The golden life at Valentine's pavilion lasts, we are told, for fifteen months: "Fifteen months of tranquility and happiness in the lives of five persons is almost supernatural. Yet so it was" (30:254/274).

The silence that surrounds these remarkable months not only points to the unsaid of a woman's pleasure that may or may not take place in the blanks; it codes the paradox of a female pastoral where women's verbs—predicates of doing—are disguised as states of *being,* the better to pass unnoticed. Indeed, Sand's transformation of an essentially frivolous place (in eighteenth-century France this sort of construction was called a *folie*) into a scene of artistic and intellectual production is the crucial piece to my reading of the pavilion as a feminist appropriation of the pastoral matrix. Thus, Valentine, who has chosen to pursue painting over music— her "natural" vocation, but one that "puts a woman too much in evidence" (6:50/52)—imagines that this talent will help her to "support herself in society" if one day her patrimony again becomes state property. Located in the pavilion of an asocial (artistic) productivity that would bring an active identity and autonomy to woman in society, this fantasy, I think, is no less the anguished alibi of the woman who would justify her passage to writing.[15]

Can the fable survive its insertion within the structure of the novel? Bénédict and Valentine seem to wish to remain outside literature, through they are perpetually cast into the standard plots of sexual destiny. To Bénédict, who like Saint-Preux before him claims to prefer virtue to beauty, mind to body, Valentine replies that she, like Julie, has learned through his teaching that the "nonmaterial alliance" they have formed is "preferable to all earthly ties" (30:258/278). Can one contract a nonmaterial alliance [*une alliance immatérielle?*] While an "alliance" can be understood in nonmaterial terms (theologically, for example), the more common and more compelling sense of the word in this context is of course that of the social bonds relating families through marriage. And as Valentine should know but refuses to acknowledge, such an alliance, for example her own with Lansac, is nothing but material: grounded in the quantifiable, the concrete, the real.

The husband's unexpected return—he arrives to sell the very property that supports his wife's fantasy—brings Valentine abruptly up against the reality of her relation to Bénédict as well. After (blindly) signing papers that will dispossess her of all property and fortune, Valentine, on the eve of her husband's departure, determines to implore his assistance in her vain struggle to avoid the abyss she sees before her: "a sublime and romantic project," the narrator underlines, "which has tempted more than one wife at the moment of committing her first error" (33:281/305). Like the princess of Clèves before her, Valentine confesses: "There is still time to save me. Do not let me succumb to my destiny; rescue me from the seduction that environs me and presses me close. . . . I am a poor weak woman, left alone, abandoned by everybody; help me!" (34:289/312). Unlike the prince of Clèves, the count of Lansac remains unmoved by this archaic rhetoric of pathos, and he replies in the wordly language of circulation that condemned the princess within her fiction: "All this is sublime, my dear, but it is absolutely ludicrous. You are very wrong; take a friend's advice: a woman should never take her husband for her confessor; that is asking of him more virtue than is consistent with his profession" (34:291/314). With this failed repetition of heroic female plot, Sand's novel swerves away from the fierce sublimation of Lafayette's solution and moves toward a dysphoric closure.[16] Unlike the princess, Valentine, seduced by the discourse of a Rousseauist erotics, will finally succumb to a sexual fate. In the face of a Bénédict literally swooning from the struggle to repress his passionate nature, "Valentine, vanquished by pity, by love, and above all, by fear, did not again tear herself from his arms" (36:307/331). Thus, some two years after her marriage, and in the thirty-sixth chapter of thirty-nine, Valentine, who had sworn she would die "rather than belong to any man" (32:277/298), loses her virginity within the very walls of Raimbault, in the room said to be her own.

The timing and the language of the "fatal moment" (36:307/331) both score and underscore the Rousseauist intertext: Valentine's fall, her capitulation to the laws of "natural" desire, repeats Julie's virginal lapse, the filial transgression which in Rousseau's novel is repaired by a proper marriage docile to paternal authority. But unlike Rousseau, Sand writes the act of adultery only fantasized under the cover the incest in *Julie* into her plot. She thus takes her distance from Rousseau here—and by the same token from the erotics of the Lafayette text admired by Rousseau.[17] However deferred, her novel finally inscribes the rights of the body driven from its own fictions, from Elysium. But the gesture cannot rewrite its own consequences: what is the proper space for adulterous love?

No reader of nineteenth-century fiction would expect to see this union integrated legitimately within the novel. Nor is it. Valentine must leave the château, which has become the property of a usurer, and she takes refuge with the Lhéry family at the farm within whose walls the novel opened. With the evacuation of the primary signifiers of the spatial oppositions—the pavilion as the scene of chaste love outside time, the château as the incarnation of the historical confirmation of social difference—how is desire to be figured?

The husband dies, killed according to the hazards of his class, in a duel. And Bénédict renews his claim for pastoral union:

> Do you not remember that one day you regretted that you were not a farmer's daughter, that you could not escape the slavery of a life of opulence, to live like a simple village maiden beneath a thatched roof? Well, now your longing is gratified. You shall be *queen in the cottage* in the ravine; you shall raise your own flowers, and sleep without fear or anxiety on a peasant's breast. (38:327/353; emphasis added)

In this play with the codes of social difference—"queen in the cottage"—Bénédict seeks to will into existence through language the collapse of referential polarities that have structured the novel throughout. But the power of narrative overrides the iconography of his poetic representations.

Bénédict is killed by his old rival with the weapons of their class—by the thrust of a pitchfork—and dies on Valentine's breast. Valentine dies a week later. Bénédict's murderer dies exactly one year later, having drunkenly mistaken a river for a road. Athénaïs, the farmer's daughter to whom Bénédict originally was engaged, now widowed, through an inheritance buys the Château de Raimbault; her father exchanges his land for the remaining estates. And closure?

The final chapter of the novel—two pages that serve as an epilogue to the flurry of events—opens with the return to the Black Valley (from Paris) of Louise and her son Valentin, who has become, with the passage of time, a "man"—and a doctor. They are housed by the Lhérys in the pavilion, returned to its original function as a guesthouse. It was "a sad consolation for them," the narrator comments, "to live in the pavilion."[18] What is at stake in the melancholy of this penultimate destination must be understood, I think, in its relation to the tradition into which Sand inserts herself. To the extent that one can claim that the French novel after the *Princess of Clèves* always looks back nostalgically to the universe figured there as one which "reconciles fantasy with reality" for the last time, one can also argue that the dominant desire of that tradititon is for an aristocratic universe within which the only destabilizing difference is sexual (Rustin, 222).[19] That "reality" is a homogeneous aristocracy defined by wars with a national Other—like the Homeric universe; it is a "consoling" universe. By the 1750s the model of an "aristocratic Eden" has become an ironic point of reference for novelists, the golden age irrevocably past. Rousseau, in 1761, fantasized a modern rewriting, relocating Elysium in Switzerland. But the dream cannot resist the dysphoric encroachment of bourgeois reality.[20]

In the case of Sand after the Revolution, closure looks back out of time. The Raimbault name returns to the property. Valentin— returning without the suffixal *e* of the feminine to compensate nevertheless for the feminine loss of the inheritance—through a detour becomes the heir Valentine had always and earlier wished him to be.[21] And through the descendance of a second *mésalliance,* the second alliance of old names and new money (Valentin Raimbault and Athénaïs Blutty), a second Valentine continues in the *image* of the Other. In some sense the child legitimately inscribes the outlawed love of Bénédict and Valentine. She could thus be read as the sign of historical difference come to interrupt the pastoral continuity of the Black Valley. But little Valentine is not the direct issue of rebellion. She is, rather, its doubled displacement through docile reproduction. Therefore we must wonder whether the perpetuation of "the beloved name of Valentine" (39:336/363) is the mark of social transformation or the sign of circularity—Valentine/Valentin/Valentine—an empty repetition that might also be called a "defunct ideological sign, incapable of constituting an arena for the confrontation of living social inflections" (Voloshinov, 44), something like the fate of the feminist pavilion.

Sand's novel takes as the site of its closure the place marked off for death in the architecture of social life.[22] And the last sentence of the novel takes up again the perspective of the traveler with which it began: "The traveler, as he passes the village cemetery, frequently sees the lovely child playing at Louise's feet, and plucking the cowslips that grow on the double grave of Valentine and Bénédict" (39:336/363). Here the traveler observes a scene empty of any *local* meaning, for the flowers, which by their name—*primevère*—signal youth and renewal, growing as they do on a tombstone, overcode the already formulaic conjunction of life and death achieved by placing a beautiful, fair-haired child in a cemetery. The novel thus marks in its closing moves the shift of emphasis away from the natural setting of pastoral "onto the child" that Empson has located in the nineteenth century (254). But if this shift, like the emergence of the graveyard within the pastoral dominion—following the familiar iconography of the memento mori—

confirms in the end the staying power of the pastoral *code,* is there
a feminist inscription to be read there as well? It the little girl
Valentine the figure of liminal difference, of a rewriting to come?
Or does her presence at this site reinscribe the power of repetition?

If by not marrying the duke of Nemours, the princess of Clèves
forestalls what she feels to be a certain destiny of unhappiness, she
also forecloses another form of repetition. Unlike her mother—
who may have been in the world of the court the only woman to
have enjoyed the love of a husband and a lover without being found
out, but who nonetheless *like other women* has a child—the princess is a final daughter.[23] As such, she makes an end *in her person*
to the continuation of female plot. Whatever his admiration for
Lafayette, Rousseau after Lafayette returns to the reproduction of
daughters, and "continues" his Julie through her cousin Claire's
Henriette. Joan DeJean argues convincingly that "at the close of
*Corinne,* Staël evokes Rousseau's family novel, the most important
eighteenth-century forerunner of the nineteenth-century genealogical fictions that seek to confine woman to a subordinate role in
the time of generations." But in Staël's evocation of the male precursor, there is also, DeJean notes, "an act of revenge on the paternal literary order" (87). Corinne's text will be continued by
Juliette. In Sand's play of intertexts, we have to wonder which text
she revises. It is clear that the fate of the dead heroine's living
image is proposed as the figure to the answer, but it is equally
clear that the answer is withheld. After unveiling the feminine past,
the veil of narrative covers up the tropes of a feminine future.

It is not altogether surprising that Sand proposes no clues to
the story to come, no more than Eliot, say, writes a future for
Gwendolen Grandcourt on the verge of a new life at the end of
*Daniel Deronda.* Sand writes in 1842 in preface to a new edition
of her first novel *Indiana* that for years she had sought to resolve
an "insoluble problem": *"to reconcile the happiness and dignity
of individuals oppressed by society without modifying the constitution of society itself"* (16; Sand's emphasis). The Sandian solution in the face of this radical insolubility is to stage a protest
against what she describes in this same text as "the injustice and
barbarity of laws governing women's existence in marriage, family
and society." The protest takes the form of a not so subtle attack
on what we have been calling female plot: "Marriage, society, all
existing institutions, I hate you!" is Bénédict's silent cry (22:182/
198). And the narrative of Valentine's wedding night in itself rep-

resents the refusal of a mythified female destiny. But is that an end to repetition? It is impossible, I think, to know whether little Valentine will in her turn become the eponymous heroine of a novel about marriage and desire that ends in a graveyard. But it is also the case that this hermeneutic impasse is largely overdetermined: Sand's antiproleptic closure *is* her vision for the future, or at least its metaphor.

I want now to move away from the dead end of the cemetery and back to the pavilion for the elements of a conclusion.

When the count returns to Raimbault with his creditor, he asks the man what the pavilion is worth: "Almost nothing," was the reply. "These luxuries and fancy buildings are worth nothing on a country estate. . . . In a city it's different. But when there's a field . . . around this building, or . . . a meadow, we'll say, what will it be good for? Just to tear down for the stone and lumber that are in it" (31:269/290). The disparity between the man's marketplace evaluation of the pavilion and Valentine's private one— "the secret hiding-place of pure and modest happiness" (31:270/ 290)—is the measure of the founding incompatibility between a *new* fictional female plot and the "laws governing woman's existence in marriage, family and society," to reinvoke the terms of Sand's analysis. Thus necessarily Valentine's aristocratic fantasy of a female-controlled stasis that could withstand both the telic pressure of male desire and the contiguities of the dominant narratology is written off by the laws of economic circulation and back into an older plot.

Nonetheless, the desire for another temporality—a night that never ends—and another topography in which to live it has been written. That the time of perpetual deferral and its space in the end are subsumed by the necessities of fictional closure does not erase the inscription, just as the narrator's ambiguous injunction at the end of *Villette* to "picture union and a happy succeeding life" does not erase our sense that Monsieur Emmanuel has drowned, nor—more to the point—that Lucy Snowe has found her voice. Although in the end Sand's fiction pulls back before the radical solution put in place by Lafayette—the refusal of male sexuality as a plot, and a patriarchal plot destined to repetition— it revises the Rousseauist fascination with the filial by placing Elysium *outside* the paternal sphere. *Valentine* is female plot in Restoration France: mired in nostalgia for what can never be again, hesitating on the threshold of what might yet be.

## NOTES

I WOULD LIKE to thank Peggy Brawer, Carolyn Heilbrun, Sandy Petrey, and Peggy Waller for their critical responses to an earlier version of this essay.

1. In her autobiography, Sand comments on the reception of *Indiana* in terms of her writing identity: "The newspapers all spoke of M. *G. Sand* with praise, insinuating that a woman's hand had to have slipped in here and there in order to reveal to the author certain delicate matters of the heart and mind, but declaring that the style and the judgments were too virile not to be those of a man. They were all a little (like) Kératry" (2:174). Although she goes on to claim that this reaction didn't bother her, but did hurt Jules Sandeau's pride, I think we can read Sand's personal investments here clearly enough. (For more on Kératry, see "Writing Fictions.")

The most interesting work on Sand's difference is being done by Naomi Schor. See "Female Fetishism: The Case of George Sand," and "Reading Double: Sand's Difference."

I would like to thank Judith Kates for encouraging me to read *Valentine* as the novel of another pavilion.

2. Both *Le Rouge et le Noir* (1830) and *Eugénie Grandet* (1833) depend for the economy of their fiction on a figured relation between the local history of the provinces in its intersections with a recognizable event and the story of its (local) characters. The *Vallée-Noire,* which is Sand's invented toponym, derives its importance here from another system of connotation: that of genre. The Berri, we are told, is *picturesque.* On the possible implications of Sand's topographics, see Ellen Moers's all too brief, provocative chapter on female landscape, "Metaphors: A Postlude," in *Literary Women* (243–64).

Unlike *Indiana* and *Lélia, Valentine* is not available in a scholarly (Garnier) edition. An 1869 edition (Paris: Lévy) and a 1976 edition (Paris: Aujourd'hui) exist: the latter is the reedition of an 1843 edition. I will be quoting from the English translation by George Burnham Ives (Chicago: Cassandra, 1978), which is a reprint of a 1902 edition. References to chapter and page are noted parenthetically; the French pagination corresponds to the 1976 edition.

3. I allude to the circulation of daughters at the heart of the social contract as described by Claude Lévi-Strauss.

In an episode that embodies the cost of repression, Blutty, the jealous groom, provokes Bénédict, taunting him about his feelings for Valentine. The fallout of their quarrel has Blutty, in a rage, throw a glass of wine at Bénédict which misses its object and instead covers "the bride's lovely dress with indelible stains" (21:177/190). Bénédict catches the glass, however, thereby saving Athénaïs from bodily injury; but the consummation of the marriage is momentarily suspended. (At the end of the novel, Blutty corrects his aim and succeeds for the wrong reasons.)

4. I borrow the term "chronotope" from Mikhail Bakhtin. "We will give the name *chronotope* (literally "time space") to the intrinsic connectedness of temporal and spatial relationships that are artistically expressed in literature. . . . In the literary artistic chronotope . . . time, as it were thickens, takes on flesh, becomes artistically visible; likewise space becomes charged and responsive to moments of time, plot and history. . . . The chronotope

as a formally constitutive category determines to a significant degree the image of man in literature as well. The image of man is always intrinsically chronotopic" (*The Dialogic Imagination,* 84–85).

5. Peggy Kamuf has provided a compelling, psychoanalytic account of the Rousseau material in "Inside *Julie's* Closet."

I will be quoting from Jean-Jacques Rousseau, *La Nouvelle Héloïse: Julie, or the New Eloise,* part 1, letters 54 and 55, pp. 122–24. The corresponding French pages in the Garnier, 121–25.

6. I'm referring to Valmont's troping of "to the moment" in letter 47 and 48 of Choderlos Laclos's *Les Liaisons dangereuses,* where he writes literally *on* one to another: "But I must leave you for a moment to calm an excitement which mounts with every moment, and which is fast becoming more than I can control" (111). The confusion of presence and absence whereby one woman's circulating body allows the desire for the Other to be sustained will ultimately confound the libertine—but too late.

7. Tanner brings useful etymologies from Vico: "The second solemnity is the requirement that the woman be veiled in token of that sense of shame that gave rise to the first marriages in the world. This custom has been preserved by all nations; among the Latins it is reflected in the very name 'nuptials,' for *nuptiae* is from *nubendo,* which means 'to cover.' . . . The third solemnity—also preserved by the Romans—was a certain show of force in taking a wife, recalling the real violence with which the giants dragged the first wives into their caves" (59).

8. Tony Tanner identifies a similar construction in Goethe's *Elective Affinities:* "The kiss [between Charlotte and the Captain] is *almost* returned . . . In that *almost* lies all the felt constraints of the marriage vows, the restraining pauses that law can put on passion" (198).

9. On what did or didn't happen and the relation of Valentine's virginity to Jacques Derrida's trope of the hymen see "La Double Séance" in *La Dissémination.* Parts of Derrida's analysis follow: "The hymen is located between the inside and the outside of woman, consequently, between desire and fulfillment. It is neither desire nor pleasure but between the two. The hymen only takes place when it doesn't take place, when nothing really happens" (41). In the course of her analysis of the famous scene of interrupted defloration in *Salammbô,* Naomi Schor provocatively interrogates the Derridean discussion of the hymen (*Breaking the Chain,* 118–19). Although the neither/nor of the hymen allows Flaubert to play with what may or may not be known, Sand insists that we (do) know. Leslie Rabine takes Derrida's "The Double Session" as a scene in which to reconsider the relation between feminism and deconstruction in "The Unhappy Hymen Between Feminism and Deconstruction." She identifies what remains undeconstructed in Derrida's metaphorics: "the lexical network that marks the hymen not as what belongs to woman, but as what makes woman into the property of man, and that comes into play whether acknowledged or not." The hymen, she pointedly observes, is "an organ of the male imagination through which man has related to woman as to something to be owned." In this sense, we might say, Valentine's wedding night also allows us to deconstruct deconstruction through feminism.

10. This project interests women writers other than Sand. Daniel Stern (Marie d'Agoult), George Sand's contemporary, provides an unambiguously dys-

phoric account of a wedding night (seen from the heroine's perspective) in her novella *Valentia* (1847). The heroine is given bouillon which produced a drugged stupor: "Then he approached me. I wanted to speak but I felt it inconceivably difficult to move my lips. My head suddenly felt very heavy; my mind became jumbled, and my eyelids drooped. In vain I tried to open them. The wall coverings seemed to leap off the walls, come toward me, envelop me. . . . My limbs grew numb. Soon after, I felt nothing at all but my heavy breath in my throat . . . and I fell into a deep sleep." The next morning the heroine observes the disorder of her hair and the pallor of her complexion and draws the "humiliating" conclusions. Leslie Rabine, who cites this passage in her interesting essay "Feminist Writers in French Romanticism," comments on the disparity between the Gothic code "which evokes supernatural and extraordinary experiences, and, on the other hand, a common, ordinary experience (of the bride on her wedding night), familiar to many readers but which is never talked about and which is extraordinary . . . as the subject of a literary passage" (499–500).

Colette supplies a brief, barely oblique description of a wedding night in *Claudine en ménage* (1902): Claudine bravely claims not to be afraid and insists on undressing herself; then, embarrassed by Renaud's gaze, she throws herself on the still-made bed: "He joins me there. He holds me there so tightly that I can hear his muscles trembling. Completely dressed, he embraces me, keeps me there,—Good Lord, what is he waiting for to get undressed too?— and his mouth and his hands keep me there, without his body touching me, from my quivering rebellion up to my frantic consent, up to the shameful moans of pleasure that I wanted to hold back out of pride." That night, though Renaud ultimately undresses, the bed remains made, and Renaud "asks me for nothing, except for the freedom to give me as many caresses as I need to sleep, at daybreak" (13–14).

This kind of writing becomes possible only in the twentieth century, but it should not be seen as the whole story either. There is also Colette's invocation of the room that awaits the newly married couple in "La Noce," *La Maison de Claudine* (1922): "the massive shutters, the door, all the exits of this stifling little tomb will be closed upon them" (70); and Isak Dinesen's story "The Blank Page" tells a tale of silence, of framed virginities.

11. In a further indictment of bourgeois marriage, in Sand's plot, once the count assures the payment of his considerable debts by taking possession of his wife's property (what she thinks of as her patrimony), the contractual enjoyment of her person becomes a matter of complete indifference. As a husband, Lansac "insists" no further; classically, he finds his pleasure elsewhere. On the other hand, when, as a result of the altercation between Bénédict and Blutty, Athénaïs wants to remain with her father, the necessity of possessing a wife's body is made clear. The father exclaims: " 'I am still at liberty to shut the door on you and to keep my daughter. The marriage is not consummated yet. Athénaïs, step behind me'. . . . And she clung with all her strength to her father's neck. Pierre Blutty, whose title as his father-in-law's heir was not assured as yet by any legal document, was struck by the force of these arguments" (21:179/192–93). The variants are a matter of class.

12. In this opposition of ellipsis to periphrasis, I am following the categories of Pierre Fontanier in *Les Figures du discours*. Ellipsis is a figure of understatement, periphrasis, of emphasis.

13. Kate Chopin's *The Awakening*, Carolyn Heilbrun has reminded me, figures a similar refuge: "The 'pigeon-house' stood behind a locked gate, and a shallow *parterre* that had been somewhat neglected. There was a small front porch, upon which a long window and the front door opened. The door opened directly into the parlor; there was no side entry. Back in the yard was a room for servants, in which old Celestine had been ensconced" (99).

14. Rousseau, *La Nouvelle Héloïse*, 11:313. See Tanner's section on Elysium, *Adultery in the Novel*, 143–65. In this same letter, Saint-Preux comments on two hours he spent dreaming in Julie's garden, "two hours *to which I prefer no other time in my life*" (emphasis added). And he characterizes these extraordinary feelings as being due to "the enjoyment of virtue" [*la jouissance de la vertu.*] It is interesting to consider the intersection between this privileged moment of pleasure in Julie's *virtuous* space and the hour "after" we discussed above.

15. The scorn heaped upon a woman who merely wishes to think is scored by Sand when she has Lansac comment on the activities in the pavilion: "Tell me, are you in search of the philosopher's stone, or the most perfect form of government? I see that we are wasting time out in the world cudgelling our brains over the destiny of empires; it is all pondered and arranged in the pavilion in your park" (31:268/289).

Colette ends her pastoral novel *Break of Day* on the word *oasis*: a space of production that reshapes the sexual into a book, open and without limits [*livre sans bornes ouvert.*] What is the space of the female self who would imagine?

16. It could also be argued, of course, that while the prince is moved by his wife's plea to be saved from the telos of her desire—after all, he was the one who had encouraged her to do so—he no less leaves her to find her own (re)solution. In this sense, the "good" husband can't be distinguished from the "bad."

17. "I am not afraid to compare the Fourth Part [of *Julie*] with the *Princesse de Clèves*" (Jean-Jacques Rousseau, *Confessions*, book 11, 505).

18. For altogether mysterious reasons, this line, "Ce fut une triste consolation pour eux que d'habiter le pavillon," which should be the second line of the second paragraph, is deleted in the English translation.

19. Sylvère Lotringer has argued the point in his article "La Structuration romanesque."

20. Jacques Rustin ends the argument of *Le Vice à la mode* on that failure, reading in Rousseau "the instinctive refusal of the very future he outlines, the passionate denial of the great bourgeois dream that his dear Robinson had concretized in his flourishing desert island: the absurd and wonderful, naive and diabolical dream of a *profitable paradise*" (242).

21. To a Bénédict worried—for her—that Valentine will foolishly sign away her wealth, Valentine explains the symbolic project animating her: "It is true that, for my own part, I would be content with this pavilion and a few acres of land. . . . But this property of which my sister was defrauded, this, at all events, I propose to bequeath to her son after my death: Valentin will be my heir. I propose that he shall be Comte de Raimbault some day. That is the object of my life" (32:276/297).

22. The inaugural paragraph of the narrative had already proposed, after a brief tour of the scene, "a cemetery a few rods square, enclosed by a quick-

set hedge, five elms arranged in a quincunx and a ruined tower" as the exemplary social space of a *bourg* (1:3/2).

23. In "A Mother's Discourse," Marianne Hirsch speculates interestingly about reading the exceptional woman at the court as the mother and the effect this positioning might have had on the daughter (85–86). I continue to see the daughter's repositioning as going *beyond* the mother's discourse. Beth McGroarty, in the course of a seminar on the "Female Protagonist" at Barnard, helped me see the subversive power in the trope of the "final daughter."

# [ 9 ]

## *Woman of Letters:*
## *The Return to Writing in Colette's*
## The Vagabond

It is not that the Author may not "come back" in the Text, in his text, but he then does so as a "guest." If he is a novelist, he is inscribed in the novel like one of his characters, figured in the carpet; no longer privileged, paternal, aletheological, his inscription is ludic. He becomes, as it were, a paper-author: his life is no longer the origin of his fictions but a fiction contributing to his work; there is a reversion of the work on to the life. . . .

Roland Barthes, "From Work to Text"

She had been looking all along for a friend, and it took her a while to discover that a lover was not a comrade and could never be—for a woman. And that no one would ever be that version of herself which she had sought to reach out and touch with an ungloved hand.

Toni Morrison, *Sula*

### BIOGRAPHICS: WRITING AS A WOMAN

IN THE opening scene of *The Vagabond,* the persona the heroine calls that "painted mentor" [*cette conseillère maquillée*] returns her gaze from the mirror and addresses her double waiting in the dressing room for her turn to go on stage:

Is that you there? All alone, there in that cage where idle, impatient, imprisoned hands have scored the white walls with interlaced initials and embellished them with crude, indecent shapes? On those plaster walls reddened nails, like yours, have unconsciously inscribed the appeal of the forsaken. Behind you a feminine hand has carved *Marie,* and the name ends in a passionate mounting flourish, like a cry to heaven. (5–6/1067–68)

Why, the mentor goes on to ask, are you there all alone? Why there and not elsewhere?

The dialogue of identity—"Is that you there?" "It really is me there"—that becomes the story of the vagabond whose wandering is fixed (in the feminine) in the novel's title,[1] begins at the site of these indoor graffiti, under the emblem of a classically female signature; the anguished cry of abandonment signed *Marie*, the most significant and at the same time most ordinary name a woman can have in a Catholic country. Against this gesture of anonymous femininity that marks and remarks upon the pain of being alone and waiting, Colette maps the trajectory of a woman who will choose, precisely, not to embrace the solution of the couple—"the interlaced initials" of heterosexual salvation—but to *remain* alone and on the move; to return to the solitude of writing.

Locating the question of female identity in a theatrical setting—the heroine, Renée Néré, is a mime (also a dancer and actress)—is itself a way of restaging the literature of female destiny summarized in the handwriting on the wall. The conventions of the scene behind the scenes—the dressing room, the madeup gaze that flirts with the clichés of mask and reality—overcode the already stylized figuration of woman's identity, its status in representation *as* representation. The novel thus asks from within these familiar tropological zones: what might there be for women *beyond* a representation of identity that depends upon the truth of the mirror and the passionate flourish of female script?

In *A Room of One's Own* Woolf offers a reading of a novel she has invented to embody her discussion of women and fiction. What interests me specifically here in that famous exercise of practical criticism is first the figure of the imaginary author of that novel, Mary Carmichael. Because of the dual legacies of money and space provided by Mary Beton and Mary Seton, the Mary of the twentieth century is in a position to write a new kind of fiction, one that breaks with the literature of the past by "tampering with the expected sequence" (DuPlessis, 31–32, *A Room*, 85). That rupture of expectations is captured in the sentence "Chloe liked Olivia" and its sequence: "They shared a laboratory" (*A Room*, 87). Together the sentences (much glossed by feminist critics) articulate and generate the possibility of a subjectivity constituted not through the old scenarios of love and marriage but through new topographics of work and friendship (DuPlessis, 34). For Colette, writing before and after *A Room of One's Own*, the implications of that displacement are inseparable from a coming to signature, and a matrix of rhetorical moves away from the inevitabilities (the maxims) of female plot. In *The Vagabond,* this "poetics of critique" (DuPlessis, 20) first put in place by the dialogics of the looking-glass, then undercut by the banal markers of feminine traditions (*Marie*'s passion), becomes a form of commentary on the dominant discourse on woman (in 1910) that in turn structures the novel and engenders the terms of its closure.

Like Woolf's Mary Carmichael, Colette's Renée Néré refuses the sequence of fixed expectations and available identities implicit in the signature of love and its italics. In that desperate chirographics (Ong, 2) nails *like her own* have tried to express an original desire, but they have been able only to repeat an already familiar story: the initials of names linked together in a figured embrace are the shorthand of female plot. The reddened nails inscribe a need for something, something that mounts from the unconscious and ends in an ellipsis of deferred closure. In Colette's fiction there is no way out for *Marie,* but it will fall to Renée Néré, whose name anagramatically embodies the signifiers of renewal, to break the "expected sequence" in her own writing. By proposing in the material support of her heroine's name a symmetry that points to the logic of the mirror and its reversals, Colette plays with the gender asymmetry of specular economies.[2]

Much of Colette's work is a meditation on solitude, on the possibility—for a woman—of living alone beyond despair. In the 1928 narrative, *Break of Day,* the heroine, a writer, reflects upon "a second place," emblem of the daily life of the couple: the plate, the glass, the other's napkin ring. On the days this place is not set, she reflects, "I am merely alone, and not abandoned" (10/44). In *The Vagabond,* in many ways a rehearsal for the later text, the heroine is less able to draw such neat distinctions in the self-portrait of female autonomy. When Renée returns home after her performance and looks in the mirror again, she no longer sees the "painted image of an itinerant music-hall artiste": the mirror reflects "only—myself." But this self—"just as I am!"—is a woman more ambiguously, more conventionally alone: "Behold me then, just as I am! Alone alone, and for the rest of my life no doubt. Already alone; it's early for that. . . . Alone! Indeed one might think I was pitying myself for it! . . . Alone . . . and for a long time past" (11–13/1072–73). As she interrogates the meaning of her state, she returns to the mirror, but the gaze in turn passes through the dialogue that constitutes the dominant voice of this novel: "And if I talk to myself it is because I have a writer's need to express my thoughts in rhythmical language" (13/1073). It is this rhythm *as text* within the weave of the novel that challenges the regime of reflection: "Facing me from the other side of the looking-glass, in that mysterious reflected room, is the image of 'a woman of letters who has turned out badly'" (13/1073). At this moment in the narrative, the images of the "artiste" and the "woman of letters" are out of phase, and seem to be incompatible. But I want to argue that the story of the vagabond, of the "artiste" on the road, is the account of a return to letters—a rerighting of the original version—that incorporates the rhythms of performance *in writing*.[3]

At the beginning of *The Vagabond,* however, being a performer means unbecoming a writer: " 'A woman of letters who has turned out badly': that is what I must remain for everyone, I who no longer write, who deny myself the pleasure, the luxury of writing. . . ." What is the status of this writing? "To write, to be able to write" [*Ecrire! Pouvoir écrire!*] (14/1074). The exclamation generates its own and three more paragraphs of explanations which begin: "To write is . . ." The definitions of writing, the pleasures and passions of the hand, the pen, and the page, are lyrical accounts of the internal negotiations between the "scribbling unconsciously" [*griffonnage inconscient*] that becomes its own arbitrary graffiti and "need to note and describe." Both modes have ambivalent effects: the "joy and torment of the idle."

Against the generalized luxury of writing under the regime of idleness, the heroine itemizes the costs of writing as work: "It takes up too much time to write. And the trouble is, I am no Balzac" [*Et puis, je ne suis pas Balzac, moi*] (15/1074). The reference to Balzac is glossed immediately to mean faced with the intrusions of everyday life, the demands of the tradespeople, shoemaker, lawyer, agent, I am not able to keep on writing. But not to be Balzac— the accounts of whose uninterruptable productivity are inseparable from his authority as *the* novelist of the nineteenth century in the French mythology of its own literary history—is not only a matter of a (female) vulnerability to interruption.[4]

To say "I'm no Balzac" is to say several things at once. If Balzac stands for the triumph of a realism in the novel that entails a certain relation of mastery over the world of things, the codes of reference that support his realism also depend upon a certain gendered relation of writer to reader; of male author to female reader. Thus when the partisans of the *nouveau roman* close the book on the literature of the past with disdain for its authors' belief in the power of the sign to secure meaning, it is to Balzac that they turn for their example. But not simply as the representative of an old guard of writing; more problematically as the emblem of an older and pernicious tradition of *reading*. The new novel denigrates the old by identifying the latter's reception and circulation with the scene of the feminine: a literature marked by its solicitation of the *lectrice*—the woman reader; or perhaps more inclusively, the reader, male or female, as woman.[5] Colette, we know, was a great reader and admirer of Balzac. "No body of novel writing can be compared to Balzac's" [*Aucune oeuvre romanesque ne se compare à celle de Balzac*] Colette writes in 1944 (cited in *Oeuvres*, 1297). What does it mean for a writer of fiction, looking back on a career, to take Balzac as the measure of a body of work? What would the grounds of value and comparison be?

Perhaps this is to pass too quickly from the reader to the writer. In *Claudine à Paris*, reading functions as a transitional object: "I read, I read. Everything. Anything. It's the only thing that distracts me, that gets me away from here and out of myself" (*Oeuvres*, 322). Removed from the lessons of schoolwork, from *explications de texte*, reading belongs to pure idleness and a certain anxiety: "You wander in the vast apartment, you abandon the old and dear Balzac, you stop, your gaze vague and lost, before the looking-glass of your room which shows you a long slim young girl . . ." (*Oeuvres*, 347). Reading in *The Vagabond* is also situated between the mirror and the escape from reflection; but it becomes associated more specifically with the escape of travel and the metaphors of displacement: "This evening I shall not feel sleepy, and the spell of the book—even a brand-new book with that smell of printer's ink and paper fresh from the press that makes you think of coal and trains and departures—even that smell will not be able to distract me from myself" (11–12/1072). Although for Renée Néré reading is a matter of the new as *diversion*, for Colette (and Claudine) the volumes of Balzac, like her own writing, are a continuum of present, past and future: "my cradle, my forest, my journey" ("Le Képi," cited in *Oeuvres*, 1297). These words represent for Colette the network of affective values which constitute the work of writing as a scene that paradoxically retrieves origins in a fantasmatic projection of future identities. As we will see, in the novel of travel called *The Vagabond*, Renée has stopped reading, the better, it seems, to daydream, to drift; and the dreams circle around the material attached to these terms of identity. Here in the context of a writer's biography the woman of letters who has turned out badly dwells on the material obstacles that stand in the way of a career of writing *as a woman*.[6] Renée Néré describes the fate of a heroine *after* the solutions of closure that historically have terminated the vicissitudes of female plot: "The problem is, since I have been living alone, that I have had first to live, then to divorce, and then to go on living. To do all that demands incredible activity and persistence. And to get where?" (15/1074–75) Where is there to go after the ending? Is it a question of *arriving* somewhere?

In the discussion of the *Peruvian Letters* I argued that "coming to writing" as a trope of self-authorization supplies an alternative figure for female autonomy, an opening onto a world beyond the limits put in place by the heroine's text. At the same time, however, I suggested that this figuration of a radical change in representation—the woman alone, not merely reading for pleasure in the library but translating and writing—offered itself as the metaphorical account of a less strictly literary project. By this I meant the process through which female subjectivity might constitute itself within a scene of work. In *The Vagabond* as in *Corinne* that project operates on two levels: how to imagine a different scene of desire; and how to perform it, bringing its effects into the more complex public arena of what Jane Tompkins has called "cultural 'work' " (xv).

I think it is important to consider the ways in which the jubilation of earning one's living—"On my good days I joyfully say over and over again to myself that I earn my living!" (28/1085)—alters the economy of identity beyond the pleasure and unpleasure of work: "The music-hall where I became mime, dancer and even on occasion, actress, turned me also, despite my astonishment at finding myself reckoning, haggling and bargaining, into a tough little business woman. The least gifted of women soon learns how to be that when her life and liberty depend upon it" (28/1085). In this sense, *The Vagabond* as the fiction of a return to writing materializes the rhetoric of *A Room of One's Own*: Renée's performing career enacts the fragility of being without the five hundred pounds and room of her own that would permit a woman to write.

Another way of thinking about Colette's staging of female subjectivity is offered by Teresa de Lauretis's important discussion in *Alice Doesn't* of "experience." I cite her elaboration of the concept at some length here because it theorizes the constructed nature of subjectivity, and because the relations it posits between the subject and the social seem very close in spirit to Colette's account of a performing (sometimes performative) identity:

> I use the term [experience] not in the individualistic, idiosyncratic sense of something belonging to one and exclusively her own even though others might have "similar" experiences; but rather in the general sense of a *process* by which, for all social beings, subjectivity is constructed. Through that process one places oneself or is placed in social reality, and so perceives and comprehends as subjective (referring to, even originating in oneself) those relations—material, economic, and interpersonal—which are in fact social and in a larger perspective, historical. The process is continuous, its achievement unending or daily renewed. For each person, therefore, subjectivity is an ongoing construction, not a fixed point of departure or arrival from which one then interacts with the world. (159)

Although de Lauretis's definition of subjectivity does not delimit an exclusively or uniquely female process, the logic of her argument grounds an understanding of what women's subjectivity might mean; or rather *how* it might come to mean, come to gather meaning.

De Lauretis begins the discussion in "Semiotics and Experience" with the passage in *A Room of One's Own* in which Woolf's "I" comes to learn what it means to be a woman. As in most academic institutions, the problem is one of turf: "This was the turf; there was the path. Only the Fellows and Scholars are allowed here; the gravel is the place for me" (159). This coming to consciousness of one's *place* "as a woman"; not a Beadle (or a Fellow or a Scholar); the gravel of the path, the steps to the library, not the library itself ("ladies are only admitted to the library if accompanied by a Fellow of the College or furnished with a letter of introduction"); this interaction, central to the constitution of women's subjectivity, can be read in Colette's writing thematically—as the narrative of a woman's apprehension of a world that plays with the gestures of identity—and structurally, as a fractured linearity punctuated by a rhythm of reverie and return.

In a passage toward the end of *A Room of One's Own,* Woolf offers another way of getting at that process of identification, of *becoming a woman* through exclusion and disenfranchisement: "if one is a woman one if often surprised by a sudden splitting off of consciousness, say in walking down Whitehall, when from being

the natural inheritor of that civilisation, she becomes on the contrary, outside of it, alien and critical" (101). This passage has become something of a locus classicus for feminist critics. Thus Rachel
DuPlessis, expanding upon Mary Jacobus's earlier work on the
implications of this experience for the woman writer of "not only
exclusion, but an internalized split" (Reading Woman, 38), deciphers a "contradictory quiver" set in motion by the tension between the seductions of ideological conformity ("natural inheritor") and the coming to consciousness of its ("alien and critical")
costs (39). For the woman writer (or the figure I have called the
"female critical subject") this awareness produces "a rewriting of
gender in dominant fiction" (43), a rewriting that is seen most clearly
in the "transgressive invention of narrative strategies, strategies that
express critical dissent from dominant narrative" (5). DuPlessis reads
this "poetics of critique" in the work of twentieth-century American, British, and Canadian writers. I think we can read the "critique of story" (43) in earlier (and later) European writing as well.
(This is also the point of "Emphasis Added.")

As Renée reviews her current situation, she begins, like a heroine, with the available love stories. One is offered by a young
admirer who writes a twelve-page letter imagining himself as a
"Prince Charming, poor lad, rich and powerful too" (23/1080).
Renée contrasts herself with the "wretched youth," who, "lost in
his azure palaces and enchanted forest, could dream of someone."
Beyond dreams and letters, she imagines herself alone and una-
waited: "But there is no one waiting for me on the road I follow,
a road leading neither to glory nor riches nor love" (23/1081). The
Colettian text looks forward and backward in the complex negotiations between a past marked both by the perfect past of childhood imaged in the bonds with the mother; the imperfect past of
the catastrophic first love and marriage; and the question of the
future, that can never match the past in either domain, and that
is never evoked without a return on itself. Thus the metaphorics
of the road seem always to reverse directions:

> What remains of my life reminds me of the pieces of a jigsaw
> puzzle. Have I got to try and reconstruct, piece by piece, the
> original scene of it [le décor primitif]: a quiet house in the
> middle of a wood? No, no, I can't, someone has jumbled to-
> gether all the outlines of that sweet landscape; I should never
> be able to find again the bits of blue roof patterned with yel-

low lichen, nor the virginia creeper [*la vigne vierge*], nor the
*deep forest without birds*. . . . (24/1081; emphasis added)

The story of coming to writing, its interruption, return, and daily
reinscription throughout Colette's career, depends on the *impossibility* of returning to this scene. The pieces, fragments of the fantasy of the perfect origin, remain as testimony to another order
and another economy against which every new construction is
measured. But in a way, because the original scene never is deconstructed—merely disassembled and jumbled [*brouillé*]—the
reconstruction can never bring about an entirely new scene: in this
economy the new landscape remains marked by the nostalgia (with
an emphasis on the etymology of return) of an archaic order, a
lost horizon. In this retrospective of the career of the woman of
letters who has turned out badly, the lost landscape is placed between the lovers of the present and the ruin of love that constitutes
the past; a marriage of seduction and betrayal. Writing, in Renée's
fiction, comes as a way of compensating for the infidelities that
regulated the marriage: "I settled down to suffering with an un-
yielding pride and obstinacy, and to producing literature" [*à faire
de la littérature*] (27/1083–84).[7] The literature consists of three titles: *The Ivy on the Wall* [*Le Lierre sur le Mur*], *Next Door to
Love* [*A côté de l'amour*], and *The Forest Without Birds* [*La Forêt
sans oiseaux*]. The first, described as being "a little provincial novel"
written as a refuge from the suffering of the present, is located in
a "still recent past" and metaphorically placed *as* a piece of landscape: it is in spirit like "the pools in [her] part of the world"
and is extravagantly successful, an overnight success (like Sand's
*Indiana*). If in the fiction, unlike the life, the author signs alone,
"Renée Taillandy," and is immediately recognized for her talent,
the success (in this biography) nonetheless becomes a production
of the couple (like that of Colette and Willy); or in the terms of
the fiction, *produces* the couple: they become " 'the most interesting couple in Paris' " (3:27–31/1084). But if the account of worldly
recognition is marked ironically by the use of inverted commas,
the language describing the act of writing (the second book) is
lyrical: "Yet in giving birth to it [*en mettant celui-là au monde*] I
had savoured the voluptous pleasure of writing [*la volupté d'écrire*],[8]
the patient struggling with a phrase until it becomes supple and
finally settles down, curled up like a tamed animal, the motionless
lying in wait for a word by which in the end one *ensnares* it"

[*l'affût qui finit par* charmer *le mot*] (27–28/1084). This very bodily account of the mating of words and sentences as a negotiation
between pleasure and struggle in which both agent and material
are animated and animal may be seen to constitute the specificity
of Colette's language about writing: a modern(ist) insistence on
the agency of the letter, the physicality of language, the material
force of its signifiers. It is the recovery of this writing that the
finally solitary signature of *The Vagabond* enacts.

The third book, *The Forest Without Birds,* was a flop, and yet
this is the author's favorite: her "unrecognised masterpiece" (28/
1084).[9] The more she likes her work, the less the public does, and
the writer inveighs against the inadequacy of readers:[10]

> Incomprehensible? Perhaps it is for you. But for me its warm
> obscurity is clear as day; for me a single word is enough to
> create again the smell and colour of hours I have lived through.
> It is as sonorous and full of mystery as a shell in which the
> sea lives, and I should love it less, I think, if you loved it too.
> But rest assured, I shall never write another like that, I never
> could. (28/1084)

Like the physical act of writing, the book is a record of sensations:
or rather, memory is located in the signifiers beyond their signifying function. This writing of the self, from the self in which the
author coincides with the subject of its prose, is now relegated to
the past. At the end of *The Vagabond* Renée Néré will return to
the pleasure of this text. In the space between those two points,
travel and performance stand in for the solitary passion of words
on the page: "At present other tasks and cares fill my time, especially that of earning my living, bartering my gestures, my dances
and the sound of my voice for hard cash" (28/1084). In this system
of exchange, gestures and miming do the work of words.

But there is a moment of biography to be accounted for in Renée's
narrative of the apprenticeship to writing, and that is the passage
from the immobilized suffering of the "abandoned woman" to the
liminal figure of the woman on the stage. After eight years of en-
during the infidelities of Taillandy, Renée, pushed out of her own
house ("shown *my own* door"), finally leaves to become a woman
alone. The "story" (we are reading) "ends—or begins" at that
moment of no return (30/1086), in the twist on the model of seduction and betrayal which locates the abandonment within marriage, as though Ariadne had left Theseus at home with the other

woman. Despite the variation, the heroine passes through the classical poetics of pain.

The temptation of the maxim that punctuates Colette's own prose comes to structure the account of suffering *as a woman*. It is not the tears that interest her—"that is the most ordinary part of my story"—nor what follows: "the retreat into themselves, that patient withdrawal which follows their rebellious tears!" What interests the female narrator is woman's capacity for suffering: "I will do [women] this justice, which flatters me too: it is only in pain that a woman is capable of rising above mediocrity. Her resistance to pain is infinite" (31/1087).

To what extent does Colette underwrite this naturalization of suffering? What, for example, does she make of her beloved Balzac's discourse on the subject: "in love and sorrow, feeling and self-sacrifice, will always lie the theme of women's lives" [*Sentir, aimer, souffrir, se dévouer sera toujours le texte de la femme*] (*Eugénie Grandet*, 182/129). When in the place of an Ariadne dissolved in tears on Naxos her narrator offers the Medea-like figure of female excess and rage, does the counter example inscribe *another* essentialism? "She grows supple in the practice of suffering and dissimulation, as if they were daily exercises full of risks. . . . Sometimes, if she is too weak or too loving, she kills. And when that happens she will be able to astonish the whole world with an example of that disconcerting feminine resistance" (32/1087). The fate of the imaginary woman continues to unfold as the narrator places her subject on trial. People will say: "she's made of steel!" [*Elle est en acier!*] (32/1088). But the narrator immediately transposes this commonplace expression, like the clichés of the minimal dysphoric female plot—"She's dying of grief. . . . She has died of grief" (31/1087)—rejected earlier, into the discourse of another, homelier mythology: "No, she is merely made 'of woman'—and that is enough" [*Elle est en femme*] (32/1088).

What is the status of this insider's knowledge of the truth of femininity? Where is the woman in this text?[11]

In one of the more famous footnotes in the brief history of French feminist literary criticism, Hélène Cixous asserts that in the body of twentieth-century French (as opposed to Anglo-Saxon) writing, "the only inscriptions of femininity" she has seen "were by Colette, Marguerite Duras . . . and Genet" (879). Cixous has never further elaborated on the femininity of these three writers; and given her own personal demonstrated preferences for Clarice Lispector, Kleist, and Joyce, it is hard to know what marks of femininity she has found there. But in a way, Cixous's discovery of the feminine in Colette is perhaps best articulated in the rhythms of her own writing. In "The Laugh of the Medusa," for example, the call to writing—"Write your self"/"To Write" (880)—the rhetoric of writing as an emancipatory strategy for women, to get back what belongs to her, "her goods, her pleasures, her organs, her immense bodily territories which have been kept under seal" (880)—rewrites the passages on the writing from the body that open *The Vagabond*: "the orgy of inspiration from which one emerges stupefied and aching all over, but already recompensed and laden with treasures that one unloads slowly on to the virgin page in the little round pool of light under the lamp" (14/1074). One might see in the pleasure of the signifier enlisted in the exposure of a female subjectivity, the fluency of a certain femininity.

Arguably, Colette's texts self-consciously describe a female nature; they in fact constitute a discourse *on woman*, a kind of *Second Sex* in fiction, an "*écriture féminine*" *avant la lettre*. Added together, Colette's own maxims make up a kind of handbook or compendium of practical wisdom; female lore that ranges from a girl's childhood to the psychological preparation for death.[12] But if her works are studded with details of a female materialism, they are not necessarily the stuff of a female essentialism—if by this one means the kind of fatalism, the always already of female destiny, that delimits an unchanging map or biological tracking of possibility and impossibility. Rather, the *oeuvre* in its variety— fiction, memoirs, journalism, theater, correspondence—constructs a record of *experience* that in its concern for the idiosyncratic calls into question the clichés of sexual difference, and by the same token, the truth of gender.[13] (Having said this, I want to bring to bear here Mary Russo's sharp remarks on the subject of essentialism in a crucial footnote: "The dangers of essentialism in posing the female body, whether in relation to representation or in relation to 'women's history,' have been well stated, so well stated, in fact, that 'anti-essentialism' may well be the greatest inhibition to work in cultural theory and politics at the moment, and must be displaced" [228].)

Against Balzac's mythology of obligatory female (self-)sacrifice seen from the outside, or at least from the precincts of a masculine realism, Colette offers feminist fables of resistance and self-preservation seen from within, "naturally," as it were, but also critically revised. In Colette's human comedy, the figure of woman takes her distance from the classical text of femininity. In that gesture, Colette negotiates the space for a writing of another point of view: I'm not Balzac. But in that space of differentiation, in the move away from identity and toward a female subjectivity, an asymmetry is produced: Colette becomes a woman writer. As she is described in the most recent edition of *Le Petit Larousse illustré*: "French woman of letters . . . painter of the feminine soul . . . and of the nature we know." A "woman of letters," is no Balzac: "French writer . . . author of *The Human Comedy* . . . fresco of French society." To be sure, Colette's scenes of private life, her portraits and types, her resisting reader—"Man, my friend"—are appreciated within the culture as a form of self-reference (a national treasure): the naming of a Place Colette in Paris to mark her location in the Parisian landscape; the creation of a museum in her native village. But the work nonetheless remains marginal to the canon of twentieth-century writing, or perhaps more exactly, it is perceived as local, appreciated as a kind of a vernacular realism.[14] In 1984 the Pléiade edition of Colette's works began to be published. It will be interesting to see whether this high-culture recognition will have a significant effect on her *place* in the body of writing retained for the transmission of values within the purview of dominant institutional organizations—curricula, anthologies, literary history.[15]

The question, of course, turns on the issue of the universal, the body of its representation. Is it possible for the voice of female subjectivity to occupy the position of writer—not woman writer? Is the resistance to the particular appeal of female subject matter susceptible to a breaking down without a massive coming to consciousness about the *gender of reading?* These questions are represented *en abyme* in Colette's novel. In *The Vagabond* Colette demonstrates the ways in which structures of reception and destination—who addresses whom—are inseparable from the *reading of gender*. Renée's return to writing has everything to do with the destination and reception of the "difference of view" embodied by a feminist subjectivity. Challenged (amorously) by the masculine universal, the woman writer replies with a counter text.

In her essay on *The Vagabond*, Erica Eisinger argues that "the self Renée discovers behind the mask of the heavily made-up music hall *artiste* is the writer. The two professions are alike; both are creative and rhythmic" (101): "Nothing is real except making rhythm of one's thought and translating it into beautiful gestures" (47/

1099). But if in this translation from thought to gesture the body's effect is to *charm* the creatures in the audience (48/1099), like the taming of the word she learned to do in the dance of writing (27–28/1084), at least one important difference radically distinguishes the two gestures both as an activity and as a profession.

On stage, whatever her gestures of control and powers of seduction, the actress by definition is subjected to the classifying scrutiny of the gaze: here the men "crane forward with that curiosity, that cynical courtesy which men of the world display towards a woman who is considered 'déclassée.'" Despite her will to render the spectators imaginary—"Do these people really exist, I ask myself? No, they don't. The only real things are dancing, light, freedom and music"—by the logic of the gaze that thinks it possesses what it sees, Renée is "real" for them: the real woman "whose finger-tips one used to kiss in her drawing-room and who now dances, half naked, on a platform" (47/1099). The actress's vulnerability to the spectators' gaze is aggravated by the ambiguous intimacy of the setting—"le cachet en ville," "the social engagement at the house of some people of very good position but not in the habit of paying large fees" (15/1074)—in contrast to the theater where this authorized intrusive scrutiny is mediated by the "barrier of light" that separates the actors from "*them*" (44/1096). On stage, the material world of the theater offers Renée a scene of control: "The harsh light sustains me, the music governs my gestures, a mysterious discipline controls and protects me . . . all is well" (8/1069). Nonetheless, despite the supports of theatricality, the performing body of the woman in public, like Virginia Woolf's fictional "I" crossing the turf of the campus of Oxbridge, is subject to interpellation:[16] "At the back of the room a man's silhouette gesticulates and calls out 'Bravo!'" (48/1099). Unlike the hand on the page exercising its powers in the circle of light that illuminates its sphere on the writing table, and that reaches out in a gesture of mastery to an imaginary reader through words, the body on the stage is an object of sight, and therefore subject to the "disequivalence between sexual and symbolic differentiation" (Silverman, 272) produced by the male gaze.

One might, I realize, want to object that the gesticulations of the Beadle, who, as "the enforcer of academic patriarchy" (*Alice Doesn't,* 155), is entitled by his role to bar the woman's way and show her her place, have little in common with the conventionally enthusiastic responses to what is after all a public performance that calls for a response. On what grounds can I argue that the

Big-Noodle's (as he is dubbed by Renée—*le Grand-Serin*) gestures and shouts of "Bravo," despite the theatrical codes of behavior that would seem to naturalize them, work to delimit Colette's fictional "I" in the novel as "woman" (*Alice Doesn't*, 159) as powerfully and surely as the man in the "cut-away coat and evening shirt" designates the proper path for a woman to take? How is "Bravo" genderizing? Perhaps the male spectator is simply (generically) enthusiastic?

The answer is in part bound up with the traditional representations of the actress in fiction: the performer *as woman*, which, as we saw with Corinne, is a theatrical variant of the structuring power of the male gaze. We could here say of Dufferein-Chautel, as we did earlier of John Bretton's conventionally gendered appraisal of Vashti in *Villette*, that "he judged her as a woman, not an artist" (322). Two models of the actress are rewritten here; two classic texts of the gaze through which we might usefully situate Colette's project: Zola's *Nana* and Staël's *Corinne*. In radically different modes, and to different ends, both texts mythologize the figure of the woman as performing artist, and locate her in the inevitable oscillations between the public stage and private life, spectators and lovers. Between the actress of hyperbolic powers of seduction and the artist who transcends seduction through her genius, Colette creates a nonheroic artist. In Colette's rewriting, the figuration of the actress is grounded in a historical moment in which it becomes possible to imagine tropes of identity that emerge from a daily scene of work.

Once the man who cries "Bravo" determines to enter the life of the actress (forc[ing] the door of my dressing room!" [79/1123]) the play of gazes becomes more complex. The man with the ridiculous name, Maxime Dufferein-Chautel, who sends flowers and cards, is not completely master of the prerogatives of the (male, aristocratic) gaze he by birth inherits: for he must also learn to wait "like a woman"—"Happy because he has seen from my look that I have recognised him, he follows my movements, my comings and goings on the stage, with his head, just as my dog Fossette does when I am dressing to go out" (56/1105)—to be acknowledged by another's gaze. The figuration of desire in this passage operates as an emblem both of their relation and of the structure of the novel. Unlike the classical model glorified by Ovid in the *Heroides*, according to which the woman waits as the man appears, disappears, and sometimes reappears, her life suspended between waiting rewarded and waiting forever installed; here the man

waits in the position of the feminine although in the dialogics of
their couple, his identity finally is located within a conventional
masculinity: "It's because . . . this fellow is *a man*. I cannot forget
that he is *a man*" (81/1125). (In the same way she will write: "There
is nothing new in my life except a patient man lying in wait for
me" [56/1106].)

The crux is formed: once the man comes on the scene, what
happens to the woman's scene? What denouement can come from
the knot of this criss-cross: the woman on stage/the man in the
audience? On the one hand, like Oswald faced with Corinne's admirers, Max hopes to capture Renée by making his gaze replace
the others. On the other, the woman sees the man as inseparable
from the story of conventional destiny she is determined to resist:
for Renée, at home on the road, "*home*" also means "*homme*."
(The choice of the English signifier is key, since in French mythology the English embody the conventional, and in particular,
the dream of a domestic ideal.)[17] Like Corinne in Rome, Renée in
Paris is tempted by the notion of attachment—English comforts—
but pulled by another figure of herself, and torn between *home*
and *abri*: a "shelter, and not a home, that is all I leave behind
me. . . . Hotels of every type, and sordid music-hall dressing rooms
. . . have been more familiar and benevolent to me than this place
which my love calls 'a charming, cosy nest' " (170/1194). The logic
of the plotting in the novel derives from the competing claims of
these places.

## THE DROPPED STITCH

*The Vagabond* is divided into three unequal parts. The first, as we
have seen, opens backstage in a dressing room, and closes at home
as the scene of future departures: "My lately acquired and rather
artificial liking for uprooting [*déplacements*] and travel fits in happily with the peaceful fatalism natural to the bourgeoise that I am"
(73/1119). This double truth results in a contradiction in terms that
embodies the novel's narrative tension: "A vagabond, maybe, but
one who is resigned to revolving on the same spot like my com-
panions and brethren" (74/1119). The paragraph that ends this
section of the novel glosses the paradox of the traveler who remains behind:[18]

It is true that departures sadden and exhilarate me, and whatever I pass through—new countries, skies pure or cloudy, seas
under rain the colour of a gray pearl—something of myself
catches on it and clings so passionately that I feel as though
I were leaving behind me a thousand little phantoms in my
image, rocked on the waves, cradled in the leaves, scattered
among the clouds. But does not a last little phantom, *more
like me than any of the others,* remain sitting in my chimney
corner, lost in a dream and as good as gold [*rêveur et sage*]
as it bends over a book *which it forgets to open?* (74/1119;
emphasis added)

Is the "last little phantom" the self that belongs to the woman
writer who neither stays nor leaves in any simple or singular way?

The second part of the novel opens on the interior of the "woman
of letters who has turned out badly" seen from the eyes of her
"admirer": "What a charming, cosy nest! I must say it's hard to
imagine your existence in the music-hall when one sees you here
between this rosy lamp and that vase of carnations" (75/1120). To
Max's view from the outside, Renée opposes the view from within;
she mocks his failure to perceive the shabbiness behind the glow
of her arrangements; his failure to read the signs: "to think that
all that can so dazzle the casual visitor as to make him imagine,
between these faded green walls, the secluded, contemplative and
studious life of a gifted woman [*une femme supérieure*]. Ah, but
he hasn't noticed the dusty inkpot, the dry pen and the uncut book
on the empty box of stationery!" (75/1119). If the image of retirement and study may be read for irony, the details that counter
the vision may not, for they are the material emblems—inkpot,
pen—of the writer's activity Renée has abandoned. Max's difficulty in understanding, after a first evening spent with Renée at
home, how she could live privately the way she does and yet choose
to appear on stage is a problem of *vision* that will be given its full
weight at the end of the novel, in Renée's refusal to see the world
reflected in a lover's gaze (222/1232). But before Renée turns away
definitively from the desire of that gaze to map her identity in the
world, the narrative sets in place two tracks of more or less successful resistance to its powers: she tries to negotiate her way around
Max's gaze by catching it at work (78–79/1123); and she retrieves
the power of her own through a return to childhood visions.

What are we to make of the woman who has stopped reading,

who does not even bother to cut the pages? Who is she to the "last little ghost," "good as gold," who sits dreaming over a book it forgets to open; and to the child, a girl of twelve, whose gaze is "almost sexless"? The "last little ghost" is the most like her, and yet not her.

> The train very slowly followed a track under repair. . . . A child, standing at the edge of the wood, watched us pass, a little girl of twelve whose resemblance to myself struck me. . . . Her unsociable look, too, and those ageless, almost sexless, eyes which seemed to take everything seriously, were mine also, really mine. It was indeed my own shy childhood which stood there, dazzled by the sun, at the edge of that coppice and watched me pass. (92/1132)

If the heroine has split off from her childish self but recognizes herself in it, what is the relationship between the two looks: the unselfconscious and "natural," the self-conscious and "critical"?

In the second and longest segment of the book, the heroine remains in Paris, rehearsing for the tour, fantasizing about travel, about leaving and staying. She falls asleep one afternoon and awakens from a dream in which she had returned to her origins, to the forest, to the vision and voice of the daughter.

> Who was it, while I slept, who loosened the coronet of plaits coiled about my brows like the tresses of a grave young Ceres? I was . . . I was . . . there was a garden . . . a peach-coloured sunset sky . . . a shrill childish voice answering the cries of the swallows . . . yes, and that sound like distant water, sometimes powerful and sometimes muffled: the breath of a forest. I had gone back to the beginning of my life. What a journey to catch up with myself again, where I am now! (119/1154)

If there is no return to the originary space except in dream, is there anywhere to go, except in circles? Are these trips on the road the fulfillment of childhood dreams or their mockery: what is it to be Renée Néré?

> As for the new cities and new countrysides, so briefly glimpsed, so quickly passed that they grow blurred in the memory, are there such things as new countries for one who spins round and round in circles like a bird held on a string? Will not my pathetic flight, begun anew each morning, inevitably end

up each evening at the fatal "first class establishment" which Salomon and Brague praise so highly to me?

I have seen so many *first class establishments* already! . . . Must I discover and perpetually renew in myself that rich fund of energy which is essential to the life of wanderers and solitaries? Must I, in short, struggle—ah, how could I forget it?—against solitude itself? And how to achieve what? What? What? (120–21/1154–55)

We might say that the task of Colette's novel is to invent for the heroine a form and scene of work that would avoid the disappointment that follows from the failure of promises held out in childhood—"Effort brings its own rewards"—to come true in adulthood—"I am still waiting" (121/1155), and a plot that would provide a detour from the equally unreliable commonplaces of grown-up economies: the offers that come from the man who proposes as a husband to replace her work with himself through his money (143/1173).

As Renée vacillates between the rehearsals of the tour and the fixed destination of *home* and *homme* that Max represents,[19] she evokes for her friend Hamond a landscape glimpsed from a train window, and in which she imagines herself grounded with "him" in a life of available satisfactions, "within reach of my mouth and my hands" (150/1178):

At noon, the farm girls would be milking the cows in the fields: I could see, in the deep grass, pails of burnished copper where the foaming milk squirted in thin straight jets . . . I want to enjoy, all at the same time, everything I lack: pure air, a generous country where everything is to be found, and my love. (150–51/1178)

In the face of this representation of plenitude, fixed in the lush iconography of timeless pastoral, Hamond asks the question of history, or at least of story: "And then, my child, afterwards?" (151/1178). And then what? Will she give up the road? Will she pick up "that witty pen which is growing rusty"? (151/1179) And then, with the instincts of an "ex-genre painter," Hamond paints in the details of domestic life; a child, for instance.

If Renée can't see the scene of reproduction in representation, Maxime gets the point immediately: "And then, at least, you'd never be able to leave me . . . you'd be caught [*prise*]" (153/1180). The domestic scenarios of woman's destiny—the faithful husband, the beautiful baby (152/1179)—produce a familiar narrative of male and female roles under patriarchy's roof: "And he shall ask me: 'Where are you going?' as though he were my master. A female I was and, for better or worse [*pour en souffrir et en jouir*], a female I find myself to be" (158/1184). Within these arrangements of mastery and pleasure, the essentialist positioning of the couple engenders an equally familiar literature of female despair. The heroine—once, as we saw, in the biographical figures of her self-representation, an "abandoned woman," here still bears the mark of its pain: " 'Everyone leaves me, I'm all alone.' Loving me as he does, he well knows that there is no need of words or reasonings to calm me, but only cradling arms, a warm murmur of vague caressing words, and kisses, endless kisses" (157/1183). Despite the panic that seems to underwrite this mode of attachment figured by the "hands of a drowning [woman]" (156–57/1183) drenched in tears and clinging to her lover, Renée finally leaves for the tour.

Thus, the second part of the novel ends on the departure rehearsed and reviewed:

> How many times, in fleeing from myself, have I not fled from this ground floor? Today when, beloved and in love, I am leaving, I would like to be still more loved, still more loving, and so changed as to be unrecognisable in my own eyes. No doubt it is too soon, and the time has not yet come. But at least I am leaving with a troubled mind, overflowing with regret and hope, urged to return and reaching out towards my new lot with the glorious impulse of a serpent sloughing off its dead skin. (170/1194)

The stakes of this departure lie in the question of its difference from the others, of her difference from herself; if she is loved and loves enough no longer to resemble herself. Leaving in love at least allows for a change in genre. Indeed, the third part of the novel opens on a letter, her first, she says, love letter. This third brief section may be read as an epistolary novel revised. Or rather, one could argue that through the return of the letter, Colette rejoins a feminist epistolary tradition: against the erotic paralysis of the Portuguese nun, Renée Néré, like Graffigny's Zilia and Riccoboni's Fanni Butlerd, will write her way out of the standard plots.[20] More specifically, and perhaps more usefully, we could say that by letter writing Renée returns herself to literature, to the older mastery of a hand moving across a page.

As the train moves away from Paris, Renée, half-asleep, is agitated by the tiring rhythm of "childish arithmetical dreams": "If you have left half of yourself behind, does that mean you have lost fifty per cent of your original value?" (173/1197). The problems of childhood math are of course adult calculations: what is the value of a woman not attached to a man? And that question about female identity also has a specificity for Colette's symbolic mapping, which, we have seen, is bound up with place. In her third letter she writes:

> My darling, I've just passed through, without stopping, a region which belongs to me because I spent my childhood there. . . .
>
> Nothing has changed there. A few new roofs, bright red, that's all. Nothing has changed in my part of the world—except me. Ah, my darling love, how old I am! Can you really love such an old young woman? I blush for myself, here. Why did you not know the tall child who used to trail her regal braids [*ses royales tresses*] here, silent by nature as a wood nymph? All that, which I once was, I gave to another, to another than you! (175–76/1198)

There is a way in which this novel make sense only in terms of the values of that place; and the fascination of the lost story, the *tresse* or weave of narrative inseparable from its topography. The story, perhaps in fact no story at all, but a scene, a stance, a gaze.

In Colette's text that child exists in a scenario of abandonment fatally interwoven with the story of the woman's desire. Inside the woman's body, "the female body lying there, which bars my way . . . that brute bent on pleasure, is I myself." But if one can do battle with that enemy, there is one worse: "the lost child [*l'enfant abandonnée*] who trembles inside me, weak and nervous and ready to stretch out her arms and implore: 'Don't leave me alone!'" (203/1217–18). In the *Critical Inquiry* issue on "Canons," Lawrence Lipking has argued that the cries of that female child constitute the sentence that might generate a woman's poetics: "Abandoned women know that the world can shift too fast to be imitated, that the harmony of art is made to be broken. Hence their poetics obeys another law of nature, the unsatisfied craving of children who cry to be held" (78).

While one can agree with Lipking's general claim that a "woman's poetics" would probably valorize a modality of imitation different from Aristotle's, an imitation based upon another appre-

hension of the natural, it would not, I think, found itself in a
naturalization of female suffering, and an identification of "the
lost child" with adult women. In *The Vagabond,* for example, if
this "need" prevails inside a woman's body, it is also transformed,
reworked by language.

The poetics of the return to writing involves displacing the cries
of the child afraid of the dark; and also of the woman immobilized
by her own desire, whose body stretches out "barring the way"
of the woman on the move. Although the heroine speaks of *overcoming* the "lost child" (203/1218), I don't think we should see
this so much as a gesture of repression as the rezoning of an economy that would allow for a permanent oscillation between the
rhythms of childhood and the orders of adult life.

As Renée travels and Max waits and writes for her to return
and become his, "the woman of letters who has turned out badly"
suddenly can't stop writing:

> with a fullness and a freedom difficult to explain. I write on
> wobbly pedestal tables, sitting sideways on chairs that are too
> high, I write with one foot shod and one bare, the paper lodged
> between the breakfast tray and my open handbag, all among
> the brushes, the bottle of scent and the button-hook; I write
> sitting at a window that frames part of a courtyard, or the
> most delicious gardens, or misty mountains. I feel myself at
> home amid this disorder of a camp, this no matter where and
> no matter how, and freer than among my haunted furniture.
> (209/222)

The return to writing begins with letter writing about returning to
Max, but the return to writing will also require the displacement
and transformation of that epistolary fiction through letter writing. How does this happen? The process of writing itself undoes
the structure of destination: just as Renée suddenly finds herself
at home *(chez moi)* on the move, in the same way, movement itself
takes her past the notion of return.

In a moment of absence to herself, "half asleep, like the sea, and
yielding [*abandonnée*] to the swaying [*bercement*] of the train, I
thought I was skimming the waves, so close at hand, with a swallow's cutting flight" (207/1220); in this state between sleeping and
waking, awash in the vague rhythms of the maternal,[21] Renée suddenly realizes—through the work of *memory*—that she has forgotten Max: Max suddenly becomes brutally subordinated to another desire: "to seek for words, words to express how yellow the

sun is, how blue the sea, and how brilliant the salt like a fringe of white jet. Yes, forgotten him, as if the only urgent thing in the world were my desire to possess through my eyes the marvels of the earth" (207/1220–21). The writing that returns as desire is not, at least in this moment of almost physical urgency, a desire for story, for another plot. Rather it is a more literal apprehension of the material of language: the yellow sun, blue sea—almost a child's vocabulary and coloring book images of the beach, but for the writerly flourish that signs the seascape with a contradiction: "the fringe of white jet." To come to this writing requires a forgetting and a refusal of the "natural."

I have been reading this third epistolary section as a *mise en abyme* (with an internal signature that marks the self-consciousness of the structure) of the novel as a whole, in the sense that it rehearses and replaces the questions of the fiction iconographically, or metaphorically within the text as a matter of vision. But the figure that finally comes to name the process of reconstruction that results in Renée's decision to bypass the destination of female plot derives from another thematics. Not surprisingly, the metaphor chosen to bear the weight of the heroine's choice comes from a childhood scene:

> If only I could wind back again the months that have expired up to that winter day when Max walked into my dressing room. . . . When I was small and learning to knit, they made me undo rows and rows of stitches until I had found the little unnoticed fault, the dropped stitch, which at school was called "a lapse." A "lapse"! That's all he would have been in my life, then, this poor second love of mine whom I used to call my dear warmth, my light. He is there, quite close at hand, I can take hold of him—and I flee. (214/1225)

The term that Renée chooses to characterize the love affair with Max, in French *une manque* (a regionalism), supplies the feminist measure of the decision not to take what is at hand, since the most common use of this noun is in the masculine, which is how Freud's notion of lack as the constitutive female experience is translated in French: *le manque*. When Renée finally "drops" Max, it is precisely against that sense of lack and from a posture of plenitude.

It is as though the unconscious self-abandonment to the (maternal) rhythms of the train had "organized" in her a desire for escape, "far away, down in the depths of my being, without my taking so far any direct part in it" (214/1225). The effects of this

internal event lead to a reversal of the old story—*"what I was"*—
in which "horribly alone" now emerges as the definition of a positive freedom. In the story of abandonment she would have said:
"take me." Here she asks: "What are you giving me? Another myself? There is no other myself" (214/1226). The move from female
to feminist, knitting to unknitting, entails a revalorization of economies: "A look of his can rouse me and I cease to belong to myself
if he puts his mouth on mine? In that case he is my enemy, he is
the thief who steals me from myself." Against the theft of herself
through the body is the offer of a material gain: "I shall have
everything that money can buy" (215/1226). But Max's offer of a
place at the "edge of a white terrace" from which to see others
pass misses the language of Renée's desire. When he beseeches her
to return to live among her "equals," she replies: "I have no equals,
I have only my fellow wayfarers" (215/1226).

To choose the terms which might locate a subjectivity outside a
lexicon of hierarchy—master, equal—but within a notion of fellowship and movement is to pose the possibility of a female identity self-consciously constructed through work. (In Irigaray's utopian vision this is the sort of demystification that might occur "if
the 'commodities' refused to go to 'market,' " if they "maintained
'another' kind of commerce, among themselves" [196/193].) The
shift from the discourse of sex to that of class (or from the body
to real estate—the white terrace vs. the shabby ground floor) is a
move toward unsettling the problematics of the gaze; displacing
the emphasis from the sexual axis along which the man's look
circumscribes the woman as object to the material experience of
a producing subjectivity. To refuse to look down and contemplate
the wanderers is only one piece of the revision: the other is to look
in order to record.


## CHANGING SUBJECTS: WOMAN OF LETTERS

RENÉE WRITES her first love letter from the road from her ground-
floor rooms as though she had already left, as though she were
already on the road; hoping, as she puts it, to become *unrecog-
nizable* in her own eyes. The question of the epistolary "novel"
that completes the fiction of *The Vagabond* is almost exactly that:
whether Renée can *see herself* otherwise. As she hesitates between
continuing as she is and becoming "no longer . . . Renée Néré
but My Lady Wife" (191/1209), she focuses her doubts and suf-

fering on an image: the snapshot Max sends her of himself playing
tennis with a girl. This image of youth becomes the text and pretext of the decision finally produced not to return to Max, not to
marry (him). In a long letter about the *girl,* the inevitable unknown
younger woman rival, that anticipates the language and structures
of *Chéri,* Renée rehearses a refusal comprehensible to Max's masculinity; a classically feminine insecurity about appearance that leads
Max to reply, like the king in "Snow White," with the discourse
of authority derived from the mirror: "You will always be the most
beautiful!" (206/1220). The conventionality of this reply shows Renée
that Max has not understood the gravity of her resistance; that
she has written only "almost sincerely!" and principally for herself: "I hope it may bring me relief, that sort of interior silence
which follows a sudden utterance, a confession" (199/1214). In this
writing, which she describes as a mode that like her "mobile face"
that in Max's words expresses too much, the excess of language
serves to carry its subject beyond the requirements of communication as dialogue. This becomes a writing that returns itself to
the sender; though without the fiction of destination (the lover as
receiver) it would not come into being.

Against the anxiety crystallized in the fixed image of Max and
the (generic) girl at the tennis court, against the familiar logics of
possession in which woman fatally is seen, and evaluated in her
feminine identity (199/1215), Renée opposes the need to see for
herself: "I want to see again, under this heavy sky, my Elysian
refuge, the Gardens of the Fountain" (201/1216). The site of this
garden is the scene of the struggle discussed earlier in this chapter
in which the child within the woman's body cries out in anguish
her panic at being left alone. In this garden, which is Renée's
"kingdom," but only to the extent that she identifies with the pas-
sersby, the "wanderers and solitaries" who stop there on their way
elsewhere, the struggle to free herself from Max's story finally comes
to consciousness: "this dispute is slowing rising up and forcing its
way into the daylight" (202/1217). What emerges from the economy of the unconscious is a sentence; a sentence that like that of
the writing on the wall at the beginning of the novel seems fatal:
"This time the formula is clear. I saw it written in my mind and
I see it there still, printed like a judgment in small, bold capitals"
(203/1217). The message of this writing is contained in the hope
offered by the single word "escape" [*l'évasion*] (203/1217).[22]

I suggest in "Arachnologies" that what Ellen Moers called "female landscape," the mapping and iconography of privileged places

in women's writing, may also be read as a desire for a revision of story, in particular of closure; a desire, as we have seen, that falls outside the masculinist conventions of plausible narrative. In *Indiana*, Sand takes her heroine to the ravines of an island in the Indian Ocean; in *Valentine*, closer to home, she designs an Elysian retreat, an "enchanted island in the midst of real life," a scene of escape from the demands and violence of heterosexual plotting. In *The Vagabond* as in *Valentine*, to invoke Elysium is to conjure a space immune to the passage of time. Last year's spring is still this year's: "It is so fairy-like in this place where the spring hangs motionless over all things" (201/1216).

In this garden where "nothing changes" (201/1216), Renée peers into the "baths of Diana," which return to her gaze not the image of her face but the "Judas trees, the terebinths, the pines, the paulownias with their mauve flowers, and the double purple thorns" (201/1216): a garden of reflections that do not evoke Narcissus' mirror. But in the text of a writer who rarely borrows from a classical library, what is the reading effect of the classical reference to Diana in the context of this exquisite retreat of gardens and fountains protected by black gates?[23] Perhaps the most pertinent of the myths surrounding Diana is that which records her fierce protection of the precincts of her own space; her resistance to the male gaze that seeks to penetrate her boundaries. Here no spectator impinges upon Renée in the borrowed virginal enclosure— "the approach of the storm has driven away all intruders" (202/1217)—that is her kingdom for the time of her passage. Diana, we know from the myth, turned against the violation of the gaze as self-depossession and through her divine powers caused Acteon's destruction, his dismemberment and dispersal. In *The Vagabond*, against the equally intrusive gestures of an arrogant masculinity, in a double move of self-repossession, Renée Néré will reclaim the authority of her own vision and reconstruct her powers through a dispersal of her imaged self.

As we saw in *Corinne*, the male spectator who aligns himself with the legacy of patriarchy poses a threat to the security of female authority, to the extent that the (performing) woman is tempted by the look of love. Thus, Renée at a crucial moment in the unfolding affair with Max admits to herself: "I must confess, that in allowing this man to return tomorrow, I was giving way to my desire to keep, not an admirer, not a friend, but an eager spectator of my life and my person. . . . Could I sincerely declare that, for a few weeks past, I have not taken pleasure in the attention of this passionate spectator?" (111–12/1148). In her chapter on "The Woman in Love," Beauvoir cites this passage as an example of woman's joy "to find in her lover a witness" (717). "Love," she writes, "is the development that brings out in clear, positive detail the dim negative, otherwise as useless as a bland exposure" (718). In her choice of the metaphorics of photography, Beauvoir points to the double message effect of the male gaze: on the one hand, the spectator of one's life confers meaning on existence by focusing it, composing it lovingly as a spectacle, a performance—hence the possible occasion of a responsive, mobile exchange; on the other, because the spectator's gaze is classically gendered, it tends to fix its object as an image of woman, within the conventions of an eternal femininity.

To some extent, of course, the threat of the male gaze in Colette's novel is always tempered by its recontainment within a feminine and feminist discourse, the vigilant eye and self-conscious voice of the narrator. Writing "as a woman," the narrator is scrupulous about the complications of heterosexual positionings within the gaze. There is first the conventional displacement of onstage, off-stage dialectics of recognition and misrecognition. Max turns up unexpectedly after rehearsal and Renée feels uncomfortable being seen,

> under the strong, noonday light, with my hair out of curl under my fur cap, my nose shiny for lack of powder, and my mouth dry with hunger and thirst . . . [T]he Big Noodle is looking me over as if he had never seen me before.
>
> I stifle a sudden childish longing to cry and instead I ask him, as if I were about to bite him: "What is it? Have I got a smut on my nose?"
>
> He takes his time to reply: "No . . . but . . . it's odd . . . when one has only seen you in the evening one would never believe you have grey eyes. They look brown on stage."
> . . . Come to that, I too had never seen him so well, in full daylight. His deep-set eyes are not black, as I thought, but a rather tawny brown, like the eyes of sheep-dogs. (66/1113)

In this exchange, which begins with a classically Colettian self-consciousness about a woman's unmadeup appearance (that reaches hyperbolic form in *Chéri* and in the critique of it performed by *La fin de Chéri*), the woman ends by equalizing what she takes as a negative judgment, by returning the observation—as though looking were merely seeing; as though looking entailed reciprocity and a mark of intimacy. Early in their affair, Renée will say, as she observes Max in her apartment unbeknownst to him: "To be entirely honest, let me mention what I like best in him: a look that is sometimes absent and seeking, and that kind of private smile in the eyes which one sees in sensitive people who are both violent and shy" (78/1123). As the love story that structures *The Vagabond* starts to fall apart, that look changes for Renée from a source of improvised, personal pleasure, a self-confident play of glances meeting and not meeting that confirms one's necessity for the other, to the images of a stereotypical masculinity, framed in the black and white record of the photograph, and framing with its text an anxious and rebellious prose of dissent.

The scene in the garden in which Renée comes to read the "sentence" of her deepest desires is framed at the beginning with the letter to Max about the photograph of the girl on the tennis court. It ends with a refusal—"my first victory"—to call him to comfort the abandoned child who "pines merely because she is not cherished enough" (203/1218). Although in some sense one could argue that the whole third part of the novel is about the power of landscape to revise story in this way, I think that the pause at Diana's fountain—the "warm stone of the ruined temple" (201/1216) that Renée lovingly caresses, the silence of the water's dispute—is the moment at which I would locate its emblematic turn; a moment of signature to be articulated subsequently with the writing of forgetting, the "lapse" discussed earlier, but that occurs later in the narrative. Although Renée is moved by the discourse on solitude of her friend and mentor, Margot—"One has to get terribly old . . . before one can give up the vanity of living in the presence of someone else" (111/1148)—and forced as we have just seen, to admit its truth—"Could I sincerely declare that, for a few weeks past, I have not taken pleasure in the attention of this passionate spectator?" (112/1148)—in the end, like the princess of Clèves, she will choose to remain outside its surveillance. The vanity of living in the presence of someone else presents its own dangers to a woman's vanity.

Toward the end of the tour, which is also to say toward the end of the novel, as Renée prepares to return to Paris, she and her fellow travelers are offered the possibility of a tour in South America. The "sound of those two words," their "glittering names," dazzle Renée as she imagines their possibilities of pleasure and excitement. But the images Brazil and Argentina evoke for her (because of a picture her friend Margot gave her) of "a spider with a silver

stomach and a tree covered with fireflies" are stopped by "but
. . . what about Max?" Max becomes a "question mark" around
which she turns looking for an answer to the problem of destination—"What about me, then, do I exist merely to bother my
head about this cumbersome capitalist?" In her hesitation, she
contrasts the "enchanted web of falling stars, giant flowers, precious stones and humming birds," the clichés of the New World,
with a less appealing, old world vision of domestic life: "what will
you do" in "that tub of a houseboat,"[24] demands to know the
"foul-mouthed ancestor" whose voice carries on with a will of her
own inside her (211/1223). That voice, like the mentor's in the
mirror in the opening scene of the novel is part of the dialogism
that structures Colette's writing. When it grows dark, Renée suddenly thinks "how good it would be to lean now against the shoulder of the man [she] was humiliating a moment ago" in her mind
(212/1224). Faced with the contradiction, she sets out to write a
letter:

> I switch on the ceiling-light and, for something to do, try a
> temporary arrangement of the writing-table, opening the blot-
> ter between the cheval-glass and the bunch of narcissus; I'm
> trying to make the place look like home [*un semblant de home*]
> and what I long for is hot tea, golden bread, my familiar lamp
> with its pink shade, the barking of my dog and the voice of
> my old Hamond. A large sheet of white paper lying there tempts
> me, and I sit down. (212/1224)

The temptation of the blank page moves the heroine into the decision to move on and to choose the improvised, the mobile, and
the approximate—"*un semblant* de home"—as opposed to the
"sunny enclosure, bounded by solid walls" that marriage represents to her (191/1208). But if the improvised home offered by an
anonymous hotel room, like the public train carriages of a traveler's journey, are the valorized scenes of a performer's life, we
may also understand them in relation to the fragile walls of the
princess of Clèves's pavilion and the elaborately private spaces of
Zilia's library. At stake, then, in Renée's refusal of marriage and
the reclamation of autonomy is not so much life on the road for
its own sake as the imagination of new domains of subjectivity,
an elsewhere without "patriarchal laundry" (1223). Thus, the desire to escape from the conventional arrangements the man Maxime
wants to offer along with his name (194/1211) comes to "continue" the precursor's plot and revises it as coming to writing.

## FEMINIST MODERNISM

THE THIRD PART of the novel operates through a series of re-
fusals and reversals that in the end replace the fixed identity of
woman with the *improvised mobility* of a feminist subjectivity, a
feminist modernist whose desires in language remain subject to
change. In these pages Renée glosses and translates her last letter
to Max, the one she will call "unfinished" (221/1231). If she explains to him that she could not "resume the habit of loving" (220/
1230), when she addresses him through the reader outside the
structure of the "real" destination, she is less kind: "Dear intruder,
whom I wanted to love . . . I reject you and I choose . . . all
that is not you" (222/1231). The logic of the sweeping rejection is
bound up with a feminist critique of the economics of the male
gaze: "I refuse to see the most beautiful countries of the world
microscopically reflected in the amorous mirror of your eyes." Unlike Woolf's patriarch who relies upon the reflecting powers of
woman as looking glass (35), who depends on its lying gaze for
his "vitality," Colette's "beggar-woman" (222/1232) wants to see
for herself unprotected by the play of mirrors.

In the same rhetoric of critique, Renée refuses the values of Max's
vision—or point of view: "You wanted to brighten me with that
commonplace dawn, for you pitied me in my obscurity. Call it
obscurity, if you will: the obscurity of a room seen from without.
I would rather call it dark, not obscure." At stake in this redefinition of terms is nothing less than a rearticulation of and challenge to the grounds of subjectivity: what (and whose) interest determines the apprehension of experience itself. Thus, as she rejects
Max's offer of a happiness which would "illuminate [her] with its
commonplace dawn," Renée proposes, almost pedagogically, a gloss,
a poetic text on the theme of darkness that concludes: "Dark, with
the red gleams of an agonizing memory. But you are he in whose
presence I should no longer have the right to be sad" (223/1232).
Renée's room is illuminated according to an economy in which
reflection is generated by an ethic of passion and memory, not by
the optics Max's view maintains: the specular judgment of authorization that banishes or admits the right to feeling. We might
think of the "difference of view" produced by women's writing as
emerging from the zones of this darkness within.

When Renée returns to her rooms from the tour in order to leave
again without seeing Max, she passes through her refuge "without

writing a name on the bloom of dust" that covers the furniture;
she leaves the "unfinished letter" for her lover "signed and dated"
(221/1231), but resists the automatic gesture of the graffiti artists
whose scrawls marked their passage on the walls of her dressing
room at the opening of the novel. The reticence in face of a commonplace sentimentality is of a piece with the choice to move on:
at one with a desire beyond a notion of plot that requires the destination of "home." The novel thus ends on the invocations of a
desire separable from the definition of a single place:

> I shall desire you as I desire in turn the fruit that hangs out
> of reach, the far-off water, and the blissful little house that I
> pass by. In each place where my desires have strayed, I leave
> thousands and thousands of shadows in my own shape, shed
> from me: one lies on the warm blue rocks of the ledges in my
> own country, another in the damp hollow of a sunless valley,
> and a third follows a bird, a sail, the wind and the wave. You
> keep the most enduring of them: a naked and undulating
> shadow, trembling with pleasure like a plant in the stream.
> But time will dissolve it like the others, and you will no longer
> know anything of me until the day when my steps finally halt
> and there will fly away from me a last small shadow. (223/
> 1232)

The novel closes on these images of a multiplicity of selves made
up of sites of desire; on the ellipsis (the final punctuation of the
French version) that also leaves the process of dispersion open. It
is possible to read this refusal of the master narratives, the images
and structures of fixed identity as the culmination of a modernist
strategy to dissolve the guarantees of subjectivity and selfhood in
the free play of language. It is equally possible to shore up such
an argument with an insistence on the disjunctive effects of landscapes like these: the interruption and suspension, displacement
and deferral performed by the accumulation of images and metaphors of movement, dispersal, and vision. But does the language
of multiple desires signal modernly the deconstruction of the subject?

I think not. Rather, the refusal of the props of identity [*cher
appui*] which both "rest and wound" [*repose et blesse* (223/1232)];
of the nostalgia for integrity that locates itself in a "home" and
the signature of patriarchal law—*Mme ma femme*—are displaced
by modalities of desire and being that attach to another project:
the project of a subjectivity that on the one hand experiences its
desires "in turn," in a nonlinear heterogeneity—the man, fruit,

water, house—all marked by the trait of their unavailability; and
on the other, that leaves traces of identity behind, like so many
shadows of its author's body to become the vagabond of its own
fiction.[25]

For Colette, then, the multiplicity of desires scattered across the
landscape is not *finally* random, figured by the "unbridled (pan-
demic) circulation of signs, of sexes, of forces" (*S/Z*, 216/222) that
characterizes the modernist project; the relentlessly self-referential
engagement with language. To the extent that modernism involves
the struggle with the dead father, and panic at the powers of the
archaic mother, female modernism, or at least feminist modernism, as one might imagine, emerges from rather different alliances
and romances.[26] For Colette, thinking back through her mother,
the mapping of sites of desire is an act of reconstitution.

In the penultimate paragraph of *Break of Day* Colette reads her
mother's last letter like one of those "haunted landscapes where,
to puzzle you, a face lies hidden among the leaves, an arm in the
fork of a tree, a body under a cluster of rock" (142/185). It is the
mother's lesson about renunciation in the face of death that teaches
the daughter about the ethics of desire. Thus the writer/heroine
of *Break of Day* banishes her lover—"Fly my favourite! Don't
reappear until you have become *unrecognisable*" (140/182; emphasis added)—with the words, we recall, Renée in *The Vagabond* had used for herself: that she would leave and return "unrecognisable" in her own eyes (74/1194). In *Break of Day*, as the
fiction reaches closure, the heroine reveals the transformation to
be an act of literature: "But I only have to help him and lo! he
will turn into a quickset hedge, spindrift, meteors, *an open and
unending book*, a cluster of grapes, a ship, an oasis . . ." (143/
185; emphasis added).

What should we make of these permutations between subject
and object, female artist and its other self, female artist and male
lover, subject and landscape? Self or lover, the authority of vision
returns to the artist who from her posture of solitary observer reshapes desire and replaces it in an "open and unending book."
The "woman of letters who turned out badly" in *The Vagabond*
is the writer Renée Néré becomes and who will, as we saw in
"Writing Fictions," reclaim her signature in *Break of Day*:

> in them I called myself Renée Néré or else, prophetically, I
> introduced a Léa. So it came about that both legally and fa-
> miliarly, as well as in my books, I now have only one name,

which is my own. Did it take only thirty years of my life to reach that point, or rather *to get back to it?* I shall end up by thinking that it wasn't too high a price to pay. (19/53; emphasis added)

In both cases, the signature of the woman writer aligns itself incorrigibly with the material of the love story—"chapters dedicated to love, or regret for love, chapters blind with love" (*Break of Day*, 19/53). But at the same time the feminist signature authorizes a reflection on woman's contradictory relation to its limits as a story, a critique of the plots that define women's plausibilities in fiction and draw the boundaries of their lives around the "home." To the extent that the formation of new subjectivities takes place as a continual negotiation within and against those limits, Colette's writings are its own open and unending book.

## NOTES

1. Colette tried to use "The Vagabond" as the title of fictions featuring Annie, who appeared in *La Retraite sentimentale* and *Claudine s'en va;* she had also thought of calling *Claudine s'en va* "Je m'évade," but Willy wanted the name Claudine to remain in the title in order to exploit the success of the previous Claudines. In 1944, in a note written to Maurice Goudeket about the original edition of the novel, Colette writes: "I took back, not without a major struggle, the title that suited the novel at hand, the first novel I signed" (in *Oeuvres*, 1582).

We may perhaps read the signature of the feminine hand as a stand-in for the signature of the writer for whom the name of the signature was from the beginning part of struggle about an identity in writing.

In *Le Petit Robert* the title of Colette's novel is given as an example for the feminine form of the noun. The measure of innovation in creating a female vagabond may be taken in Agnès Varda's 1986 much remarked upon film "The Vagabond"—in French, "Sans toit ni loi"—in which the escape, more modernly, proves to be only an impasse.

2. On the self-reflexive nature of Renée Néré's name and mirror images, see Joan Hinde Stewart's *Colette*, 47 ff.

3. In the preface to the Fleuron edition of *La Vagabonde, L'Entrave,* and *L'Envers du music-hall*, Colette celebrates the pleasures of her life as a performer, and describes its effects on her writing: "It was then that I undertook to submit my work as a writer to the rhythm of my existence as an artist. The odd thing is that I succeeded. . . . When I look back on my past, I never contemplate this period of healthy and simple labor without gratitude" (in *Oeuvres*, 1236).

4. Woolf's famous remarks in *A Room of One's Own* on the relationship

between writing and physical conditions, and the significance this might have for a theory of sexual difference, seem particularly apt here: "The book has somehow to be adapted to the body, and at a venture one would say that women's books should be shorter, more concentrated than those of men, and framed so that they do not need long hours of steady and uninterrupted work. For interruption there will always be" (81). The form of *The Vagabond* embodies this mode of discontinuity.

5. I am grateful to Alice Y. Kaplan for references to Robbe-Grillet's remarks on this subject: see especially, in *Pour un nouveau roman,* the connection of Balzac with Lafayette as origin of psychological analysis (15, 22; and the association, negative of course, of the novel and women, 33).

6. Sido remarks in a letter shortly after the novel's publication: "I can't help thinking you are writing your biography, because, because . . . these things are lived and all the more interesting" (in *Oeuvres,* 1583).

7. One would have to turn to *Mes Apprentissages* (1936) for a detailed autobiographical account of the marriage with Willy, and the terms of the original coming to writing, imposed on her by Willy and his finances (his Book). Here these relations of force are passed over in silence.

8. We might contrast here Zilia's description of the "volupté délicate" she experiences in writing (see chapter 5, p. 144).

9. I take this to be another tribute to Balzac, whose *Le Chef d'oeuvre inconnu* is famously the story of an artist's struggle.

10. To what extent is the mystification of the readership a function of gender? As in *Break of Day:* "Man, my friend, you willingly make fun of women's writings because they can't help being autobiographical. On whom then were you relying to paint women for you . . . ? On yourself?" (19). See chapter 2, "Writing Fictions," on the "marked" readership of women's writing.

11. I am of course playing around with Mary Jacobus's argument in "Is There a Woman in this Text?"

12. Colette self-consciously comments on this aspect of her writing, by quoting one of her husband's recommendations within the fiction of *Break of Day:* "When you're about fifty you ought to write a sort of handbook to teach women how to live in peace with the man they love, a code for life as a couple" (22).

13. Beauvoir in *The Second Sex* turns to Colette as an authority on women's experience. Colette is the only woman writer she refers to systematically.

14. Thus in the Lagarde and Michard literary manual (1966) for twentieth-century literature, for example, Colette appears under the large general rubric, "The Novel from 1919 to 1939," under "Man and Nature" [*L'homme devant la nature*]. The entry begins with a quotation from Colette's own work locating her as the queen of the earth. To her accounts of nature, her mother, children, and daily life is added her skill as a portraitist of Paris 1900.

15. Certainly the existence of a Pléiade edition affects a writer's fate as an object of study. The first volume of the new edition has brought together writing and information about Colette's early writing career never before assembled in one place. In the case of this chapter, I can say that this material, especially the accounts of reception, importantly changed my sense of the novel's position in the *oeuvre.*

As for Colette's place before the Pléiade (and perhaps after), Henri Peyre writes in *French Novelists of Today* (1967): "Her niche is probably assured in anthologies of French prose, but her place as a French novelist is not secure" (39).

16. In her reading of Althusser's famous notion of interpellation, Kaja Silverman argues that "the family plays as central a role within the Althusserian scheme as it does in the Freudian or Lacanian ones. It remains to determine," she then asks "whether that role is seen as ideological or as transcultural, as it is in the other two models. Needless to say," she writes "this is a critical determination since it includes the all important issue of sexual difference" (219). Silverman concludes that Althusser perceives family as "elaborately mediated by ideological representations" (220), hence implicitly attentive to that issue. It seems to me, nonetheless, that the cultural context of "hailing" by the police, given by Althusser as an exemplary *commonplace* occurrence, is blind in its metaphorics to the unequal positionings of male and female subjects within the commonplace itself. In other words, the model of "interpellation" as the constituting moment of subjectivity does not necessarily render the specificities of female subjects in the social text. To return to the text at hand: when the Beadle interpellates Woolf's "I," and Max, the female performer, they reenact the specific positionings of dominant and subdominant.

17. Like Lucy Snowe, Renée Néré remains outside the comforts "plaited" by little Polly Home; a patriarchal identity attached to a fetishized place of origins. On plaiting and female plot, see Christine Froula's "Out of the Chrysalis: Female Initiation and Female Authority in Virginia Woolf's *The Voyage Out*" (71).

18. The same formulation appears in the earlier *Claudine en ménage*: "Renaud called me a seated vagabond. Laughing, I replied that his *home* could be put into a valise" (*Oeuvres*, 415) and in the prologue to *La Retraite sentimentale*.

19. See also, this bit of dialogue, an exchange between the homosexual character, Marcel, and Claudine that in *Claudine en ménage* sets up the play on words *home/homme*:

— For whom are you leaving me?
— For me. I'm on honeymoon with my little home [in English in the text].
— You have a new little . . .
— Yes, with one *m*. Didn't you know? (494)

20. On the epistolary tradition that informs Colette's novel, see Joan Stewart's *Colette*, 36–48.

21. The French makes the associations of *mer* and *mère* inevitable, and it is doubled by the associations of *bercement*—the rocking of a cradle, etc.

22. We recall that the term of escape appeared in one of the versions of titles Colette imagined for the history of Renée Néré's authorship—*L'Esclavage-L'Evadée*—and that *Je m'évade* was the original title of *Claudine s'en va* (*Oeuvres*, 1607). In all of the versions the title articulates a particular thematics of refusal—an escape from the constraints of marriage.

23. In a letter to Hamel, dated April 26, 1909 (*Lettres de la Vagabonde*) Colette describes "the marvelous gardens here, and the Roman baths and the temple of Diana, in this green shade and exuberant spring" (*Oeuvres*, 1635). The local reference, however, doesn't stop the flow of associations for the reader.

24. Deleted from the English translation is the phrase that follows directly,

*où l'on blanchit une lessive partriarcale.* This is a rare use of explicitly feminist discourse in Colette's writing.

25. Earlier in the novel, Renée writes, "How far away I feel, as if I had already left, cut adrift [*disperseé*] and taken refuge in my journey!" (103/1141)

26. On these issues, see Christiane Makward's essay, "Colette and Signs: A Partial Reading of a Writer 'Born *Not* to Write.'"

# Works Cited

Albistur, Maité and Daniel Armogathe. *Histoire du féminisme français*. Paris: des femmes, 1977.

Altman, Janet. *Epistolarity: Approaches to a Form*. Columbus: Ohio State University Press, 1982.

Anderson, William S. *Ovid's Metamorphoses: Books 6–10*. Norman: University of Oklahoma Press, 1972.

Ascher, Marcia and Robert Ascher. *Code of the Quipu: A Study in Media, Mathematics, and Culture:* Ann Arbor: University of Michigan Press, 1981.

Auerbach, Nina. "Why Communities of Women Aren't Enough." *Tulsa Studies* (Spring–Fall 1984), 3(1–2):153–57; rpt. in *Feminist Issues in Literary Scholarship*, ed. Shari Benstock. Bloomington: Indiana University Press, 1987.

Bakhtin, Mikhail. *The Dialogic Imagination*. Ed. Michael Holquist. Austin: University of Texas Press, 1980.

Bal, Mieke. "Mise en abyme et Iconicité." *Littérature* (1978), 29:116–28.

——*Lethal Love*. Bloomington: Indiana University Press, 1987.

Balzac, Honoré de. *Eugénie Grandet*. Paris: Garnier-Flammarion, 1964. *Eugénie Grandet*. Trans. Marion Ayton Crawford. Harmondsworth: Penguin, 1976.

——"Autre étude de femme." In *Les Secrets de la Princesse de Cadigan*. Paris: Folio, 1980.

Barthes, Roland. "Style and Its Image." In *Literary Style: A Symposium*, ed. Seymour Chatman. London: Oxford University Press, 1971.

——*Sade, Fourier, Loyola*. Paris: Seuil, 1971. *Sade-Fourier-Loyola*. Trans. Richard Miller. New York: Hill and Wang, 1976.

——*Le Plaisir du texte*. Paris: Seuil, 1973. *The Pleasure of the Text*. Trans. Richard Howard. New York: Hill and Wang, 1975.

——*S/Z*. Trans. Richard Miller. New York: Hill and Wang, 1974.

——*Roland Barthes par Roland Barthes*. Ecrivains de Toujours. Paris: Seuil, 1975.

——"The Death of the Author"; "From Work to Text." In *Image/Text/Music*. Trans. Stephen Heath. New York: Hill and Wang, 1977.

——*Prétexte: Roland Barthes. Colloque de Cerisy*. Paris: Union Générale d'Editions, 1978.

Beauvoir, Simone de. "Interroge Jean-Paul Sartre." *L'Arc* (1975), 12:3–12.

——*Le deuxième sexe*. Paris: Gallimard-Folio, 1976. *The Second Sex*. Trans. H. M. Parshley. New York: Bantam, 1970.

——*The Prime of Life*. Trans. Peter Green. New York: Harper, 1976.

Benstock, Shari. "Reading the Signs of Women's Writing." *Tulsa Studies* (Spring 1985), 4(1):5–15.

Benstock, Shari, ed. *Feminist Issues in Literary Scholarship*. Bloomington: Indiana University Press, 1987.

Berg, Elizabeth. "Iconoclastic Moments: Reading the *Sonnets for Helene*, Writing the *Portuguese Letters*." In *The Poetics of Gender*, ed. Nancy K. Miller. New York: Columbia University Press, 1986.

Berger, John. *Ways of Seeing*. London and New York: Penguin, 1973.

Béteille, Arlette. "Où finit Indiana? Problématique d'un dénouement." In *Recherches Nouvelles*. *Groupe de Recherches sur George Sand*. C.R.I.N. 6–7, 1983, pp. 62–73.

Borowitz, Helen. "The Unconfessed *Précieuse*: Madame de Staël's Debt to Mademoiselle de Scudéry." *Nineteenth-Century French Studies* (Fall–Winter 1982–83), pp. 32–59.

Braidotti, Rosi. "Patterns of Dissonance: Women and/in Philosophy." Manuscript.

Brée, Germaine. *Women Writers in France: Variations on a Theme*. New Brunswick: Rutgers University Press, 1973.

——"The Fictions of Autobiography." *Nineteenth-Century French Studies* (Summer 1976), 4(4):438–49.

Brody, Jules. "*La Princesse de Clèves* and the Myth of Courtly Love." *University of Toronto Quarterly* (1969), 38:105–35.

Brontë, Charlotte. *Villette*. 1853. Rpt. New York: Penguin, 1983.

Brooks, Peter. *The Melodramatic Imagination*. New Haven: Yale University Press, 1976.

——"Freud's Masterplot." *Yale French Studies* (1977), nos. 55–56, pp. 280–300; rpt. in *Reading for the Plot: Design and Intention in Narrative*. New York: Knopf, 1984.

Brownstein, Rachel Mayer. *Becoming a Heroine*. New York: Viking, 1982.

Burney, Frances. *Camilla, or A Picture of Youth*. Ed. Edward A. Bloom and Lillian D. Bloom. Oxford: Oxford University Press, 1983.

Butor, Michael. "Sur *La Princesse de Clèves*." In *Répertoire*. Paris: Minuit, 1960.

Calder, Jenni. *Women and Marriage in Victorian Fiction*. New York: Oxford University Press, 1976.

Catullus. *The Poems of Catullus*. Harmondsworth: Penguin, 1982.

Caws, Mary Ann. "Centennial Presidential Address 1983: Realizing Fictions." *PMLA* (May 1984), pp. 312–21.

Chateaubriand, René de. *Mémoires d'outre-tombe*. Vol. 1. Paris: Flammarion, 1948.

Chopin, Kate. *The Awakening and Selected Stories of Kate Chopin*. Ed. Barbara H. Solomon. New York: Signet, 1976.

Cipriani, Fernando. "Mme de Graffigny: Dalle *Lettres de Cirey* alle *Lettres d'une Péruvienne*." *Rivista di letterature moderne e comparate* (1980), 33:166–86.

Cixous, Hélène. "The Laugh of the Medusa." Trans. Keith Cohen and Paula Cohen. *Signs* (1976), 1(4):875–94.

Cixous, Hélène, Madeleine Gagnon, and Annie Leclerc. *La Venue à l'écriture*. Paris: Union Générale d'Editions, 1977.

Colette, Sidonie Gabrielle. *La Maison de Claudine*. Paris: Livre de Poche, 1960.

——*Claudine en ménage*. Paris: Livre de Poche, 1963.

——*La Naissance du jour*. Paris: Garnier-Flammarion, 1969. *Break of Day*. Trans. Enid McLeod. New York: Farrar, Straus, and Cudahy, 1961.

——*The Evening Star*. Trans. David LeVay. London: Peter Owen, 1973.

——*La Vagabonde*. In *Oeuvres*, ed. Claude Pichois. Paris: Gallimard, 1984. *The Vagabond*. Trans. Enid McLeod. New York: Farrar, Straus, and Giroux, 1980.

——*Oeuvres I*. Ed. Claude Pichois. Paris: Gallimard, 1984.

Coulet, Henri. *Le Roman jusqu'à la Revolution*. New York: McGraw-Hill and Armand Colin, 1967.

Culler, Jonathan. *On Deconstruction*. Ithaca: Cornell University Press, 1982.

Danahy, Michael. "Social, Sexual, and Human Spaces in *La Princesse de Clèves*." *French Forum* (September 1981), 6(3):212–24.

Daugherty, Beth Rigel. "The Whole Contention Between Mr. Bennett and Mrs. Woolf, Revisited." In *Virginia Woolf: Centennial Essays*, ed. Elaine K. Ginsberg and Laura Moss Gottlieb. Troy, N.Y.: Whitson, 1983.

Deforges, Régine. *O m'a dit*. Paris: Pauvert, 1975.

DeJean, Joan. "Lafayette's Ellipses: The Privileges of Anonymity." *PMLA* (October 1984), 99(5):884–902.

——"Staël's *Corinne:* The Novel's Other Dilemma." *Stanford Literature Review* (Spring 1987), 10(1):77–88.

——"Fictions of Sappho." *Critical Inquiry* (Summer 1987), 13(4):787–805.

De Lauretis, Teresa. *Alice Doesn't: Feminism, Semiotics, Cinema*. Bloomington: Indiana University Press, 1984.

De Lauretis, Teresa, ed. *Feminist Studies/Critical Studies*. Bloomington: Indiana University Press, 1986.

Derrida, Jacques. *La Dissémination*. Paris: Seuil, 1972.

——*Of Grammatology*. Trans. Gayatri Chakravorty Spivak. Baltimore: Johns Hopkins University Press, 1976.

——"Becoming Woman." Trans. Barbara Harlow. *Semiotext(e)* (1978), 3(1):128–37.

*Dictionnaire des antiquités grecques et romaines d'après les textes et les monuments, Le*. Ed. Charles Darenberg and Edmond Saglio. Paris: Hachette, 1877–1919.

Didier, Béatrice. "Femme/Identité/Ecriture: A propos de *L'Histoire de ma vie* de George Sand." *Revue des Sciences Humaines: Ecriture, Féminité, Féminisme* (1977), no. 168, pp. 561–76.

Doane, Mary Ann. "Woman's Stake: Filming the Female Body." *October* (Summer 1981), 23:36.

Donoghue, Denis. "A Criticism of One's Own." In *Men in Feminism*, ed. Alice Jardine and Paul Smith. New York: Methuen, 1987.

Doubrovsky, Serge. "*La Princesse de Clèves:* Une Interprétation existentielle." *La Table ronde* (1956), 138:36–51.

DuPlessis, Rachel Blau. *Writing Beyond the Ending: Narrative Strategies of Twentieth-Century Women Writers*. Bloomington: Indiana University Press, 1985.

Duras, Marguerite. *The Ravishing of Lol Stein*. Trans. Richard Seaver. New York: Grove Press, 1966.

Eagleton, Terry. "Text, Ideology, Realism." In *Literature and Society: Selected Papers from the English Institute*, ed. Edward Said. Baltimore: Johns Hopkins University Press, 1978.

Ecker, Gisela, ed. *Feminist Aesthetics.* Trans. Harriet Anderson. Boston: Beacon Press, 1985.

Eisinger, Erica. *The Vagabond:* A Vision of Androgyny." In *Colette: The Woman, the Writer,* ed. Erica Mendelson Eisinger and Mari Ward McCarty. University Park: Pennsylvania State University Press, 1981.

Eliot, George, *The Essays of George Eliot.* Ed. Thomas Pinney. London: Routledge and Kegan Paul, 1963.

——*The Mill on the Floss.* New York: New American Library, 1965.

Ellman, Mary. *Thinking About Women.* New York: Harcourt, 1968.

Empson, William. *Some Versions of Pastoral.* London: Chatto and Windus, 1950.

Flaubert, Gustave. *Madame Bovary.* Trans. Paul De Man. New York: Norton, 1965.

Florenne, Yves, ed. *Lettres de la religieuse portugaise.* Paris: Librairie Générale Française, 1979.

Fontanier, Pierre. *Les Figures du discours.* Paris: Flammarion, 1977.

Foucault, Michel. "What Is an Author?" *Language, Counter-Memory, Practice,* ed. Donald F. Bouchard. Ithaca: Cornell University Press, 1980.

Fréron, Elie Catherine. *Lettres sur quelques écrits de ce temps.* Vol. 1, April 15, 1749; vol. 5, March 12, 1752. Nancy: Duchesne, 1752–54.

Freud, Sigmund. "Femininity." *New Introductory Lectures on Psychoanalysis.* Trans. James Strachey. 1933. Rpt. New York: Norton, 1965.

——"A Special Type of Choice of Object Made by Men"; "The Relation of the Poet to Day-Dreaming." In *On Creativity and the Unconscious.* Trans. I. F. Grant Duff. New York: Harper, 1958.

Froula, Christine. "Out of the Chrysalis: Female Initiation and Female Authority in Virginia Woolf's *The Voyage Out.*" *Tulsa Studies* (Spring 1986), 5(1):63–90.

Gallop, Jane. *The Daughter's Seduction.* Ithaca: Cornell University Press, 1982.

——"Annie Leclerc Writing a Letter, with Vermeer." In *The Poetics of Gender,* ed. Nancy K. Miller. New York: Columbia University Press, 1986.

Garcilaso de la Vega. *The Incas: The Royal Commentaries of the Inca, Garcilaso de la Vega, 1539–1616.* Trans. Maria Jolas; from the French, trans. Alain Gheerbrant. New York: Orion, 1961.

Gass, William. "Three Photos of Colette." *New York Review of Books,* April 14, 1977.

Gaudin, Colette, Mary Jean Green, Lynn Anthony Higgins, Marianne Hirsch, Vivian Kogan, Claudia Reeder, and Nancy Vickers, eds. "Feminist Readings: French Texts/American Contexts," *Yale French Studies* (1981), no. 62.

Genette, Gérard. "Vraisemblance et motivation." *Figures II.* Paris: Seuil, 1969.

Gilbert, Sandra. "From *Patria* to *Matria:* Elizabeth Barrett Browning's Risorgimento." *PMLA* (March 1984), 2(99):194–210.

Gilbert, Sandra and Susan Gubar. *Madwoman in the Attic: The Woman Writer and the Nineteenth-Century Literary Imagination.* New Haven: Yale University Press, 1979.

——"Sexual Linguistics: Gender, Language, Sexuality." *New Literary History: A Journal of Theory and Interpretation* (1984–85), 16:515–43.

Godwin, Gail. "One Woman Leads to Another." *New York Times Book Review,* April 28, 1985, pp. 13–14.

Graffigny, Françoise de. *Lettres d'une Péruvienne*. In *Lettres Portugaises, Lettres d'une Péruvienne, et autres romans d'amour par lettres*, ed. Bernard Bray and Isabelle Landy-Houillon. Paris: Garnier-Flammarion, 1983. *Peruvian Letters*. Trans. R. L. Whitehead. London: Harchard, 1805.

——*Lettres d'une Péruvienne*. Ed. Gianni Nicoletti. Bari: Adriatica, 1967.

Grossvogel, David. *The Limits of the Novel*. Ithaca: Cornell University Press, 1971.

Guilleragues, Gabriel de Lavergne. *Lettres Portugaises traduites en français*. In *Lettres Portugaises, Lettres d'une Péruvienne, et autres romans par lettres*, ed. Bernard Bray and Isabelle Landy-Houillon. Paris: Garnier-Flammarion, 1983.

Gusdorf, Georges. "Conditions et limites de l'autobiograhie." *Formen der Selbstarstellung*. Berlin: Duncker and Humbolt, 1956.

Gutwirth, Madelyn. *Madame de Staël, Novelist: The Emergence of the Artist as Woman*. Urbana: University of Illinois Press, 1978.

——"*Corinne*, or the Appropriation of Allegory." Manuscript.

Hadas, Pamela White. *Designing Women*. New York: Knopf, 1979.

Haraway, Donna. "A Manifesto for Cyborgs: Science, Technology, and Socialist Feminism in the 1980s." *Socialist Review* (March–April 1985), 15(2):65–107.

Heilbrun, Carolyn G. *Toward a Recognition of Androgyny*. New York: Knopf, 1973.

——"James Joyce and Virginia Woolf: Ariadne and the Labyrinth." Manuscript.

Heilbrun, Carolyn G., and Margaret Higonnet, eds. *The Representation of Women in Fiction: Selected Papers from the English Institute, 1981*. Baltimore: Johns Hopkins University Press, 1983.

Hellman, Lillian. *An Unfinished Woman*. New York: Bantam, 1974.

Henderson, Mae. "Black Women Writers: Speaking in Tongues." Manuscript.

Hirsch, Marianne. "A Mother's Discourse: Incorporation and Repetition in *La Princesse de Clèves*." *Yale French Studies* (1981), 62:67–87.

——"Female Family Romances and the 'Old Dream of Symmetry.'" *Literature and Psychology* (1986), 32(4):37–46.

——*Speaking For Her: Mothers, Daughters, and Narrative*. Bloomington: Indiana University Press, forthcoming.

Herrmann, Claudine. *Les Voleuses de langue*. Paris: des femmes, 1976.

Hoggsett, Charlotte. *The Literary Existence of Germaine de Staël*. Carbondale and Edwardsville: Southern Illinois University Press, 1987.

——"Graffigny and Riccoboni on the Language of the Woman Writer." Manuscript.

Homans, Margaret. *Bearing the Word: Language and Female Experience in Nineteenth-Century Women's Writing*. Chicago and London: University of Chicago Press, 1986.

Huyssen, Andreas. "Mapping the Postmodern." *New German Critique* (Fall 1984), 33:5–52.

Irigaray, Luce. *Ce Sexe qui n'en est pas un*. Paris: Minuit, 1977. *This Sex Which Is Not One*. Trans. Catherine Porter. Ithaca: Cornell University Press, 1985.

Jakobson, Roman. *Essais de linguistique générale*. Paris: Minuit, 1963.

Jacobus, Mary. "Is There a Woman in This Text?" *New Literary History*

(Autumn 1982), 14(1):117–42; "The Question of Language: Men of Maxims and *The Mill on the Floss,*" *Critical Inquiry* (Winter 1981), 8(2):207–22; rpt. in *Reading Woman: Essays in Feminist Criticism.* New York: Columbia University Press, 1986.

James, Henry. "George Sand." *French Poets and Novelists.* 1893. Rpt. London and New York: Macmillan, 1977.

Janeway, Elizabeth. "Women's Literature." In *The Harvard Guide to Contemporary American Writing,* ed. Daniel Hoffman. Cambridge: Harvard University Press, 1979.

——"On the Power of the Weak." *Signs* (Autumn 1981), 1(1):111–18.

Jardine, Alice. *Gynesis: Configuration of Woman and Modernity.* Ithaca: Cornell University Press, 1985.

Jardine, Alice and Paul Smith, eds. *Men in Feminism.* London and New York: Methuen, 1987.

Jehlen, Myra. "Archimedes and the Paradox of Feminist Criticism." *Signs* (Summer 1981), 6(4):575–601.

——"Against Human Wholeness: A Suggestion for a Feminist Epistemology." Manuscript.

Johnson, Diane. "Ghosts." *New York Review of Books,* February 3, 1977.

Jones, Ann Rosalind. "Surprising Fame: Renaissance Gender Ideologies and Women's Lyric." In *The Poetics of Gender,* ed. Nancy K. Miller. New York: Columbia University Press, 1986.

Joplin, Patricia Klindienst. "The Voice of the Shuttle Is Ours." *Stanford Literature Review* (Spring 1984), 1(1):25–53.

Kael, Pauline. Review of *Julia. The New Yorker,* October 10, 1977, pp. 100–1.

Kamuf, Peggy. "Inside *Julie's* Closet." *Romanic Review* (November 1978), 69(4):296–306.

——"Writing Like a Woman." In *Women and Language in Literature and Society,* ed. Sally McConnell-Ginet, Ruth Borker, and Nelly Furman. New York: Praeger, 1980.

——"Replacing Feminist Criticism." *Diacritics* (Summer 1982), 2(12):42–47.

——*Fictions of Feminine Desire: Disclosures of Heloise.* Lincoln: University of Nebraska Press, 1982.

Kaplan, E. Ann. "Is the Gaze Male?" In *Women and Film: Both Sides of the Camera.* New York and London: Methuen, 1983.

Kelly-Gadol, Joan. "Did Women Have a Renaissance?" In *Becoming Visible: Women in European History,* ed. Renate Bridenthal and Claudia Koonz. Boston: Houghton Mifflin, 1977.

Knight, Diana. "A Feminist Paragraph." *Paragraph* (October 1986), 8:1–5. Special Issue in Honour of Simone de Beauvoir (1908–1986), ed. Diana Knight.

Knoepflmacher, U. C. "Fusing Fact and Myth: The New Reality of Middlemarch." In *This Particular Web: Essays on Middlemarch,* ed. Ian Adams. Toronto: University of Toronto Press, 1975.

Kolodny, Annette. "Dancing Through the Minefield: Some Observations on the Theory, Practice, and Politics of a Feminist Literary Criticism." *Feminist Studies* (Spring 1980), 6(1):1–25; "A Map for Rereading; or, Gender and the Interpretation of Literary Texts." *New Literary History* (Spring 1980), 11(3):451–67; rpt. in *The New Feminist Criticism,* ed. Elaine Showalter. New York: Pantheon, 1985.

Krantz, Rachel. " 'Qu'est-ce que c'est que Corinne?': Erotic Plot and Ambition in Mme de Staël's *Corinne or Italy.*" Unpublished MS, 1985.

Kristeva, Julia. "Questions à Julia Kristeva." *Revue des Sciences Humaines.* (1977), no. 168, pp. 495–501.

——*Pouvoirs de l'horreur: Essai sur l'abjection.* Paris: Seuil, 1980.

——"Women's Time." Trans. Alice Jardine and Harry Blake. *Signs* (Autumn 1981), 7(1):13–35.

——*Revolution in Poetic Language.* Trans. Margaret Waller. New York: Columbia University Press, 1984.

Laclos, Choderlos de. *Les Liaisons dangereuses.* Trans. P.W.K. Stone. New York: Penguin, 1961.

Lafayette, Marie-Madeleine, comtesse de. *La Princesse de Clèves.* Paris: Garnier-Flammarion, 1966. *The Princesse de Clèves.* Trans. Nancy Mitford. Harmondsworth: Penguin, 1978.

Lagarde, André and Laurent Michard. *Textes et Littérature: Le XXᵉ siècle.* Vol. 6. Paris: Bordas, 1966.

Lanham, Richard A. *A Handlist of Rhetorical Terms.* Berkeley and Los Angeles: University of California Press, 1969.

Lanser, Susan Sniader. *The Narrative Act: Point of View in Prose Fiction.* Princeton: Princeton University Press, 1981.

Lanser, Susan Sniader and Evelyn Torton Beck. "[Why] Are There No Great Women Critics? And What Difference Does It Make?" In *The Prism of Sex: Essays in the Sociology of Knowledge,* ed. Julia A. Sherman and Evelyn Torton Beck. Madison: University of Wisconsin Press, 1979.

Larnac, Jean. *Histoire de la littérature féminine.* Paris: Kra, 1929.

Lauguaa, Maurice. *Lectures de Mme de Lafayette.* Paris: Armand Colin, 1971.

Lejeune, Philippe. *L'Autobiographie en France.* Paris: Armand Colin, 1971.

——"Le Pacte autobiographique." *Poétique* (1973), 14:137–62.

Lentricchia, Frank. *After the New Criticism.* Chicago: University of Chicago Press, 1980.

Lipking, Lawrence. "Aristotle's Sister: A Poetics of Abandonment." *Critical Inquiry* (September 1983), 10(1):61–81.

Lotringer, Sylvère. "La Structuration romanesque." *Critique* (1970), 26:498–599.

MacArthur, Elizabeth J. "Devious Narratives: Refusal of Closure in Two Eighteenth-Century Epistolary Novels." *Eighteenth-Century Studies* (Fall 1987), 21:1–20.

McConnell-Ginet, Sally. "Intonation in a Man's World." *Signs* (1978), 3(3):541–59.

McDonald, Christie V. *The Dialogue of Writing: Essays in Eighteenth-Century French Literature.* Waterloo, Ontario: Wilfrid Laurier University Press, 1984.

Makward, Christiane. "Colette and Signs: A Partial Reading of a Writer 'Born Not to Write.' " In *Colette: The Woman, the Writer,* ed. Erica M. Eisinger and Mari Ward McCarty. University Park: Pennsylvania State University Press, 1981.

Marcus, Jane. "Liberty, Sorority, Misogyny." In *The Representation of Women in Fiction: Selected Papers from the English Institute, 1981,* ed. Carolyn G. Heilbrun and Margaret R. Higonnet. Baltimore and London: Johns Hopkins University Press, 1983.

——"Still Practice, A/Wrested Alphabet: Toward a Feminist Aesthetic." *Tulsa*

*Studies* (Spring–Fall 1984) 3(1–2):79–98; rpt. in *Feminist Issues in Literary Scholarship*, ed. Shari Benstock. Bloomington: Indiana University Press, 1987.

——*Virginia Woolf and the Languages of Patriarchy*. Bloomington: Indiana University Press, 1987.

Marcus, Jane, ed. *Virginia Woolf: A Feminist Slant*. Lincoln: University of Nebraska Press, 1983.

Marks, Elaine. *Colette*. New Brunswick: Rutgers University Press, 1960.

——"Women and Literature in France." *Signs* (1978), 3(4):832–42.

Marks, Elaine and Isabelle de Courtivron, eds. *New French Feminisms*. Amherst: University of Massachusetts Press, 1980.

May, Georges. *Le Dilemme du roman au XVIII^e siècle*. New Haven: Yale University Press, 1963.

Mercier, Michel. *Le Roman féminin*. Paris: Presses Universitaires de France, 1976.

Miller, J. Hillis. "Ariadne's Thread: Repetition and the Narrative Line." In *Interpretation of Narrative*, ed. Mario J. Valdes and Owen J. Miller. Toronto: University of Toronto Press, 1976.

——"Ariachne's Broken Woof." *Georgia Review* (Spring 1977), 31(1):36–48.

——"The Clarification of Clara Middleton." In *The Representation of Women in Fiction: Selected Papers from the English Institute, 1981*, ed. Carolyn G. Heilbrun and Margaret R. Higonnet. Baltimore: Johns Hopkins University Press, 1983.

Miller, Nancy K. "Creating Feminist Works." Proceedings of "The Scholar and the Feminist IV," Barnard College Women's Center, April 1978.

——" 'I's' in Drag: The Sex of Recollection." *The Eighteenth Century* (1981), 22(1):45–57.

Millett, Kate. *Sexual Politics*. New York: Doubleday, 1970.

Mitchell, Juliet. "Femininity, Narrative, and Psychoanalysis." In *Women: The Longest Revolution*. New York: Pantheon, 1984.

Moers, Ellen. *Literary Women: The Great Writers*. New York: Doubleday, 1976.

Moi, Toril. *Sexual/Textual Politics*. London and New York: Methuen, 1985.

Montesquieu, Charles Secondat de. *Persian Letters*. Trans. C. J. Betts. Baltimore: Penguin, 1973.

Morrison, Toni. *Sula*. New York: Knopf, 1974. Rpt. New York: New American Library, 1982.

Naylor, Gloria. "Famous First Words." *New York Times Book Review*, June 2, 1985, p. 52.

Nesbit, Molly. "What Was An Author?" *Yale French Studies* (1987), 73:229–57. Special issue on "Everyday Life," ed. Alice Y. Kaplan and Kristin Ross.

O'Neale, Sondra. "Inhibiting Midwives, Usurping Creators: The Struggling Emergence of Black Women in American Fiction." In *Feminist Studies/Critical Studies*, ed. Teresa de Lauretis. Bloomington: Indiana University Press, 1986.

Ong, Walter. *Orality and Literacy: The Technologizing of the Word*. London and New York: Methuen, 1982.

Ovid. *Metamorphoses*. Trans. Frank Justice Miller. Cambridge and London: Harvard University Press and William Heinemann, 1966.

——*Heroides*. Trans. Grant Showerman. Cambridge and London: Harvard University Press and William Heinemann, 1971.

Pascal, Roy. *Design and Truth in Autobiography.* Cambridge: Harvard University Press, 1960.

Peterson, Carla. *The Determined Reader: Gender and Culture in the Novel from Napoleon to Victoria.* New Brunswick: Rutgers University Press, 1986.

Peyre, Henri. *French Novelists of Today.* New York and Oxford: Oxford University Press, 1967.

Phelps, Robert. *Earthly Paradise.* New York: Farrar, Straus, Giroux, 1966.

Prescott, Peter. In *Newsweek,* October 16, 1978.

Rabine, Leslie. "Feminist Writers in French Romanticism." *Studies in Romanticism* (Fall 1974), 16(4):491–507.

——"George Sand and the Myth of Femininity." *Women and Literature* (1976), 4(2):2–17.

——"The Unhappy Hymen Between Feminism and Deconstruction." In *The Other Perspective on Gender and Culture,* ed. Juliet Flower MacCannell. Forthcoming.

Réage, Pauline. *The Story of O.* Trans. Sabine d'Estrée. New York: Grove Press, 1967.

Register, Cherri. "American Feminist Literary Criticism: A Bibliographical Introduction." In *Feminist Literary Criticism: Explanations and Theory,* ed. Josephine Donovan. Lexington: University Press of Kentucky, 1975.

Rich, Adrienne. "When We Dead Awaken: Writing as Re-Vision (1971)"; "Toward a Woman-Centered University (1973–74)." In *On Lies, Secrets, and Silence: Selected Prose, 1966–1978.* New York: Norton, 1979.

——"Blood, Bread, and Poetry: The Location of the Poet"; "Notes Toward a Politics of Location." In *Blood, Bread, and Poetry: Selected Prose, 1979–1985.* New York: Norton, 1986.

Richardson, Samuel. *Pamela.* New York: Norton, 1958.

Rigolot, François. "Les 'sutils ouvrages' de Louise Labé, ou: Quand Pallas Devient Arachne." *Etudes Littéraires* (Autumn 1987), 20(2):43–60.

Robbe-Grillet, Alain. *Pour un nouveau roman.* Paris: Minuit, 1963.

——"What Interests Me Is Eroticism." An Interview by Germaine Brée. In *Homosexualities and French Literature: Cultural Contexts/Critical Texts,* ed. George Stambolian and Elaine Marks. Ithaca: Cornell University Press, 1979.

Robinson, Lillian. "On Reading Trash." In *Sex, Class, and Culture.* Bloomington: Indiana University Press, 1978.

Rosand, David. " '*Ut Pictor Poeta*': Meaning in Titian's '*Poesie*'." *New Literary History* (1971–72), 3:527–46.

Rose, Phyliss. "Women Writers and Feminist Critics." *Atlantic Monthly* (August 1985), pp. 88–91.

Rossum-Guyom, Françoise van. "Les Enjeux d'*Indiana* I: Métadiscours et réception critique." In *Recherches Nouvelles.* C.R.I.N. 6–7, 1983, pp. 1–35.

——A propos d'*Indiana:* La Préface de 1832. Problèmes du métadiscours." *George Sand.* Colloque de Cerisy. Paris: Société d'Editions d'Enseignement Supérieur Réunis, 1983.

Rousseau, Jean-Jacques. *Julie, ou la Nouvelle Héloïse.* Paris: Garnier, 1960. *La Nouvelle Héloïse: Julie, or the New Eloise.* Trans. and abr., Judith H. McDowell. University Park: Pennsylvania State University Press, 1968.

——*Les Confessions.* Paris: Garnier-Flammarion, 1968.

Rousset, Jean. *Forme et signification*. Paris: Corti, 1962.

Rubin, Gayle. "The Traffic in Women: Notes on the 'Political Economy' of Sex." In *Toward an Anthropology of Women*, ed. Rayna R. Reiter. New York: Monthly Review Press, 1975.

Russo, Mary. "Female Grotesques: Carnival and Theory." In *Feminist Studies/Critical Studies*, ed. Teresa de Lauretis. Bloomington: Indiana University Press, 1986.

Rustin, Jacques. *Le Vice à la mode: Etude sur le roman du XVIII$^e$ siècle de Manon Lescaut à l'apparition de la Nouvelle Héloïse (1731–1761)*. Paris: Ophrys, 1979.

Said, Edward W. "The Problem of Textuality." *Critical Inquiry* (Summer 1978), 4:673–714.

Sainte-Beuve, Charles-Augustin. *Portraits contemporains*. Paris: Michel Lévy Frères, 1870.

Sand, George. *Lélia*. Ed. Pierre Reboul. Paris: Garnier, 1960. *Lélia*. Trans. Maria Espinosa. Bloomington: Indiana University Press, 1978.

——*Indiana*. Ed. Pierre Salomon. Paris: Garnier, 1962. *Indiana*. Trans. George Burnham Ives. 1900. Rpt. Chicago: Cassandra, 1978.

——*Histoire de ma vie*. In *Oeuvres autobiographiques*. 2 vols. Paris: Gallimard, 1970.

——*Valentine*. Paris: Aujourd'hui, 1976. *Valentine*. Trans. George Burnham Ives. Chicago: Cassandra, 1978.

Sansone, Melinda. *"Lettres d'une Péruvienne:* The New Sentimental Plot and Its Feminist Implications." Manuscript.

Schor, Naomi. "La Pérodie: Superposition dans *Lorenzaccio*." *Michigan Romance Studies* (1982), 2:73–86.

——*Breaking the Chain: Women, Theory, and French Realist Fiction*. New York: Columbia University Press, 1985.

——"Introducing Feminism." *Paragraph* (October 1986), 8:94–101.

——"Female Fetishism: The Case of George Sand." In *The Female Body in Western Culture: Contemporary Perspectives*, ed. Susan Rubin Suleiman. Cambridge: Harvard University Press, 1986.

——"Reading Double: Sand's Difference." In *The Poetics of Gender*, ed. Nancy K. Miller. New York: Columbia University Press, 1986.

——"Dreaming Dissymmetry: Barthes, Foucault, and Sexual Difference." In *Men in Feminism*, ed. Alice Jardine and Paul Smith. New York and London: Methuen, 1987.

——"Portrait of a Gentleman." *Representations* (Fall 1987), 20:113–33.

Sedgwick, Eve Kosofsky. *Between Men: English Literature and Male Homosocial Desire*. New York: Columbia University Press, 1985.

Showalter, Elaine. *A Literature of Their Own*. Princeton University Press, 1977.

——"Feminist Criticism in the Wilderness." *Critical Inquiry* (Winter 1981), 8(2):179–206; "Toward a Feminist Poetics." In *Women Writing and Writing about Women*, ed. Mary Jacobus. London: Croom Helm, 1979. Rpt. In *The New Feminist Criticism: Women, Literature, Theory*, ed. Elaine Showalter. New York: Pantheon, 1985.

——"Women's Time, Women's Space: Writing the History of Feminist Criticism." *Tulsa Studies in Women's Literature* (Spring–Fall 1984), 3(1–2):29–

44. Rpt. in *Feminist Issues in Literary Scholarship,* ed. Shari Benstock. Bloomington: Indiana University Press, 1987.

——"Women Who Write Are Women." *New York Times Book Review,* December 16, 1984, pp. 1, 31–33.

Showalter, English. "Les *Lettres d'une Péruvienne:* Composition, Publication, Suites." In *Archives et Bibliothèques de Belgique* (1983), 54:14–28.

Shroder, Maurice Z. *The Image of the Artist in French Romanticism.* Cambridge: Harvard University Press, 1961.

Silverman, Kaja. *The Subject of Semiotics.* New York: Oxford University Press, 1983.

——"*Histoire d'O:* The Construction of a Female Subject." In *Pleasure and Danger,* ed. Carole S. Vance. Boston and London: Routledge and Kegan Paul, 1984.

Smith, Barbara. "Toward a Black Feminist Criticism." *Conditions: Two 1* (October, 1977), no. 2. Rpt. in *The New Feminist Criticism: Essays on Women, Literature, Theory,* ed. Elaine Showalter. New York: Pantheon, 1985.

Snitow, Ann. "Mass Market Romance: Pornography for Women Is Different." *Radical History Review* (Spring–Summer 1979), pp. 142–161; rpt. in *The Powers of Desire,* ed. Ann Snitow, Christine Stansell, and Sharon Thompson. New York: Monthly Review Press, 1983.

Spacks, Patricia Meyer. *Imagining a Self.* Cambridge: Harvard University Press, 1976.

Spivak, Gayatri Chakravorty. "French Feminism in an International Frame." *Yale French Studies* (1981), 62:154–84.

——"The Politics of Interpretations." *Critical Inquiry* (September 1982), 9(1):259–78.

——"Displacement and the Discourse of Woman." In *Displacement: Derrida and After,* ed. Mark Krupnick. Bloomington: Indiana University Press, 1983.

Staël, Germaine de. "De l'influence des passions sur le bonheur des individus et des nations." *Oeuvres Complètes.* 17 vols. Vol. 4. Paris: Treuttel et Wurtz, 1820–21.

——*Corinne ou L'Italie.* Edited and with a preface by Simone Balayé. Paris: Folio, 1985. *Corinne, or Italy.* Trans. Avriel H. Goldberger. New Brunswick: Rutgers University Press, 1987.

——*An Extraordinary Woman: Selected Writings of Germaine de Staël.* Ed. and trans. Vivian Folkenflik. New York: Columbia University Press, 1987.

Stambolian, George and Elaine Marks, eds. *Homosexualities and French Literature.* Ithaca: Cornell University Press, 1979.

Stanton, Domna C. "The Ideal of 'Repos' in Seventeenth-Century French Literature." *L'Esprit Créateur* (1975), 15:79–104.

——"Language and Revolution: The Franco-American Dis-Connection." In *The Future of Difference,* ed. Hester Eisenstein and Alice Jardine. Barnard College Women's Center. Boston: G. K. Hall, 1980.

Starobinski, Jean. *L'Invention de la liberté; 1700–1789.* Geneva: Skira, 1964.

Stendhal. *De l'amour.* Paris: Cluny, 1938.

Stern, Daniel. *Mémoires.* 1833–1854. Paris: Calmann-Lévy, 1927.

——*Mes Souvenirs.* Paris: Calmann-Lévy, 1880.

Stewart, Joan Hinde. *Colette.* Boston: Twayne, 1983.

Stimpson, Catharine. "Ad/d Feminam: Women, Literature, and Society." In *Selected Papers from the English Institute: Literature and Society,* ed. Edward Said. Baltimore: Johns Hopkins University Press, 1978.

Sukenick, Lynn. "On Women and Fiction." In *The Authority of Experience,* ed. Arlyn Diamond and Lee R. Edwards. Amherst: University of Massachusetts Press, 1977.

Swallow, Noreen. "The Weapon of Personality: A Review of the Sexist Criticism of Mme de Staël, 1785–1985. *Atlantis* (Fall 1982), 8(1):78–82.

Tanner, Tony. *Adultery in the Novel: Contract and Transgression.* Baltimore: Johns Hopkins University Press, 1979.

Thompson, Patricia. *George Sand and the Victorians: Her Influence and Reputation in Nineteenth-Century England.* New York: Columbia University Press, 1977.

Tompkins, Jane. *Sensational Designs: The Cultural Work of American Fiction, 1790–1860.* New York: Oxford University Press, 1985.

Vallois, Marie-Claire. "Voice as Fossil, Madame de Staël's *Corinne or Italy:* An Archaeology of Feminine Discourse." *Tulsa Studies* (Spring 1987), 6(1):47–60.

——*Fictions féminines: Mme de Staël et les voix de la Sibylle.* Saratoga: Anma Libri, 1987.

Varga, A. Kibédi. "Romans d'amour, romans de femmes à l'époque classique." *Revue des Sciences Humaines* (1977) no. 168, pp. 520–30.

Vier, Jacques. *La Comtesse D'Agoult et son temps.* Paris: Armand Colin, 1961. Vol. 4.

Voloshinov, V. I. *Le Marxisme et la philosophie du langage.* Paris: Minuit, 1977.

Waller, Margaret. "The Male Malady: Gender, Power, and the *Mal du siècle* Novel." Ph.D. diss., Columbia University, 1986.

Watson, Barbara Bellow. "On Power and the Literary Text." *Signs* (1975), 1(1):111–18.

Weed, Elizabeth. "A Man's Place." In *Men in Feminism,* ed. Alice Jardine and Paul Smith. New York and London: Methuen, 1987.

Welles, Marcia. *Arachne's Tapestry: The Transformation of Myth in Seventeenth-Century Spain.* San Antonio: Trinity University Press, 1985.

Wittig, Monique. "The Straight Mind." *Feminist Issues* (Summer 1980), 1(1):103–12.

——"The Mark of Gender." In *The Poetics of Gender,* ed. Nancy K. Miller. New York: Columbia University Press, 1986.

Woolf, Virginia. *The Common Reader.* New York: Harcourt, 1953.

——*A Room of One's Own.* New York: Harcourt, Brace, and World, 1957.

——"Mr. Bennett and Mrs. Brown." In *Collected Essays.* Vol. 1. New York: Harcourt, Brace, and World, 1967.

——*The Letters of Virginia Woolf.* Vol. 6, 1936–41. Ed. Nigel Nicolson. London: Hogarth, 1980.

# Index